HD9710.A2 M376 2007

01

Mas
ch

Mastering
AUTOMOTIVE
CHALLENGES

Professor Bernd Gottschalk and Ralf Kalmbach

London and Philadelphia

With special thanks to the co-authors who helped in making this book: Axel Koch, Dr Sari Abwa, Juri Wagenleitner, Norbert Dressler and Thorsten Mattig, Roland Berger Strategy Consultants.

Publisher's note

Every possible effort has been made to ensure that the information contained in this book is accurate at the time of going to press, and the publishers and authors cannot accept responsibility for any errors or omissions, however caused. No responsibility for loss or damage occasioned to any person acting, or refraining from action, as a result of the material in this publication can be accepted by the editor, the publisher or any of the authors.

First published in Great Britain and the United States in 2007 by Kogan Page Limited

Apart from any fair dealing for the purposes of research or private study, or criticism or review, as permitted under the Copyright, Designs and Patents Act 1988, this publication may only be reproduced, stored or transmitted, in any form or by any means, with the prior permission in writing of the publishers, or in the case of reprographic reproduction in accordance with the terms and licences issued by the CLA. Enquiries concerning reproduction outside these terms should be sent to the publishers at the undermentioned addresses:

120 Pentonville Road
London N1 9JN
United Kingdom
www.kogan-page.co.uk

525 South 4th Street, #241
Philadelphia PA 19147
USA

© Bernd Gottschalk, Ralf Kalmbach and individual contributors, 2007

The right of Bernd Gottschalk, Ralf Kalmbach and individual contributors to be identified as the author of this work has been asserted by them in accordance with the Copyright, Designs and Patents Act 1988.

ISBN-10   0 7494 4575 0
ISBN-13   978 0 7494 4575 1

British Library Cataloguing-in-Publication Data

A CIP record for this book is available from the British Library.

Library of Congress Cataloging-in-Publication Data

Mastering automotive challenges / Bernd Gottschalk, Ralf Kalmbach, [editors].
    p. cm.
  Includes index.
  ISBN-13: 978-0-7494-4575-1
  ISBN-10: 0-7494-4575-0
 1. Automobile industry and trade -- Management. I. Gottschalk, Bernd, 1943 – II. Kalmbach, Ralf.
  HD9710.A2M376 2007
  629.222068--dc22
                                          2006030580

Typeset by Saxon Graphics Ltd, Derby
Printed and bound in MPG Books Ltd, Bodmin, Cornwall

Contents

Preface by Bernd Gottschalk and Ralf Kalmbach		v
Part I Major challenges		**1**
1	The automotive industry sets the course for the global economy *Bernd Gottschalk*	3
2	The automotive power play moves into its next round *Ralf Kalmbach*	25
3	The globalization challenge – is the automotive industry raising the champions of tomorrow? *Dr Thomas Sedran*	46
4	The value chain challenge: networks, the strategy for success *Marcus Berret*	69
5	The technology challenge: progress or pitfall? *Silvio Schindler*	103
6	The market challenge: who will gain strategic control? *Jürgen Reers*	146
7	The sales and after-sales challenge: capturing value along the car lifecycle *Dr Max Blanchet and Jacques Rade*	171
Part II Case studies		**217**
8	Partnership as a model for success *Franz Fehrenbach*	219

9	Brand differentiation on the basis of platform and module strategies *Dr Bernd Pischetsrieder*	241
10	New impetus for General Motors in Europe *Carl-Peter Forster*	252
11	How electronics is changing the automotive industry: from component suppliers to system partners *Peter Bauer*	270
12	The next evolutionary step for the automotive industry is just around the corner: factors for sustainable success in the interplay of OEMs and suppliers *Siegfried Wolf*	290
13	BlueTec: the path to the world's cleanest diesel *Thomas Weber*	314
14	Bharat Forge: emerging players from emerging regions *Babasaheb N Kalyani*	334
	Conclusion *Ralf Kalmbach*	345
	Index	*368*

Preface

The automotive sector is the key industry in almost all industrialized economies. It is one of the driving forces behind globalization. Major macroeconomic factors, including economic growth, employment, technological progress and the pace of innovation, are all strongly influenced by the automotive industry, whose products are both produced and sold worldwide. Globalization, however, is accompanied by radical changes that present serious challenges to automotive companies.

Production in the Eastern European and Asian growth markets is constantly expanding, while the global footprint is increasingly determined by cost efficiency. Not only traditional production sites, but also tried and tested development and manufacturing structures are in inexorable decline. At the same time, political developments such as EU enlargement are creating new opportunities to redesign the global footprint, as companies seek to exploit the advantages now opening up in other locations.

Component suppliers are increasingly responsible for creating value and providing expertise. Some already have the capability to develop and manufacture entire vehicles, and they are making full use of their engineering design skills. In fact, some of these companies are visibly catching up with the vehicle manufacturers in terms of know-how.

Partnerships between original equipment manufacturers (OEMs) now require an active exchange of important vehicle modules such as the engine or the gearbox. This makes it much easier for new competitors to enter the market or reposition themselves within the market.

The automotive industry develops and produces highly complex products. Driven by the dynamic innovation of recent years, this new level of complexity demands a new management approach. Without it, companies will not cope. We are also seeing important changes in customer behaviour, as consumers abandon their traditional car-buying habits. In addition to mobility criteria, customers are increasingly guided by lifestyle choices when selecting their vehicles. And companies are also adjusting their product lines in response to this change.

Sales structures are also facing upheaval. With competition getting ever tougher and markets ever tighter, sales, customer service and financial services are becoming increasingly important. Retail is the face to the customer. It is here that the foundations are laid for brand perception, and ultimately profitability. And now that the new rules under the Block Exemption Regulation are in force, auto makers must reexamine and overhaul their retail strategies.

Manufacturers and suppliers are investing increasingly in greener technologies. Manufacturers are redoubling their development efforts to improve environmental and safety features. This is partly because their customers expect cleaner cars, and partly because they need to respond to legislative initiatives by the EU or, for example, the state of California. And this trend is creating new areas of technological competition.

So far, the automotive industry has always been able to take on and overcome similar challenges. It has responded successfully to oil crises, sluggish economic growth and difficult market conditions. But the present situation is special: it now looks as if many different underlying economic, political and ecological factors are changing simultaneously.

Most publications on the subject of automotive management deal only with individual aspects and questions raised by the management agenda. A wider, holistic perspective on the industry is still lacking. The aim of our book is to fill this gap. It is intended to provide guidance for automotive managers and to offer practical help for practical management by giving examples of best practice and recommendations for action.

The first section presents a number of contributions on the central problems to which automotive managers must find answers. In the second part, top managers from major auto makers present some case studies to illustrate their strategies for tackling the challenges already outlined – strategies that have won international acclaim. The final section sums up the key success factors for overcoming these challenges and presents concrete recommendations for practical implementation.

We believe this book can provide significant support in meeting the challenges you face in the automotive industry.

Bernd Gottschalk
President OICA and VDA
and
Ralf Kalmbach
Roland Berger Strategy Consultants

Part I

Major challenges

1

The automotive industry sets the course for the global economy

Professor Bernd Gottschalk, President of the International Organization of Motor Vehicle Manufacturers (OICA) and the German Association of the Automotive Industry (VDA)

THE GLOBAL AUTOMOTIVE INDUSTRY – THE SIXTH BIGGEST ECONOMY

The growth prospects of a national economy are largely determined by its key industries. In recent decades, the automotive industry in many triad countries has proven to be one of the strongest drivers of technology, growth and employment. If it were a single country's economy, the global automotive industry – with total sales of around €1,900 trillion – would be the world's sixth largest national economy. More than 8 million people are directly employed in the process of manufacturing vehicles and parts alone. That equates to over 5 per cent of all people directly employed in industrial manufacturing, and many times more than that if those indirectly employed in the automotive industry are included. More importantly, though, the automotive industry is now the world's biggest innovator, investing an estimated total of just under €70 billion a year in research and development. This makes it a driver of technical progress and is the main factor behind the increasing technological connectivity between industry segments. Original equipment manufacturers (OEMs) are also among the biggest contributors to national revenue, pumping some €450 billion a year into state coffers in 26 countries. This proves that the automotive industry has also assumed sociopolitical responsibility, and its contribution to the future of our national economies is greater than that of almost any other industry. The car is indispensable to society, and the automotive industry is equally indispensable to the development of our communities.

GERMANY AS A BUSINESS LOCATION: A TRADITION AND A FUTURE

Germany has the world's leading automotive industry, and not just because the car was invented there. The country is also a major automotive production location and sales market. The automotive industry alone accounted for €235 billion of the manufacturing sector's €1,300 billion total sales in 2005, not including the sales generated in upstream industry segments, from plastics to steelmaking. Of Germany's €162 billion export surplus in 2005, the automotive industry alone was responsible for €89 billion. The external component accounted for 0.7 percentage points of the 0.9 per cent 'growth' of GDP in 2005. This means that approximately 0.3 percentage points of this rise – or a third of the previous year's increase – would not have been possible if the automotive industry had not been so successful on external markets. Moreover the automotive industry is one of Germany's biggest employers, providing 766,600 jobs. If the indirect workforce employed in the automotive-related upstream and downstream industries is counted, the total rises to 5.3 million jobs.

The structure of Germany's economy and industry is dependent on the automotive sector. For this reason, the conditions for doing business in Germany have to support the automotive industry's further success. There are some heartening signs of progress on this count in the wake of EU enlargement, which has increased competition between countries:

- Unit labour costs have been slashed in the last three years, mainly due to lasting productivity gains, but also because Germany has finally stopped granting workers sizeable pay rises. As a result, the country now leads the field 'only' in absolute wage figures. This was a necessary step by unions and management, and one that will gradually improve Germany's ability to compete on cost.
- At the same time, the average operating time in the German metal working and electrical engineering industry rose from 45 hours a week in 1989 to just under 59 hours in 2004.

- The Pforzheim 2004 wage agreement in the German automotive industry laid down a number of special rules. These opened the door to more flexible solutions, longer working hours to suit individual business requirements and flexible working hours, particularly in the area of research and development.
- 'Plant protection agreements' between manufacturers or suppliers and their employee-elected representatives, designed to keep a plant alive in exchange for worker concessions, also contain provisions that represent important steps toward regaining past levels of competitiveness.

However, we must bear in mind that these positive changes are late in coming and are being made in an environment where the countries competing to attract new businesses are not letting up in their attempts to become more competitive. That is why the right strategy and a consistent business promotion policy cannot be based solely on companies' restructuring efforts and the improvement of the taxation regime. Nor can it centre only on cutting bureaucracy and regulation, improving conditions in the labour market and lowering non-wage costs. Trade unions and company management must also take responsibility as the parties to wage agreements. Now more than ever, wage agreements must help make sure that the country remains an attractive place for companies to do business.

The crucial factor – and this is a tricky aspect of the public discussion in Germany – is not only how much effort is put into correcting mistakes, liberating companies from outmoded burdens that the market is no longer willing to bear the cost of, and making the framework for wage agreements more flexible. The key is the relative speed with which the conditions for business in Germany change compared with conditions in other countries. It is about how quickly Germany manages to stay competitive compared with new and attractive potential business locations in Eastern Europe. The latter may, of course, see their cost advantages erode – albeit very slowly – as wages and price levels approach those in Western Europe. But they have correctly recognized the need to offset the smaller gap in labour costs by redoubling their efforts to attain a more highly qualified workforce, by strengthening their R&D capacities, by developing their infrastructure and by improving the conditions for production logistics.

This is why the factor that determines Germany's relative competitive position is not the next round of wage agreements alone; it is the whole package of moves that set the political framework. Will Germany be able to stay one step ahead with first-rate road and transport infrastructure? Will German universities and their graduates remain some of the best in the world? And will manufacturers and suppliers still be able to maintain the technological lead in the automotive market that they have achieved together over the past decades? It is not just the 'automotive business model' that will decide how much of the industry's future value is created in Germany – a comprehensive 'Germany business model' is what will determine this.

One thing is certain: political attempts to talk Eastern Europe into raising taxes and wages, or to label foreign investments by German industry (which depends on global networks) as unpatriotic, are not likely to protect jobs in Germany, and nor are penalties on value created overseas. These are actions by countries that have already admitted defeat in the battle to stay competitive. Germany has no need for them.

CAPACITIES AND NEW COMPETITORS

The pressure on Germany as a location for building cars is on the rise for a number of reasons:

- Passenger car plants in Germany are still far from working at optimal capacity. And production capacities in Europe will go up from 18.6 million to 20 million cars by 2011, an 8 per cent rise.
- The new production sites being opened by French/Japanese and Korean OEMs in Central and Eastern Europe (with additional capacities in excess of 1 million cars a year) present a new challenge for the competitiveness of the German automotive industry, especially in the lower and mid-range price segments.
- National boundaries are becoming blurred: value chain links that would previously have been clearly allocated along national lines are becoming 'multidomestic'.

The cost competition affects the main car-producing nations of Europe in the wake of 'European globalization' that has followed EU enlargement and the increase in competition it has brought between member states. But it also affects the North American OEMs, who face enormous competition from the Japanese, Koreans and Germans. In the not too distant future, the presence of Chinese or Indian car makers and brands on the world's other car markets will cause competition to intensify once again, just as the presence of German products in China or India is creating new market opportunities for German industry.

As one of the world's biggest industries, with production of its global brands accounting for some 22 per cent of worldwide production, the German automotive industry is an example of a growth industry in a state of flux. The 1992/93 crisis was more a crisis of R&D and production processes, which resulted in full-scale reengineering that saw the focus firmly placed on the core manufacturing activities, and processes reorganized. Today, though, we are rather faced with a process of adjustment caused by globalization. However – and this does not make the strategic answers easier – the pressure to adjust to globalization is accompanied by a number of other challenges. While these may not be new, they do require many different answers for many different companies.

CHINA AND INDIA – THE NEW GROWTH CHAMPIONS

In 2005, battles over prices and terms were fierce and companies saw their market shares fluctuate rapidly. This proved how difficult it is to predict how the emerging markets are going to develop. It also showed how fast previously successful strategies need to be modified under massive time pressure, and huge efficiency-boosting programmes need to be implemented even in a market like China, which is supposed to offer the benefit of rising volumes.

German car makers and suppliers were among the first to do business in China, long before the market took off. However, the structural shifts in the Chinese market, the rapid differentiation of market segments, and of course the attractiveness of new providers, have caused German OEMs' share of the Chinese market to decline in recent years. This was absolutely to be expected, as a large share of a sheltered market can never be maintained to the same extent after the market has been opened up. But German OEMs are rising to the new challenge by renewing their product range, adjusting their structures in procurement and sales, and organizing their cooperation with their Chinese partners and their German partners on the supply side.

The Indian market has reached a volume of more than 1 million cars, putting it on a par with Mexico and Russia. The number of commercial vehicles sold in India already exceeds that sold in Turkey and Russia. German OEMs entered the Indian market at a later stage than they did China, but their Indian business is now ramping up nicely.

Another way in which India differs is perhaps still more important. At present, China is the scene of a major fight for the Chinese domestic market, though vehicles and parts are not yet being exported from the country in any magnitude. India, on the other hand, is becoming a real and relevant global player, particularly in the supply industry. India is already delivering just-in-sequence parts to German car makers, and Japanese and Korean cars are being manufactured on the subcontinent and shipped to the European Union. These examples illustrate India's consistent global orientation and development of export capabilities, and show that India is now a player in the global automotive business. This is driven by consistent orientation toward competitive prices and a remarkable R&D focus, now visible in areas other than India's global IT supremacy. As a result, and quicker than many had expected, India is not merely in the process of becoming an important and fast-growing market, it is exploiting the opportunities that the global market and the markets in Europe, including Germany, offer Indian manufacturers and suppliers. And it is doing this more conspicuously than any other Asian growth market.

The German automotive industry has taken up the challenge offered by the Indian market. In Skoda, a company from a German conglomerate already holds a leading position in the Indian market's premium segment, and BMW is now joining the likes of DaimlerChrysler in the top segment. More will follow. MAN's entry in the Indian commercial vehicles market is an indication of the growth of the market for technically complex, state-of-the-art vehicles.

German companies and their partners account for 15 per cent of the sales generated in the parts industry in India. What is more, these firms saw sales jump by 20 per cent last year, which testifies to the opportunities the country holds for the German automotive supply trade. And these opportunities will be seized; this much is proven by the contacts between small and medium-sized enterprises in particular, which are set to intensify greatly in the coming years.

Nevertheless, a systematic rise in exports from China can be expected in the next few years. The eleventh five-year plan sees the automotive industry not merely as a key industry, but as a growing automotive export nation. Furthermore, China can be expected to make ambitious plans with regard to modern, environmentally friendly engine concepts. This will turn China and India into global players to be reckoned with – and challengers to established competitors.

EXPORT STRATEGY AND GLOBAL BUSINESS LOCATION STRATEGY: THE GERMAN AUTOMOTIVE INDUSTRY IS FORGING ITS OWN PATH

Of the passenger cars produced in Germany, 71 per cent are destined for the export market. In the past 10 years, exports from the German automotive industry have risen 54 per cent. This sounds like the traditional model of 'Germany, the export champion', but it is only one aspect of the full picture. In future, the picture will be marked more by global presence, operating production plants directly in foreign countries with a close relationship to research and development activities at home.

- The number of German OEMs' foreign production sites and licensees has increased by more than 250 per cent since the early 1990s, to over 2,000 today.
- German companies alone supply 600 production sites in Western Europe, 300 sites in Central and Eastern Europe and 300 throughout NAFTA.
- The extent of their presence in China and the rest of Asia has also skyrocketed in recent years.

This development is not without consequence for the value chain structure. Today, 40 per cent of the value created from exports is a direct result of purchased materials and services that were previously imported, primarily from low-cost countries. This import volume – and this is the telling figure – has risen by 143 per cent in the last 10 years. Engine and automotive parts imports also grew by 9 per cent last year (worth some €32 billion), more than double the growth of exports, which saw a mere 4 per cent rise. This shows that the importance of internationally purchased materials and services is still growing; and it will continue to grow, the longer it takes for the conditions for business in Germany to improve. Or, to put it in positive terms, there will be no automatic process of deindustrialization in Germany as long as it can actively improve its standing in the key competitiveness factors of labour costs, working hours, flexibility and non-wage costs.

While 130,000 new jobs have been created in the German automotive industry since the mid-1990s, it is important to point out that 160,000 new jobs have been created at its manufacturers and suppliers in Eastern Europe. This, in turn, has created a global manufacturing network, which, by combining the advantages of Germany with the low costs of Eastern Europe in particular, has brought product costs down to competitive levels.

By moving early, consistently and quickly into Central and Eastern Europe, German companies have given themselves an advantage over their global competition. Without it, they would have lost their ability to compete on cost. In the automotive industry more than any other, the idea that new jobs in low-wage countries destroy jobs in Germany is completely unfounded.

However, the restructuring programmes present no prospect of continuing the upward trend in employment in Germany to bring quick productivity gains. But it is worth noting that although the manufacturing sector has seen 15 per cent of its jobs disappear in the past decade, the German automotive industry has proved to be a 'job machine'. At the same time, productivity has improved dramatically thanks to investments in technology and capital stock. Sales per hour worked have risen by 66 per cent. The rise in production in the automotive industry in the past decade is not a result of rationalization investments, but is rather due to the fact that sales have doubled.

THE GERMAN MARKET

The weak market of the past five years is a key factor in Germany's relative importance as an automotive market, and indeed production in this country coming under pressure. Although 2004 and 2005 saw the first small signs of growth returning, the danger has not passed. This growth was generated exclusively by growth in the commercial customer segment. No fundamental U-turn can be seen yet in the private car owner's decision to continue saving rather than buy a new car, resulting in the further ageing of the vehicle population. German OEMs' and their suppliers' success in boosting sales and revenues in Germany can therefore not be attributed to higher volumes. Rather, it is a result of the higher value of each car: in other words the result of qualitative growth. The premium segment, the greater numbers of diesel cars and the higher standards of driving comfort and safety have led to substantial value growth in the German market. This growth has exceeded that indicated by the low-volume development.

The commercial vehicle segment did see genuine growth in the German market, though. The export-driven investment dynamic in Germany's industry has also hit commercial vehicles in their capacity as capital goods. For the second year in a row, Germany's commercial vehicle market is seeing a significant upturn. In the last two years, new vehicle numbers have risen by 20 per cent. Supported by the rise in demand for low-pollutant vehicles and the launch of digital tachographs and new vehicle concepts, 85,500 vehicles over 6 tonnes were sold in Germany in 2005. In the international markets, German car makers achieved a new export record in 2005, selling 115,800 vehicles over 6 tonnes. Thanks to their strong international business and the continuing positive sales balance in Germany, manufacturers of vehicles over 6 tonnes saw their production in 2005 increase by a further 5 per cent, to a record volume of 168,800 vehicles. This took them past the 400,000 mark for the first time, with a total of 407,500 commercial vehicles manufactured in Germany. Internationally, too, German OEMs produced more commercial vehicles than ever before.

Trans-European logistics and the need for modern commercial vehicles that meet the latest emissions standards even before they become law are forcing commercial fleet operators to renew their fleets. German commercial vehicle manufacturers have been extremely successful because they meet these growing demands and focus rigorously on technology leadership.

THE GERMAN SUPPLY INDUSTRY: A FAVOURITE IN THE COMPETITION

A consistent focus on technology leadership is also what made the German supply industry strong. Big corporations and small firms alike are among the global technology leaders of the day. An export ratio of 42 per cent and a high worldwide presence through production sites and joint ventures underscore this point, with German suppliers engaging in almost 1,800 business arrangements across 74 countries.

With sales of €68 billion in 2005, Germany's supply industry is the world's third biggest, behind Japan and the United States. In the past 10 years, it has proven to be a growth engine: since 1994, revenues have grown by more than 8 per cent a year on average. And 90,000 new workers (net) have been taken on. Over the last 10 years, the supply industry has, first and foremost, helped the automotive industry beat the downward trend seen in other industries in terms of employment figures. The number of jobs in the industry increased by 31 per cent between 1995 and 2005, rising approximately 3 per cent a year.

So the doubling of the scale of the industry's foreign involvement clearly did not have a negative impact on employment at home. On the contrary, it strengthened the production sites in Germany by making them more competitive. This is the only explanation for the exceptional rise in export sales. In Germany, too, the industry's revenues grew much faster than their customers' revenues.

Besides the substantial improvements in vehicle equipment, particularly the improvements in safety, comfort and environmental friendliness, this can be traced back to the suppliers' greater integration in value creation processes. Since 1994, German OEMs have reduced their vertical integration levels by 10 percentage points thanks to outsourcing. They have transferred one third of their original value creation onto their suppliers, and the supply industry's share of value creation in Germany now exceeds 75 per cent.

The process of outsourcing is expected to continue on a global scale in the years to come. This promises more good growth opportunities for the German supply industry, both in the growth markets and in Germany. Despite the sacrifices that may have to be made in the short term, the German supply industry is expected to be a stabilizing factor in the development of the economy in the medium to long term. It will also be a driver of technological innovation.

Still, the press is full of stories of industry consolidation trends. With OEMs having already gone through this process, the supply industry offers considerable scope for consolidation, as it is characterized by a high proportion of small and medium-sized enterprises, international as well as national. The liberalization of markets and the possibility of linking up international activities reinforce these tendencies. This is exemplified by the increasing involvement of international capital funds, even with smaller suppliers. Nevertheless, there has not been a significant reduction in the number of supplier companies.

Nor does this seem surprising in view of the industry's attractiveness. Impressive growth rates and technological progress, particularly in the field of electronics, tend to attract companies in adjacent industries. No industry has such a varied range of materials and products as the automotive supply industry. From steel to software, almost all branches of industry are involved in the manufacturing of a car. The industry is diverse – what binds it together are the challenges it faces from competitors, customers and the economic framework.

For the German supply industry, sustaining technology leadership is the key factor in competition. This alone is what will allow production to continue in a high-wage country that is also marked by a high tax burden on businesses. Another major challenge is the fierce competition in the automotive markets, which sees customers faced with rising cost pressure, and higher material costs squeezing revenues. The equity ratio in German companies is low by international comparison, which makes the position even more difficult. Investments in new products and process improvements, as well as spending on research and development, are high and need to be financed. Ultimately, suppliers and car makers need to work together to maintain their competitive position.

A TESTING TIME FOR SUCCESS STRATEGIES

It is true that 'end of days' prophecies, like those issued by the Club of Rome, or 'winner and loser' predictions, as developed by James P Womack, Daniel T Jones and Daniel Ross, the authors of *The Machine that Changed the World* (Rawson, New York, 1990), have been overtaken by reality. But it is equally true that the changes set in motion by globalization necessitate a different economic and political framework, call into question conventional location structures, and make new business models imperative for automotive companies.

That is why so many strategies, decisions on the location of production sites, and historic supply and production structures in the German automotive industry are currently being put to the test. And that is why diverse cost-cutting and restructuring programmes are ultimately the answer to the challenges that globalization is throwing at us. Regardless of which strategy is best for each individual company, there are certain clear development lines that will shape the coming years:

- Productivity at traditional production sites in the home market must be increased to safeguard the basis of Germany as a business location – still attractive overall – and at least soften the trend in production offshoring to low-wage countries. The actions to increase efficiency that companies are now implementing minimize the difference in unit costs that sets us apart from alternative business locations when taken together with all cost factors. In spite of the strengths of Germany's car manufacturing sites – outstanding technological performance and flexibility combined with a direct line to the innovation process – there is only justification for bringing large production volumes to the country if car makers cut production costs and make working hours more flexible. These are difficult processes and some of them are painful, particularly for the workforce in Germany. Interestingly, the so-called traditional automotive plants – some of which have their own in-house wage agreements but all of which certainly have elements far in excess of national wage rates – are under growing pressure from modern, leaner plants and efficient working models, such as 5000 x 5000 at Volkswagen.

The adjustment processes currently under way prove that the industry is being proactive and optimizing its organization in the face of much tougher global competition. Some companies are already proving that they can regain market share and achieve stronger revenues after such a process of restructuring. But what is also clear is that foreign manufacturing is also on the increase, and it will grow at a faster rate than domestic production.

The German automotive industry will increase its global presence. In 2005, German OEMs were already producing more cars worldwide than ever before, with 10.7 million vehicles built in 23 countries. That was 3 per cent more than the previous year. The passenger car segment beat its previous year's record by 2 per cent, taking the total number of cars produced to 9.6 million. Commercial vehicle production leapt 16 per cent to a total of more than 1.1 million. Including Chrysler, German OEMs increased their 2005 production volume by 3 per cent to 13.45 million automobiles. This means that more than one in five (21 per cent) of all vehicles manufactured in the world were built in the production halls of German automotive corporations. The automotive industry's strategy is basically a network strategy: thanks to its strong position in the German home market, it is strong on exports. This protects additional jobs, while simultaneously safeguarding business through a network of production sites in low-wage countries. These enable car makers to gain access to local markets and achieve a better production cost level. Improved competitiveness now sees as much as 40 per cent of the export value originating from supplies shipped from low-wage countries to traditional German production sites.

▎ German OEMs will defend their role as world champions in diesel. The Germans hold 51 per cent of the Western European market for diesel vehicles, which now accounts for 49.5 per cent of the total automotive market. This means that German brands are responsible for 63 per cent of the market's 4.1 million growth in vehicle numbers over the past 10 years. Accounting for 47.4 per cent of passenger car production in Germany, the diesel has also dramatically increased the relevance of Germany as a production location. Today, it is the Germans' key technological advantage over their competitors, particularly as demand is growing in this sector.

The fact that German car makers now account for 82 per cent of the market for vehicles with diesel particulate filters in Germany underlines the contribution to future competitiveness made by clean exhaust emissions technologies. Selective catalytic reduction (SCR) has already prepared the ground for the next technological leap in the reduction of nitrogen oxides (NOx), which can help the diesel engine make a decisive breakthrough in other markets, primarily the United States. Clean diesel is the key buzzword that will boost the presence of this technology in emerging markets that do not yet have a sizeable diesel segment, such as China. The growth market of India already has a high share of diesel vehicles, and this represents an opportunity that will be exploited by German OEMs. Some of our global competitors may be putting their efforts into other engine technologies. Admittedly, they will gain a positive image as early starters, but this is because they do not have the same technological potential with the diesel, on either the manufacturing or the supply side. SCR technology combined with the additive Ad Blue® (VDA's Ad Blue trademark is now registered worldwide as a fuel as well as the related vehicle technology) or the Bluetec technology show that the German automotive industry was also the first to tackle the tricky subject of removing NOx from diesel emissions, the last remaining environmental questionmark.

- The global market for premium products has grown at double the pace of the global automotive market since 2000, registering 10 per cent growth. A market potential of almost 10 million vehicles worldwide seems realistic for 2010. This growth is primarily down to the ever wider distribution of models with premium features outside the traditional domain of premium and executive cars as well as sports cars. Premium features are increasingly being offered successfully in the compact and sport utility vehicle (SUV) classes. And growth is set to continue in the years to come.

- No other industry sector invests as much in new technologies as the German automotive industry. It has invested €16 billion and employs 86,000 people in R&D, including one-fifth of all the engineers working in German industry. Most importantly, the German automotive industry occupies the top spot in the number of automotive patents. Giving up this position, or letting cost, quality and technology leadership do battle against each other, is unthinkable. Although electronics have been particularly helpful in developing safety features – ABS, ESP, airbag, collision avoidance radar, night vision and so on – doing away with them would lead directly to simpler technology. This would make it easier to achieve stable processes, which is a basic requirement for quality. However, it would meet neither the heightened demands of the customers nor the general framework in high-wage Germany. Treading this path would already be very difficult for the German, and even for the European or North

American automotive industry. In the future, it would be completely impossible because of the new competitors from China or India: we would find ourselves stuck in a no-escape situation as the Asians played out their cost advantage against us. The German OEMs' premium position requires them to be a step ahead of the market on technology while at the same time ensuring good quality and acceptable cost levels.

- The homogeneous economic cycles in the automotive industry that we saw in the 1970s and 1980s are more or less a thing of the past. They have been replaced by individual economic cycles for each OEM, created by model cycles or innovations. Consequently, 30 to 50 per cent of 2005's market demand in Germany was created by new vehicles and engines. So new models are one thing; concept innovation is a decisive step further. Concept innovation will continue to hold a significant and probably growing relevance for the German automotive industry in the future. Social change – be it in the age structure, the population or consumer habits – has fragmented or individualized the product offering and differentiated the product range. While there were 340 models available in Germany in 1990, by 2005 the number was already up to 510. The supermini segment is growing, largely driven by the wider range of models. The compact class is also gaining weight, while the traditional midsize category is shrinking slightly. The biggest winners are SUVs, 4×4s, innovative spatial concepts, four-seater convertibles, new models straddling the line between passenger car and commercial vehicle, and the new cross-utility category. While niche vehicles made up just over 15 per cent of all new cars five years ago, they now account for almost 27 per cent.

The upshot of this development is that the complexity that car makers eliminated by reducing their vertical integration back in 1992/93 has now returned, with all of its consequences for higher costs, especially overheads. Manufacturers must ask themselves how they can continue to exploit economies of scale in view of the growing variety of niche vehicles. Another method of keeping costs under control in the face of growing complexity and differentiated niche products, besides the intelligent mix of production locations mentioned above, is so-called modular, platform or unit assembly strategy. Such a strategy enables smaller, yet still economical, batch sizes to be produced, although this does necessitate a higher degree of flexibility. Intelligent outsourcing and the integration of various partners – all the way through to the logistics stage – are a suitable way of keeping complexity down and at the same time handling product diversity, international procurement and site management.

- The market for cars costing less than €10,000 is growing in Europe, and even more so globally. Many of the world's markets, like India, will increasingly focus on vehicles around the €5,000 and perhaps even the €2,000 mark. These categories are only feasible on the cost side if considerably more value is generated in low-wage countries. However, even in Germany, this market segment is more than 50 per cent served by German products – although some are made in Brazil – so there are clearly considerable opportunities to be had here. Behind this development lies the fundamental question whether Germany might only be able to manufacture premium cars in the future, perhaps being forced to give up the production of volume vehicles.
- In the automobile business, finance and leasing are unavoidable to enable large swathes of the population to fulfil their desire to have their own car. Cheap financing deals are driving the new growth markets in particular. Around 75 per cent of new cars registered in Germany are bought through leasing or financing, with half of the deals arranged by automotive banks. This activates an important area of growth and employment potential in this key industry, which is basing more and more of its future business on automobile-related services. In addition to the 770,000 people directly employed by car makers and automotive suppliers in Germany, a further 18,000 work at financial subsidiaries in Germany, 11,000 of them at manufacturers' own banks and leasing companies.

Financial services have thus become a significant source of revenue. Even when automobile sales have been slow, automotive banks have still enjoyed good growth rates. Automotive banks and leasing firms have more than doubled their total assets in the past 10 years, and they now total almost €80 billion. The total assets of Germany's five automotive banks and leasing firms alone exceeded €63 billion in 2004. OEMs' own banks account for more than 70 per cent of financial services sales, with 85 per cent of that amount coming from the leasing business. Car insurance, the third largest segment in the insurance industry, represents a further pillar of automotive financial services, with annual sales in excess of €22 billion. Insurance brokerage by car dealers now accounts for about 30 per cent of policies taken out – a figure that continues to rise.

Car-related services are one of the most important trends to have been recognized by the German automotive industry early on. The growing separation of car ownership and car usage is another. 76,000 people were registered with car-sharing organizations in 2005, their numbers rising by more than 10 per cent over the previous year. This market is growing disproportionately fast, although for the time being it remains a small part of the total market.

THE POLITICAL FRAMEWORK: CARS 21

The success of a strategy is not decided by the market alone. In developed economies, the automobile is now the most regulated product of all. In emerging markets, the degree of regulation is growing faster than most of the markets are. In the past, it was largely the self-regulation and creativity of engineers that kept giving the development of the automobile a technology push at ever shorter intervals. Nowadays, progress is determined by the targets politicians set for the industry in the belief that these targets will reduce fuel consumption or cut emissions faster.

New environmental and safety regulations can be out of sync with the car industry's innovation cycles, and sometimes they are even mutually exclusive. The latter can occur when, say, regulators require additional safety features on the one hand while insisting on weight reductions and lower CO_2 emissions on the other. In the fiercely European markets, this gives car makers a major disadvantage over those in countries with much lower levels of competition, such as Japan or Korea. In these countries, companies sometimes even receive government support.

The CARS 21 process, spearheaded by European Commission Vice-President Günter Verheugen, clears the way for the global competitiveness of an industry to become one of the key criteria determining the direction and speed of new EU regulations. The CARS 21 group was made up of high-ranking representatives from the European Commission, Member State ministries, the European Parliament, the automotive and the oil industry, as well as other non-governmental organizations (NGOs) such as consumer protection organizations. The result is a series of joint recommendations aimed at improving the European automotive industry's ability to compete on a global scale, but also supporting further improvements in road safety and lessening the impact of the car on our environment. CARS 21 defined an integrated approach that will be used to bring the diverging requirements, many of which are only ever seen together when they reach the developer's desk, into line with each other. Their consequences will then be assessed during the legislative procedure itself.

The group's recommendations are intended specifically to improve the legislation governing new vehicle registration by simplifying the processes involved. This includes, for example, integrating the ECE regulations into the body of European law, which at the moment contains almost identical EU directives that are meant to run in parallel. The plan is to replace 38 EU directives with ECE regulations. In addition to this, vehicle and parts manufacturers will be allowed to self-test their products' compliance with certain regulations, and the use of 'virtual' testing (such as computer simulation) will also be permitted. Work on international harmonization of vehicle regulations will be intensified, with key markets and growth markets being more closely involved in the harmonization. Furthermore, the comprehensive approach also means that transitional rules based on product lifecycles will be defined for when new regulations come into force or existing ones are modified. Moreover, the impact of regulations already in force will be reviewed after a certain period has elapsed.

The group also discussed a number of ways of reducing exhaust emissions for light vehicles (Euro 5) and heavy vehicles (Euro 6). Commission proposals are planned for both of these regulations, and will be presented in 2006 (in the case of light vehicles) and 2007.

The integrated approach is particularly thorough when it comes to efforts to reduce CO_2 emissions, with all stakeholders being addressed (the automotive and the oil industry, automobile workshops, as well as drivers and the relevant authorities). Besides engineering the vehicles themselves to be more efficient, the introduction of information systems such as gear change indicators and consumption meters, and even training in eco-driving, are among the solutions being considered. Biofuels (mainly admixed with regular fuels) will play a key role, with special emphasis being placed on what are known as second-generation biofuels (for instance BTL, biomass-to-liquid), since these are expected to provide the greatest potential at acceptable cost levels.

Hence, the recommendations of the CARS 21 group provide a new basis for optimizing the political environment in Europe. They aim to safeguard the competitiveness of Europe's automotive industry and simultaneously bring further improvements in road safety and environmental protection by applying a comprehensive and integrated approach. The CARS 21 road map of upcoming legislation to be initiated by the European Union in the automotive sphere brings the chance of greater reliability and predictability on the part of European lawmakers. It remains to be seen how the European Union performs on this count in real legislative action.

WELCOME TRENDS IN BETTER VEHICLE SAFETY

The automotive industry has been successful at constantly improving the automobile's safety and impact on the environment. In spite of increasing traffic on our roads, the number of deaths in road traffic accidents since

1991 has more than halved, with just under 5,400 people killed in Germany in 2005, and the downward trend is continuing.

However, there is increasing evidence that the most important potential for further improvements in vehicle safety can only be realized if partners work together and share the workload intelligently. That is why CARS 21 advocates an integrated approach in this area too, involving not just vehicle technology but the road infrastructure and road users as well. The Commission will present suggestions for the successive introduction of vehicle regulations. These include things like the electronic stability programme (ESP), safety belt warning indicator, brake assistant, as well as direct and indirect visibility, ISOFIX child restraint systems and daytime running lamps. In terms of road infrastructure, it will recommend a monitoring and evaluation system that will help all parts of the road system adjust to the more exacting standards. It will even include the criminal prosecution of those driving under the influence of alcohol or drugs, or speeding, especially since these are among the main causes of accidents. And finally, positive opportunities like the e-Call system should be used to make a big improvement to emergency services callouts. It is of the utmost importance that the injured are treated within the first hour of an accident.

In the past, German automobile manufacturers and suppliers were pioneers when it came to road safety, and road safety has since become a key means of differentiation, proof of technology leadership and therefore of a brand's position. Efforts to improve safety will therefore continue to be one of the Germans' strategic priorities.

THE GERMAN AUTOMOTIVE INDUSTRY SETS ITS SIGHTS ON BIOFUELS

Keeping our society supplied with energy is one of the greatest challenges for the future. We have no choice but to reduce our dependency on oil. This is also part of the industry's responsibility toward climate protection, nationally and globally. At the same time, making sure that resources remain available and affordable in the long term is one of the keys to remaining competitive. Being less dependent on energy supplies and thus achieving greater supply security coupled with price stability are therefore long-term, primary goals. Innovation is the industry's alternative to regulation, and to prices rising to new thresholds and increasing the burden on drivers.

German OEMs are not about to put all their eggs in one basket in the hope that it is the right one. What they will adopt is a more varied approach:

- greater use of first-generation biofuels, such as biodiesel and bioethanol, and admixtures of up to 10 per cent (that is, going further than the European Union's target of 5.75 per cent by 2010);
- introducing alternative, second-generation biomass fuels (BTL);
- further efficiency improvements in highly efficient clean diesel and gasoline engines;
- customized application of all hybrid technology options;
- using natural gas as a fuel;
- developing and introducing alternative engine systems;
- considering hydrogen as a long-term prospect.

The Germans are not starting from scratch. On the contrary, increasingly efficient engines have been reducing our dependency on oil for years. The average fuel consumption of a new German car is 25 per cent lower than it was in 1990 and a massive 40 per cent lower than in 1970. Half of all new cars made by German OEMs in 2004 run on less than 6.5 litres per 100 kilometres. More than 250 models of German cars consume less than 6.5 litres, with 48 models even managing to keep their fuel consumption under 5 litres. These cars have played a big part in the continuous reduction of CO_2 emissions from road traffic since 1999. By 2004, CO_2 emissions were 15 million tonnes lower than in 1999. This makes road transport the sector with the highest CO_2 reduction over this period. Furthermore, exhaust emissions were also cut by up to 97 per cent.

Hybrid technology represents another focus for R&D activities in the coming years. The German automotive industry sees the hybrid being used primarily in areas where it can play to its advantages. Where there are rapid changes in driving speed, such as driving in city traffic, a hybrid engine can save fuel and cut emissions. The American and Japanese markets are leading the way in terms of hybrid vehicles. By 2015, hybrid vehicles are expected to account for about 15 per cent of cars on the road in the United States. In Europe, the hybrid is competing against a strong diesel market, which is making its breakthrough much more difficult.

German car makers are already working in partnership with each other and in collaboration with global partners in this area. And it is not true that they are late in starting, or that they have the wrong strategic priorities. The United States, for example, has two to three diesel cars to every hybrid vehicle. Therefore, manufacturers that have a lower than average presence in the diesel segment should be the ones asking themselves if they missed the boat.

In the long term, environmentally friendly hydrogen from renewable sources is set to become the main energy carrier. In the short to medium term, the German automotive industry is focusing on combining a whole range of different technologies. Moving away from oil involves more than the cars themselves; it entails looking at the fuels that power them. The German automotive industry is therefore pushing the use of alternative, renewable sources of fuel energy.

Admixtures with 10 per cent biofuel can cut the amount of CO_2 released into the atmosphere by the cars on the road today by more than 15g/km. For this reason, the German automotive industry has already begun getting cars ready to take admixtures of up to 10 per cent. So the German car industry has clearly started doing its homework for the future. Fuel standards will need to see further development in parallel.

The German automotive industry will continue to offer vehicles that can run on even higher admixtures. German car makers are world leaders in the production of bioethanol vehicles. With their so-called flex fuel vehicles, they have cornered almost 70 per cent of the market in Brazil, the world's biggest bioethanol market. Some OEMs are even selling these cars in Europe, including Germany.

To leverage this potential for the benefit of our climate, the task now is to tackle the challenges on the raw materials side:

- Biofuels already account for 3 per cent of fuels in Germany today. By 2020, the German agricultural sector alone will, with the right focus and suitable production methods, be able to substitute as much as 10 per cent of the fossil fuels it uses, with the figure rising to over 15 per cent by 2030. Translated into carbon dioxide emissions, this equates to potential savings of over 10 million tons for Germany alone by 2030.
- European Commission calculations indicate that almost 10 per cent of the fuel used in the European Union can already be substituted by biomass. In 2040, the figure should exceed 35 per cent.
- The global market holds even greater potential for substitution, with a larger quantity of usable space and more favourable climatic conditions in many cases.

Cutting CO_2 emissions by 80 to 90 per cent is a realistic proposition for the fuels of the future. Key factors are the profitability of energy crops, the intensity with which raw materials and their waste products are used, and the conversion rate – that is, the efficiency with which fuel is produced from biomass. In this respect, synthetic BTL fuels and fuels made from ligno-cellulose fibres have shown the best results. The return per hectare can be optimized through the cultivation of energy crops. These fuels are also capable of processing a wide range of biomass products. Moreover, the biomass is converted into fuel at an effective rate – especially since every part of the plant can be used.

However, technological suitability and a good environmental balance are not enough. New fuels must also be economically feasible. Some biofuels can already be produced at prices similar to those of fossil fuels. In most cases and particularly in Europe, biofuels can only be produced competitively because they qualify for tax exemption, but almost all biofuels display the potential to reach the price level of fossil fuels.

Ethanol is already at least as cheap as comparable gasoline, if you consider the global market price. Biodiesel too can already be produced at a competitive price if it is made from waste fats that would otherwise have to be disposed of at considerable cost.

The raw materials market is of key significance for biofuels. As the materials used to make biofuels cannot exclusively be bought in Germany, the raw materials market should be considered both nationally and internationally. It is important to successively prepare the global business of selling raw materials to meet this new demand. The growing number of potential raw materials suppliers represents a considerable advantage, from farmers in Germany to agricultural markets the world over. Long term, this provides a broader basis for our energy supplies and enables us to be less affected by political crises or OPEC-style monopolies.

Finally, the right legal and, even more importantly, fiscal framework must be in place. The focus must be placed firmly on a reliable policy of promoting biofuels – one which is based on a clear set of criteria such as the potential for reducing CO_2. Trying to manage the transition to biofuels with compulsory conversion rates and forced admixture ratios will not result in success and is likely to lead to higher prices for drivers. Taxation based on CO_2 efficiency and sustainability criteria is the best approach – this will put the market entry requirements in place for the second generation of biofuels, and prevent funds being misallocated in the future to promote biofuels that have no impact on CO_2 levels.

THE GERMAN AUTOMOTIVE INDUSTRY: EQUIPPED FOR THE FUTURE

Lasting success in the automotive industry will depend on comprehensive and highly complex integration processes. Hence, automotive companies and suppliers are facing enormous challenges because they must:

- integrate the requirements of the markets in completely different stages of the development process and different structures;
- manage a global production and supply network that can no longer be organized along the lines of home and export markets;
- integrate the requirement for ever greater levels of innovation in the supply chain and ensure reliable quality of the highest level;
- keep core competencies in Germany, from R&D to production, while also optimizing efficiency levels;
- develop several technologies at once to cut emissions and consumption levels and provide greater security in terms of highlighting synergies and overlaps, as well as show when incompatible or competing targets are being pursued;
- take society and the political world's changing expectations of the product development process into account from an early stage, and conversely, work proactively to shape the general framework.

If companies nowadays are looking at their established organizational structures and processes and adjusting them faster than they did in the past, this is primarily because they know they need to stand up to the requirements of the future. The German automotive industry is on the ball and is, in spite of all the challenges, well equipped to tackle the intensifying international competition.

2

The automotive power play moves into its next round

Ralf Kalmbach, Partner, Roland Berger Strategy Consultants

Automotive engineering is one of the key industries in virtually all developed economies. It has a profound impact on economic output, employment, technological development and a raft of other factors that are critical to a nation's economic performance. It is also one of the driving forces behind globalization. Car makers have long been marketing and selling their products around the world. Accordingly, the industry's worldwide networking strengths and global presence are way ahead of those in other sectors.

Automobiles are very special products to the individual too. Highly complex in terms of the technology they embody, they meet the basic human need for mobility, which in turn is a prerequisite for the intensive exchange of goods. On another level, cars are also status symbols that awaken desires and make dreams come true. They are (or can be) both an expression and an integral part of their owner's lifestyle. They are also expensive: in many cases, they are one of the single largest items their owner will ever buy.

The tremendous importance of the automotive industry both to developed economies and to the individuals who drive cars makes it very prone to change. A given market's propensity to invest may shift. Purchasers' preferences may vacillate. Operating costs may rise. Governments may introduce new laws that alter the playing field. All these factors – and many more besides – have a direct impact on the complex business systems and value chains that characterize the automotive industry. This fact alone presents a significant challenge to an industry that is so capital-intensive and whose tributary systems mean that it can only respond slowly to change. The corollary is that the automotive industry can only operate successfully in a stable context that is conducive to reliable planning.

Over many decades, far-reaching changes have repeatedly shaken and challenged the industry: the oil crisis in the 1970s; Japanese superiority in the early 1990s, which posed a massive threat to European and American manufacturers; the severe political and economic crisis in South America that abruptly put a line through everyone's astronomical sales expectations – the list could go on indefinitely.

Today, however, a new dimension of challenge is emerging. Fundamental political and economic changes are coinciding, and automotive companies are feeling the full force of both shifts. Traditional structures and 'rules of the game' no longer apply. The entire global industry is in transition.

The automotive power play, in other words, has moved into its next round. Managers in the industry now have but a brief window of opportunity – one or two years at most – in which to lay the foundations for their companies' future survival and success. It is time for them to find strategic answers, and to focus business systems on the new challenges that lie ahead. First, however, they must grasp the nature of the changes that are currently buffeting their industry.

GLOBAL SHIFTS IN AUTOMOTIVE MARKETS

Just a few years ago, the car industry knew for sure which markets interested it. The United States, Japan and Western Europe – the 'triad markets' – stood at the centre of all strategies and plans mapped out by vehicle manufacturers and their component suppliers. Indeed, a 70 per cent share of global vehicle sales in 2000 certainly justified this keen focus. New markets such as South America had frequently aroused great expectations in the past, yet such expectations seldom translated into successful strategies. Many manufacturers had to learn this lesson the hard way. Some, in fact, are still suffering from the legacy of misplaced investments back in those heady days.

The triad markets have been stagnating for years, however. And this is forcing the automotive industry to realign its strategic thrusts and concentrate more on up-and-coming countries and economic areas: China, India, the Asian 'tiger economies', and Eastern Europe. All these markets have grown rapidly in recent years and are the only ones that will, in future, continue to post significant growth rates (Figure 2.1).

The next round 27

China, India, Indonesia, Malaysia, Philippines, Thailand, Eastern Europe

- 2000: 6.5
- 2004: 10.8 (CAGR +13.5%)
- 2010E: 19.2 (CAGR +12.5%)

Western Europe, United States, Japan (the 'triad')

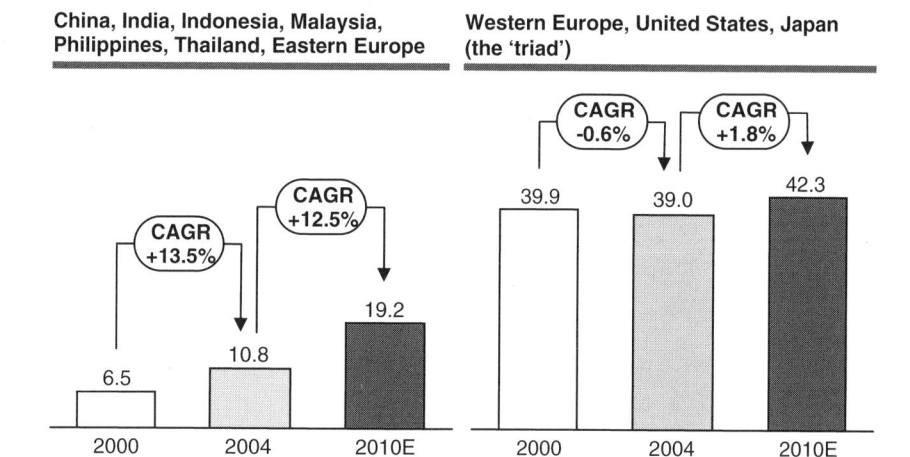

- 2000: 39.9
- 2004: 39.0 (CAGR -0.6%)
- 2010E: 42.3 (CAGR +1.8%)

Figure 2.1 *Vehicle sales in selected regions, 2000–10 (millions of units)*
Sources: JD Power, Roland Berger Strategy Consultants

There is a catch, however. Auto makers and component suppliers who turn their attention to these new markets will only meet with success if they do not see them as new sales regions only. Each one of these markets has its own highly individual economic structures, sociodemographic layers and customer needs. The example of the four tiger economies – Indonesia, Malaysia, the Philippines and Thailand – powerfully underscores this contention (Figure 2.2). Which vehicle types people most prefer varies considerably. Pick-ups are the most popular purchase in Thailand, against SUVs/minivans in Indonesia and the Philippines, for example. Also, the import quota in three of these countries (Malaysia is the only exception) is upward of 80 per cent (Figures 2.3 and 2.4).

	Population 2004 (million)	GNP per capita, 2004 (US$)	GNP growth 2004 (%)	Cars per 1,000 inhabitants
Indonesia	242	970	5.1	15
Malaysia	24	4,601	7.0	207
Philippines	87	975	6.1	9
Thailand	65	2,490	6.2	39

Figure 2.2 *Macroeconomic data in selected East Asian countries*
Sources: CIA World Factbook, Deutsche Bank Research

28 *Major challenges*

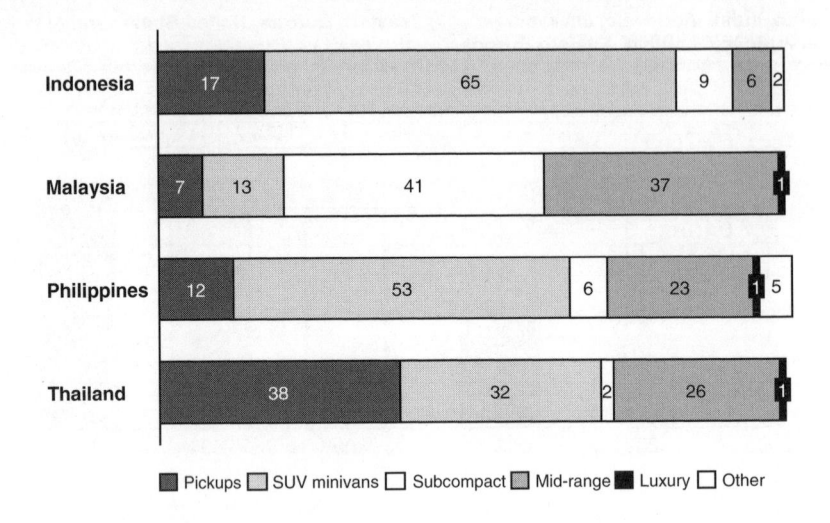

[Bar chart showing market segmentation by vehicle type:
- Indonesia: Pickups 17, SUV minivans 65, Subcompact 9, Mid-range 6, Other 2
- Malaysia: Pickups 7, SUV minivans 13, Subcompact 41, Mid-range 37, Other 1
- Philippines: Pickups 12, SUV minivans 53, Subcompact 6, Mid-range 23, Luxury 1, Other 5
- Thailand: Pickups 38, SUV minivans 32, Subcompact 2, Mid-range 26, Other 1
Legend: Pickups, SUV minivans, Subcompact, Mid-range, Luxury, Other]

Figure 2.3 *Market segmentation by vehicle type (per cent)*
Source: JD Power

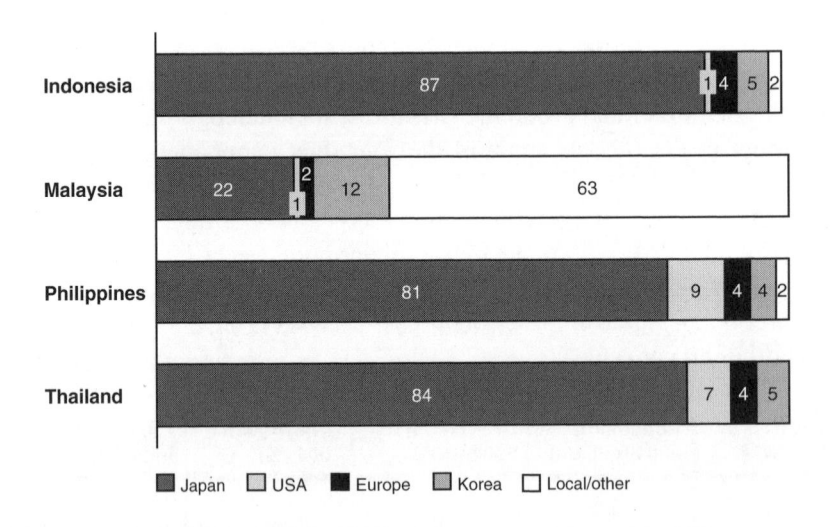

[Bar chart showing market share by country/region of origin:
- Indonesia: Japan 87, USA 1, Europe 4, Korea 5, Local/other 2
- Malaysia: Japan 22, USA 2, Europe 1, Korea 12, Local/other 63
- Philippines: Japan 81, USA 9, Europe 4, Korea 4, Local/other 2
- Thailand: Japan 84, USA 7, Europe 4, Local/other 5
Legend: Japan, USA, Europe, Korea, Local/other]

Figure 2.4 *Market share by country/region of origin (per cent)*
Source: JD Power

It follows that viable strategies for these markets necessitate specific products for specific countries or regions, suitable sales channels, and appropriate communication with the buyers. It is vital to accurately anticipate both demand structures and the factors that influence purchase decisions, and then to supply products tailored to precisely these needs. In Asia's upwardly mobile economies, vehicles do not normally need quite so much elaborate technology. The technology they do have must not be obsolete, however. Vehicles sold here must be functional and have a modern design. Behind this 'profile' is the standard buying pattern that low disposable income still dictates in all emerging markets: people want 'value for money'. Accordingly, entry-level segments in particular are experiencing above-average growth, while concurrently exerting heavy cost pressure on manufacturers.

This trend is most evident in China. In the years ahead, the low-end segments will continue to enjoy above-average growth. Vehicles in the classes A00 through A will therefore corner 70 per cent of the market by 2010 (Figure 2.5).

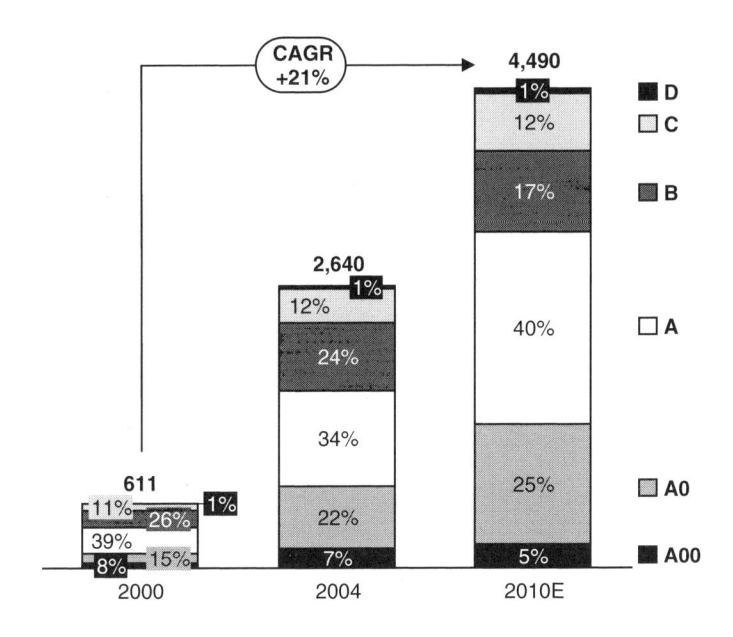

Figure 2.5 *Sales of passenger cars in China, 2000–10 (millions of units)*
Sources: CAAM; Roland Berger Strategy Consultants

China's home-grown car industry is enviably positioned in this segment. It has made stunningly fast progress in the past few years, energetically asserting its place on the Chinese market – and also laying plans to export the fruit of its labours. Collaboration with established auto makers is enabling Chinese original equipment manufacturers (OEMs) to develop and build attractive products in short order. The reason is that they have recourse to the same external links in the value chain (component suppliers, development service providers etc) as foreign OEMs. As a rule, they can also tap substantial cost advantages by sourcing and manufacturing locally. This configuration enables them to sell attractive products at prices well below the cost of their imported counterparts (Figure 2.6).

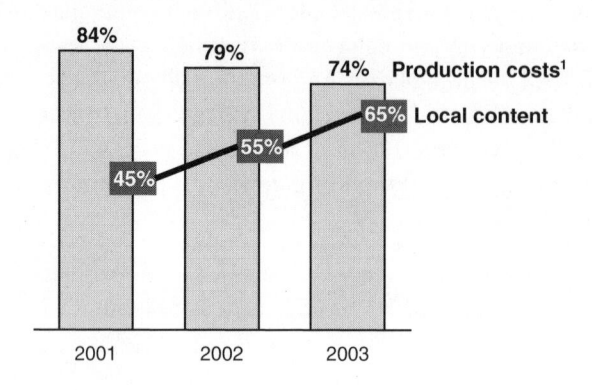

```
        84%
              79%
                    74%  Production costs¹
                    65%  Local content
              55%
        45%
        2001  2002  2003
```

1) Assumption: Production costs = 100% if local content = 0

Figure 2.6 *Correlation between production costs and local content*
Source: Roland Berger Strategy Consultants

Production of the Chery QQ in China provides a good illustration of how vehicles can be positioned very successfully, and at the same time, trigger price erosion across entire market segments. This subcompact model sells for less than the equivalent of €3,000 and was, in the first quarter of 2005, the best-selling car in China. Volkswagen's cheapest model right now – the Brazilian-built Fox – costs more than twice as much, at the equivalent of €7,000.

European and American OEMs' hopes of selling their products in these new growth markets and absorbing excess capacity will therefore come to nothing. The problem of overcapacity in their traditional markets must be dealt with at source. Meanwhile, new business models are needed for the new markets (Figure 2.7). Without local development and production, foreign OEMs will not be able to gain a foothold.

The battle for the emerging markets is therefore still wide open. Established auto makers will only score lasting successes in these markets if they can formulate and systematically apply suitably adjusted business models (in terms of brand positioning, product portfolios, pricing strategies and delivery systems). The winners in this race will be few in number.

Region	Capacity growth, 2004–10 (000 units)	Capacity utilization in 2004 (%)
Asia and Pacific	4,814	78
EU	1,209	78
North America	504	79
Eastern Europe	439	63
South America	384	55

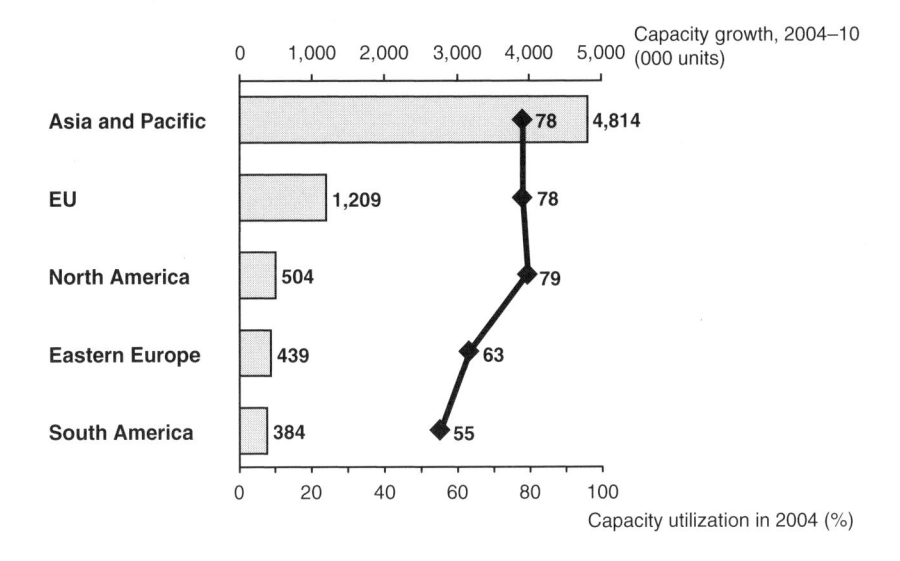

Figure 2.7 *Global capacity growth through 2010 and capacity utilization in 2004*
Sources: PricewaterhouseCoopers, Roland Berger Strategy Consultants

THE SHIFTING BALANCE OF POWER IN THE AUTOMOTIVE INDUSTRY

New markets are not the only factor that is forcing the automotive industry to adapt. The balance of power within the industry itself is likewise experiencing a shift of seismic proportions:

- New suppliers are rewriting the rules of the game.
- Traditional customer segments are dissolving.
- As the level of outsourcing increases, car makers and component suppliers are becoming more and more heavily dependent on each other.
- External conditions and constraints (a more environmentally aware public, the limited availability of fossil fuels, more pronounced political interventions in the form of laws, taxes and tolls) are forcing the industry to address new issues.

New suppliers are rewriting the rules of the game

Whenever the automotive industry engages in trials of strength, it always does so on a global scale. In the 1980s, 'cheap' Japanese cars posed an existential threat to the American and European incumbents. In the mid-1990s, highly successful Korean manufacturers brought a new challenge into the fray, whose market share rose to 4 per cent in North America and 3 per cent in Western Europe in a few short years.

In building up production capacity in their target markets (North America, Western and Eastern Europe, China and India), these companies have already done the groundwork for further expansion. They are thus gradually establishing themselves as local vendors. In many cases, their superior business models or production systems enable them to supply vehicles whose prices and quality are more attractive. The challenge to home-grown car makers' market share is obvious. As if that were not enough, these new upstarts are actually defining new success factors in the markets they target. Local players thus have no choice but to face up to their new rivals and accept that the rules of competition have changed.

Toyota, for example, is currently rolling up market after market and is well on the way to becoming the world's leading auto maker. Even General Motors (GM) and Ford are being cast in the Japanese giant's shadow in the United States (see Figure 2.8).

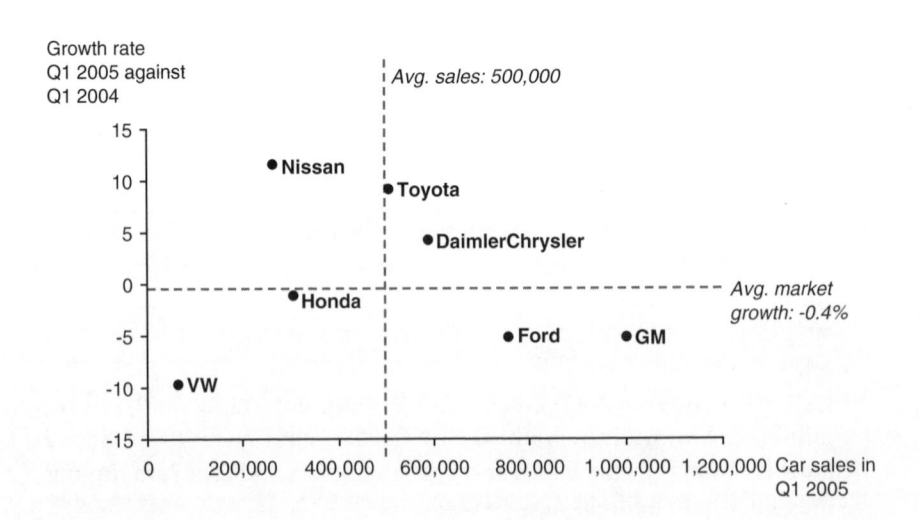

Figure 2.8 *Passenger car sales and growth rates for the largest OEMs in the United States, first quarter 2005*
Source: Roland Berger Strategy Consultants

Hyundai is likewise in the process of becoming one of the leading manufacturers in North America and Europe. Over the next few years, it is forecast to achieve 6 and 10 per cent growth respectively in these two markets. The company has a very powerful presence in China in particular. Here, its market share has shot up from zero to 8 per cent in just three years. Anticipated average annual growth of 40 per cent in the next three years will give Hyundai an even firmer foothold.

A number of other vendors are already on the starting blocks. It is only a matter of time before Chinese OEMs begin to penetrate the triad markets with knock-down prices, and before consumers begin to regard vehicles from India or the ASEAN countries as viable, economical alternatives.

Traditional customer segments are dissolving

Only a few years ago, marketing experts in the car industry could still delimit their target groups fairly clearly on the basis of social strata and purchasing power. Today, customer behaviour no longer fits into neat little patterns and decision modes, and is therefore much more difficult to predict. Traditional segmentation patterns are simply no longer valid.

Two interlocking developments have precipitated the erosion of traditional customer segments. One is buyers' growing penchant for 'smart shopping'. The other is the increasing supply of niche products from manufacturers.

Smart shopping has become a discipline that shapes every purchase a buyer makes. That naturally also applies to such major investments as the purchase of a car. Smart shoppers trawl multiple sources to retrieve copious information about products and market prices. Ever keen to secure the best value for money, they tend to shrug off the influence of past purchasing decisions. This undermines customer loyalty, forcing vendors constantly to create attractive new offerings if they want existing customers to buy successor models too.

In the fierce battle for new market segments and niches, auto makers have no choice but to pursue creative new strategies in order to set their vehicle ranges apart. To retain existing customers and win new ones, they thus market all kinds of niche products that hold out the promise of 'personal' mobility and lifestyle solutions. These offerings go far beyond regular, off-the-peg products and are designed to lure buyers irrespective of status and purchasing power. Examples of such successful niche products include the BMW Mini and the Toyota Prius.

Even so, it is becoming ever more difficult to predict whether and to what extent buyers will accept new products. Not every purchase decision can be explained in rational terms. An automobile is, after all, still a very emotionally charged product whose benefit is perceived to far surpass the mere guarantee of mobility. Seen from this angle, every planned product launch is in effect a gamble whose probability of success or failure can at best only be guessed. And big gambles inherently go hand in hand with high risks.

The growing economic implications of these risks pose a serious problem to car makers. With competition merciless and profit margins often razor-thin, one or two flops can often spell doom for the company. Without the financial backing of DaimlerChrysler, the Smart subsidiary, for instance, would long since have suffered this fate.

The crucial issue is therefore the ability to devise visionary brand and product strategies for highly unpredictable markets. Solid planning structures and processes are a must, obviously. To anticipate the trends that will really take off and translate these into just the right products nevertheless also demands a good nose, the ability to take bold entrepreneurial decisions – and a decent helping of good fortune.

The key focus should, however, always be on clear answers to two questions. What exactly does the brand stand for? And what attributes can and do existing and potential buyers want to associate with the brand? This issue has often been neglected in the past. Jaguar, for example, learnt the painful lesson that 'British luxury' cannot simply be mapped onto the volume segment, even if the brand itself rightly belongs in the premium segment. Conversely, the VW Phaeton shows how hard it can be and how long it can take to gain a foothold in new premium segments that break with brand tradition. Interestingly, customers evidently perceive that the VW Touareg – itself an expensive, luxurious sport utility vehicle (SUV) – is more authentic and fits better with the brand. Although the Phaeton and Touareg share a lot of the same technology, it is the latter that is scoring impressive sales successes.

True, there are no patent recipes. Even so, formulating a successful brand and product portfolio strategy remains the pivotal challenge to car makers today.

Car makers and component suppliers are becoming ever more interdependent

Specialization in the automotive industry goes back a long way. In today's heavily integrated and tightly networked value chains, car makers naturally still bear responsibility for development and production. A good 70 per cent of product value is added by external component suppliers, however.

Relentless pressure to cut costs and innovate in this industry will drive up the proportion of outsourced value further still. By focusing on their specific core competencies, specialized component suppliers can improve quality and achieve scale effects that benefit the entire value chain.

This compulsion to specialize throws up a series of strategic questions to which auto makers must again find clear and consistent answers:

- What does the brand stand for?
- What technological unique selling points (USPs) does the brand demand?
- What systems, modules and components are needed to realize these USPs?
- Which links in the value chain must be handled in-house?
- Which component suppliers and partners can take care of the other links?
- How should collaboration with component suppliers and partners be designed?

This pronounced shift in the value chain has, however, already triggered extensive consolidation in the component supply market. In terms of size, global footprint, skills and innovative strengths, many of today's component suppliers certainly rank as equals with the car makers they serve. In many cases, they dominate certain systems, functions and technologies to such an extent that OEMs have no choice but to live with the resultant dependencies (see Figures 2.9 and 2.10).

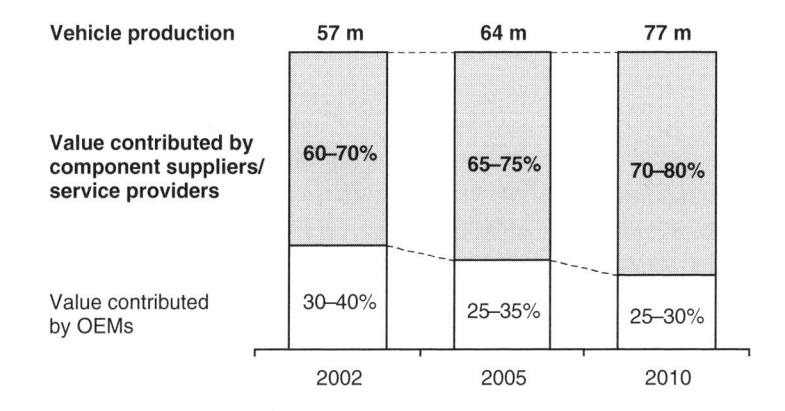

Vehicle production	57 m	64 m	77 m
Value contributed by component suppliers/ service providers	60–70%	65–75%	70–80%
Value contributed by OEMs	30–40%	25–35%	25–30%
	2002	2005	2010

Figure 2.9 *Trends in the automotive production value chain, 2002–10*
Source: Roland Berger Strategy Consultants

36 Major challenges

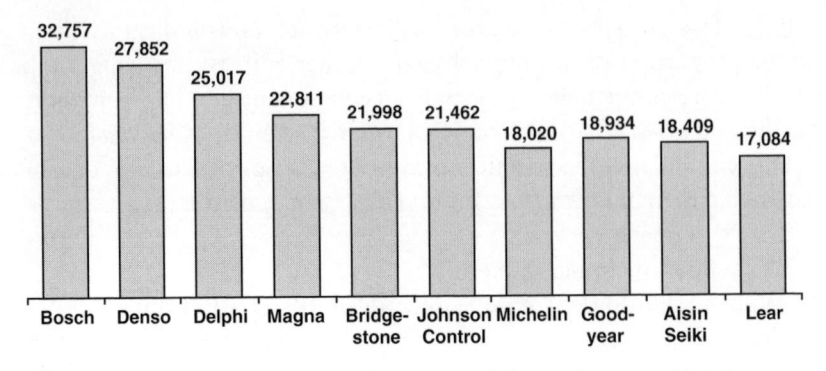

Company	Sales
Bosch	32,757
Denso	27,852
Delphi	25,017
Magna	22,811
Bridgestone	21,998
Johnson Control	21,462
Michelin	18,020
Goodyear	18,934
Aisin Seiki	18,409
Lear	17,084

Note: Currencies are translated at the value dates for the financial statements in each financial year.

Figure 2.10 *The 10 largest automotive component suppliers, 2005/06 (sales in US$ millions)*
Source: Bloomberg, company information

If anything, auto makers will in future have to give even greater consideration to component suppliers than in the past. Complementing their core competencies in development and production, OEMs will also have to concentrate heavily on forging strategic partnerships and designing efficient collaborative processes and structures. Success will, by definition, become a collaborative achievement.

Tighter conditions and constraints impose limits – and create opportunities

The future of personal mobility will not be shaped first and foremost by faster or more powerful vehicles. Social and environmental issues will instead be the determining factors. Traffic density and pollution have already reached or exceeded critical thresholds in many places (see Figure 2.11). Innovative solutions such as London's city-centre toll zone bear witness to governments' attempts to prevent private transport infrastructures from collapsing altogether. Other large cities and conurbations will follow suit.

Political regulation takes effect via the ratification of prescribed pollution thresholds and safety standards, via taxation and via prohibitions. At the same time, consumers too are fuelling demand for more economical, environment-friendly cars. This bottom-up trend is therefore likewise obliging automotive firms to adopt a greener stance.

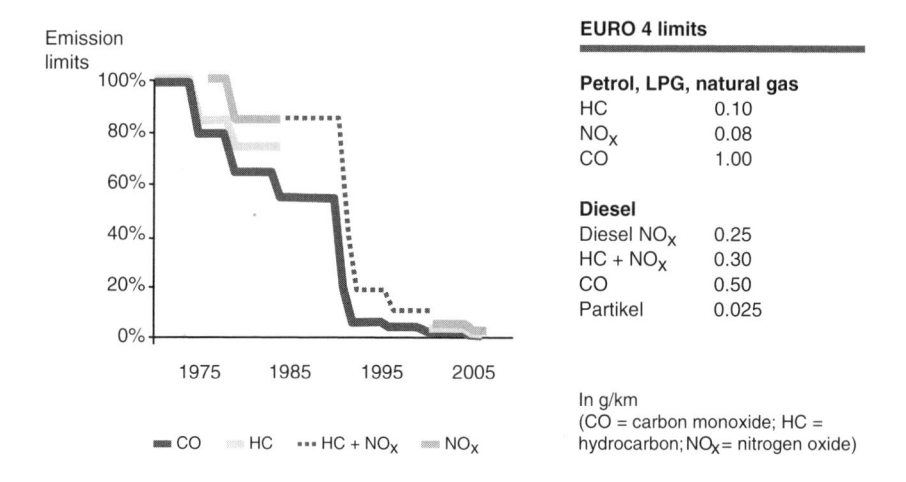

Figure 2.11 *Trend in vehicle emissions in Europe, 1975–2005*
Sources: Volkswagen, VDA website

The industry has long since accepted such political influence. Accordingly, traditional selling points such as performance, design and price are increasingly being complemented by environmental and safety aspects. Today's key innovations revolve around the need to optimize fuel consumption, reduce harmful emissions and improve vehicle safety.

The ever greater traffic density, and in particular the higher volume of traffic in major conurbations, nevertheless often more than offset any positive effect from such innovations. Further norms, prescriptions and regulations are therefore bound to follow. The recent EU directive on particulate matter is only one example.

The automotive industry will accept this development too. Indeed, it will have to throw its weight behind the initiative. After all, the industry itself benefits from regular statutory decrees that oblige drivers to fork out for new features if they want to avoid stiff penalties relating to obsolete car technology. In a similar vein, safety and environmental issues provide car makers with new ways to set themselves apart through innovation, and thereby to strategically reposition their brands. Thanks to its Prius model, Toyota, for instance, has successfully cultivated an image as an environment-conscious brand. Rivals worldwide have been forced to respond to this astute move. Peugeot achieved a comparable effect by quickly and systematically introducing diesel particle filters.

THE WINNER TAKES IT ALL

Such upheavals bring fundamental change to whole industries. Not all companies handle or, in particular anticipate, the corresponding opportunities and threats with the same measure of success. Few are able to adapt to changed conditions and bring their business systems into line with new constraints.

Current developments will bring lasting change to the automotive industry. There will be winners and losers. Some companies will lose or have to relinquish their independence. Others will grow faster than ever, and above all profitably. The gap between 'good' and 'bad' will widen. Mediocre firms – and this goes for auto makers and component suppliers alike – will be the first to hit the wall (see Figure 2.12).

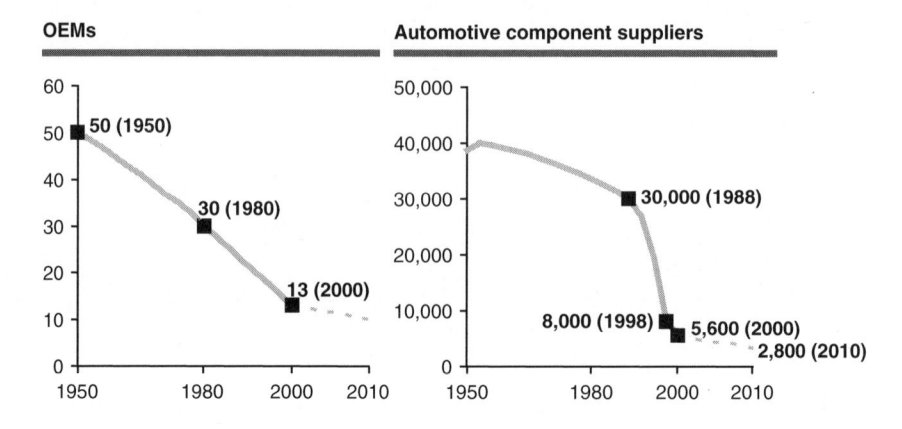

Figure 2.12 *Number of independent OEMs and independent automotive component suppliers, 1950–2010*
Source: Automobilproduktion

The process of concentration in the automotive industry will continue. New players, especially those with roots in emerging markets, may take the field in the short term. In the medium term, however, they too will experience the workings of global market mechanisms that are even now separating the men from the boys.

The example of China

The Chinese car industry presents a fine study of the early stages in this development. Issued in 2005, the new Chinese automobile directive will considerably speed up the pace of market concentration. Small, local OEMs will no longer be competitive under the new provisions. They will either be absorbed by larger indigenous companies that are able to compete in the international arena, or they will be forced out of the game. Merger activity will increase – witness SAIC's acquisition of China National Automotive Industry Corporation and the current talks between Hafei and Changhe.

Global OEMs will play a part in driving this development. Rather than go under in the wave of consolidation, they will reassess whether existing partnerships will help them to survive and remain competitive. Where necessary, they will have to revector their collaborative activities.

Consolidation in the industry will probably leave four or maybe five big players that dominate the market. Hundreds of smaller firms will not survive. The same goes for other 'new' markets such as India and the ASEAN countries, where just a handful of companies will likewise rule the roost. These winners will not necessarily be today's incumbents, however. Some new players have the potential to overtake their less agile predecessors and outmanoeuvre them at their own game and on their home turf.

This story reminds us of how the dinosaurs died out, albeit with one crucial difference; back then, the smaller, more nimble mammals survived. By contrast, the global auto business requires companies to achieve a certain critical mass if they are to operate profitably. Only large companies can exploit the economies of scale, fully utilize their production capacity, build up expensive, ubiquitous sales and service networks, and deliver the volume needed to keep them running. The ability to combine size and agility will therefore be decisive in the battle for survival.

A comparison of Toyota and GM underscores the point. Toyota has already risen to second slot in the worldwide automotive business and is giving GM a hard race for pole position. Though both groups are of a similar size, the discrepancy in terms of performance could not be more striking. While GM is fighting to stay alive, Toyota is smashing record after record.

For all its size, GM right now looks ill-placed to survive in the face of fierce global competition. Company pensions and other pension commitments add US $1600 to the cost of every vehicle that rolls off its production lines. Following mistakes in model policy, GM cannot even sell its cars on its home (US) market without conceding heavy discounts, and not even this sales strategy is paying off: in 2004, the company sold only 50,000 more vehicles than in the preceding year. Its market share in the United States is dropping toward 20 per cent. Margins are dwindling and cashflow is negative. As things stand, the Detroit-based giant cannot compete with the Koreans on price, with the Japanese on quality, or with the Europeans on technological performance.

Toyota, however, has managed to position itself as the quality and environmental technology leader. It is selling cars that customers want to buy. It is also growing profitably: In 2004, volume sales jumped 10.5 per cent year on year, while sales revenues were up 7.3 per cent. Another plant is slated for construction in the United States in the near future in order to accommodate growing demand in this market (see Figure 2.13).

	GM	Toyota
Year founded	1908	1937
Employees in 2004 (000)	321	260
Vehicles sold in 2004 (million)	8.1	6.7
Number of brands 2005	13 (Chevrolet, Pontiac, Buick, Cadillac, GMC, Saturn, Hummer, Saab, Holden, Opel, Vauxhall, Daewoo, Isuzu)	5 (Lexus, Toyota, Hino, Daihatsu, Scion)
Sales in 2004/2005 (US$ billion)[1]	162[2]	165[3]
EBT 2004/2005 (US$ billion)[1]	-6.6[2]	15.1[3]
Market cap. at June 15, 2005 (US$ billion)	20.3	128.9
Rating in June 2005 (S&P)	Junk bond	AAA

1) Financial years end December 31, 2004 (GM) and March 31, 2005 (Toyota)
2) Automotive and other operations
3) Non-financial services business

Figure 2.13 *Comparative view of GM and Toyota*
Sources: Company data, Bloomberg, Roland Berger Strategy Consultants

Top performers and low performers

Toyota may be a classic example of a successful company, but it is by no means the only one. Many car makers and component suppliers are evidently succeeding in their attempts to establish and refine business systems that keep them prospering in the long run. Other companies are falling at precisely this hurdle (see Figures 2.14 and 2.15).

What makes the difference between top performers and low performers? What do the former have in common? What are the obvious success factors? Which business systems are superior? Which need to be revamped if companies are not to drift into oblivion?

The next round 41

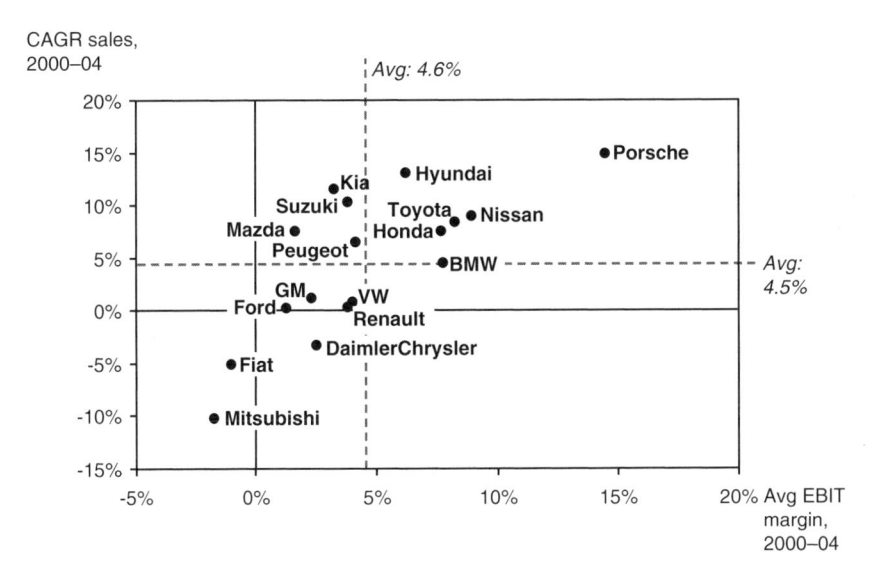

Figure 2.14 *Sales and profits at selected OEMs, 2000–04*
Sources: Bloomberg, Roland Berger Strategy Consultants

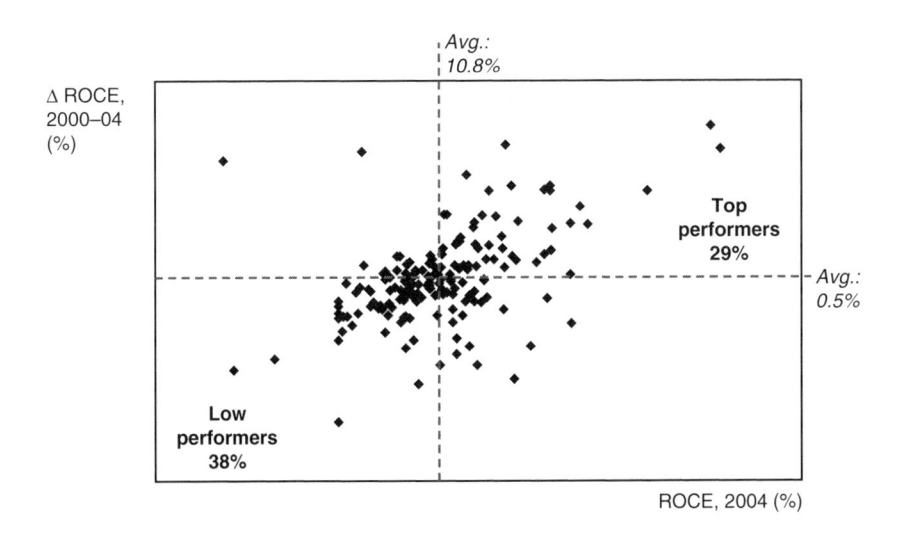

Figure 2.15 *Change in return on capital employed (ROCE), 2000–04 and 2004, at the largest component suppliers*
Sources: Bloomberg, Roland Berger Strategy Consultants

The top performers' success factors

In a large number of projects, Roland Berger has been able to identify certain features that are common to all top performers:

- in-depth customer knowledge;
- a clear vision and clear goals;
- a long-term perspective;
- a strong focus on customer loyalty;
- consistent delivery on the promise of value for money in the low price and premium price segments;
- consistently high quality;
- a global presence but a regional orientation;
- an entrepreneurial spirit.

We have already singled out Toyota as a fine example of a top performer. BMW too belongs in the same bracket. Ever since the German car maker got rid of Rover, it has consistently posted earnings before interest and tax (EBIT) of over 8 per cent. Sales revenues have risen 15 per cent since 2001, while volume sales of group-owned brands have leapt 33 per cent.

BMW's key strengths are its ability to innovate and its successful premium brand strategy. The company covers every premium segment, from the compact class to luxury sedans, and nets high margins across the board. The BMW brand has become synonymous with something special – an achievement reflected in its vehicle strategies. Dynamism, agility, the joy of driving, exceptional design and technology on the highest level are BMW's typical values. And customers believe them. For years, the company has ranked top in the ADAC AutoMarxX ratings on driving attributes and design.

BMW's vision and goals are determined by a sharp focus on the premium segment. The longevity of its goals and decisions is underpinned above all by the company's shareholder structure: 47 per cent of BMW's stock is family-owned. The company remains rigorously committed to the demands of its customers, who expect a great deal in terms of technology, quality and safety. Target groups are analysed very precisely and products are tailored specifically to them. (Occasional exceptions, such as the iDrive system, only confirm this rule.) BMW customers' satisfaction expresses itself in above-average loyalty, as evidenced once again by Cap Gemini's Car Online Study in 2005.

The problems of low performers

The low performers have a hard time activating these levers of success. Many of them fall at the same hurdles:

- failure to identify fundamental trends;
- failure to redesign business systems (too little or too late);
- no long-term corporate strategy;
- a lack of vision;
- a focus on short-term profitability;
- no distinctive profile;
- failure to deliver value for money;
- inconsistent brand management;
- a lack of entrepreneurial courage;
- no early-warning systems.

DaimlerChrysler, Fiat, Ford, GM, Mitsubishi and Volkswagen all figure below-average stock market performance. These companies' recent history clearly shows where the problems lie.

DaimlerChrysler's global strategy has not worked. The merger with Chrysler and its acquisitions in Asia have destroyed value instead of creating it. Expensive corrective action has been and still is necessary as a result. Since the merger with Chrysler, the value of the company has plunged by 60 per cent.

Fiat has been struggling with quality, brand and image problems for years. Compared with other market players, its dealer network also underperforms. The group has been spilling red ink since 2002. Rumours of a takeover by Chinese OEMs are doing the rounds in the press.

Ford is straining under three main burdens: the spin-off of Visteon, unimaginative models (especially in the United States) and the unprofitability of Jaguar. The factories that Visteon handed back to Ford in 2005 are generating added costs of some US $2 billion. And although cars sold in the United States are subsidized to the tune of around US $3,500 on average, market share is continuing to shrink. PAG subsidiary Jaguar received an injection of US $750 million in 2004, and more is still needed. Jaguar is not scheduled to break even until 2007. Ford's market capitalization has sunk to just US $20.6 billion, and Standard & Poor's has downgraded its stock to junk bond status.

The brands in the GM group do not have a clear enough profile, either in customers' perception nor in the way the group itself demarcates its brands. Vehicles whose appearance and content is very similar give customers little incentive to buy. Recently, GM's share of the US market slid to 25 per cent.

While the other Japanese manufacturers have occupied niche positions in Europe, Mitsubishi has tried to build an image as a volume provider. Since 1998, the company's sales volume in Western Europe has fallen by around 28 per cent. Over the same period, the sales of the four other major Japanese OEMs have grown by 14 per cent.

Volkswagen was too slow to move into forward-looking niche segments. Until recently, the company had no SUVs (only multi-purpose vehicles, MPVs) and no attractive soft-tops in its portfolio. In China, VW has lost ground because it had no solution that was agile and flexible enough to accommodate local developments. Once other Western and Japanese OEMs had flooded the Chinese market with new models, the successful but aging Santana was no longer able to defend its once-impressive market share. In 2005, only 17 per cent of all new vehicles on the streets of China bore the VW logo – against 46 per cent in 2000.

Success factors for component suppliers

Most of the success factors discussed above apply to both vehicle manufacturers and component suppliers. In a 2004 study entitled *Patterns of Success for Automotive Component Suppliers*, Roland Berger investigated the requirements that specifically concern the component supply industry. Top and low performers were identified on the basis of their return on capital employed (ROCE) for the years 1997 to 2002. Their strategic orientation was also examined. The study found that successful component suppliers differ from the others in five specific areas:

- Company size: the largest companies succeed thanks to economies of scale and their powerful negotiating position. The smallest succeed by occupying niche positions.
- Product portfolio: on average, the top performers account for 90 per cent of sales revenues with just one product group.
- Customer portfolio: on average, the top component suppliers earn 66 per cent of revenues from their top three customers, against 45 per cent for the low performers.
- Research and development spending: successful component suppliers invest 70 per cent more in R&D than low performers.
- Vertical integration: successful component suppliers add more value in-house (see Figure 2.16).

The question is, how can these success factors be condensed into a framework that can provide clear orientation to managers in the auto-

1 Company size	Sales < US$ 0.5 bn		Sales < US$ 5 bn	Sales > US$ 0.5 bn
2 Product portfolio	Focused			Diversified
3 Customer portfolio	Focused			Diversified
4 R&D spending	Low (< 2% of sales)		Medium (2–4% of sales)	**High (> 4% of sales)**
5 Vertical integration	Low		Medium	**High**

☐ Successful component suppliers ☐ Less successful component suppliers

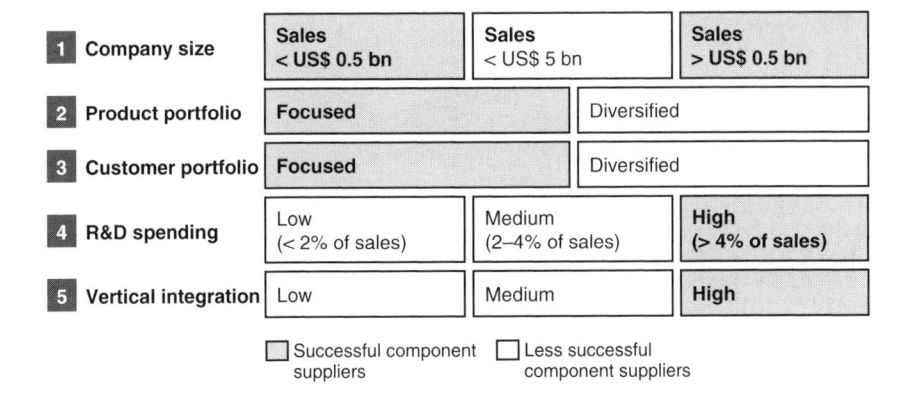

Figure 2.16 *Key areas in which top-performing component suppliers differ from low performers*
Source: Roland Berger Strategy Consultants

motive industry? Answering this question and the questions outlined below is the purpose of this book.

Part I outlines the main challenges to which industry managers and their companies must find answers today:

- The globalization challenge – is the automotive industry raising tomorrow's winners?
- The value chain challenge – networks: the strategy for success.
- The technology challenge – progress or pitfall?
- The market challenge – who will gain strategic control?
- The social challenge – increasing social and political acceptance of the automobile.

In the case studies featured in Part II, top managers of leading auto makers describe how they are rising to these challenges, what problems have to be surmounted, and what opportunities are opening up.

3

The globalization challenge – is the automotive industry raising the champions of tomorrow?

Dr Thomas Sedran, Partner, Roland Berger Strategy Consultants

General Motors (GM), Ford and Chrysler have lost more than 15 percentage points of their North American market share since the early 1980s. It has gone primarily to Toyota and other Japanese original equipment manufacturers (OEMs), but also to the Koreans. Apparently, even in their home market, the 'big three' of yesteryear are putting up little opposition to the Japanese invasion, as evident in their continued loss of market share. Even in Europe, Asian brands have passed the 17 per cent mark in terms of market share.

Now Chinese and Indian manufacturers such as Geely and Tata have declared their intention to conquer the world's key automotive markets. On the supplier side, new competitors are springing up in emerging markets as well. They are growing at incredible speed through joint ventures and acquisitions. Buying the latest technologies, they are going up against established vendors and snapping up orders.

Is the automotive industry raising the champions of tomorrow as globalization progresses? Who will emerge triumphant out of the globalization battle – only those who buy and drive the cars? What are the key challenges established suppliers and newcomers face as a result of globalization, and how can both groups master them?

GLOBALIZATION IN CHANGING TIMES

Although globalization has taken on a growing importance in recent years, the topic is as old as the Industrial Revolution when it comes to developing new sales, production and sourcing markets. The British East India Company, which acquired the exclusive right to trade between the Cape of Good Hope and the Strait of Magellan on 31 December 1600, is a good example. Despite – or perhaps because of – the fact that executing this right necessitated sometimes lengthy and fierce conflicts with other colonial powers, the East India Company evolved into a key source of wealth and power for the British Empire in the centuries that followed. Some of the effects of this can still be felt today. Similarly, the globalization activities of the Venice of the 17th and 18th centuries contributed significantly to the city's prosperity and power.

THE AUTOMOTIVE INDUSTRY – TRADITIONALLY A GLOBAL INDUSTRY

With the exception of its very earliest days at the end of the 19th century, the automotive industry has been a global industry almost from the start. The pioneers of globalization were GM (see Figure 3.1) and Ford, which established distribution companies in numerous countries in the early 20th century. In the 1920s and 1930s they set up or bought production sites in one country after another across Europe and Asia to be better able to serve these 'remote' sales markets. This globalization was driven by three key motives that still apply today:

- developing sales potential in growing markets;
- taking full advantage of lower wages and factor costs;
- leveraging the high fixed costs in vehicle R&D and production.

Ford, GM and Chrysler's global presence gave them access to competitive advantages. By the mid-1960s they dominated 52 per cent of the world market, with their plants manufacturing around 10 million vehicles in total. However, at the time, the vast majority of the automotive demand – more than 90 per cent – stemmed from North America and Western Europe. As demand for vehicles grew in Japan, Korea, Brazil, China and other countries, the regional focus shifted enormously. Today, Japan and the new sales markets make up more than 35 per cent of the world market,

1912	• GM Export Company established to handle sales outside the United States
1920	• Manila branch established dedicated to Far East marketing (relocated to Shanghai in 1922)
1924	• Chevrolet production site opened in Copenhagen to supply Scandinavian, Eastern and Western European markets
1925	• Vauxhall Motors Ltd, England, acquired • General Motors do • Additional sales branches opened in Europe
1926	• Subsidiary in South Africa established • Five Australian production plants built
1927	• Plants in Berlin, Germany and Osaka, Japan, built
1928	• First car plant in India opened
1929	• Adam Opel AG acquired
1930	• GM Overseas Operations (GMOO) established to coordinate production and marketing activities outside of North America

Figure 3.1 *General Motors globalization milestones 1912–30*
Source: General Motors

and this tendency is likely to rise considering the growth rates being observed in China, India, Russia and the ASEAN countries.

Moreover, Figure 3.2 highlights the growing amount of networking in the automotive industry across the regions. While just 8.7 per cent of the worldwide demand was handled cross-regionally in the mid-1960s, the figure exceeds 15 per cent today. As excess capacities grow in China and Eastern Europe, this rate will continue to increase in the years to come.

The Japanese and Koreans conquer North America and Europe

With the increasing demand, particularly in Asia, the balance of power in the global automotive industry has shifted massively in recent decades. The biggest winners were the Japanese and Korean OEMs. This development was bolstered by the recession of the early 1980s, when Toyota and other Japanese auto makers acquired many new customers outside their home markets thanks to attractively priced, high-quality and low-consumption vehicles.

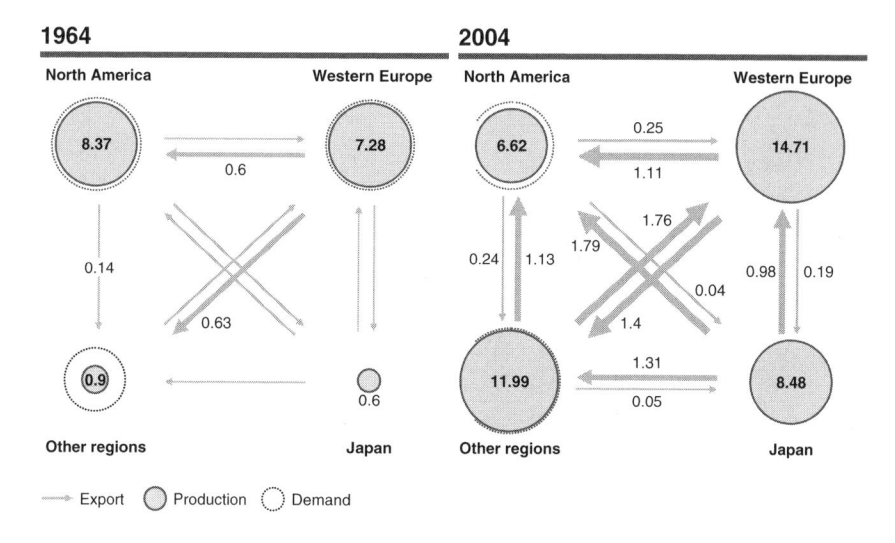

Figure 3.2 *Regional distribution of car production and demand worldwide 1964–2004 (million vehicles)*
Sources: R L Polk Marketing Systems, Global Insight, VDA, Roland Berger Strategy Consultants

North America – an easy game

Established car makers did not have any competitive offerings ready in these segments, specifically in North America, and opted instead to bypass the issue by focusing on larger vehicle segments (primarily pickups, sport utility vehicles (SUVs) and vans), which at the time delivered excellent margins and substantial growth. The strategic importance of these portfolio gaps then – and now – is shown in the development of market share over the past 10 years. Thanks to the good experience car buyers have had and the ability of Asian manufacturers to gradually adapt their vehicle offerings to American tastes, they have since been able to boost their North American market share to over 30 per cent.

Asian OEMs no longer depend on price for their business success. Price was their main selling point up until the early 1990s, when their 'cheap' cars taught the 'big three' the meaning of fear. The Asians successively took advantage of the flexibility afforded by the quality image they had created, which is extremely important in North America, and increased their prices. Toyota and their Asian counterparts can now afford to keep out of the crippling price wars, and still succeed in gaining market share.

Emulating the successful strategy of the Japanese OEMs, Korean brands managed to get a foot in the door and quickly expand their position in the US market. With more than 30 per cent and 10 per cent compound

50 Major challenges

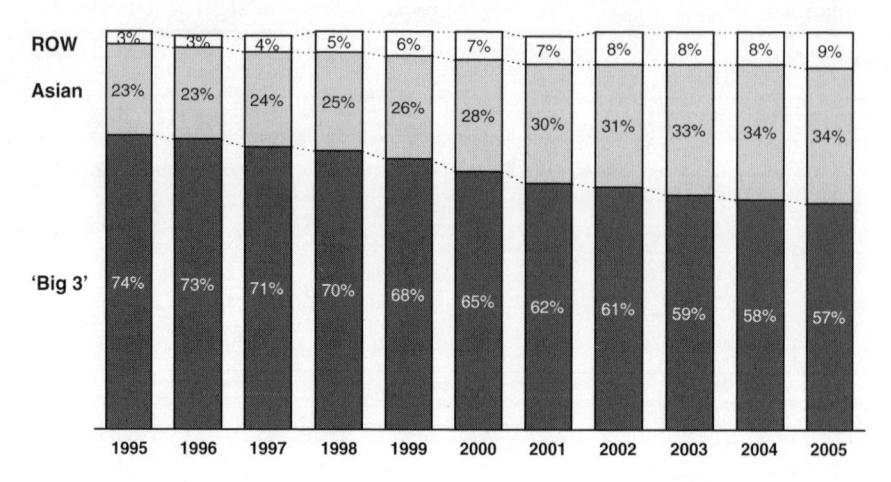

	1995	1996	1997	1998	1999	2000	2001	2002	2003	2004	2005
ROW	3%	3%	4%	5%	6%	7%	7%	8%	8%	8%	9%
Asian	23%	23%	24%	25%	26%	28%	30%	31%	33%	34%	34%
'Big 3'	74%	73%	71%	70%	68%	65%	62%	61%	59%	58%	57%

Note: The 'big three' are GM, Ford and Chrysler. Asian = Japan + other Asian OEMs

Figure 3.3 *Market share by brand in North America 1995–2005*
Sources: JD Power, Roland Berger Strategy Consultants

annual growth rate (CAGR) respectively in the period from 1994 to 2004, Kia and Hyundai were the fastest-growing car brands in the United States. Similar to Toyota, the Koreans are also upgrading their brand perception on the back of quality, which consequently enables them to raise their prices. Kia and Hyundai have already progressed to the lower midsection of the market in terms of price. The entry-level market segments they have 'freed up' extend an open invitation to the burgeoning Chinese auto makers, which will soon begin to follow these proven patterns to develop a presence in the American market. Besides the growing market opportunities created by the upward price movement of the established Asian manufacturers, the development is accelerated by the current excess capacities of 2.5 to 3 million vehicles in China (with a rising tendency), as well as the growth of the market in China itself, which is lagging behind expectations. Initial announcements of companies' intentions to import hundreds of thousands of vehicles into the United States to sell locally have set things in motion.

Increased pressure on the European fortresses

Japanese and Korean brands have also launched a broad frontal attack on European markets. No segment is being spared. Even in the premium category – traditionally a segment dominated by European OEMs – Lexus is in the process of completely repositioning itself, defining a new brand core with hybrid engine technology. According to the press releases, Nissan's premium brand Infinity is about to be introduced in Europe. In the medium term, Nissan is planning to exceed Lexus's present market share. Thus competition is set to intensify, even in the premium segment. Yet 'escaping upmarket' into ever more complex technology does not seem to do the trick these days given the recent experience of Mercedes-Benz and others.

As a result, Asian auto makers have established themselves as permanent players in the European market as well. There are, however, some significant differences between Europe and the United States, which have so far restricted their success in the world's second largest economic zone. These are:

- Europe has a strong local car-making industry with traditionally high brand and customer loyalty.
- Europe is the home base of the biggest premium OEMs.
- European volume manufacturers maintain a stronghold in the entry-level segments and defend their market positions with product blitzes and, in some cases, very successful cost-cutting programmes.
- Innovation and brand perception still play a significant role in people's purchase decisions.

However, since Europe's economy has become stuck in a rut and the big nations have begun reforming their social security systems, the consumption climate and customer priorities have shifted in favour of lower-priced offerings. Asian OEMs are also reaping the benefits of failed strategies implemented by some European OEMs, such as Volkswagen, which wanted to sell ever more technology at ever higher prices. In some instances, such strategies have resulted in a dilemma. Although customers demand cost-intensive features (for example airbags), they are not very keen to pay a premium for them.

Moreover, Asian companies have cleverly adjusted their designs to suit European tastes – frequently with the assistance of Italian automotive body engineers such as Pininfarina, which have greatly influenced automotive design trends for many years. Simultaneously, Asian auto makers are getting an additional boost from their superior quality positioning, which often drives critical purchase impulses in the embattled volume segment. As a result of these factors and developments, Asian OEMs, after suffering a setback in 2001, have been able to expand their European market share to 19 per cent as of 2005.

Just like in the United States, there is a certain time lag between Korean OEMs and their Japanese competitors in terms of market launch.

52 Major challenges

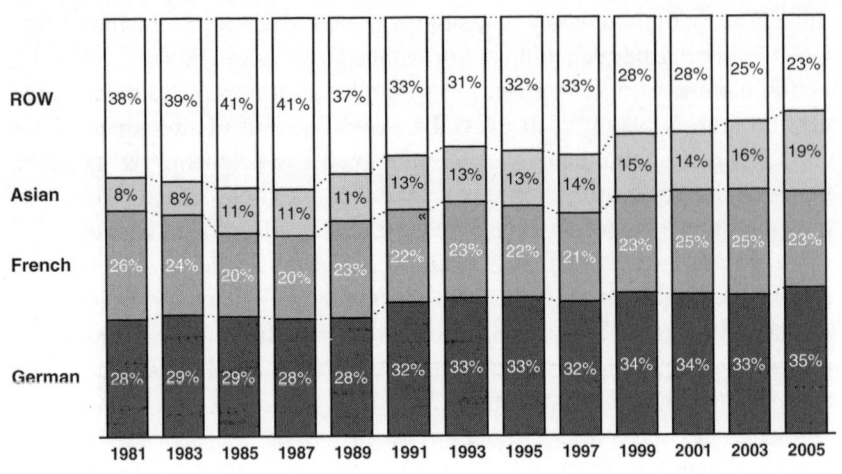

Figure 3.4 *Market share based on OEM origin, Europe*
Sources: VDA, JD Power, Roland Berger Strategy Consultants

	1981	1983	1985	1987	1989	1991	1993	1995	1997	1999	2001	2003	2005
ROW	38%	39%	41%	41%	37%	33%	31%	32%	33%	28%	28%	25%	23%
Asian	8%	8%	11%	11%	11%	13%	13%	13%	14%	15%	14%	16%	19%
French	26%	24%	20%	20%	23%	22%	23%	22%	21%	23%	25%	25%	23%
German	28%	29%	29%	28%	28%	32%	33%	33%	32%	34%	34%	33%	35%

Note: Cars only

Recently, however, they have displayed dynamism. In Europe as well as the United States, Kia and Hyundai are now the fastest-growing brands. Nonetheless Toyota, globally considered the toughest competitor for European and American OEMs, will continue to produce unfettered growth rates of around 8 per cent in Europe over the next few years.

In a stagnating market, this obviously means that some players will be forced out. Consequently, four Asian auto makers now rank among the world's top 10. In 2006, Toyota will very likely overtake GM as the world's biggest OEM. With total market capitalization of €150 billion, it exceeds the combined value of GM, Ford and DaimlerChrysler. Other leading Asian manufacturers have pulled into the fast lane as well. Selling 2.5 million vehicles (an increase of 11 per cent year on year), Hyundai, for example, generated after-tax profits of €1.9 billion (up 7 per cent) in 2005 – another record-breaking result. And the company is budgeting for even more growth – at least another 10 per cent in 2006.

Is this a case of déjà vu *with new OEMs from China, India and Eastern Europe?*

The rapid growth of the automotive markets in China and India goes hand in hand with the emergence of new car makers that are also receiving support through government policies. What opportunities do these newcomers have in competing with the big automotive conglomerates globally? Will the meteoric rise of the Japanese and Koreans now be followed by the decade of the Chinese and Indians?

There are certain arguments to support this assumption. Asian manufacturers have used the growing acceptance of Japanese and Korean brands in North America and Europe to adjust their prices upwards. In recent years, this has created a gap in the price spectrum, which now opens the door for Chinese, Indian and Central and Eastern European OEMs. Initial indications that they will fill the gap are emerging.

China's largest auto maker, SAIC, has secured key technology and brand rights from Rover. Nanjing Automobile bought the Rover plant, complete with its English workforce with their automotive industry experience. Brilliance, BMW's joint-venture partner, will offer its flag ship 'ZhongHua' car, with its C and D class ambitions, for the incredibly low price of €19,000 on the German market. The Dacia Logan, built in Romania, exceeded Renault's first year sales forecasts by far, selling almost 13,000 vehicles. Theoretically at least, Chinese and Indian manufacturers benefit from very low-cost production factors, especially personnel costs but in other cost areas too, given that statutory regulations concerning the equipment and safety of workstations, for example, are minimal. Indian car makers Tata and Maruti are also preparing to enter the European market.

Another catalyst that will aid the rapid rise of Chinese and Indian manufacturers is their easy access to know-how. Thanks partly to mandatory government requirements (such as licence regulations) and supported by the outstanding growth opportunities in emerging markets with no existing brand loyalties, new car makers from the emerging markets are finding partners at minimal cost who will help and guide them in the low-cost production of good cars that are also suitable for selling in established markets. The current stagnation of the triad markets further aids this development, given that the growing demand in China and India makes it possible to continue to employ highly competent workers in the short term at reasonable cost.

At first glance, very little seems to contradict the fast emergence of the Chinese, Indian and Central European newcomers, especially in view of the enormous progress made in recent years coupled with the will that these countries have to propel themselves into a better future. On the other hand, many ambitious companies' expansion strategies have failed in the past. With the exception of Hyundai, no newcomer has made it into the premier league in the past 20 years. The list of those that failed to make the grade is long: Proton from Malaysia, Avtovaz/Lada from Russia, Kia and Daewoo from Korea and Mahindra from India. Many others have been taken over or play only a regional role.

What special challenges do newcomers have to overcome to be able to play a critical role in the global race for success? How can established manufacturers take advantage of the opportunities in the emerging markets without fostering unwanted competition? What options do European and US manufacturers have to defend their home markets and market share against increased attack from Asian manufacturers? Can established manufacturers utilize new markets to improve their cost base and thus their competitive positioning on a global level?

SURVIVING BY SUCCEEDING IN THE NEW EMERGING MARKETS

In a liberalized world without major restrictions to trade, the future of OEMs and automotive suppliers will be decided in the newly developing markets of Asia and Eastern Europe. These are the only places where demand will grow in terms of absolute volumes and sales; they are the only places where auto makers will find the low-wage workers they need to remain globally cost-effective and competitive in their traditional triad home markets in the era of hybrid costing. Those who miss the opportunities in these booming markets will be left with very little room to manoeuvre in the continued consolidation of the automotive industry.

Growing demand is restricted to emerging markets

While the demand for vehicles continues to stagnate on a high level in North America, Western Europe and Japan, demand will increase significantly over the next few years in emerging markets, especially in China and India, but also in Brazil and Russia. The key drivers of this development are rising household incomes among the population, the stabilization of basic economic indicators, and the continuous expansion of (highway) infrastructures, as in India. Moreover, citizens of these countries have a strong desire not only to meet their individual mobility needs by purchasing a vehicle, but also to express their growing prosperity. The sum total of these factors translates into average growth rates of more than 7 per cent until 2015 in these emerging markets.

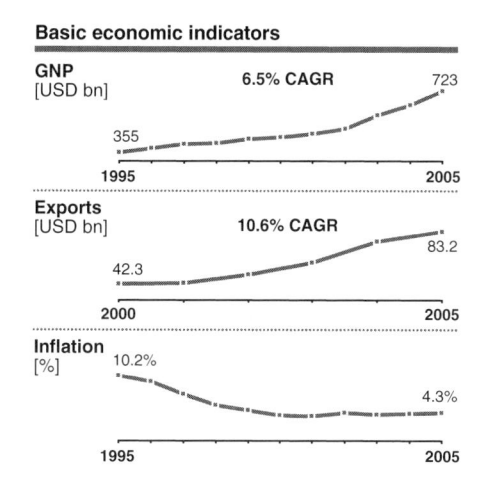

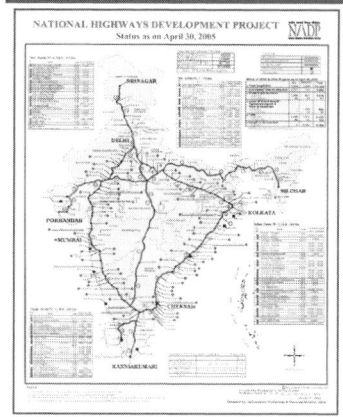

Figure 3.5 *Development of basic indicators and highway infrastructure in India*
Sources: Economist Intelligence Unit, Investment Brief (Indian Embassy)

Sustained cost advantages in emerging markets

In addition to the development of local sales potential, labour cost savings of a factor of 10 to 20 are the primary drivers behind companies offshoring the manufacturing part of the value chain to emerging markets or establishing production sites there. Differences in the education levels of the available staff, infrastructure deficits (such as unreliable power supply), added logistical costs and measures to protect the firm's legal position (such as intellectual property rights) wipe out a substantial part of the impact that labour cost savings have on production costs. Nonetheless, even considering these factors and risks, clients' projects still yield savings potential of 15 to 20 per cent over the total cost of production and development at sites in established markets. From a Western European or North American perspective, complete offshoring to China or India is unavoidable or expedient in very few cases only. It frequently makes the most business sense to develop sites in Central and Eastern Europe or Central and South America. For instance, absolute savings at a production site in Central China compared with one in Eastern Romania total just 50 cents per hour. In other words, the labour cost savings would be offset by the higher logistical costs.

Experts project that the difference in hourly wages will hardly change in the medium term, even if wage rises continue at their present rate. This is because of the higher starting level in industrialized nations, which means that the absolute rate of wage increases is already higher here than in emerging markets. According to an EIU scenario (see Figure 3.6), the absolute difference between hourly wages will actually grow in the coming years. Moreover, the anticipated productivity increase in emerging markets will be significantly higher than in the triad markets. As a result, product cost advantages will shift even further in favour of the emerging markets.

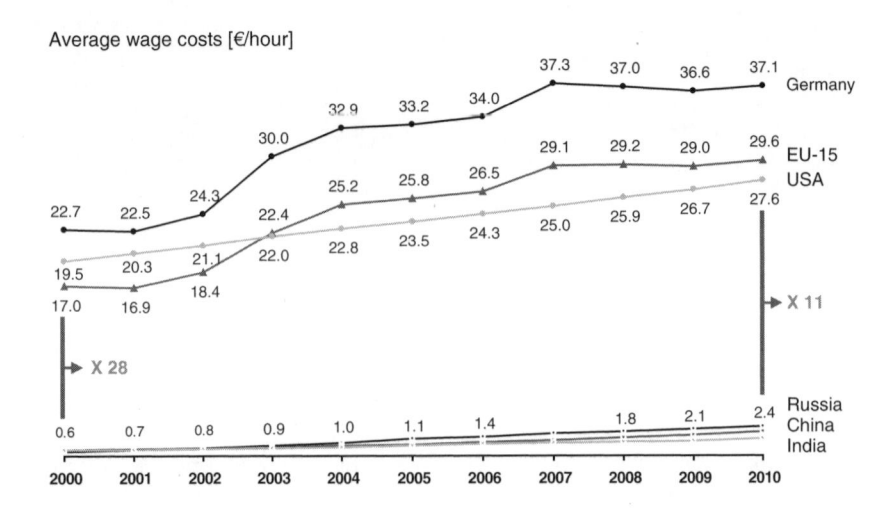

Figure 3.6 *Comparison of wage cost development in industrialized nations and emerging markets*
Sources: Economist Intelligence Unit (EIU), Roland Berger Strategy Consultants

Challenges for established OEMs and newcomers

It is not easy to keep exploiting the comparative growth and cost advantages of emerging markets sustainably. Established OEMs and newcomers alike will have to address a wide range of challenges. These are:

- a large number of first-time buyers and minimal brand loyalty;
- high levels of price sensitivity and diversity in regional markets;
- high fixed costs and operations that lack critical size;
- demand volatility, exchange rate fluctuations and trade barriers.

High number of first time buyers and minimal brand loyalty

The vast majority of customers in emerging markets are first-time buyers, and many of them have no experience with cars. The only exceptions are first-time buyers making the transition from two-wheelers to cars. They do, however, represent a relatively large segment of the market. In India, for example, more than 5 million two-wheelers are sold each year. About 25 per cent of these customers plan to buy a car in the next few years, which translates into a total market volume of more than 1 million cars. In India, a total of 80 million people will have the financial wherewithal to purchase an automobile in 2007.

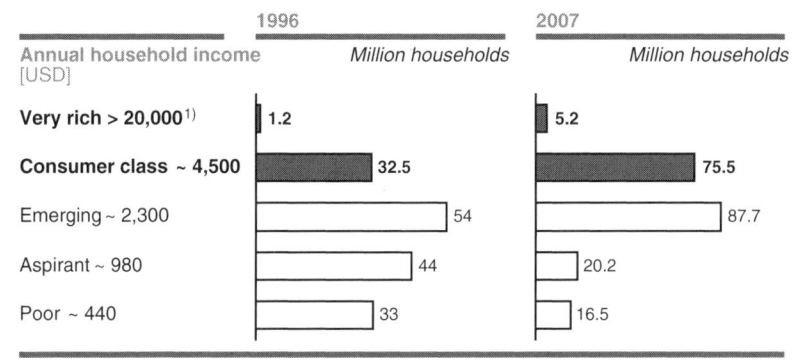

Annual household income [USD]	1996 Million households	2007 Million households
Very rich > 20,000 [1]	1.2	5.2
Consumer class ~ 4,500	32.5	75.5
Emerging ~ 2,300	54	87.7
Aspirant ~ 980	44	20.2
Poor ~ 440	33	16.5

- In 2007, more than 80 million households will have adequate disposable income to afford a car
- The impact of increasing disposable income is evident in consumer goods markets

1) Based on purchasing power parity, this is the equivalent of US$100,000 per household

Figure 3.7 *Demographic structure and disposable incomes in India*
Sources: Economist Corporate Network, Roland Berger Strategy Consultants

Similar to East German car buyers after German reunification, first-time buyers in emerging markets are indeed brand oriented, but not as brand fixated as customers in established markets. Although disposable incomes have increased, they are still limited, so people opt for the car that delivers the best combination of low upkeep costs and modern design and features for a price that falls under their personal limit. The car's resale value plays only a minor role in purchasing decisions at this time.

These buying patterns create equal selling opportunities even for brands that do not play a leading role in the big automotive markets of today. Buick's success in China is a good example. This brand does not generate much market share for GM in the United States but in China, where it has

Feature	Ranking[1]	
Driving comfort	1	
Maintenance	2	
After-sales service	3	Total lifecycle cost
Fuel consumption	4	
Price	5	
Equipment	6	
Appearance	7	
Other	8	
Resale value	9	

- The **total lifecycle costs** of the vehicle are critical criteria in the decision-making process.
- A typical Indian buyer expects European quality at Asian prices.
- Resale value plays a very minor role given that cars remain with the first owner for a long time. Nonetheless, the **used car market is beginning to grow**.
- **Driving comfort** is **a must**, given that long **traffic delays** are common and the **infrastructure is still inadequate**.
- Only car makers with a **strong presence** in the country emphasize vehicle maintenance and **after-sales service**.

1) Rediff.com survey, 2004; 8841 responses from 25 Indian cities

Figure 3.8 *Factors influencing purchase decisions in the midsize segment in India*
Sources: Rediff, Roland Berger Strategy Consultants

been given a fresh, modern positioning and offers solid product/performance ratios, it is a yardstick for the midsize-premium segment.

High levels of price sensitivity and diversity in regional markets

Even though Mercedes-Benz, BMW and Audi are establishing assembly and production sites in emerging markets, the majority of cars sold into emerging markets go for less than €8,000. In India, for example, such cars make up more than 60 per cent of the total market. Obviously, the performance and features of these vehicles are not identical with those of more expensive models that are also sold in the triad markets. Nonetheless, the level of the established competitors has to be reached – at least visually – especially in terms of design and comfort.

In the wake of a growing model portfolio and rising local production capacities, price pressure has entered the Chinese market. Even in the mid-range and higher price segments, the past 12 months have seen list prices and transaction prices fall by more than 20 per cent in some cases.

The specific vehicle properties that drive customers' decisions to buy a car not only depend on individual buyer segments, they also vary considerably between regional sales markets. In keeping with the old adage 'China is more than China', customers in the north-east place more

Overview prices of selected A segment models

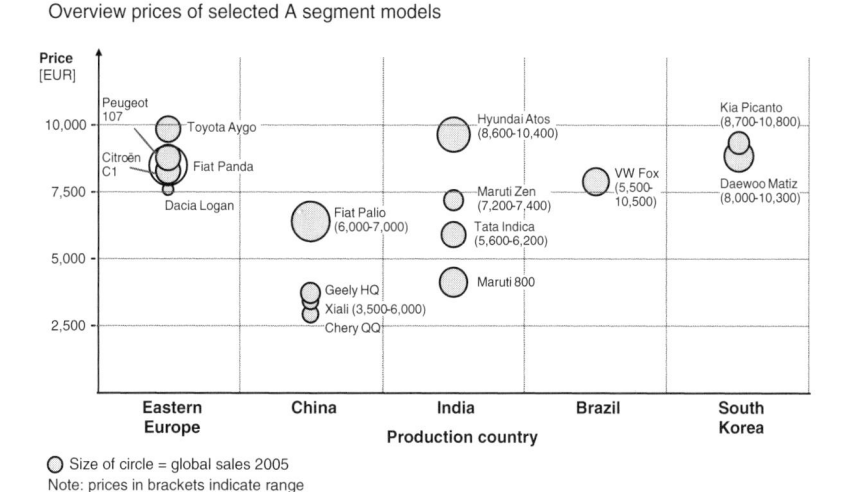

Figure 3.9 *Volume car prices in key emerging markets*
Sources: JD Power, Roland Berger Strategy Consultants

emphasis on vehicles and brands that are especially known for durability and reliability, whereas people in the south and south-east tend to go for international brands.

High fixed costs and operations that lack critical mass

Research and development, production, sale and service in the automotive business remain capital-intensive activities. Even if production changes over from fully automated assembly lines to more manual processes to exploit the labour cost advantages of the emerging markets, hundreds of millions of euros worth of investment will still have to be pumped in to ensure that production remains competitive on cost and quality. To justify such investments, annual production volumes of at least 100,000 or ideally 200,000 vehicles per model or model family have to be churned out. Given that not even China – the largest of the emerging markets with about 4 million vehicles sold in 2005 and very strong competition – is able to absorb such volumes, plants in emerging markets can be competitive only if export strategies for these vehicles targeting neighbouring and triad markets are developed simultaneously.

Substantial investments are also required in sales and service to ensure vehicles are presented and maintained in a way compatible with the brand. Even though such investments are usually not made by auto makers but by independent car dealerships, they too require certain minimum volumes to justify their investments. One of the biggest financial and operational

60 Major challenges

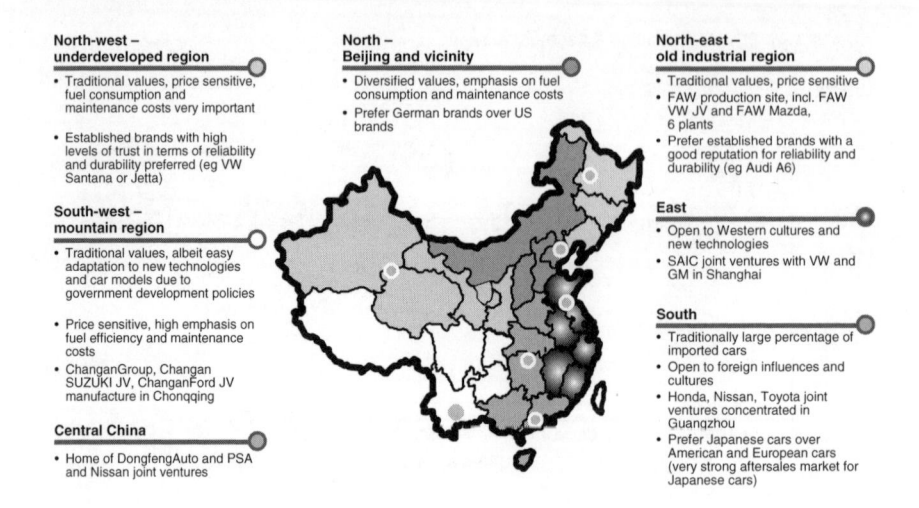

North-west – underdeveloped region
- Traditional values, price sensitive, fuel consumption and maintenance costs very important
- Established brands with high levels of trust in terms of reliability and durability preferred (eg VW Santana or Jetta)

South-west – mountain region
- Traditional values, albeit easy adaptation to new technologies and car models due to government development policies
- Price sensitive, high emphasis on fuel efficiency and maintenance costs
- ChanganGroup, Changan SUZUKI JV, ChanganFord JV manufacture in Chonqqing

Central China
- Home of DongfengAuto and PSA and Nissan joint ventures

North – Beijing and vicinity
- Diversified values, emphasis on fuel consumption and maintenance costs
- Prefer German brands over US brands

North-east – old industrial region
- Traditional values, price sensitive
- FAW production site, incl. FAW VW JV and FAW Mazda, 6 plants
- Prefer established brands with a good reputation for reliability and durability (eg Audi A6)

East
- Open to Western cultures and new technologies
- SAIC joint ventures with VW and GM in Shanghai

South
- Traditionally large percentage of imported cars
- Open to foreign influences and cultures
- Honda, Nissan, Toyota joint ventures concentrated in Guangzhou
- Prefer Japanese cars over American and European cars (very strong aftersales market for Japanese cars)

Figure 3.10 *Regional customer preferences in China*
Source: Roland Berger Strategy Consultants

OEM JV: 123; Direct wages: −17; R&D: −2; Components: 20; Overheads: 19; Sales: 8; Taxes: 6; Depreciation: 5; Energy: 3; Chinese model: 165

Cost advantages of Chinese OEMs | Cost disadvantages of Chinese OEMs

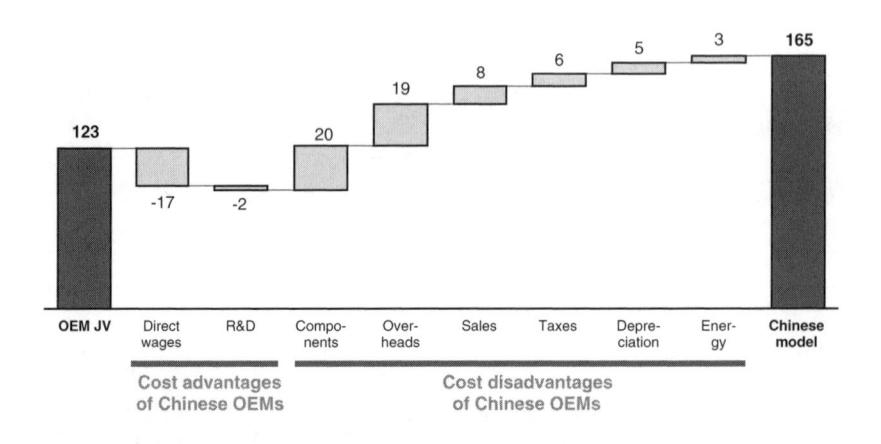

Figure 3.11 *Cost disadvantages in China as against the global benchmark (in CNY 000)*
Sources: Expert interviews, Roland Berger Strategy Consultants

challenges in this context is ensuring the availability of service centres and spare parts supplies across the huge geographical expanses of countries such as China and India.

While economic minimum volumes are fairly irrelevant in protected markets given that prices and margins are well above global market levels, the kinds of volume that need to be sold increase dramatically when such markets are liberalized. This is currently very well demonstrated in China, where prices are falling significantly while vehicle sales and service standards are rising to allow companies to differentiate themselves from the competition.

Demand volatility, exchange rate fluctuations and trade barriers

Young, dynamic economies are always subject to special risks resulting from virtually unforeseeable shifts in their financial system and political situation. Drastic drops in demand as well as substantial changes in currency exchange rates and government trade restrictions (import duties, local content provisions) may follow such seismic shifts. They have a grave impact on the profitability of investment decisions. In an increasingly networked and globalized world, the domino effect cannot be ruled out. The Asian crisis of 1998 and the subsequent devaluation of multiple currencies, for example, resulted in as much as a 40 per cent drop in demand in Brazil at the end of the 1990s.

Success strategies for established auto makers

To successfully develop the potential of emerging markets, established OEMs will have to master a whole series of specific challenges. The first of these is to gain a thorough understanding of local market conditions and customer requirements. The second is to develop specific low-cost competencies. Then they will need to integrate emerging market activities into the operations of a global R&D, production and sourcing system. Most importantly, they must safeguard intellectual property rights. All of these aspects and more also need to be embedded in management structures and personnel development systems that have been modernized with a view to the special challenges of globalization.

Understanding and meeting local market requirements

Up until a few years ago it was sufficient, and indeed very lucrative, to go into emerging markets such as Brazil, China or South Africa and sell vehicle models that were no longer competitive in the embattled triad markets on the grounds of outdated design and technical features. Volkswagen did this with great success for years with the Beetle in Brazil and Mexico, and continues to do so today, for example with its City Golf, a derivative of the Golf I, made and sold in South Africa. From a mere cost and liquidity angle, this strategy sometimes makes economic sense given that the production costs of older models are significantly lower because the products are less complex, and they allow manufacturers to attain market-specific objectives more easily. Naturally such strategies are also less capital-intensive, because they use machines and tools that have already been amortized.

In an era of liberalized markets, this type of approach increasingly appears to be doomed to failure. In the premium segment, the trend was evident even before this. Mercedes-Benz's attempt in the mid-1990s to continue production – in India – of the E Class type W124, manufactured in core markets from 1985 through 1994 but no longer built in Europe, failed miserably. After all, customers who were able to afford the high price tag for this E Class wanted to drive around not in a discontinued model, but in the very same one they had seen on their trips to Europe.

Overall, established car makers, particularly those in the volume segment, are facing the challenge of having to technically 'slim down' products featuring complex engineering for emerging markets in order to align their costs with local spending abilities. On the other hand, their design and features must be such that local customers do not feel they are driving an outdated model. In this context, adaptations to local customer preferences are absolutely crucial. Part of the reason that Volkswagen lost market share in China was because it simply ignored the preferences of its Chinese customers. Appropriate strategies for this booming market would have been to offer the Jetta instead of the Golf and the Fox instead of the Polo.

Developing low-cost competencies

Volume segment manufacturers must develop specific low-cost competencies if they want to take a leading role in emerging markets in the medium term. Those who do not have a competitive entry-level model in the €5,000 to 8,000 price range will lose many first-time buyers to other brands/OEMs. Moreover, this approach also means forsaking volume, sales and margin potential to finance the necessary denser sales and service networks. And those first-time buyers who can later afford to buy in higher price segments will either upgrade within the same brand or switch to premium brands.

But how does a company create such a low-cost/low-price entry-level model if the mere manufacturing costs of common entry-level models (excluding selling costs/overheads) in triad markets exceed €7,000 and are often far higher than that? Cosmetic 'de-contenting', such as leaving out airbags, xenon lamps or catalytic converters, is certainly not the answer. Our experience shows that established auto makers can deliver such vehicles only if they take a radical approach:

- forgoing redundant corporate structures and processes that drive costs;
- focusing on the technically feasible aspects that customers are willing to pay for;
- taking consistent advantage of cost benefits resulting from modularization as well as developing, sourcing and manufacturing at low-cost sites;
- assigning dedicated multifunctional teams that work largely independently of group structures;
- ensuring targeted integration of suppliers that also meet the four requirements stipulated above.

With its Dacia Logan, Renault provides a perfect example of the practical implementation of this approach. Although built on the same platform as the Renault 19, the remainder of the vehicle was newly developed with a strict focus on cost optimization. Some components from current series models were used. Others were based on completely new approaches to ensure all requirements were met. This stringent 'design-to-cost' approach resulted in a much higher percentage of manual labour being used in production than is the norm in modern car plants. As a consequence, chassis structures became less complex and had higher tolerances. Given that this was not at odds with customer requirements in this market segment, the approach yielded substantial savings.

Global R&D, production and sourcing system

Serving emerging markets locally from pure CKD assembly plants is frequently the first step to more intensive market penetration. As trade barriers decline (through World Trade Organization (WTO) membership, for instance) and demand volumes rise, the profitability of doing more of the value creation in emerging markets increases accordingly. Yet given the enormous capital intensity of certain value creation activities, such as pressing and painting equipment, the approach of developing market after market separately is still relatively uneconomical in many cases. To ensure that such equipment is used to its full capacity, there are already many automotive plants in Brazil, China, India and South Africa exporting virtually complete vehicles or expensive aggregates, such as engines, transmissions or axles, within the scope of a worldwide production system.

At this time, Hyundai is probably the most aggressive auto maker when it comes to establishing production sites in emerging markets. The new plants in China, Russia, India, the Czech Republic and Slovakia make a substantial contribution to the growth of this automotive group. In Russia, Hyundai is one of the fastest-growing manufacturers; in India the company more than doubled its production volume from 2002 to 2004. One-third of the Indian output (about 75,000 cars) is now being exported, primarily to Africa, the United States and Latin America. Consequently, India is not merely a production site for local demand; it is also being used as a hub for other markets.

Under the catchphrase 'global sourcing', a lot of effort in recent years has gone into taking advantage of supplier cost potential in emerging markets. Initially, the focus was mostly on subsidiaries of established suppliers. As suppliers increasingly consolidated and the automotive industry grew in China and India, recent attempts have been directed towards exploiting the cost savings potential of these new players in the vendor market. A few of them – Bharat Forge among them – have been highly successful in this.

As the number of available university graduates with a technical background declines and cost pressure in research and development increases, emerging markets are beginning to play a more interesting role as locations for global R&D networks. Brazil has already evolved into a key supplier of R&D services, for instance within the Volkswagen Group; India is set to move centre stage for all established auto makers in the years to come. The country will play an important role even for premium OEMs such as DaimlerChrysler, which offshored their R&D activities to Bangalore as early as 1997.

Safeguarding know-how

The more intrinsic networks with local R&D and production partners are, the higher the risk of valuable know-how that has been developed over many years being disclosed to third parties. Considering that many of the new markets are engaged in a very long-term process of playing catch-up and are very diverse, intensive knowledge transfer is often required to develop production and development resources and new suppliers. On the one hand, this transfer must be both planned and accepted to prevent sometimes insurmountable hurdles from being erected in day-to-day business operations. On the other hand, it has to be absolutely clear whenever such transfers are made that there is a risk of critical know-how being communicated to partners who still have to learn how to handle and protect other people's intellectual property. The lack of legal safeguards, and perhaps even the existence of protectionism, can sometimes result in confidentiality and non-disclosure agreements becoming virtually worthless. The aim must be to find the right level of know-how transfer to develop the business without weakening the company's own knowledge base.

'Globalizing' management structures and personnel development

Management structures and personnel development systems will also have to reflect the importance and challenges of successfully developing opportunities in emerging markets. Given the liberalization of emerging markets, it is completely inadequate to approach these countries with a 'second-rate' team. Moreover, executives should not be encouraged to rotate to new positions too quickly. Especially in Asian cultures, long-term relationships are key to successfully negotiating contracts with business partners and are even more important in implementing them properly. Recruiting, personnel planning and personnel development teams should increasingly integrate staff and executives from the emerging markets. The value of emerging markets must be reflected in corporate hierarchies by allocating management positions accordingly. Responsibility for the operational business in emerging markets such as China and India absolutely must be assigned at top management level.

Success strategies for newcomers

Newcomers such as Chery, FAW, Geely, SAIC and Tata have taken up advantageous positions in their respective home markets in recent years – through joint ventures and increasingly also through autonomous efforts. This development was and is being supported by local governments. As markets continue to be liberalized, newcomers are, however, increasingly being subjected to the tough competition of the global market. To survive as independent companies through the long-term consolidation of the automotive industry, these newcomers will have to master a series of specific challenges. They will have to:

- develop independent brands;
- develop products fit for the global market and autonomous technology competencies;
- implement export strategies.

Developing independent brands

Only a few Asian OEMs have successfully built up the kind of brand awareness in Europe and North America that would allow customers to develop emotional connections with them. Despite being active in Europe for many years, Asian car makers regularly rank near the bottom of the list when consumers are asked how much they like a certain brand. However, this fact did not negatively affect the Asians' overall success, because they were able to win over customers with rational arguments. Nowadays, Japanese OEMs and Hyundai stand for quality and good value for money. The new competitors will first have to work hard to build up this kind of image while simultaneously striving to create a differentiated brand perception. Being recognized as a car maker with 'reasonable prices and OK quality' is not enough on its own, not even in the emerging markets. How important a brand can be is evident in the sudden sales boost experienced by former Daewoo vehicles when they started being sold under the Chevrolet brand. In any event, auto makers must understand that creating true brand value is a process that can take years, even decades, in the automotive industry.

Developing products fit for the global market and autonomous technology competencies

There is no doubt about it – Indian, Chinese and Russian car makers do not yet possess the technological competencies to allow them to compete with European or Asian OEMs. Highly public failures such as the crash test of the Chinese Landwind SUV and the low sales figures of Tata in Great Britain underscore this fact. To be able to keep up in the increasingly liberalized global competition as autonomous suppliers, the newcomers will have to close these competency gaps. Buying up patents and production facilities, as SAIC and Nanjing Motors did when they legally acquired Rover's competencies, is likely to remain the exception rather than the rule.

Probably the most attractive way of closing competency gaps, in our opinion, is to intensively integrate and utilize R&D service providers such as AVL, EDAG, Karmann, Magna-Steyr, Pininfarina and others. The main focus of the know-how transfer in these business transactions is on body and overall vehicle competencies. Moreover, strategic partnerships with large, technology-driven suppliers such as Bosch, Continental, Delphi or SiemensVDO will be helpful in addressing electrical and safety issues and in closing gaps in engine and chassis-related proficiency.

Comparing the breakneck speed with which the leading newcomers are evolving with the historical development of Japanese and Korean OEMs, it is safe to assume that some of the new players will already have closed all of the key competency gaps within the next 10 years.

Implementing export strategies

To be able to finance all of the investments necessary to develop vehicles fit for the global markets and build competitive plants, newcomers from the emerging markets will also have to develop export markets. Obviously, they will not be able to export cars that are subject to legal restrictions, such as licence manufacturing agreements. At this time, independent suppliers are shipping only to export markets where the statutory and customer requirements are relatively low. The sales volumes generated in these markets will not suffice in the long term to escape the industry's consolidation pressure. The ambitious newcomers from emerging markets will therefore be compelled to export to automotive core markets as well.

Despite good long-term prospects for some of the newcomers, we shall not see any momentous shifts in market share, given that the newcomers will be confronted with much stricter safety, emissions and fuel consumption standards and will first have to build up distribution and service networks in these core markets.

A recent Roland Berger Strategy Consultants study reaffirms this opinion. While more than 40 million people in the United States have annual incomes of between US $15,000 and 50,000, which would make them an ideal target group for cheap vehicles from China, cars in this category have barely sold at all in recent years. Only Hyundai was able to exceed the 100,000 vehicles mark, which it did with two models in the same year. Against the backdrop of rising fuel prices and the fact that vehicle upkeep costs have become more important as a factor in people's purchase decisions, our survey indicates that a new market for cheap cars costing less than US $10,000 will develop in the United States. Chinese OEMs such as Chery and Geely are well positioned to move into this segment. However, they will have to sell their cars for at least US $7,500 in order to rake back the cost of adapting them to US statutory requirements and to cover additional distribution and marketing costs.

Given the lack of sales and service networks in the core automotive markets, we consider the hurdles still to be high, albeit not insurmountable. Independent dealers and fast-fit chains are waiting for their chance. *Automotive News Europe* ran the headline 'Some German Opel dealers will sell Chinese cars' on 5 August 2005. Allegedly there are already plans to utilize the Opel distribution network, currently suffering from excess capacities, to sell new brands.

CONCLUSION

The globalization challenge is, is the automotive industry raising the champions of tomorrow? The points made in this article show that the answer to this question is multifaceted. In any event, the leading OEMs and suppliers of today are indeed giving R&D assistance to new manufacturers from emerging markets. Some of these new manufacturers will evolve into competitors to be reckoned with. On the supplier side, Bharat Forge is already fit to play in the premier league.

Many of the new suppliers will, however, fall prey to continued industry consolidation. Equally, OEMs from established core markets that are currently considered leaders will become victims if they do not take the necessary restructuring action in time, or if they fail to implement it consistently enough. The current problems at Fiat, Ford and GM, as well as at Delphi and other suppliers, underscore the dramatic negative consequences of holding on to old sinecures for far too long.

Ultimately, the progress of automotive globalization will make cars more affordable and better for us – the customers and drivers.

4

The value chain challenge: networks, the strategy for success

Marcus Berret, Partner, Roland Berger Strategy Consultants

As a key sector of the global economy, the automotive industry is second to none in driving the development of new product and process technologies. Ever since car makers and component suppliers began to build up huge surplus capacity worldwide, it has also been one of the most competitive industries. As a result, pressure to cut costs and improve performance in the automotive value chain has been growing constantly in recent years.

Auto makers and their component suppliers thus found themselves forced to reinvent their value chain processes at regular intervals. Attention initially focused on perfecting the art of assembly line production in the 1970s, followed by a focus on 'lean' development and production to improve efficiency in the 1980s. In the 1990s, value chains became increasingly globalized as production plant and sourcing activities spread to countries with low labour costs.

Now, in the first decade of the 21st century, the stakes have been raised further still. To enable continued growth and catering to ever more variegated customer wishes, despite stagnating markets, manufacturers have substantially broadened the range of models they have on offer. The number of models marketed by European manufacturers has indeed more than doubled in the space of just 10 years (see Figure 4.1). During the same period, lead development times have been slashed by between 10 and 20 per cent – even as vehicles have become technologically more complex.

Cost pressure also increased as Asian vendors grew their market share and made overcapacity – currently sufficient for around 20 million units –

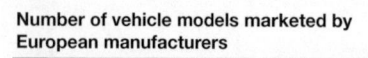

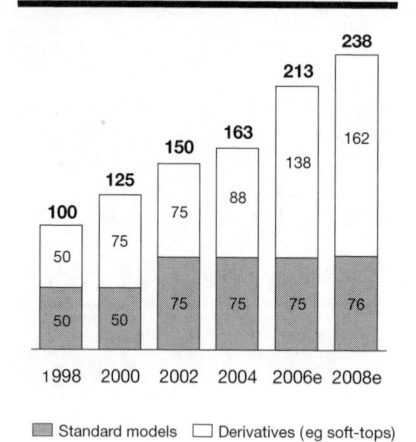

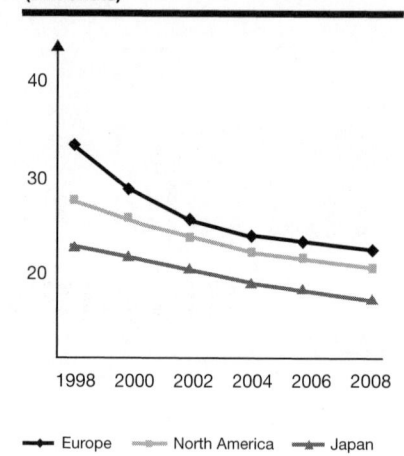

Figure 4.1 *More model ranges but shorter development cycles*
Source: Roland Berger Strategy Consultants

worse still. One fruit of this development is the less than satisfactory earnings situation at numerous car companies, including Ford, General Motors (GM), Fiat and DaimlerChrysler, not to mention many of their component suppliers.

In our view, OEMs, component suppliers and development and production service providers must therefore join forces to pull three key levers that together can optimize the entire automotive value chain (see Figure 4.2):

▎ Lever I: value chain breakdown ('what?'). This lever optimizes the part played by every link in the value chain (original equipment manufacturers (OEMs), component suppliers, development service providers and production service providers).
▎ Lever II: footprint ('where?'). This lever optimizes the physical and geographical development and production networks operated by all companies involved.
▎ Lever III: business model ('how?'). This lever optimizes collaboration between each link in the value chain, for example in the form of joint ventures or strategic partnerships.

Lever I:
Value chain breakdown

- **OEMs:** Focus on development/production activities that shape the brand
- **Component suppliers:** Positioning as integrators or cost-oriented component vendors
- **Development service providers:** Project management and standardization services
- **Production service provider:** Services to handle peaks and help OEMs enter new markets

Lever II:
Physical service provision

- Ongoing **relocation** of value links to countries with low labour costs
- **Challenges**
  - Choosing products and services that are suitable for relocation
  - Choosing the right location
- Existing plant in **countries with high labour costs can survive**, eg by becoming more flexible and reducing personnel expenses

Lever III:
Business model

- Productivity can be raised significantly only by improving **collaboration** between
  - OEMs and OEMs
  - OEMs and component suppliers
  - Component suppliers and component suppliers
- **Challenges:**
  - Choosing a suitable form of collaboration
  - Adjusting skill sets
  - Choosing the right partners
  - Sharing risks and opportunities fairly

Figure 4.2 *Levers to make the value chain more efficient*
Source: Roland Berger Strategy Consultants

LEVER I: VALUE CHAIN BREAKDOWN, A STRONGER FOCUS ON CORE COMPETENCE

In recent years, vehicle manufacturers have consistently rolled back their share of the total value chain. Whereas 70 per cent of value was added in-house in the 1960s, this figure had dwindled to just 34 per cent or so by 2004. These days, having external suppliers deliver completely preassembled modules and systems straight to the OEMs' assembly lines – and even having them fit these modules in the vehicle shell – has become business as usual. While opening up considerably more business potential for component suppliers, this trend also imposes far greater responsibility on the same firms, demands greater skills and exposes them to higher risks.

Beyond parts production, recent years have also seen OEMs outsource the development and production of entire vehicles. Engineering service providers such as EDAG and Pininfarina and production service providers such as Karmann and Magna Steyr have benefited from this practice, boosting their sales by nearly 15 per cent per year since the mid-1990s.

Notwithstanding these developments, the way roles have been split in value chains to date is far from optimal. All too often, car makers are inconsistent in the way they relocate activities, and hence also in the way they scale back internal capacity. This leads to a situation where both parties – the OEM and the component supplier – keep capacity available. Consequently, at the latest by the time when they have to decide who does what, the manufacturers often still tend to opt for in-house production to avoid wasting internal capacity.

Conversely, OEMs have already transferred too much competence to external suppliers in some areas, electronics being a good example. This makes the former more heavily dependent on the latter than ever before, especially with regard to the quality of the components and modules supplied.

One subject of heated debate in the past few months has been why German cars have become less reliable. The numbers are sobering. According to a study by the ADAC (the German automobile association), 251,000 vehicle breakdowns were recorded in Germany in 2004, against 216,000 in 1999 (see Figure 4.3). Interestingly, the mileage clocked up remained more or less constant in this period.

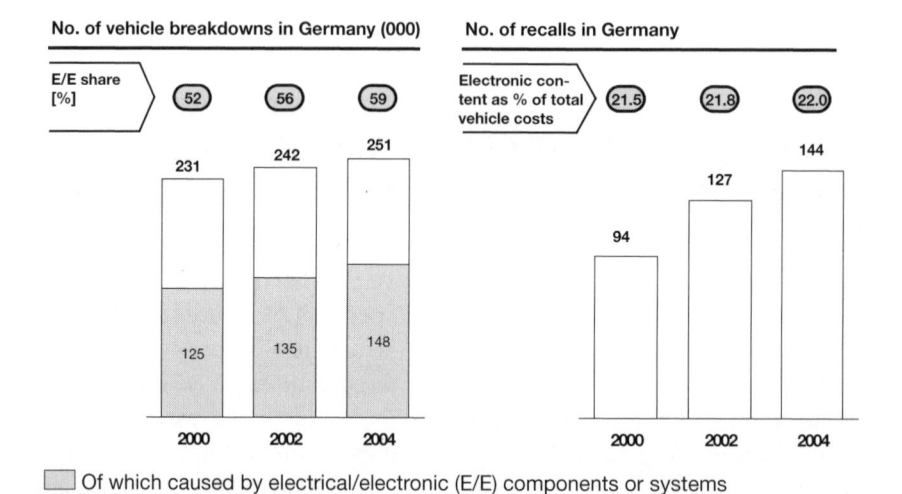

No. of vehicle breakdowns in Germany (000)			No. of recalls in Germany		
E/E share [%]	52	56	59	Electronic content as % of total vehicle costs	21.5	21.8	22.0
2000: 231 (125 E/E)	2002: 242 (135 E/E)	2004: 251 (148 E/E)	2000: 94	2002: 127	2004: 144

▨ Of which caused by electrical/electronic (E/E) components or systems

Figure 4.3 *Breakdown and recall statistics, 1994–2004*
Sources: ADAC, Roland Berger Strategy Consultants

The number of cases in which electronic problems are the cause of breakdowns has risen from 50 to nearly 60 per cent. However, this is not only because of the generally greater importance of electronics in all kinds of vehicle function, as can be seen from a direct comparison between European makers and their Asian rivals, whose figures look substantially better. According to the KBA, Germany's Federal Motor Vehicle Office, the number of recalls also more than quadrupled between 1994 and 2004.

Over the past few years, numerous vehicle makers have farmed out all aspects of the management of second- and third-tier suppliers to external systems integrators. Ironically, they are now starting to complain about losing direct contact with smaller component suppliers, a fact that is in turn putting the brake on innovative dynamism.

It is therefore high time to address one crucial question. How will the roles played by all parties to the development and production of automobiles evolve in future? A subset of this question is, what will happen to the skill sets needed by each player?

Car makers must therefore ask themselves which skills they need to keep in-house to what depth, and to what extent they want to rely even more heavily on external partners in future. On the other side of the equation, component suppliers and development/production service providers must gain a clearer understanding of what business opportunities the future holds, and what skill sets will be needed to exploit them.

Car makers: focused on core competences that shape the brand

In the years ahead, car makers will be compelled to invest even more of their scarce financial resources in design, development and sales/marketing. They will also have to pump proportionally more money into new growth markets, such as China, India, Russia and the Middle East. Consequently, fewer internal resources will remain available for capital-intensive production areas such as foundries and injection moulding plant.

In light of this situation, we expect car manufacturers' in-house share of the value chain to drop further to around 20 to 25 per cent of total development and production costs by 2015.

Most OEMs today still take each make-or-buy decision in isolation. They often lack any clear idea of what the overall value chain ought to look like in future. It is nevertheless vital for them to systematically comb through every activity they perform in-house. They must then clearly define what they want to carry on doing internally in future and what activities they want to farm out in the medium to long term. In addition, this analysis must draw clear distinctions between different assemblies, systems/modules and even individual components. It may even be necessary to draw distinctions on the basis of regional markets.

We would therefore recommend breaking the analysis down into three steps:

74 *Major challenges*

- Step 1: Define the 'candidate' blocks to be investigated. These blocks can be combinations of systems, modules or components, or they can be individual process steps (coachwork pressing, final assembly of the dashboard, and so on).
- Step 2: Determine what influence each candidate block has on the manufacturer's brand promise (such as the joy of driving at BMW or safety at Mercedes-Benz), and gauge the extent to which potential external providers for each block are in fact available on the market (see Figure 4.4).

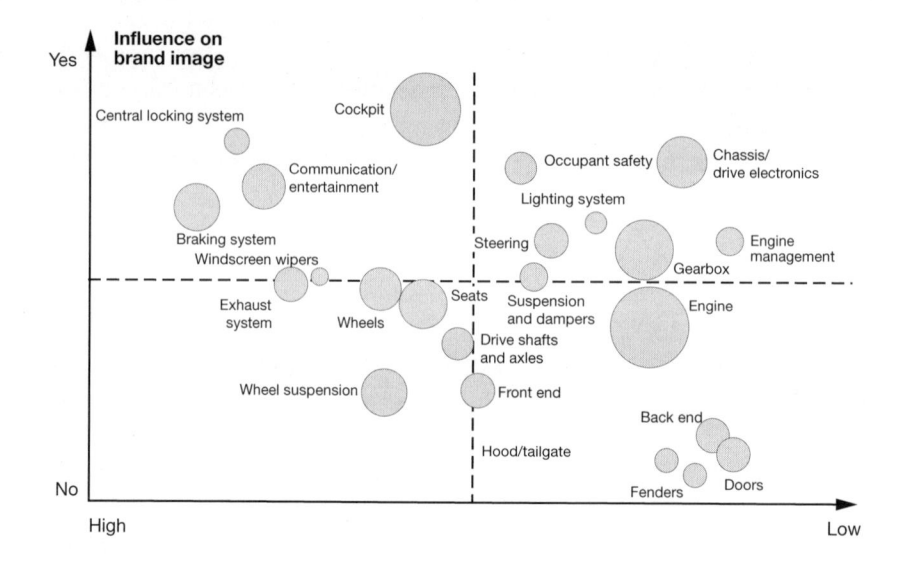

Figure 4.4 *Example of how an OEM might define its core competencies*
Source: Roland Berger Strategy Consultants

- Step 3: For any block that is not of core significance to the brand, the last step is to calculate in detail whether outsourcing would yield cost benefits. At this stage, it is critical to consider the following items: higher transportation and handling charges; the external suppliers' anticipated profit margin; and, in particular, an estimate of those overhead costs that will remain in-house in spite of outsourcing. In practice, these are precisely the areas in which mistakes are often made. One common error is to assume that overheads will be eliminated entirely if activities are outsourced. This generally causes the actual financial benefits of outsourcing to fall short of defined targets. Another mistake is to assume that overhead costs will remain static despite outsourcing. This view is equally unrealistic and often causes firms to keep activities in-house after all (see Figure 4.5).

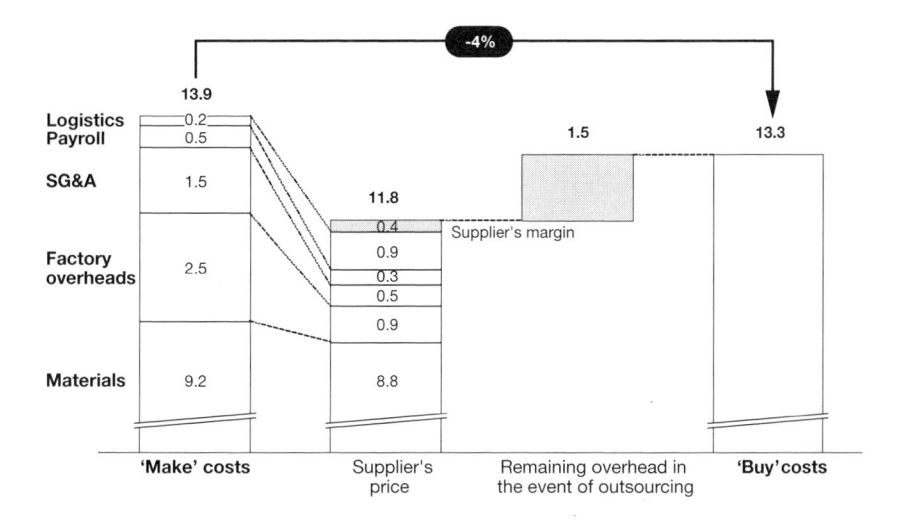

Figure 4.5 *Sample cost comparison calculation for make-or-buy decisions (in euros)*
Source: Roland Berger Strategy Consultants

As well as comparing running costs, it is naturally also important to take account of the one-off charges associated with outsourcing (such as transferring machines, drawing up a social plan to accompany the headcount reduction, and writing off plant that becomes surplus to requirements).

Once future core competencies have been defined, the company must then go on to identify the skill sets it will need and take steps to close any existing gaps.

Component suppliers: focused on components or integration

In recent years, the automotive component supply market has grown consistently at around 3 to 4 per cent per year. Better still, this growth has been profitable. The world's 500 largest publicly traded component suppliers have thus seen their return on capital employed (ROCE) rebound sharply since 2002, following the slump that lasted from 1997 through 2001 (see Figure 4.7).

76 Major challenges

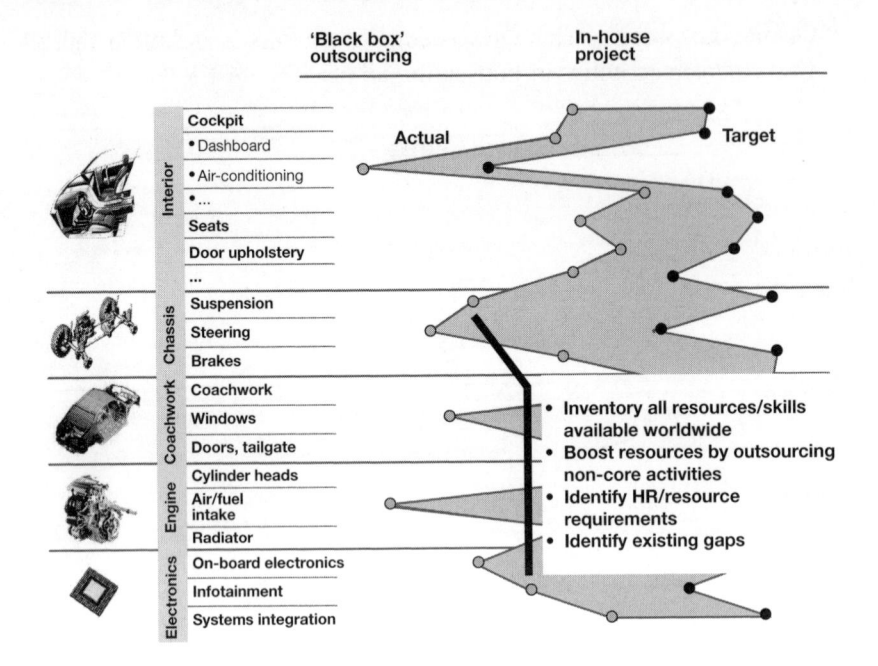

Figure 4.6 *Example of how an OEM might define its future skill sets*
Source: Roland Berger Engineering Study

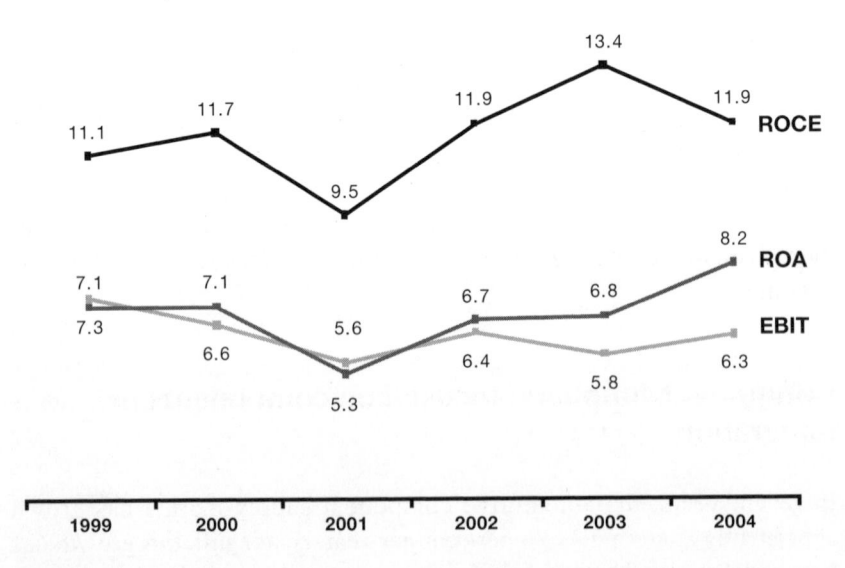

Figure 4.7 *Profitability of the world's 500 largest publicly traded automotive component suppliers*
Sources: Bloomberg, Roland Berger Strategy Consultants

As OEMs continue to farm out activities and areas of competence to external suppliers, the market for automotive components will continue to present attractive growth opportunities in the years ahead. The question is, what strategies will enable individual component suppliers to exploit this lucrative potential to the full?

To answer this question, Roland Berger Strategy Consultants have combed the global component supply industry in search of particularly successful and less successful companies. We then compared the strategies they have pursued over the past five years. Our investigation found that successful suppliers behaved differently from their less successful competitors in five key business dimensions. These dimensions are company size, product portfolio, customer portfolio, R&D spending and the degree of vertical integration.

1 Company size	Sales < EUR 0.4 billion	Sales of EUR 0.4 – 4 billion		Sales > EUR 4 billion
2 Product portfolio	Focused		Diversified	
3 Customer portfolio	Focused		Diversified	
4 R&D spending	Low (<2% of sales)	Average (2–4% of sales)		High (>4% of sales)
5 Vertical integration	Low	Average		High

☐ Successful suppliers   ☐ Less successful suppliers

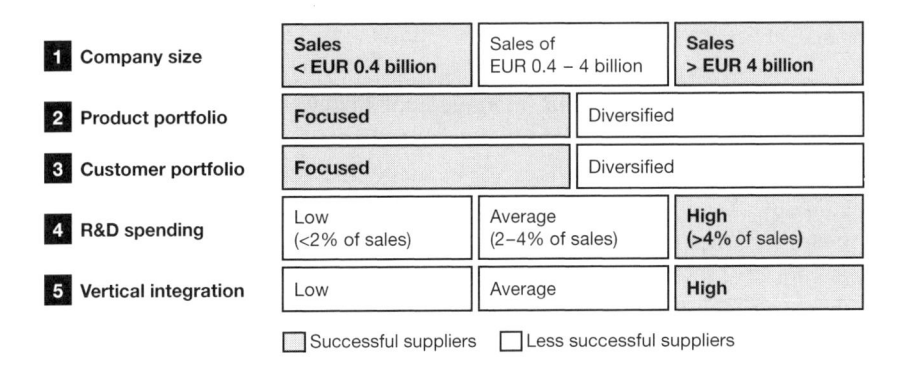

Figure 4.8 *Patterns of success in the automotive component supply industry*
Source: Roland Berger Strategy Consultants

Statistical evidence confirms a clear link between company size and earnings power, for example – although the correlation is by no means directly proportional, as business used to believe back in the days when big was always beautiful. In fact, our analysis shows that, alongside the heavyweights, small component suppliers too tend to be markedly more profitable than their medium-sized rivals.

There are several reasons for this. Many small component suppliers service highly profitable niche markets, for example, and are well protected by the patent rights they own. Moreover, owing to their relatively small sales revenue, these companies have not generally been targets for acquisition by their customers. Many of the mid-sized companies we examined are currently evolving from family-owned and/or family-run businesses to large corporations. In this transitional phase, they often lack

78 *Major challenges*

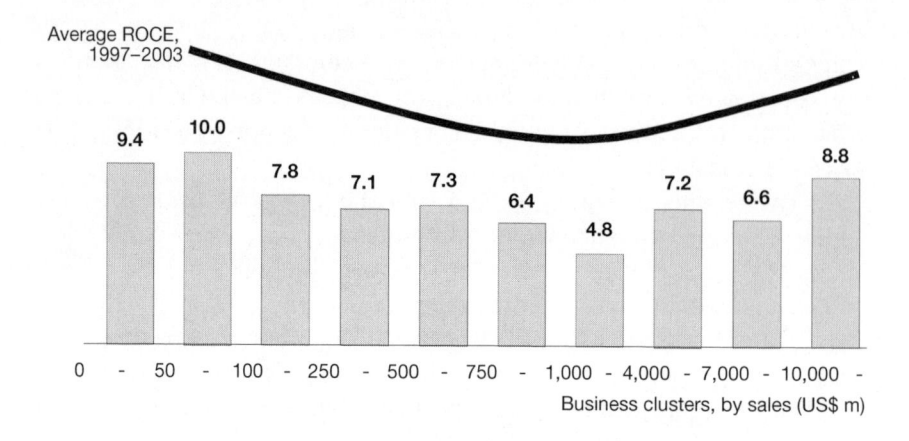

Figure 4.9 *Correlation between profitability and company size*
Source: Roland Berger Strategy Consultants

the necessary structures and management resources, or they are simply trying to service too many product groups at once.

A clear relationship can likewise be identified between profitability and the focus of a company's product or customer portfolio. Top performers generate 86 per cent of sales with their one largest product group and 58 per cent of sales with their three largest customers, for instance. Suppliers whose performance is substandard tend to have a much more diffuse product and customer portfolio.

It will doubtless come as no surprise to discover that the top-performing component suppliers are also those that invest above-average sums in research and development. The same companies also outstrip the low performers in terms of their degree of vertical integration. Apparently, numerous campaigns to shrink the value chain have not (yet) positively impacted the annual financial statements.

Many of the more successful small and mid-sized component suppliers have a strong focus on gaining a perfect mastery of individual components. The more these companies grow, however, the more important it becomes for them to acquire the skills needed to integrate individual submodules or components into complete systems or finished modules. Only then can they meet OEMs' demand for external partners that possess end-to-end value chain competence (in design, simulation, production, assembly, and in test bed, off-road and on-road testing) as well as comprehensive process management, subcontractor management and logistics skills.

One copybook example of a company that has systematically acquired these integration skills is Brose Fahrzeugteile GmbH & Co. KG, headquartered in Coburg, Germany. Since its inception in 1919, Brose has systematically and ambitiously transformed itself from a component manufacturer into an integrator of modules and systems (see Figure 4.10).

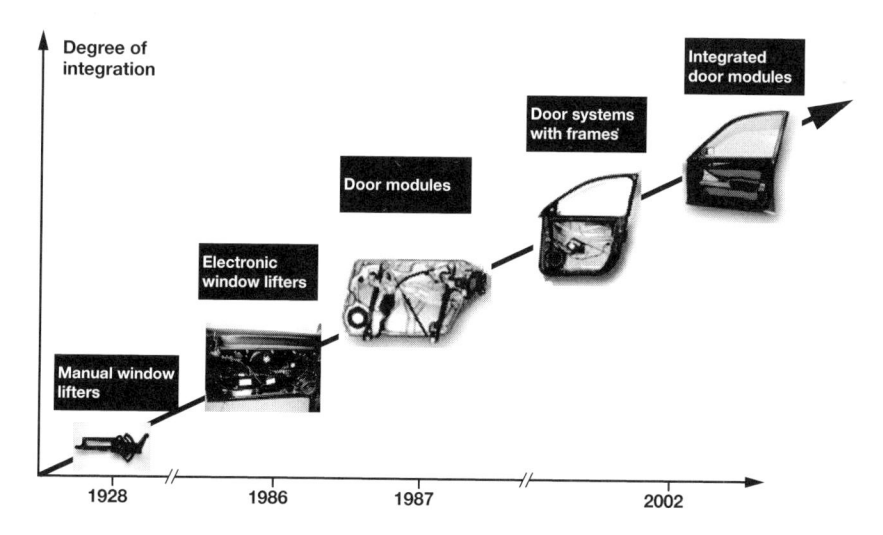

Figure 4.10 *Brose Fahrzeugteile – how a component manufacturer became a module supplier*
Source: Brose Fahrzeugteile GmbH & Co KG

Back in 1928, Brose made the first manual window lifters ever. Electric lifters came in 1963, followed by electronically controlled devices in 1986. A year later, the first door module, consisting of a window lifter, window pane, window guide and impact protection unit, was fitted in an Audi 80 Coupé. Since then, things have moved fast. Today, a Brose door module is made up of a wide range of add-on components, such as speakers, locking systems, sealing elements and control elements for the wing mirrors. To complement its window lifter and door module business, the company gradually also moved into seat adjustment and locking systems. The reward for this relentless and systematic accumulation of competencies has been impressive indeed: Brose has averaged 13 per cent annual growth for the past 50 years, expanding faster and more sustainably than virtually any other automotive component supplier.

One key success factor at Brose has been a style of management focused rigorously on the long term. Others have been optimal interplay between mechanical, electrical and electronic components, an ability to respond swiftly to changing market conditions and customer requirements, and a healthy mix of technology and cost leadership.

Engineering service providers: beginning to find their focus

Engineering service providers are a very disparate group (see Figure 4.11). Over the past decade, this corner of the supply network has enjoyed above-average growth rates, expanding on average at around 15 per cent per annum since 1996.

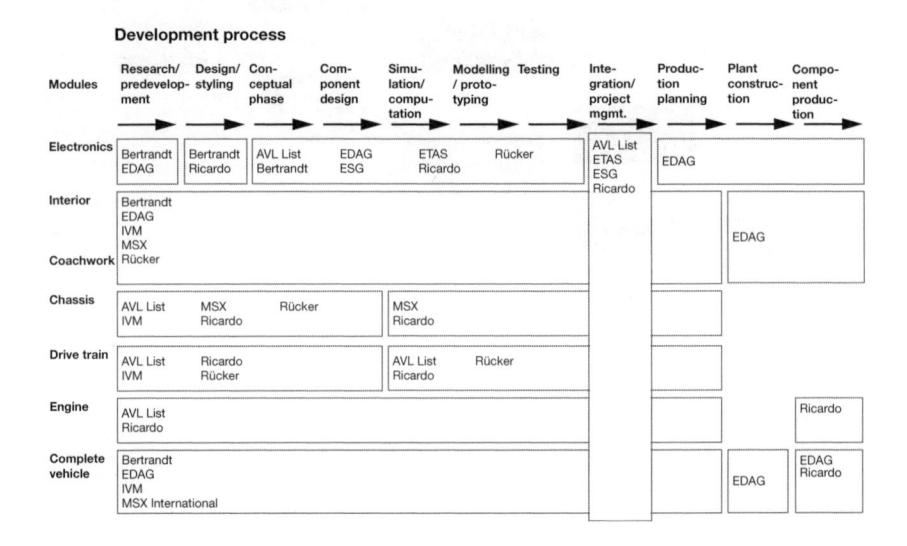

Modules	Research/ predevelopment	Design/ styling	Conceptual phase	Component design	Simulation/ computation	Modelling / prototyping	Testing	Integration/ project mgmt.	Production planning	Plant construction	Component production
Electronics	Bertrandt EDAG	Bertrandt Ricardo	AVL List Bertrandt	EDAG ESG	ETAS Ricardo		Rücker	AVL List ETAS ESG Ricardo	EDAG		
Interior	Bertrandt EDAG IVM MSX									EDAG	
Coachwork	Rücker										
Chassis	AVL List IVM	MSX Ricardo		Rücker	MSX Ricardo						
Drive train	AVL List IVM	Ricardo Rücker			AVL List Ricardo		Rücker				
Engine	AVL List Ricardo										Ricardo
Complete vehicle	Bertrandt EDAG IVM MSX International									EDAG	EDAG Ricardo

Figure 4.11 *Activities covered by engineering service providers*
Source: Roland Berger Strategy Consultants

Dark clouds have however been looming on the horizon, at the latest since the start of 2004. Demand for external engineering services has shifted into reverse, for a number of reasons. One is that a number of OEM engineering departments have moved over to a strict insourcing policy in order to absorb excess in-house capacity. Demand is also being hit by car makers' redoubled attempts to keep competence that is critical to their brands in-house. Furthermore, one of the principal drivers of the outsourcing trend – sharp growth in the variety of vehicle models – is likely to peak in the next year or two. At the same time, OEMs are now making first-tier suppliers responsible for entire systems and modules, in the hope that they will also handle and finance the necessary engineering work.

Despite all these negative effects, the market for engineering services is still likely to present lucrative business opportunities in the medium to long term. This market segment will receive positive stimulus from the fact that in-vehicle technology – especially in the field of electronics – is continually becoming more complex. Auto makers' cost-conscious efforts to standardize or at least harmonize, certain technologies (such as software engineering), modules and components across different vendors will likewise fuel further demand for these services. This is precisely where tremendous opportunities lie in store for engineering service providers.

The providers concerned will nevertheless only be able to tap this potential if they carve out a keener profile for themselves. Back in the heady years of rampant growth, many such firms tried to cover every conceivable service, from predevelopment to plant construction – and that in every single product group. This inevitably left them with a decidedly fuzzy market position, preventing many of their business areas from achieving critical mass. The pivotal challenge will therefore be to define focal areas of future activity, and to bring both qualitative and quantitative resource allocation into line with this new orientation. Our experience indicates that many development service providers could raise their efficiency by double-digit percentages if they were to optimize their capacity management in particular. A further challenge in the years ahead will be to adjust their network of locations in line with customer expectations. Above all, this will involve building and ramping up capacity in low-labour-cost regions such as China and India.

Full-service providers and dedicated production service providers: services to unplug bottlenecks and catalyze entry to new markets

A series of full-service providers for auto makers have emerged in the recent past. Today, the likes of Karmann and Magna Steyr can not only develop entire vehicles and get them production-ready: they also have the capabilities to volume-produce vehicles, which they do with the BMW X3, the Mercedes CLK and the Jeep Grand Cherokee. Alongside these flexible market players, dedicated production service providers such as Valmet (for the Porsche Boxster) have gained a foothold on the market.

For car companies, drawing on the services of such firms makes eminent sense. Capacity bottlenecks can be unplugged. Small-series and niche models can be rolled out efficiently at highly flexible plant, despite low unit volumes. By no means least, the car makers themselves have to tie up far less capital for development and production.

In this segment too, however, a few boom years have now given way to a more sober mood. Large numbers of new niche models, such as VW's soft-top and the latest 6 Series BMW, have been or are still being manufactured

82 Major challenges

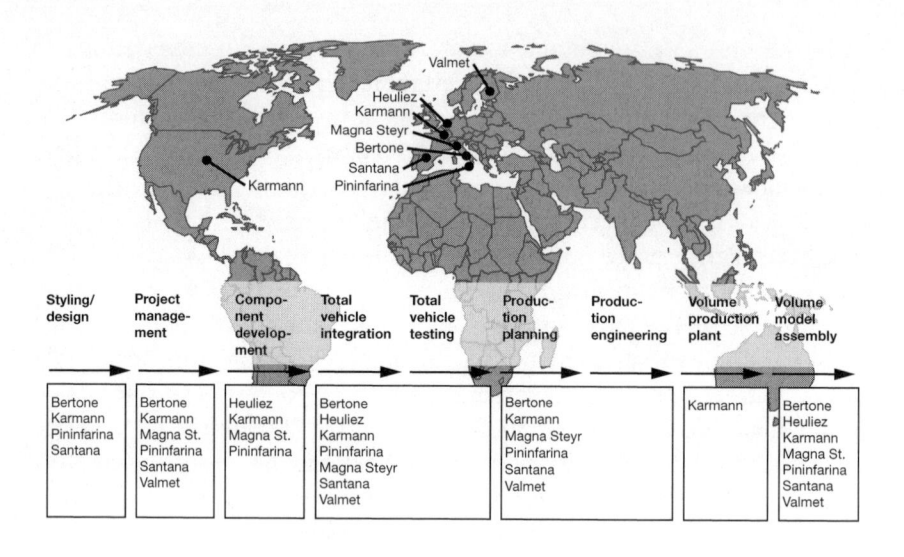

Figure 4.12 *Overview of production service providers*
Source: Roland Berger Strategy Consultants

in-house. New plants are springing up in the world's growth markets, even though existing capacity in the triad markets is not being rolled back. Current global overcapacity – enough for some 20 million vehicle units – is thus likely to remain acute until beyond 2010. Added to this is the fact that OEMs themselves have in the meantime set up more flexible production plants of their own. One direct consequence is that production service providers saw an average of two to three percentage points shaved off their profits between 2001 and 2003.

Here again, however, production service providers can continue to operate in attractive areas in future. One opportunity is to assist OEMs as they seek to penetrate new growth markets such as China, Russia, India and Iran. The idea of having service providers that absorb peaks right across the brand spectrum is also proving to be a viable option. In this area, production service providers must nevertheless make their production processes and plants more flexible than they are at present.

Section summary: attractive growth opportunities for module and system suppliers – major challenges ahead of engineering and production service providers

In future, OEMs will concentrate even more heavily on areas of competence that are critical to their brand image. Many component suppliers can therefore look forward to sustained and very attractive growth, especially in the areas of drive and chassis products. All in all, we believe that component suppliers will increase their share of the total value chain from around 64 per cent today to about 73 per cent in 2015 (see Figure 4.13).

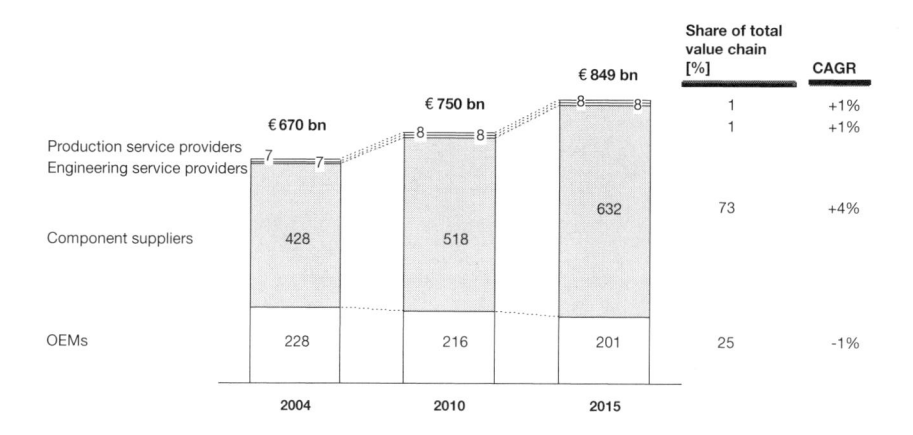

Figure 4.13 *Breakdown of the value chain in the global automotive industry*
Source: Roland Berger Strategy Consultants

The outlook is less rosy for development and production service providers, however. Most of the areas in which they operate are closer to OEMs' own core competencies than is the case for the component suppliers. Accordingly, these service providers will be hit harder by the auto makers' bias toward insourcing.

LEVER II: FOOTPRINT, GROWING PRESSURE ON EXISTING LOCATIONS

The second lever to improve efficiency in the value chain is the optimization of physical footprint. The central question here is, where can what products and services be provided most efficiently?

In recent years, capital spending in the automotive industry has headed east to the new growth regions of Asia and Eastern Europe at an astonishing pace. Manufacturers of the calibre of Hyundai, Kia, PSA and VW are currently erecting new assembly plants worth over €4 billion in

Eastern Europe alone. The established triad markets are being left behind (see Figure 4.14).

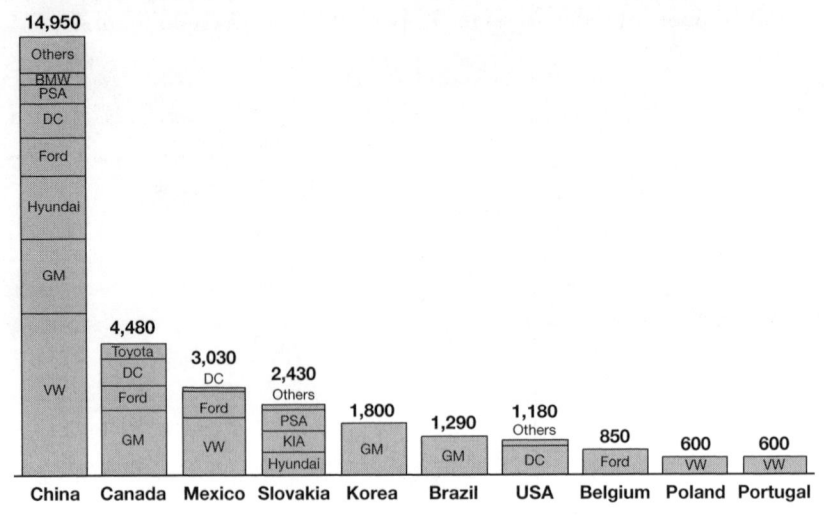

Figure 4.14 *Capital spending announced by OEMs, by country (in € million)*
Sources: JD Power, Roland Berger Strategy Consultants, OEMs' press releases

Although production jobs are the primary target, the writing is already on the wall for development activities as well. Here too, new jobs will be created only in Eastern Europe (+2,000), China (+4,500) and India and the Pacific region (+4,000) in the next 10 years (see Figure 4.15). In the coming years, car manufacturers will offshore the work of whole development teams to countries with low labour costs. China is very clearly the OEMs' favourite destination, followed by Eastern Europe and India. Simulation, machine tool construction, modelling and documentation are among the activities that will feel the impact most keenly.

The same trend can be observed among automotive component suppliers and engineering service providers. Not a week goes by without a company announcing its intention to invest in Eastern Europe while slashing capacity in Western Europe. Italy, the UK and Spain are leading the way in axing local production capacity, whereas factories in France and Germany are usually retained but downsized.

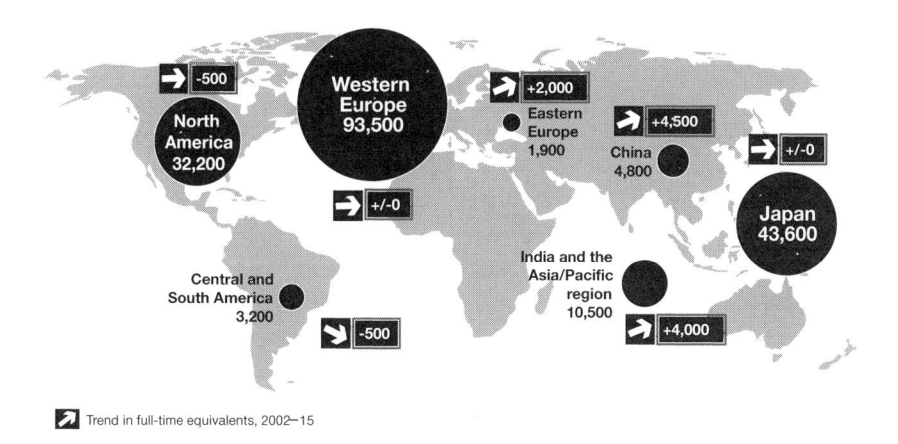

Figure 4.15 *OEMs' existing and planned development resources (in full-time equivalents)*
Sources: Roland Berger Strategy Consultants, interviews with auto makers, company information

Establishing low-labour-cost locations – a matter of survival

The widespread belief that the benefits afforded by Eastern Europe and other locations with low labour costs will be eroded by substantial annual wage increases over the next 5 to 10 years is wrong. True, annual wage rises of as much as 10 or 15 per cent are no rare occurrence in many Eastern European countries. Given the low level from which they are starting out, however, substantial discrepancies will remain in absolute terms (see Figure 4.16).

In spite of lower productivity in locations with low labour costs, companies can thus still save up to 75 per cent of their personnel expenses for a long time to come. And personnel expenses account for 25 to 30 per cent of total production costs on average. It follows that, even allowing for higher logistical and complexity costs and lower productivity, component suppliers can still expect to reduce total costs by 10 to 15 per cent by transferring production to Eastern Europe. In the hard-fought component supply business, that can make the difference between staying alive and going under (see Figure 4.17).

The trend towards building up capacity in countries with low labour costs will thus continue in the years ahead. Indeed it will accelerate, as a 2004 study by Roland Berger Strategy Consultants discovered. Of the respondent mid-sized industrial companies, 90 per cent said they planned to transfer further links in their value chain abroad in the next five years.

86 Major challenges

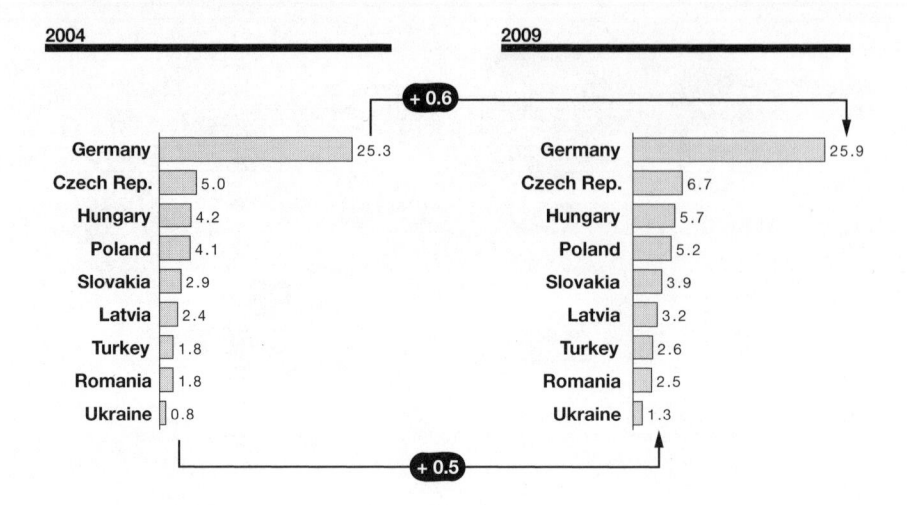

2004

Germany	25.3
Czech Rep.	5.0
Hungary	4.2
Poland	4.1
Slovakia	2.9
Latvia	2.4
Turkey	1.8
Romania	1.8
Ukraine	0.8

2009

Germany	25.9
Czech Rep.	6.7
Hungary	5.7
Poland	5.2
Slovakia	3.9
Latvia	3.2
Turkey	2.6
Romania	2.5
Ukraine	1.3

+ 0.6 (Germany)
+ 0.5 (Ukraine)

Figure 4.16 *Labour costs (including non-wage labour costs) for an unskilled worker in Germany and Eastern Europe (€/hour)*
Sources: EIU, CE research, LLP, Roland Berger Strategy Consultants

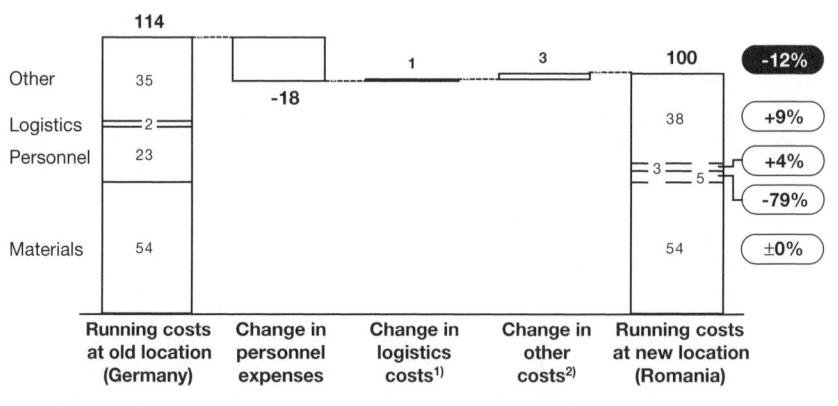

Running costs at old location (Germany): 114
- Other: 35
- Logistics: 2
- Personnel: 23
- Materials: 54

Change in personnel expenses: −18
Change in logistics costs[1]: 1
Change in other costs[2]: 3

Running costs at new location (Romania): 100
- Other: 38
- Logistics: 3
- Personnel: 5
- Materials: 54

−12%
+9% (Other)
+4% (Logistics)
−79% (Personnel)
±0% (Materials)

1) Including the cost of capital inventories 2) Coordination, tax writeoffs, more scrap, etc.

Figure 4.17 *Comparative view: average costs for a component supply factory with annual sales of around €170 million (in € m)*
Source: Roland Berger Strategy Consultants

To put that figure in context, only 69 per cent of these have relocated value chain links to low-labour-cost countries in the past. Increasingly, even highly complex technological components are being caught up in this wave.

Often enough, component suppliers have no other choice. When one of their OEM customers asks them to supply components direct to a low-cost plant, the only question is, do the volumes and prices justify investing on the ground in China or Russia?

On the other hand, a lot more preparation and careful consideration is needed when deciding to set up a site from which countries with high labour costs can import parts manufactured at low cost. Three key issues must be covered when preparing and planning to relocate production to countries with low labour costs:

- Suitable products must be chosen.
- A suitable production location must be chosen.
- A detailed relocation plan must be drawn up.

Choosing suitable products

The issue of exactly what activities are to be relocated is the most important question of all. A five-step approach to answering this question has proven its value in the past (see Figure 4.18).

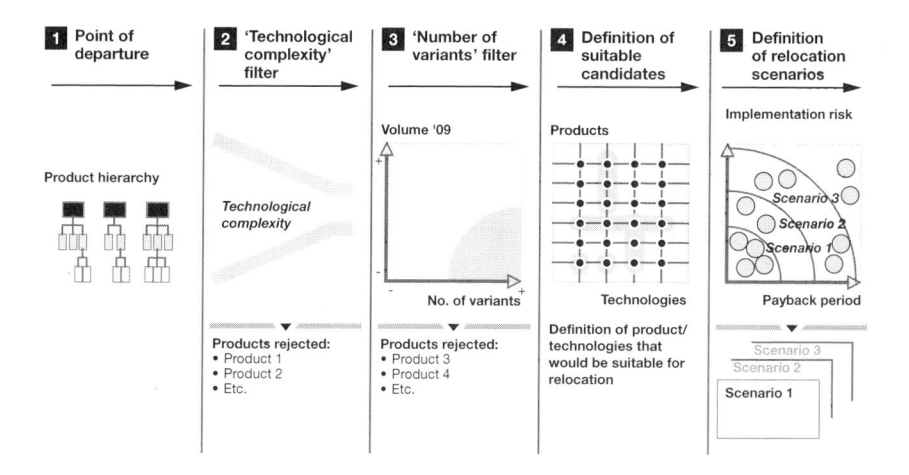

Figure 4.18 *Determining the scope of production to be relocated*
Source: Roland Berger Strategy Consultants

The first step involves drawing up a clear, understandable hierarchy of the entire product portfolio. A scoring model then enables products whose technology is too complex to be eliminated, as they are not suitable for relocation. The third step is to examine the number of variants of each of the remaining products. Depending on the relative maturity of the short-listed low-labour-cost locations, the results of this examination may vary.

Products manufactured in a wide range of variants (that is, relatively labour-intensive products) might be ideal for one candidate location but not at all suited to another.

Products that make it to step four are divided up into individual process steps. The various combinations of products and production stages are then analysed to determine both the financial impact of and the risks associated with relocation. A series of plausible scenarios are then evaluated to arrive at a final decision. When analysing the financial impact, it is important to make sure that all relevant cost items are factored in, including the cost of training new people on site, higher logistical costs, the cost of producing new samples for OEMs, and the implicit cost of any discounts granted to the auto makers.

Choosing a suitable production location

A whole raft of criteria must be considered when looking for a suitable low-labour-cost location. Practical experience has nevertheless shown that a small number of criteria carry the most weight (see Figure 4.19).

		Weighting [%]	PL	CZ	H	SLO	SK	LT	LV	EST	BG	RO	HR	SM	MK	BIH	UA	RUS	TR
Costs	• Personnel	30																	
	– Current wage costs	20	3	2	3	1	4	4	4	4	5	5	3	5	4	5	5	5	5
	– Long-term wage trend	50	2	2	2	1	3	3	4	3	5	4	2	4	4	4	5	5	4
	– Availability	30	5	5	5	2	5	2	2	2	3	4	2	1	1	1	2	4	3
	• Logistics	30																	
	– Distance	40	4	5	4	4	4	3	2	2	2	4[1)]	4	3	2	3	2	1	1
	– Reliability	60	5	5	5	5	5	4	4	4	2	3	4	2	2	2	1	1	1
Stability	• Economic and financial stability	7.5	4	4	4	5	4	4	4	4	3	3	3	1	1	1	2	3	2
	• Political and legal stability	10	5	5	5	5	5	5	5	5	3	3	3	1	1	1	1	1	1
	• Transparency	12.5	2	3	3	4	3	3	3	4	3	3[1)]	2	1	1	2	1	1	2
Duties/ taxes	• Corp. income taxes	5	3	2	4	2	3	4	4	1	4	4	3	5	5	1	2	2	1
	• Customs tariffs	5	5	5	5	5	5	5	5	5	4	4	3	3	3	3	3	3	3
Weighted score		100	3.8	3.9	3.9	3.5	4.1	3.6	3.6	3.4	3.2	3.5	2.9	2.4	2.2	2.3	2.3	2.4	2.2
Ranking			(4)	(2)	(2)	(7)	(1)	(5)	(5)	(9)	(10)	(7)	(11)	(12)	(16)	(14)	(14)	(12)	(16)

New EU member countries: PL, CZ, H, SLO, SK, LT, LV, EST
Candidates: BG, RO
Non-EU countries – Others: HR, SM, MK, BIH, UA, RUS, TR

1 Very disadvantageous   5 Very advantageous

Figure 4.19 *Simplified scoring model for choosing a location (example, Eastern Europe)*
Source: Roland Berger Strategy Consultants

Current personnel expenses at the target location, and above all anticipated wage increases in the years ahead, are naturally two of the most significant factors. Generally speaking, reliable information can only be gleaned through in-depth talks with industrial companies, job placement and investment agencies, and/or public bodies in the countries concerned. Component suppliers in particular should think about the kind of employees they will need very early on, and then conduct research to determine whether the regions they have in mind actually have a large enough pool of labour with appropriate skills.

Logistical costs are the second core issue. It is vital to ensure that transportation channels can be relied on absolutely, even in adverse weather conditions. Otherwise, the buffers that have to be factored in would tie up capital and quickly negate any savings made on labour costs, for example. It is also important to make sure that the target location is easily accessible to visitors (customers, suppliers and the company's own management). Proximity to a decent-sized airport is always expedient, for example. If a reasonable solution is not found here, huge problems can occur during start-up in particular if it is not possible to respond swiftly.

The selected country must also enjoy long-term economic, financial, political and legal stability. Taxes and customs tariffs too should never be left out of the equation. Depending on the product programme and the value chain model, it may further be necessary to critically assess the availability of suitably qualified upstream suppliers.

Once priorities have been set concerning the preferred target countries, these countries must then be divided up and analysed on the basis of individual economic regions (see Figure 4.20). A final location decision should not be taken until the investigation has drilled down to a region of no more than 200 or 300 square kilometres.

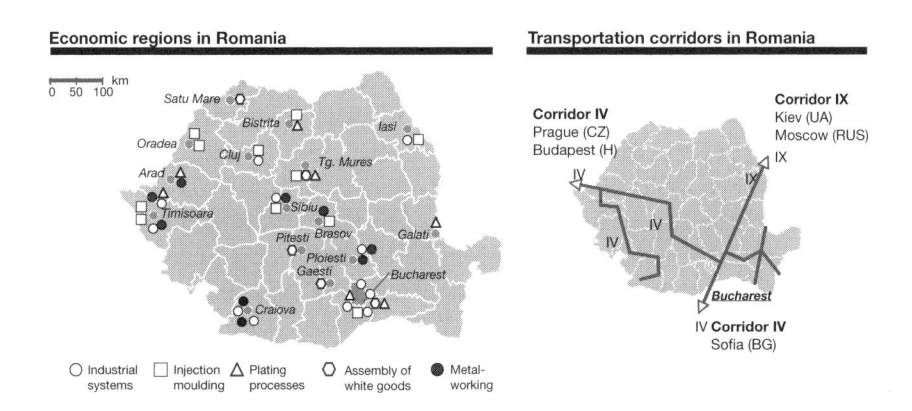

Figure 4.20 *Definition of local regions and transportation corridors (example: Romania)*
Source: Roland Berger Strategy Consultants

Detailed relocation plan

Once the scope of activities to be transferred has been defined and a target location selected, it is time to map out a detailed relocation plan. This plan will feature a number of aspects:

- layout planning for the new plant (or extension);
- punctual orders for the necessary production equipment;
- punctual recruiting/appointment of the first level of management (in particular the plant and HR managers);
- punctual build-up of inventories to ensure that shipment can continue even during relocation;
- commencement of talks with the customer to prepare for initial samples;
- preparation of communication with employees and suppliers;
- adjustment of overhead structures at the 'home' plant.

Section summary: solutions for locations in countries with high labour costs

With few exceptions, growth in the next few years will take place in countries that have low labour costs. The cost benefits involved are quite simply far too compelling. The situation is different, however, if a company wants to transfer production lines from an existing high-wage plant to a low-wage plant but has no other business to take up the slack at the original site. In such cases, social plans and sundry costs associated with plant closure can impose a crushing financial burden. It is not unusual for these expenses to add up to three or four times the projected annual savings. Experience shows that, when the cost of capital is factored in, this can extend the payback period to around four to six years.

This is precisely where factories in countries with high labour costs must seize their opportunity. Personnel expenses at home can be reduced by as much as 15 per cent by lowering payroll costs, adding greater flexibility, raising the working week from 35 to 38, 40 or 42 hours without increasing wage costs, docking overtime rates and/or cancelling vacation allowances and Christmas bonuses, for example. Since such moves add just one or two years to the payback period, relocation then scarcely makes economic sense. Numerous leading West European component suppliers have already opted to go this way in recent months and years (see Figure 4.21).

Company	Year	Plants affected	Working week	Wages/welfare benefits	Employers' concessions
Bosch		Stuttgart, Sebnitz	35 → 36-hour week	Welfare benefits and bonuses waived	No lay-offs through 2007; plans for relocation to China abandoned
Brose		All German plants	35 → 38-hour week	Under negotiation	Not known
Continental		Hanover-Stöcken	Increase to a 40-hour week	–	Not known
Continental Teves		Gifhorn	35 → 40-hour week	–	Headcount reduction limited to 200
Delphi		Wuppertal	40 → 44-hour week for white-collar empl.	–	–
EDAG		Fulda	More flexible working hours	–	Cap imposed on headcount reduction
Edscha		Remscheid	Longer working week	–	Avoidance of relocation
FAG Kugelfischer		Eltmann	More flexible overtime agreement	2% of welfare benefits waived	No lay-offs through 2006; home site saved
INA		Lahr	35 → 40-hour week	–	–
Leoni		Two German plants	35 → 38-hour week	–	–
Schuler		All German plants Würzburg	More flexible working hours	Agreed wage rise and bonuses for 2005 waived; bonus agreements more variable for subsequent years	–
Siemens VDO			More flexible working hours	Agreed wage rises postponed; vacation allowance and Christmas bonus reduced	Guarantees for 1,400 jobs through 2010

Figure 4.21 *Factory-specific agreements that have reduced personnel expenses (examples)*
Sources: Roland Berger Strategy Consultants, press releases

LEVER III: BUSINESS MODEL, MORE EXTENSIVE NETWORKING WITHIN THE AUTOMOTIVE VALUE CHAIN

The third lever to optimize the automotive value chain is improved collaboration between everyone involved.

Much work remains to be done in this area. Business relationships between OEMs and their component suppliers, for instance, have deteriorated alarmingly in recent years (see Figure 4.22). Many suppliers today complain of an unparalleled decline in the way they are treated. To take just one example, retroactive demands for one-off payments for orders that have already been completed land ever more frequently on the desks of component suppliers. Anyone who refuses to 'pay to play' can wave goodbye to follow-up orders. Since only profitable component suppliers can continue to deliver required innovations and uphold the necessary quality in the long run, this trend cannot be sustained for long.

The potential derived from optimizing the breakdown of the value chain (lever I) and optimizing physical service provision (lever II) can only be exploited to the full if all parties represented in the value work together (lever III). The forms which such collaboration takes must experience radical change (see Figure 4.23).

Major challenges

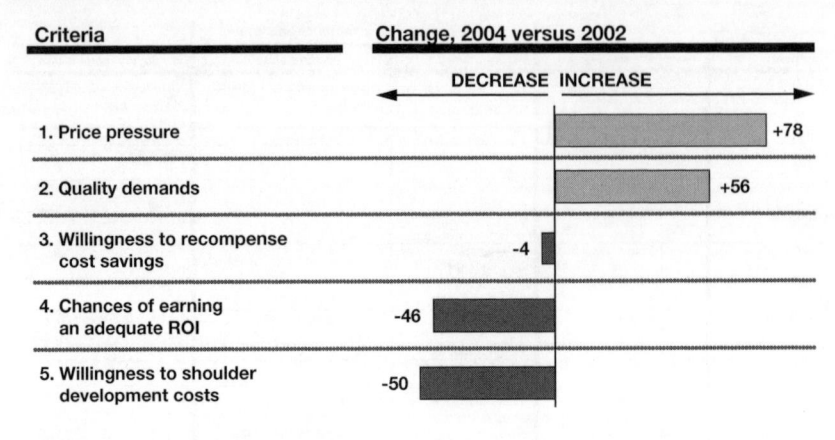

Criteria	Change, 2004 versus 2002
1. Price pressure	+78
2. Quality demands	+56
3. Willingness to recompense cost savings	-4
4. Chances of earning an adequate ROI	-46
5. Willingness to shoulder development costs	-50

Base: Average of opinions on leading OEMs

Figure 4.22 *Change in OEMs' purchasing behaviour from the perspective of their component suppliers (2004 versus 2002)*
Source: Supplier Business.com

	Today	Tomorrow
1. Innovation	• Solutions to problems mostly bilateral • No special incentives to innovate • Isolated, company-specific improvements	• Networked solutions to problems • Incentives to innovate • Improvements across and between companies
2. Leadership and communication	• Company-specific value chain strategies • Focus on strong individual processes • Communication emphasizes commitment • Hierarchic collaboration	• Integrated value chain strategies/unified and complementary competencies • Integrated processes • Intensive communication emphasizes trust • Full networking and integration of specialist knowledge
3. Access	• Local and/or company-specific standards • Independent corporate planning and control • Independent resources and capital spending • Loose collaboration	• Collaborative target agreement and escalation processes based on uniform standards • Integrated corporate planning and control • Shared resources and capital spending • Close collaboration
4. Risk	• Short-term profit maximization • Simple contractual regulation of information exchange	• Profit and risk sharing • Contractual protection of intellectual property

Figure 4.23 *Paradigm shifts in forms of collaboration*
Source: Roland Berger Strategy Consultants

To simplify matters, distinctions can be drawn between six basic types of collaboration within the automotive value chain (see Figure 4.24). The section that follows outlines one successful example of each type and summarizes the success factors for more intensive collaboration in the car industry.

The value chain challenge 93

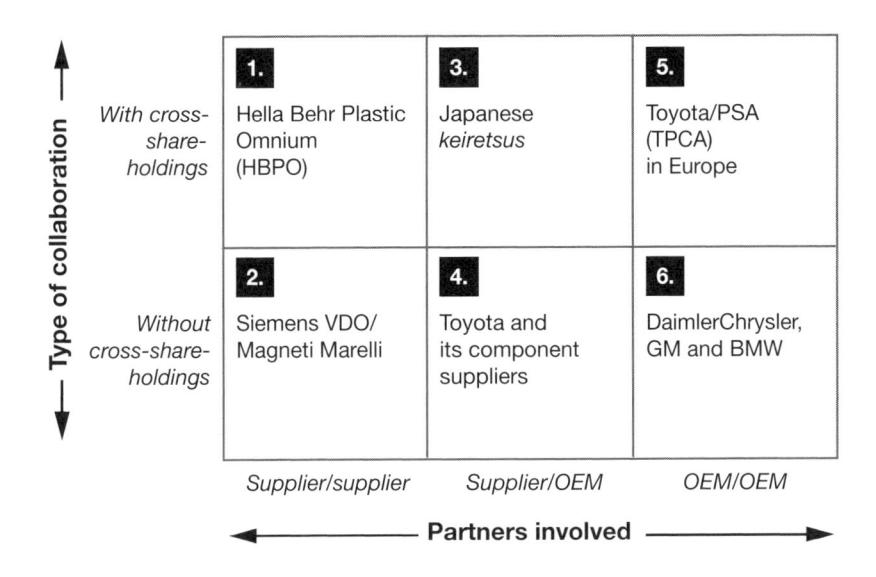

		Supplier/supplier	Supplier/OEM	OEM/OEM
Type of collaboration	With cross-shareholdings	**1.** Hella Behr Plastic Omnium (HBPO)	**3.** Japanese *keiretsus*	**5.** Toyota/PSA (TPCA) in Europe
	Without cross-shareholdings	**2.** Siemens VDO/ Magneti Marelli	**4.** Toyota and its component suppliers	**6.** DaimlerChrysler, GM and BMW

◄——— **Partners involved** ———►

Figure 4.24 *Types of collaboration in the automatic industry*
Source: Roland Berger Strategy Consultants

Joint ventures between component suppliers: the example of HBPO (Hella Behr Plastic Omnium)

HBPO is an outstanding example of successful collaboration between component suppliers that involves cross-shareholdings. What is now the leading provider of front-end modules emerged in two steps between 1999 and 2004, as parts of three component suppliers – Behr, Hella and Plastic Omnium Auto Exterior – came together. Today, these units stand together as a single, legally independent corporation with a total of eight sites in North America, Europe and Asia (see Figure 4.25).

In a very short time, HBPO became known throughout the industry as 'the module company'. It has cultivated a pronounced customer orientation and set itself the ambitious goal of becoming the clear global market leader in front-end modules. By the end of 2004, HBPO had already cornered 23 per cent of the global market.

HBPO is unquestionably a success story. Four factors have been instrumental in its astonishing rise:

▌ Attractive market segment: the market for front-end modules has witnessed very positive development in recent years. Between now and 2010, the global sales volume is expected to swell by as much as 25 per cent per annum.

Sales at HBPO (€m)

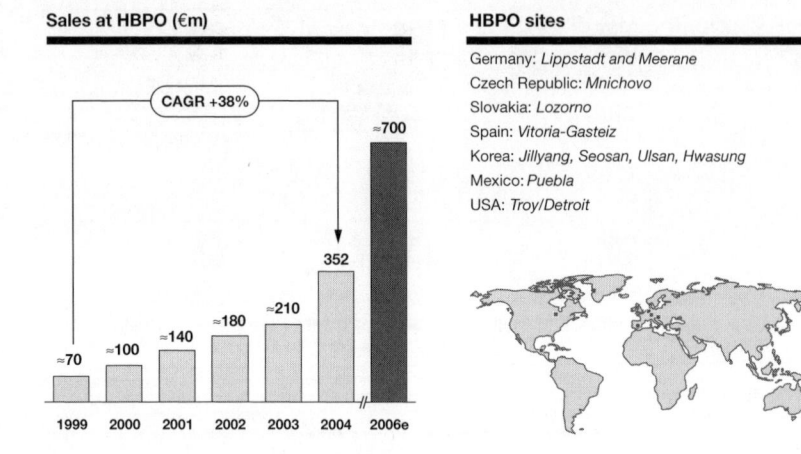

CAGR +38%

- 1999: ≈70
- 2000: ≈100
- 2001: ≈140
- 2002: ≈180
- 2003: ≈210
- 2004: 352
- 2006e: ≈700

HBPO sites

Germany: *Lippstadt and Meerane*
Czech Republic: *Mnichovo*
Slovakia: *Lozorno*
Spain: *Vitoria-Gasteiz*
Korea: *Jillyang, Seosan, Ulsan, Hwasung*
Mexico: *Puebla*
USA: *Troy/Detroit*

Figure 4.25 *HBPO at a glance*
Source: HBPO company information

- Complementary capabilities: the joint venture constitutes the ideal combination of Hella's lighting and electronics expertise with Behr's knowledge of radiators and air-conditioning and Plastic Omnium Auto Exterior's mastery of coachwork parts, bumpers and crash management. All three companies rank among the most innovative players in their respective product segments. Better still, all three also contributed complementary customer portfolios to the joint venture.
- Flexibility: the new company is extremely flexible. It focuses rigorously on customers and their needs and wants. The recent inclusion of Plastic Omnium in the organization is one fruit of this strict customer orientation.
- Cultural fit: the three joint venture partners all have comparable corporate and management cultures. All three tend to focus corporate policy on the long term, for instance. As a general rule, this kind of soft factor is hugely important to the success of joint ventures.

Analysis of numerous other joint ventures confirms the validity of these success factors.

Strategic alliances between component suppliers: the example of Siemens VDO and Magneti Marelli

The strategic alliance between Siemens VDO and Magneti Marelli is completely different from the example described above. In this case, two direct competitors decided at the end of 2004 to work together. This move came about in response to Bosch's dominance in diesel injection systems (see Figure 4.26).

Shares of the global market for diesel injection systems (2004)

- Magneti Marelli: 3%
- Delphi: 10%
- Siemens VDO: 24%
- Robert Bosch: 64%

Key data on the collaborative venture

- **Announcement**: October 2004
- **Planned production startup**: 2007
- **Object**:
  To jointly develop a new generation of diesel injection systems for smaller and mid-sized engines
- **Aim**:
  For both partner companies to sharply increase their market share

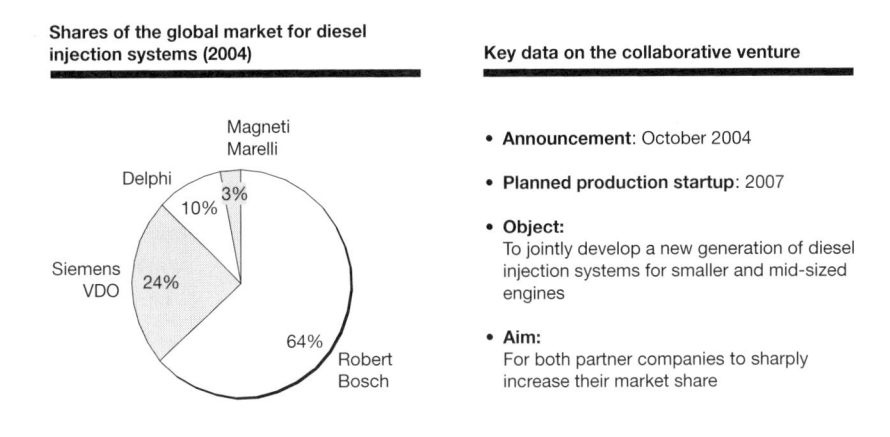

Figure 4.26 *Aim of collaboration between Siemens VDO and Magneti Marelli*
Source: Company information

The two partners have made it their goal to jointly develop a new generation of diesel injection systems for smaller and mid-sized engines by 2007. Although they are direct competitors, collaboration yields benefits for both companies:

▌ Complementary technologies: the new systems combine the magnetic fuel injectors that Magneti Marelli developed with Fiat and fuel injection technology from Siemens VDO. Magneti Marelli alone is developing the electronic control unit.
▌ Protection of intellectual property: the relevant contracts put up very high exit barriers for both parties. Effective protection is thus provided for both parties' intellectual property – usually the most critical issue in this type of collaboration.

One key challenge in collaboration between Siemens VDO and Magneti Marelli is that the two companies' customer portfolios overlap to some extent for the same product. Another issue is restricted access to the resources of the individual partners.

Close collaboration involving cross-shareholdings between OEMs and component suppliers: Japan's *keiretsus*

With the exception of a few relationships that grew up due to unique corporate histories (such as those between Faurecia and PSA or Magneti Marelli and Fiat), interlocking equity interests between OEMs and component suppliers tend to be the exception on the European and American markets. Not so in Japan, where closely interlocking interests between auto makers and component suppliers – a construct known as *keiretsu* – have been a key aspect of the automotive value chain for many decades. Toyota offers a fine example. Its extensive network involves cross-shareholdings and long-standing business relationships with and between 822 individual component suppliers. The four most important of these are Denso, Aisin Seiki, Aisin AW und Toyota Industries (see Figure 4.27).

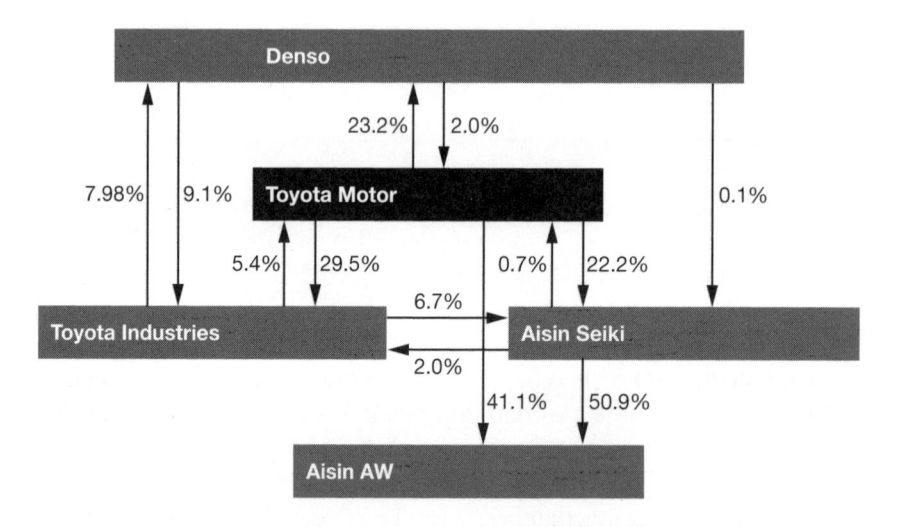

Figure 4.27 *Cross-shareholdings between Toyota and its four key component suppliers*
Source: Supplierbusiness.com

These companies often also get together to form joint ventures. Examples include Advics (Sumitomo, Denso and Aisin Seiki), FTS (Toyoda Gosei and Horie Metal) and Favess (Koyo Seiko, Toyoda Machine Works und Denso). These companies are also helping Toyota build new plants – witness the assistance provided by Denso, Aisin Seiki and Aisan Industries in relation to the new Toyota/PSA plant in the Czech city of Kolín.

Apart from interlocking capital structures, two other key factors shape the *keiretsus*:

- Collaboration in a spirit of partnership: within a *keiretsu*, a culture of trust and a willingness to learn from one another prevails. Toyota, Honda and Nissan, for example, all help their component suppliers to continually improve their performance by introducing and perfecting efficient production systems. Component suppliers that willingly accept such close collaboration generally have the assurance that they will remain partners in the long term. The probability of follow-up orders is therefore at or around 100 per cent.
- Close coordination of planning: the companies in a *keiretsu* coordinate their planning very closely. This applies both to longer-term technology and investment planning and to shorter-term changes in volume planning.

In the past, the only drawback in this system was the absence, or at best only limited presence, of competition between the individual companies. Aware of this, the OEMs have in recent years taken great pains to reorganize traditional *keiretsu* structures (see Figure 4.28).

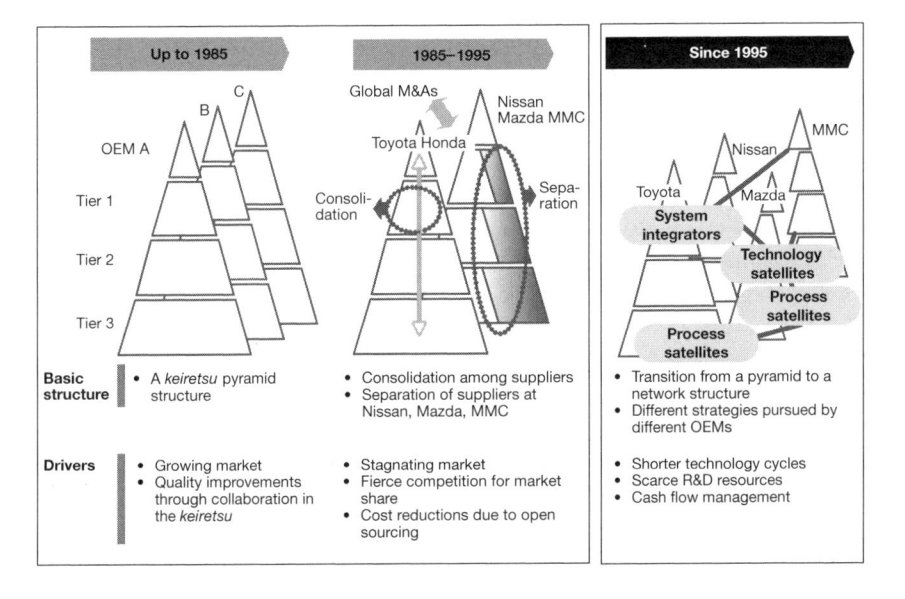

Figure 4.28 *Changes in* keiretsu *structures and the drivers of these changes*
Source: Roland Berger Strategy Consultants

Close collaboration between OEMs and component suppliers without cross-shareholdings: the example of Toyota

During its process of internationalization in recent years, Toyota has gone a long way in opening up to non-Japanese component suppliers. In doing so, it has succeeded in carrying the trusting collaboration that characterizes the *keiretsus* over into its dealings with these new suppliers. This fact is reflected in surveys that describe the extent to which component suppliers are satisfied with OEMs: Toyota regularly comes top of the league (see Figure 4.29).

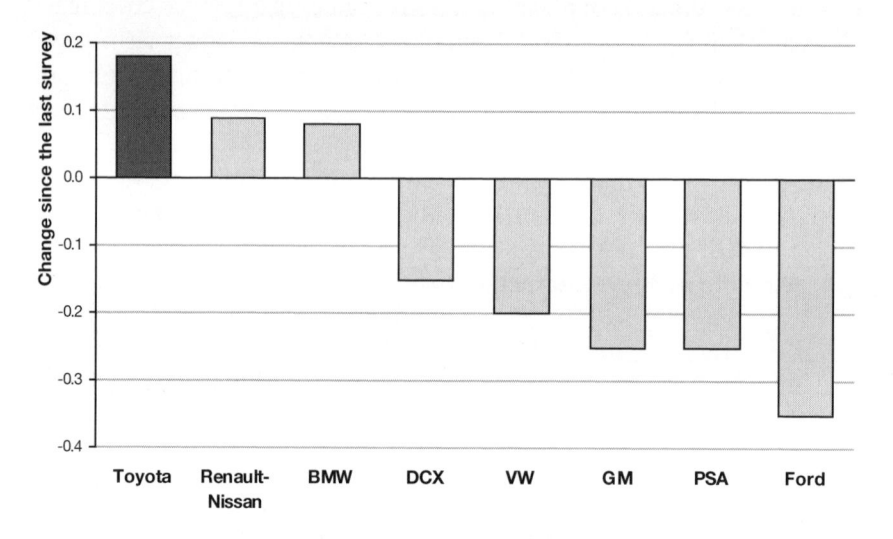

Figure 4.29 *Extent to which component suppliers are satisfied with their OEM customers, 2004*
Sources: Supplierbusiness.com

Toyota expects a lot of its component suppliers. Its quality standards are unrivalled anywhere in the automotive industry. On costs, too, it is no rare occurrence for Toyota's buyers to inform their suppliers that this or that part will simply have to cost 30 per cent less in the next product generation.

Unlike other car makers, however, Toyota is convinced that these objectives can only be realized through very close collaboration with component suppliers. In other words, Toyota doesn't just set goals: it also helps its component suppliers to meet them.

Four key tools enable all this to happen:

- Mutual understanding: Toyota takes the trouble to try to understand its suppliers' business almost as well as they do themselves. An extensive controlling system also constantly monitors and analyses suppliers' performance.
- Intensive training: Toyota has set up a group called SPM (Supplier Production Management) in its purchasing department. This group proactively helps component suppliers to fine-tune their production systems (in a process known as *kaizen*).
- Permanent technical support: each component supplier has a fixed set of Toyota engineers who are permanently assigned to it. The goal is to rectify problems before they even occur. Should problems arise nevertheless – during a new product roll-out, for example – the support team is beefed up immediately.
- Multilateral best practice sharing: Toyota organizes regular meetings and conferences to promote the systematic sharing of best practices between its component suppliers.

This kind of collaboration between the manufacturer and its component suppliers has been instrumental in Toyota's emergence as one of the most successful car makers in the world.

Joint ventures between OEMs: the example of TPCA (Toyota Peugeot Citroën Automobile)

Now that the 'merger mania' between automotive companies has subsided, collaboration that is focused on individual projects – perhaps engine construction or vehicle assembly – are coming back into vogue. One very topical and therefore very good example is PSA and Toyota's collaboration on compact cars.

In 2002, Toyota and PSA decided to build a plant in Kolín, Czech Republic, for the production of three models (the Peugeot 107, Toyota Aygo and Citroën C1) built on the same platform. The factory is scaled to cope with 300,000 units and went into production at the start of 2005. Three key factors have had a formative influence on this project:

- Homogeneous objectives between the partners: Toyota and PSA want to use the Kolín site to make small, modern, high-quality vehicles featuring attractive technology, and to sell those for low prices on the European market.

- Role-splitting in line with core competencies: in deference to its thorough knowledge of the European component supply market and its mature diesel technology, PSA is responsible for purchasing operations and diesel engines. For its part, Toyota is contributing the Toyota Production System and is also in charge of gasoline engines.
- Clear and fair ground rules: each party has shouldered its share of the development costs. By contrast, the money invested in the plant will be charged to the three brands according to manufactured units.

It remains to be seen what this joint venture delivers in the long term. Right now, however, expectations are very high indeed.

Collaboration between OEMs: the example of DaimlerChrysler, GM and BMW

At the end of 2004, DaimlerChrysler and GM announced their intention to press ahead with joint development of a 'two-mode' hybrid engine. BMW joined the alliance in September 2005. It remains to be seen whether this collaborative venture will be more successful than the Covisint electronic procurement platform launched jointly by DaimlerChrysler, GM and Ford in 1999. Back then, the entire automotive industry had high hopes for Covisint. Owing to technical problems, management mistakes and disunity among the participant car makers, the platform nevertheless failed to deliver on its promise. In 2003, the founding companies retracted their interest in the venture.

In the case of collaboration on hybrid engines, however, the outlook is not bad at all. The project already meets several of the key criteria for successful cooperation:

- Pressure to act and a win–win situation: the three manufacturers share one major problem. As hybrid technology gains an ever more secure foothold, they have fallen way behind their Japanese rivals, Toyota and Honda. While vehicles such as the Toyota Prius advance from sales record to sales record, GM, DaimlerChrysler and BMW do not have a single engine that is ready for volume production. In an age of spiralling fuel costs and ever stricter environmental legislation, that is a dangerous place to be in. This collaborative venture will reduce development costs for each of the three partners. Far more important, however, is the time they expect to make up. DaimlerChrysler and GM plan to fit the new technology in vehicles such as the Chevrolet Tahoe,

the GMC Yukon and the Dodge Durango (on the North American market) as early as 2007.
- Clear role-splitting: all parties are contributing their current state-of-the-art research to the hybrid development project. The goal is the mutual development of a modular total system. DaimlerChrysler will lead the development of rear-wheel-drive hybrid systems for saloons, while GM spearheads development for front-wheel-drive, four-wheel-drive and off-road vehicles. Each company is then independently responsible for integrating the hybrid system in its own model range.
- Clear contractual agreements: the relevant contracts set forth clear rules governing the expertise contributed, such as Mercedes-Benz's and Chrysler's 10 years of experience, and the knowledge and prototypes contributed by GM.

Section summary: closer collaboration is needed

OEMs and component suppliers will be able to improve the efficiency of the automotive value chain only if they work a lot more closely together. Collaboration between component suppliers enables them to tap new product markets and regional markets. Improved cooperation between OEMs and component suppliers helps the latter to tailor their activities even more precisely to the needs of their customers. This in turn helps them prevent the build-up of idle capacity. On another plane, collaboration between OEMs reduces the investment risk faced by all parties concerned in a marketplace that is changing ever more rapidly.

Notwithstanding these successes, any number of less successful examples likewise testify to the validity of a number of generally applicable rules:

- Clear goals must be defined for collaborative projects.
- The corporate cultures involved must be compatible.
- Roles must be split unambiguously based on each party's core competencies.
- Opportunities and risks must be shared fairly.
- Rules governing the solution of conflicts must be spelt out clearly in the contracts.

All these points require due attention when collaboration is still on the drawing board, and they must be adequately reflected in the contracts that are ultimately signed.

SUMMARY: ALL PARTIES INVOLVED IN THE AUTOMOTIVE VALUE CHAIN FACE THREE KEY CHALLENGES

In an age of ever more intensive cost pressure and fiercer competition, car makers and their component suppliers must strive for excellence more than ever before. If they fail to do so, they will not live to tell the tale.

As they go forward toward this goal, the three levers we have described in detail – the breakdown of the value chain, physical footprint and the business model – will all play a crucial role. This assertion is borne out by our investigation of numerous successful and less successful companies in the industry over the past few years.

Only those companies that define their core competencies in line with what the market demands and optimize the cost of their location networks will survive. Ultimately, however, the master key that opens the door to a secure, lucrative future will be a commitment to closer, trusting, consciously designed collaboration.

5

The technology challenge: progress or pitfall?

Silvio Schindler, Partner, Roland Berger Strategy Consultants

INTRODUCTION

Automotive companies in the established triad markets are confronted by a tricky market situation. Sales have been stagnating for years. Legal conditions and constraints have tightened, and customers are constantly becoming both more demanding and more varied in their individual preferences. The industry has responded to this growing demand for diversity by creating a wide array of new models and vehicle segments. The resulting information overkill – and the erosion of customer loyalty that goes with it – have made it all the more crucial for car makers to clearly differentiate themselves from their rivals, and to position their brands astutely in respect of their targeted customer segments. While attractive prices tend to be the main selling point for volume manufacturers, a pitched battle for technology leadership and exclusive claims has broken out among premium brands. In an attempt to differentiate themselves against the competition, car makers have used advances in sophisticated electronics in particular to repeatedly roll back the limits of what is technologically feasible. In consequence, high-tech content in premium vehicles has experienced a quantum leap as manufacturers strive relentlessly for unique selling propositions.

Numerous manufacturers have nevertheless discovered that stuffing vehicles full of technical innovations does not guarantee their market success. Wherever customers have been unable to intuitively perceive the real value added by the new technology, or when it did not line up with customers' brand expectations, sales have consistently fallen short of projections. Some manufacturers have also learnt the hard way that customers will only accept mature technologies. If technological innovations are not really mature, they can do serious damage to a brand's image.

Premium car makers thus find themselves faced with a dilemma. On the one hand, every new product launch compels them to come out with innovative new technologies as evidence of their premium position, and to position their brand successfully and differentiate it from the competition. This situation is exacerbated by the fact that new technologies nowadays spread ever faster – what ranks as 'premium' today can very quickly filter down to lower classes of cars and/or be adopted by the competition. On the other hand, the need to master alternative competing technologies is driving costs and complexity to a level that will not be sustainable in the future.

To escape from the complexity and cost trap, car makers must restrict themselves to key technologies. They must abandon the traditional 'technology creates demand' approach that is obsessed with realizing whatever is technically feasible. They must instead turn to a 'technology generates value' approach that makes customers the focus of all technological development. Leading manufacturers have understood the opportunities that rigorous adherence to this approach affords in terms of brand positioning, a keener brand profile and differentiation relative to competitors. Successes and failures in applying this strategy – in some cases at one and the same company – nevertheless highlight the very fine line that separates dream from disaster. The challenge is, therefore, to get customer orientation to permeate the entire organization, systematically and completely. In the future, the key success factor for premium auto makers will be what we call 'customer-oriented technology management'.

THE STATUS QUO: TECHNOLOGY DEVELOPMENT WITHOUT CUSTOMER FOCUS

Technology development in transition

Competitive pressure sparks a blaze of innovation

Car makers around the world are today facing a plethora of challenges that vary considerably from region to region. In growth markets such as Asia, OEMs still have every reason to be upbeat about the promising sales outlook. The most important thing here is to pick the right market strategy, choose the right local partner and build a commensurate sales network. By contrast, the established triad markets – the United States, Europe and Japan – present OEMs with far more daunting challenges. Conditions are difficult, and markets have been stagnating for years. Legal constraints have tightened up and customers are becoming ever more varied and differentiated in their individual preferences.

A macroeconomic trend toward individualism and individualization is indeed observable in society at large. This trend is sweeping all consumer markets, triggering a veritable explosion of supply-side diversity. Seiko, for example, today has over 3,000 watches in its programme. Philips markets more than 800 different televisions. The number of magazines on newsagents' shelves has doubled in the past 10 years. And the average supermarket today stocks well over 20,000 products, as against 4,000 at the end of the 1950s.

The automotive industry too has felt the impact of this trend. Car makers have substantially broadened their model ranges to satisfy customer requirements in ever more narrowly defined target segments, and to accommodate demand for more 'individualized' vehicles and vehicle concepts. The result has been a flood of new models and new vehicle segments. In the early 1980s, the vehicle segments were limited to saloons, coupés, convertibles and estates. Today, customers also have vans, minivans, multi-purpose vehicles (MPVs), sports utility vehicles (SUVs) and a wide range of cross-over vehicles to choose from. And the tide shows no sign of ebbing. A parallel development is that vehicle life-cycles have shrunk by around three to four years over the past two decades. Models used to feature in car manufacturers' programmes for 9 to 10 years on average. Now, new models are brought to market every six years.

106 *Major challenges*

To make matters even more difficult for manufacturers, introducing new model series nowadays inevitably involves upgrading the array of features fitted as standard. Customers in Europe quite simply expect safety features such as airbags, ABS and ESP. Governments too are placing ever more exacting demands on the ecological and safety aspects of vehicles. In many cases, however, the extra cost of complying with stricter emissions regulations or fitting new safety systems cannot be passed on to the customer. Customers expect – and get – 'more car for their money'. Adjusted for inflation, a comparison of mid-range saloons such as the Mercedes C180 between 1993 and 2001 shows that list prices for standard models remained virtually static in this period, despite the fact that ever more add-on features (such as ABS, ESP, airbags and immobilizers) were fitted as standard (Figure 5.1).

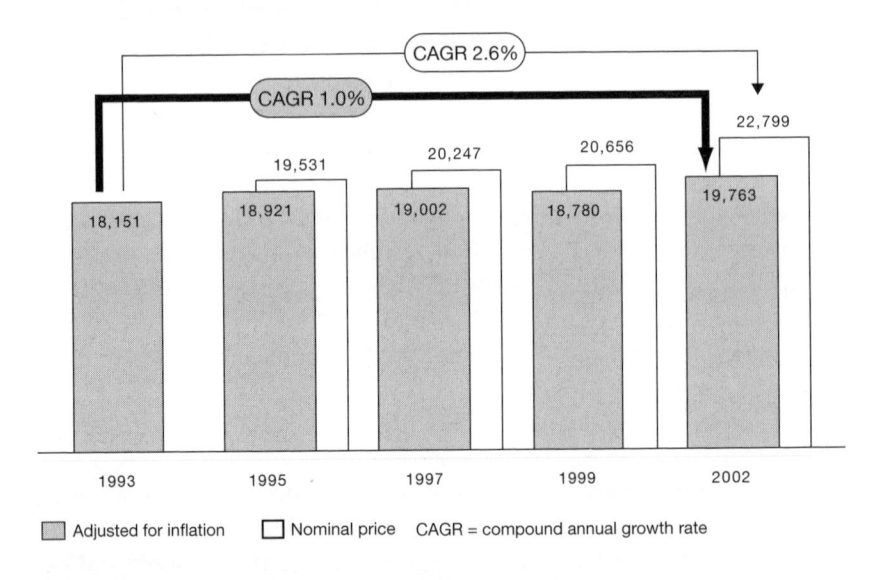

Year	Adjusted for inflation	Nominal price
1993	18,151	
1995	18,921	19,531
1997	19,002	20,247
1999	18,780	20,656
2002	19,763	22,799

CAGR 1.0% (adjusted for inflation), CAGR 2.6% (nominal); CAGR = compound annual growth rate

Figure 5.1 *Price development of a standard Mercedes-Benz C class, nominal and adjusted for inflation (ex-works list price in euros, excluding value-added tax)*
Sources: DaimlerChrysler AG, Federal Statistical Office, Roland Berger Strategy Consultants

Somehow, car makers must therefore find a solution to the following conundrum: while volumes per model line are decreasing and prices are stagnating (at least for standard versions), they still have to satisfy greater expectations of more comfort, safety and 'extras'.

Manufacturers vary the focus of their response to this dilemma depending on how their brands are positioned on the market – that is, whether a brand belongs in the premium or the volume segment. Volume brands whose primary differentiation criteria in the market are attractive prices concentrate their efforts on cost efficiency and cost effectiveness. Economies of scale (especially in purchasing, development and production), operating efficiency and a global footprint are the key issues for these firms. At the other end of the scale, premium car makers are responding to competitive pressures in a different way. In recent years, they have worked hard to position their brands precisely in specific target customer segments, thereby carving out a keener brand profile. In an age of information overkill, eroding customer loyalty and ever fiercer competition, it is supremely important to distinguish a brand from its rivals by creating an unmistakable genetic code. Brands are a source of orientation for customers. They charge what is essentially a technical product – a means of getting you from A to B – with emotion. But brands also give customers a chance to differentiate themselves from the competition, to cultivate a certain lifestyle and express a certain attitude or mindset.

Customers place their trust in brands whose brand characteristics and products best match their individual needs and wants. The basic rule is this: the more sharply a brand profile is defined, the greater will be its attraction and its ability to foster customer loyalty. In recent years, premium manufacturers have ignited a sparkling display of innovative technologies in an attempt to clearly delimit brand profiles and distinguish themselves from their rivals. Technological progress – especially in the field of electronics – has significantly improved the scope of high-tech functions in premium vehicles. Competition between innovative technologies has, however, also worsened the dilemma described above by once again sharply driving up the complexity and cost of R&D activities, for example (Figure 5.2). To remain competitive in the future, manufacturers are doing everything they can to wriggle out of this tight place. The challenge is to maintain the same level of customer loyalty and differentiation while reducing complexity and lowering costs. They will only succeed if they genuinely grasp what customers really want and need, and if they are able to focus their development activities accordingly.

Today's innovation is tomorrow's standard

Technical innovation was always the preserve of premium manufacturers. It has traditionally been the lever that lifted them above their competitors. Thanks to a series of ground-breaking new developments, DaimlerChrysler in particular has earned a reputation as an innovation leader and thus justified its position as a premium manufacturer. Examples include monocoque body construction and passenger

108 Major challenges

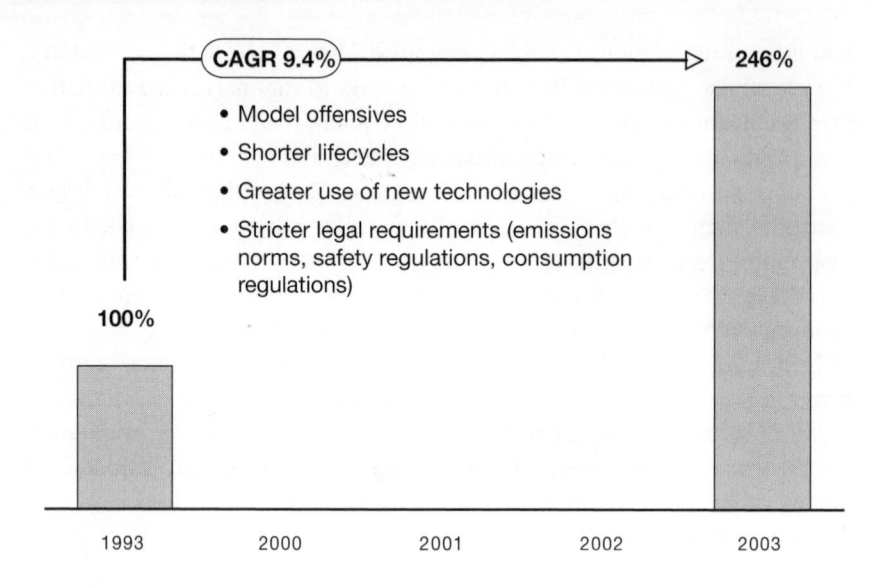

```
┌─────────CAGR 9.4%─────────▷  246%
│
│  • Model offensives
│  • Shorter lifecycles
│  • Greater use of new technologies
│  • Stricter legal requirements (emissions
│    norms, safety regulations, consumption
│    regulations)
100%
```

1993   2000   2001   2002   2003

Figure 5.2 *Development of R&D costs per vehicle (adjusted for inflation) based on the example of a premium manufacturer*
Sources: Roland Berger, DaimlerChrysler, Federal Statistics Office

protection systems in the 1960s, the introduction of ABS in the 1970s, the launch of airbags in the 1980s, and ESP in the 1990s. The period of time for which a given technical innovation gives a car maker a unique selling proposition is diminishing constantly, however. It took the ABS system around 20 years to achieve 40 per cent market penetration. Today, it is fitted as standard in just about every vehicle sold in Germany. Compare this trajectory with ESP, which was deployed for the first time in 1994 but took only 10 years to realize equivalent market penetration. This example illustrates how technological innovations that are initially designed for premium vehicles are filtering down ever more quickly into the volume segments. Technologies therefore lose their differentiating characteristics ever faster. Premium brands are particularly hard hit by this development, as it undermines their brand attraction and eats away at customer loyalty. Volume manufacturers do not face the same problem, because price is the issue on which they mainly seek to set themselves apart. They do indeed benefit from the spread of innovations since, subject to a certain time-lag, they realize new technologies in high-volume production and achieve the corresponding scale effects. Ultimately, this advantage is also passed back to premium vehicles.

The right mix of emotion and innovation

To avoid becoming expendable in this situation, premium car makers must work hard to influence the way their brand is perceived. They must occupy a credible position and clearly demarcate themselves from competitors. Also, their brand values must be coherent. If they want to be seen as innovation leaders, premium manufacturers have no choice but to repeatedly develop new technologies and get them to market as early as possible – ahead of their rivals. Eager for fatter margins, almost every car maker now wants to be regarded as a premium brand. Even manufacturers such as Subaru, until now far better known for being 'rugged and robust', are now claiming to be 'premium'. It is not enough just to produce reliable cars with the odd high-tech component here and there, however. Since the start of the 1990s, the leading European premium brands (Audi, BMW, Jaguar, Mercedes-Benz, Porsche, Saab and Volvo) have increased their share of new vehicle registrations from around 20 to around 30 per cent. Worldwide, German premium brands currently account for 40 per cent of the total premium market. In the luxury segment, this share leaps to an eyebrow-raising 80 per cent. So what is the secret of their success?

'The key to success is to combine the right mix of emotion and substance with consistent brand management,' says Kay Segler, the man in charge of the Mini brand (source: Automobilwoche). He ought to know, given that the Mini ranks as a textbook example of successful brand positioning. The people who revamped the Mini understood that Mini owners have a very special relationship with their vehicles. This meant that developers had to keep their hands off everything that was sacred to the original Mini design: go-cart-like handling, a central position squarely behind the steering wheel, and minimal overlap beyond the car wheels. What Mini customers are less concerned about are the characteristics of the engine – in stark contrast to BMW customers, for instance. The fact that BMW worked together with volume manufacturers such as Chrysler and PSA to build the Mini engine thus in no way jeopardized the vehicle's success. Above and beyond the technical blueprint, BMW took great pains to design everything else in an authentic and brand-specific manner. From sales to service, from marketing to communication, everything was specially tailored to meet the unique needs of Mini customers and carry the famous 'Mini feeling' safely over into the new generation. Even internal staff and external consultants were selected based on an assessment of whether they fitted in with the brand motto: 'Are you Mini?'

Another example of successful brand positioning – or an even greater challenge, a complete change of image – is the success story written by Audi. Over the past 25 years, Audi has managed to shake off the staid image inherited from DKW, its predecessor brand, and establish itself as one of the leading premium manufacturers. When Audi introduced the Quattro, the company rigorously translated its classic advertising slogan 'Vorsprung durch Technik' into a broad spectrum of innovations (such as the Torsen differential gear) that all customers could experience for themselves. The legendary Quattro S1 rally car set new standards in the world of motor sports and towered over its rivals for a long time. What more vivid way to demonstrate the superior performance of this technical innovation in terms of driving dynamics and driving safety to customers! At the same time, this positioning injected the necessary dose of emotion. Ultimately, it was customers' acceptance of the technological design that made the change of image a success. This feat was achieved by enabling customers to 'feel the difference' (that is, the generated value) in what, for them, were two vital areas of technology: driving dynamics and safety. Crucially, the value that was generated aligned perfectly with the Audi brand's catchphrase, and therefore helped distinguish it very clearly from its competitors.

Technology development without customer focus

High tech that doesn't generate value for customers is doomed to failure

Not all manufacturers' attempts to position themselves have met with the same success, however. Audi's parent company, for example, is having difficulty establishing 'VW' as a premium brand. Although VW's Touareg SUV has been a resounding success, its high-end flagship, the Phaeton, still lacks momentum. When the Golf V hit the market, not even a fanfare of technological innovations was able to make up for the absence of a premium bonus. Sales did not really shift into gear until prices were knocked down when the company gave away free air-conditioning systems.

The main reason for such sluggish acceleration was that customers did not intuitively grasp how they would benefit from all the technological advances, such as electromechanical steering and the elaborate four-link rear axle. In Germany in particular, advertising that focused on the new Golf's performance on bends did not at all spell out what value was being generated. Conversely, the press placed more emphasis on perceived shortcomings in workmanship – such as the appearance of the interior, which certainly does have an immediate and formative impact on brand perception, especially in a brand aspiring to 'premiumship'. As a result, what was in fact a genuinely innovative car elicited less than enthusiastic coverage in *Autobild*, a popular and influential German automotive publication: '[VW's] love for details is waning'; 'in terms of its look and feel, it's a step back, not a step forward'; and 'development on the Golf V is invisible to the eye' (an allusion to the chassis and steering).

When it introduced the iDrive concept, BMW too discovered that customers will only accept innovation if they believe it caters appropriately to their needs. Acclaimed by its maker as a trail-blazing innovation when the new 7 Series was rolled out in 2001, iDrive did not capture the hearts of drivers, who found it too complicated. BMW's basic idea had been to tidy up the cockpit while offering more functions and creating clear hierarchic structures in vehicle control. All secondary functions (such as infotainment, navigation, telematics services and audio/video offerings) were to be combined as a central functional block. BMW and its cooperation partners managed to design a knob that drivers could press or turn eight ways to control over 500 different functions. The technology was breathtaking, but the first iDrive system was extremely complex and proved too much for the company's 7 Series customers. Even younger people with a liking for technology took unusually long to learn to use the system – and they are not normally the target group for top-of-the-range saloons (which mostly consists of males aged 45 to 67). The niceties of the clever new system were often hopelessly lost on this latter group, whose affinity for information technology (IT) is known to decrease with age (Figure 5.3).

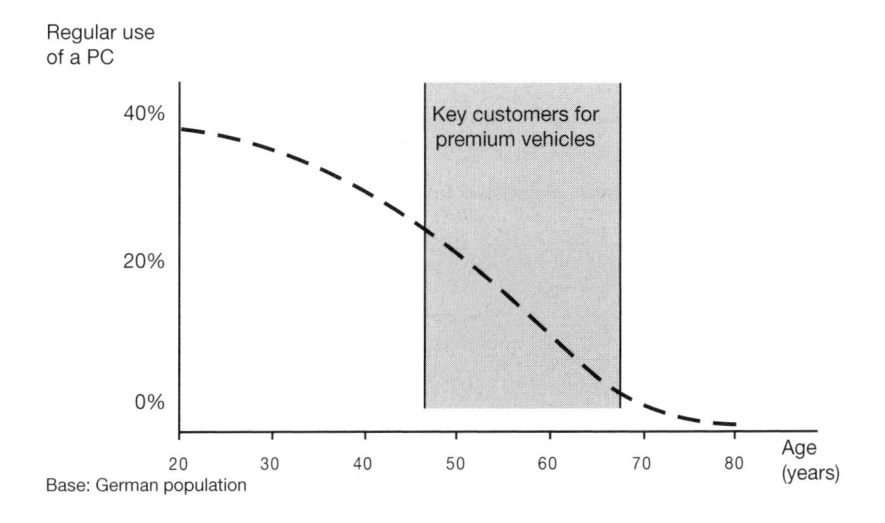

Figure 5.3 *IT affinity of key customers for premium vehicles*
Sources: DIW, Roland Berger

Customers' criticism was taken into account in later versions of iDrive. When the next generation of the 5 Series was introduced, the system was reworked and simplified extensively. Even so, the BMW system is still regarded as more complex than comparable top-end command systems. Of all the systems commonly installed in luxury saloons, the combined interface model fitted in the Audi A8, for example, is the easiest for customers to operate. Such an interface features a combination of buttons that control specific functions directly and a knob that can be turned and pressed to access multiple functions (Figure 5.4).

The command system in the new S class (W221) learnt from this object lesson and focused squarely on the needs of customers. The high-tech operating system is made up of one controller and two 8-inch screens, each in 16:9 format. It governs a whole host of technical, convenience, entertainment and navigation functions that would quickly overtax conventional forms of user interaction (switches and buttons). On the basis of extensive customer surveys, the system was designed to be very user-friendly. The most important difference is that many functions can now be operated in a number of different ways, either via the controller, through direct selection buttons, or by pressing buttons on the steering wheel. Initial tests by the press confirm that the system is indeed intuitive and very easy to use.

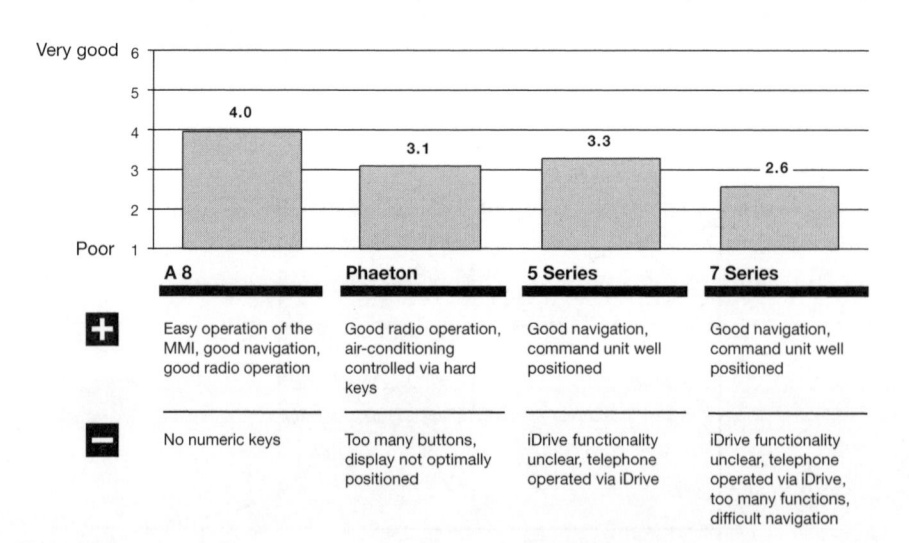

	A 8	Phaeton	5 Series	7 Series
Score (1=Poor, 6=Very good)	4.0	3.1	3.3	2.6
+	Easy operation of the MMI, good navigation, good radio operation	Good radio operation, air-conditioning controlled via hard keys	Good navigation, command unit well positioned	Good navigation, command unit well positioned
−	No numeric keys	Too many buttons, display not optimally positioned	iDrive functionality unclear, telephone operated via iDrive	iDrive functionality unclear, telephone operated via iDrive, too many functions, difficult navigation

Figure 5.4 *Convenience of command systems in premium cars*
Source: SirValUse Consulting (Germany)

The above examples show how tremendously important it is to focus technological development on what customers really want and need. If technology fails to anticipate customers' expectations, or if customers fail to perceive the value that an innovation generates, sales forecasts will be missed. Knowing the needs of the target customer segments is therefore becoming ever more crucial as a success factor in the development of new technologies.

Only mature technologies are accepted

Advances in the field of electronics have helped engineers push back the boundaries of what is technologically feasible again and again. Electronic components lay the foundation for complex applications such as active suspension, biometric recognition systems and radar-guided cruise control systems. Compliance with laws on emissions or on passenger safety, say, is no longer possible without the use of electronics. Fully 80 per cent of all innovations are already based on developments in electronics and software, and the forecast rate of growth for the next five years is 75 to 100 per cent (relating to today's value share in the entire vehicle of about 20 per cent). More and more on-board systems, such as active and passive safety systems, are becoming networked and are merging into one. This trend, coupled with ever more functionality, is making in-vehicle electronic systems hugely complex. And this in turn makes it difficult to achieve the required degree of technological maturity before innovations go to market.

A glance at breakdown statistics collated by ADAC, Germany's automobile association, highlights the impact of this trend. Electronic failures easily occupy pole position, with a share of approximately 60 per cent of all breakdowns. If we examine manufacturers' existing skill sets, a key reason for this problem quickly becomes apparent. A Roland Berger study of all leading OEMs reveals that, while electronics accounts for approximately 80 per cent of all innovations, electronic engineers account for only 14 per cent of these companies' engineering forces.

An added difficulty is that the complexity of the software development process is often underestimated. Changes to functionality are often made ad hoc, without systematic rigor. Nor has a satisfactory solution yet been found to the problem that electronics and software innovation cycles are far shorter than vehicle model cycles (Figure 5.5). This challenge is set to become even stiffer. Future customers will, for instance, no longer settle for using six-year-old on-board navigation systems or mobile phones (the average period to the next model generation) when technology in both areas has made significant strides in the meantime. Since OEMs themselves do not have the engineering skills to develop these systems, lifecycle synchronization will necessitate far closer collaboration and networking with component and system suppliers.

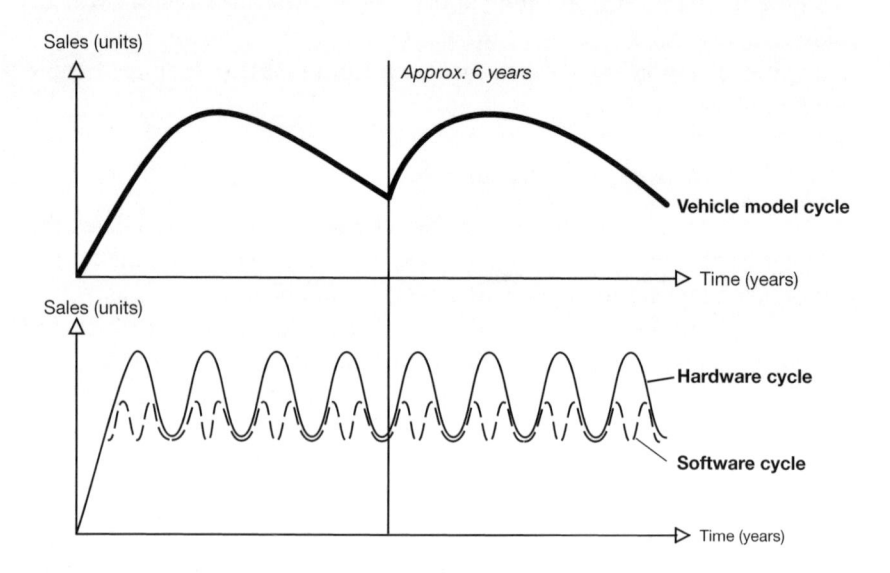

Figure 5.5 *Comparative view of vehicle model cycles versus hardware and software cycles*
Source: Roland Berger

The innovators among the premium manufacturers in particular face a kind of 'Catch-22' situation. They are under enormous pressure to satisfy the huge expectations with regard to innovative technologies with every new model launch. Yet they also have to minimize the risk that precisely these innovations – 80 per cent of which, as we have seen, have to do with electronics and software – may not be fully mature when they (literally) hit the road. Immature technologies can naturally do immense financial damage, with warranty claims and recalls quickly running up a bill into the hundreds of millions. But they also do serious harm to customer satisfaction (Figure 5.6). Mercedes-Benz knows this pitfall all too well. Investment bank Goldman Sachs estimates that services performed under warranty totalled around €2,400 for every Mercedes sold in 2004. Despite the company's enviable position as technology leader, these quality problems leave it languishing in mid-table on customer satisfaction.

By contrast, 'fast followers' such as Toyota, Honda and Nissan tend to use established technologies, have far less electronic content overall – and have far fewer problems as a result. The price they pay is that they have not yet been able to gain a foothold in the premium segment. Because of the high quality and reliability of its vehicles, Toyota remains the industry's yardstick for customer satisfaction – a reflection of customers' decreasing willingness to tolerate quality problems. The distance between leading brands is eroding all the time. If innovations are found to be immature at market launch, established market positions can shift dramatically at short notice.

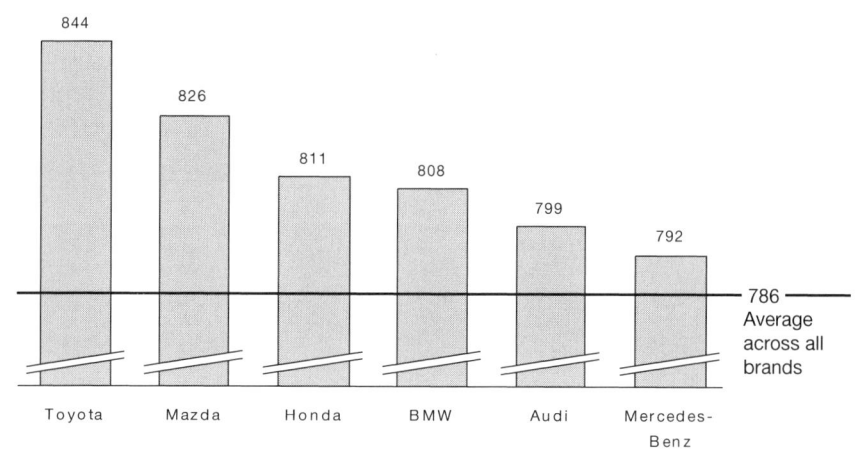

[Bar chart: Toyota 844, Mazda 826, Honda 811, BMW 808, Audi 799, Mercedes-Benz 792; Average across all brands 786. Rated on a scale of 1-1000]

Figure 5.6 *Customer satisfaction index, Germany 2004 (selected brands)*
Source: JD Power and Associates, Germany

Not all technologies become established

The purpose of technology roadmaps is to help decision makers in the automobile industry recognize when what new technologies will be introduced (Figure 5.7). However, current developments indicate that advanced technologies whose benefits to the customer cannot readily be explained have not lived up to their makers' expectations.

What are known as 'by-wire' technologies present a classic example. DaimlerChrysler recently withdrew electrohydraulic braking systems from its assembly lines – along with 600 other electronic functions. Why? Because the technologies involved are not sufficiently mature. The value they add is difficult to communicate to customers and related system costs are high. Such negative experience will also cause other by-wire technologies to slip down the priority list on development roadmaps, at least temporarily.

Yet another advanced technology – the 42V vehicle power system – will also be directly affected by this turn of events. The demotion of by-wire

	Chassis	Powertrain	Engine	Body	Exterior	Interior	Electronics
2002							
			Hybrid engine		Aluminum/ magnesium	Smart airbags	
	Ceramic brakes		Otto-engine DI	Metal foams			Bus systems
2005			Particle filter	Steel space frame	Active lighting		
		Magnesium gearbox housing		Composite materials	Pedestrian protection system	Night vision	42V vehicle power system
	Active chassis				Radar-guided cruise control system	Variable interiors	Pre-crash sensors
2010	Electro-mechanical brakes	Variable transmission		Plastic body			
	Steer-by-wire		Fuel cell engine				
		Wheel hub drive	Hydrogen engine				Driving on autopilot
2015							

Figure 5.7 *Examples of technology roadmaps*
Source: Automobil-Produktion (publication)

technologies eliminates one of the main justifications for such networks, which will therefore suffer the same fate. Innovators in the industry have long been promoting 42V technology in particular as the future trend in automotive engineering. Back in the mid-1990s, car makers were convinced that the in-vehicle need for electric power was set to rise sharply, and that existing 14V power systems would simply no longer be up to the task. The advantages of the new technology were obvious: lighter and less bulky wiring, a more reliable, efficient power supply, and the opportunity to fit vehicles with all kinds of new functions. The 42V vehicle power system was to become the platform for innovative developments such as by-wire technologies, electric turbo chargers and personalized air-conditioning systems.

Despite a very positive echo when the markets were buoyant in and around 2000, many components suppliers held back. They didn't really believe the system would make the breakthrough, and they were well aware that they themselves would have to bear most of the up-front investment in this expensive system. As early as 2000, Bosch for example voiced concerns that forecasting institutes were being too optimistic, contending that 42V would probably not be around before 2010. The current status is that no economical solution can be found to problems with the technology; that quality risks still exist; that core applications that would have needed 42V technology are now off the agenda; and that more efficient energy management has substantially reduced vehicles' need for power. It is therefore not unlikely that the 42V power system will be put on ice for the time being – or will perhaps even disappear from view altogether.

On a brighter note, development of other technologies whose benefits customers clearly understand has been accelerated. The outcomes are reaching the market earlier than expected. One example is the radar-guided cruise control system. Originally expected after 2007, this technology is already available in top-end vehicles, and is even gradually appearing in mid-range saloons, too.

TRANSITION: THE CUSTOMER AS THE FOCUS OF TECHNOLOGY DEVELOPMENT

From 'technology creates demand' to 'technology generates value'

The examples discussed, and even a cursory analysis of the technology landscape as it stands, prove a clear point: technological development is still far from focused on the customer. It is hard to shake off the impression that technology development to date has been based on the theory that technology creates demand. Accordingly, industry players have tried to develop whatever appeared technically feasible. Competitive pressure and the trend toward individualization and differentiation have doubtless also fuelled the individualization of in-vehicle functions and technologies.

An examination of the broad diversity of technology that has resulted indicates the vast spectrum covered – and gives an idea of the challenges faced by OEMs. The latter are, for example, called upon to come to terms with innovative engine technologies such as high-pressure common rail diesel systems and hybrid technology; driver assistance systems such as lane change assistants and adaptive cruise control, complete with radar and video sensors; active body control systems such as active front steering and predictive emergency braking; safety-enhancing systems such as predictive safety systems and run-flat tyres; weight-reducing materials such as steel space frame technologies, carbon fibres and composite materials; biotechnology in the context of breathable fabrics and lightweight insulating substances; and even bionics to reduce air resistance and create self-cleaning surfaces.

118   Major challenges

Since many technologies also compete with each other, OEMs find themselves confronted by almost overwhelming complexities and spiralling costs. To steer safely around the complexity and cost trap, they will in the future have to focus more narrowly on key technologies. In coming to this realization, manufacturers are learning that the 'technology creates demand' approach of the past will not get the job done. They have understood that, to master the challenges of the future, they need an approach that focuses technology development rigorously on the needs of the target customers. Only then can they reduce internal complexities while generating higher revenues by adding greater value for the customer.

Customers are indeed willing to pay for perceptible add-on benefits. Whereas buyers in Germany paid an average of around €9,500 for a new car in 1983, this figure jumped to €15,200 by 2003. The purchase of 'special extras' accounts for some two-thirds of the difference (Figure 5.8).

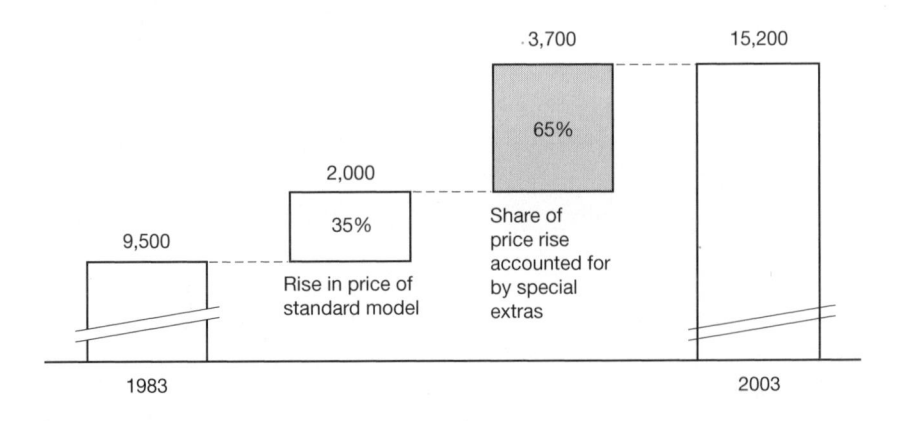

Figure 5.8 *Trend in the average price of a new car in Germany (in euros, adjusted for inflation)*
Sources: DAT Report, Roland Berger

Many car makers are now visibly shifting to a new approach. The 'technology generates value' approach assesses innovations in terms of several factors: the value they generate for customers, their degree of maturity and their compatibility with a brand profile, the fit with the product positioning and with current trends in the different technology segments. The task now facing decision makers in the industry is to investigate the myriad potential new technologies ahead of them and identify those technologies and technology segments that target customers will accept and pay for.

Ecology, safety and convenience as drivers of technology

In seeking to filter out those technologies that target customers will accept, it is vital to identify the drivers of technology – those factors that influence customers' value systems. Daily reports that fossil energy reserves are running out, the threats posed by crime and terrorism, and consumers' growing demand for comfort, availability and ease of use (in other words, convenience) have altered our system of social values. In the process, three core elements of a new value system have emerged: environmental awareness, safety and convenience. These core elements of our new value system are also having a substantial impact on the automotive industry, in which they rank as the key drivers of technological development. Perhaps even more importantly, they serve as the principal filters in determining whether or not customers accept advances in technology.

In the past, most innovations centred around the driving experience itself. Following the shift in values, however, it is only logical that three major new segments of technology have sprung up around the more elementary 'driving' segment. The three new segments are: 'the environment', which is occupied by hot topics such as particulate filters, high-pressure diesel technology and in particular hybrid engines; 'safety', which focuses on such themes as active and passive safety systems, run-flat tyres, adaptive cruise control and the kind of short-range radar sensors that only recently went into volume production; and 'convenience', involving elements such as automated air-conditioning, heated seats and seat ventilation.

In light of this situation, it is no surprise to discover that the strong growth rates which many pundits forecast for the 'communication' technology segment (focusing on functions such as DVD players, in-car PCs, internet access, remote troubleshooting and telematics services) have so far failed to materialize.

Successful technology development that focuses on the customer

As we saw earlier, leading manufacturers have woken up to the fact that the 'technology creates demand' strategy does not produce the desired results. They have begun to realize that technology must instead generate value. Indeed, a number of highly successful examples show how this shift of mindset is even now being put into practice to good effect. Analysis of these examples reveals essentially the same success factors in each case:

- Recognize key trends, technology drivers and changes in customers' value systems at an early stage.
- Identify key customer opinion leaders.
- Aim for leadership within the chosen technology segment.
- Manage the technology development process stringently with regard to the selected segment.

The new S class from Mercedes-Benz is one example that, from a technological and strategic perspective, can be categorized as an attempt to 'defend innovation leadership'. Each successive generation of this model series has traditionally set a new milestone in innovative automotive engineering. DaimlerChrysler's image and future prosperity are closely tied up with the market success of the S class. In its role as the brand's technological standard bearer, the S class affects all of the company's other model series. DaimlerChrysler is therefore compelled to pump huge amounts of money and effort into research and development work for every new S class in order to deliver on its brand promise and uphold its tradition as a pioneering innovator. The new S class indeed lives up to this role once again and is shot through with all kinds of innovations: an enhanced pre-safe system linked to ESP; radar-guided cruise control system; a braking assistant; night vision equipment, complete with two infrared headlamps and a reversing camera whose projected lines facilitate reverse parking; and a host of other smart new developments. This might all sound very futuristic, perhaps even over the top in terms of high-tech wizardry. DaimlerChrysler has, however, learned from the electrohydraulic brake episode. The lesson reads that high technology will not successfully establish itself unless it clearly generates value in a way that customers understand. On the contrary, it can make a huge dent in the brand's quality image if the technology concerned proves to be immature. Accordingly, all the innovations in the new S class have been grouped together in a package that very clearly generates value for the customer. DaimlerChrysler calls this package its 'vision of accident-free driving'.

'We focus on innovations that yield significant benefits for the customer,' says Thomas Weber, the member of the board of management in charge of research and technology at DaimlerChrysler. 'In other words, not everything that is technically feasible finds its way into our cars.' Against this background, the new technologies fitted in the S class perfectly match both Mercedes-Benz's specific brand promise (which has always been associated with advances in safety technology) and the modern value system in which 'safety' is a core element. Press commentary, such as that from the popular *Autobild* journal, confirms that the developers have struck the right chord: 'In the new S class, drivers today have a firm grip on the technology of tomorrow.'

Renault's example is especially impressive. It illustrates the vast potential even for volume manufacturers to sharply boost their brand image and carve out a more distinctive profile, provided they correctly anticipate what customers expect of new technologies. Although Renault has not been regarded as a technology leader in the past, top grades in the Euro-NCAP crash test gave a sudden and significant lift to the company's brand image. This example, too, clearly underscores the success factors for technology development in the automotive market:

- Recognize customer trends at an early stage. Renault was very quick to spot the tremendous importance that customers attach to the issue of safety – and the opportunities that a positive link between this theme and the Renault brand would open up.
- Identify key customer opinion leaders. Unlike other car makers, Renault committed to collaboration with Euro-NCAP from the beginning, an astute move that paid handsome dividends. Excessively complex and in some cases non-objective test criteria conspired with a lack of lobbying muscle to prevent other manufacturers from standardizing their test procedures. Backed by strong support from the British government, however, Euro-NCAP established itself as the leading European and OEM-independent organization for passive safety. By cleverly marketing its test results for passenger safety, and more recently for pedestrian protection, Euro-NCAP reaped the benefits of high-profile public attention and strong credibility. Equally cleverly, Renault – whose results put it at the top of the table – succeeded in co-opting this credibility for its own marketing ends.
- Aim for leadership within the chosen technology segment. Right from the outset, Renault set itself the strategic goal of becoming the first manufacturer to earn a five-star rating in the Euro-NCAP crash tests – a goal it achieved in 2001 with the Renault Laguna. To realize this ambition, the company embedded Euro-NCAP's test procedures in its product specifications and even made them a leading strategic guideline across all levels of the enterprise. Following the same rigorous logic, Euro-NCAP became a core component of Renault's marketing and communication strategy. Since then, all other car makers have likewise started to feature positive Euro-NCAP test results as a kind of 'quality seal' in their advertising campaigns. Even so, test results show that some premium vehicles have been unable to achieve five-star ratings. In one specific case, the vehicle in question undoubtedly had a superior safety concept and actually outperformed

a number of the crash test criteria. The safety concept was not applied consistently enough, though. Nor was it adapted early enough to meet the specific criteria valid for Euro-NCAP tests. Below-par test results were therefore inevitable. Strong brand positioning and a substantial premium bonus will now be needed to plug the hole that has been torn in customer opinion.

- Strictly manage technology development. Renault – not exactly a byword for innovation leadership in the past – has consistently channelled the bulk of its sizeable development spend into the 'safety' technology segment. The company has consciously refrained from spreading itself too thinly by also concentrating on other advanced technologies. Interestingly, although safety had always been an important issue to both customers and manufacturers, not all car makers grasped the significance of the Euro-NCAP crash tests to the same extent in the mid- to late 1990s. At the time, Euro-NCAP was itself striving to be accepted by the automotive industry. The permanently increasing importance of safety themes in customers' value systems thus generated a classic win–win situation for both parties. In the end, Euro-NCAP attained a leading position as an independent testing organization for passive safety, while Renault's 'lead role in passive safety' gave a lasting boost to the car maker's brand image (Figure 5.9).

		1996	1997	1998	1999	2000	2001	2002	2003	2004	2005
★★★★★ Highest crash safety score	Renault						Laguna		Megane Laguna Vel Satis Espace	Modus Megane-CC	
	VW/Audi								Touran A6	Golf Touareg	Passat
	Mercedes						C class		E class		A class
	BMW								X5	1 Series	
★★★★	Renault			Megane Espace	Megane Espace	Clio	Scenic		Kangoo		
	Audi/VW			Golf	Lupo Beetle	Polo	Passat A4	Polo A2	A3 TT		
	Mercedes			E class	A class	C class		SLK M class	Vaneo		
	BMW			5 Series			3 Series	Mini		5 Series Z4	3 Series
★★★	Renault								Twingo		
	VW/Audi	Polo	Passat A3	A6	Sharan						
	Mercedes				Smart	Smart					
★★	Renault	Clio	Laguna								
	VW/Audi		A4								
	Mercedes		C class								
★ Lowest crash safety score	BMW		3 Series								

Figure 5.9 *Euro-NCAP test results (passive crash tests)*
Sources: Euro-NCAP, 2005; ADAC

Yet another manufacturer that has understood the power of customer-focused technology strategies is likely to give sleepless nights to the incumbent technology leaders in the future. Toyota, already the front-runner in terms of growth, quality and profitability, will now also gain recognition as a technology leader. Toyota is therefore leveraging the hybrid engine technology to take the lead in the 'environment' technology segment. This core area is of crucial importance to customers. Zooming in on hybrid engines as an area of core competence, Toyota is seeking to cultivate an emotional image for the Lexus brand in particular.

Public discussion of climate change, record oil prices and particulate emissions are just some of the issues that have sensitized consumers to ecological matters, leading to calls for more environment-friendly cars. Unlike Japan's pioneers of hybrid technology, European manufacturers have elected to rely on diesel engines. Any other research they do concentrates on fuel cell and hydrogen technologies, neither of which will be ready for volume production before 2015 to 2020. To date, manufacturers and experts have led a highly technical and often polemic debate about the individual strengths and weaknesses of diesel, hybrid, natural gas and other comparatively 'green' engine technologies. Customers have perceived the heated debate as disconcerting – it has not exactly reinforced their desire for environment-friendly technologies. In the United States, tighter emissions legislation and public subsidies have fostered a trend toward hybrid vehicles that European makers quite simply overlooked for far too long. More than 80,000 hybrid autos were sold in the United States in 2004, over 50,000 of which were Prius models from Toyota. Market researchers expect the global market volume to rocket to over 900,000 hybrid vehicles by 2010 (Figure 5.10).

For the longest time, the automotive industry's corporate HQs in Europe and the United States insisted that two engines would be too expensive and too heavy. That made them hesitate to join the fray and actively address the hybrid issue. Meanwhile, Toyota had swiftly recognized what customers wanted and pressed ahead with the development of hybrid technology. It has since gained a several-year lead over the incumbent technology leaders. When the hybrid engine was first introduced in the Prius in 2000, the vehicle was derided for its stuffy design and poor driving dynamics. However, by the time the Lexus RX400h was unveiled, if not before, this attitude had changed completely. 'Runs smoothly, is great fun to drive and even appeases your environmental conscience', is how *Autobild* summed up its test drive experience – encapsulating to perfection what customers expect of hybrid vehicles.

Ever since Hollywood stars such as Cameron Diaz and Harrison Ford rolled up to the Oscar awards ceremony in a hybrid Prius, and ever since a

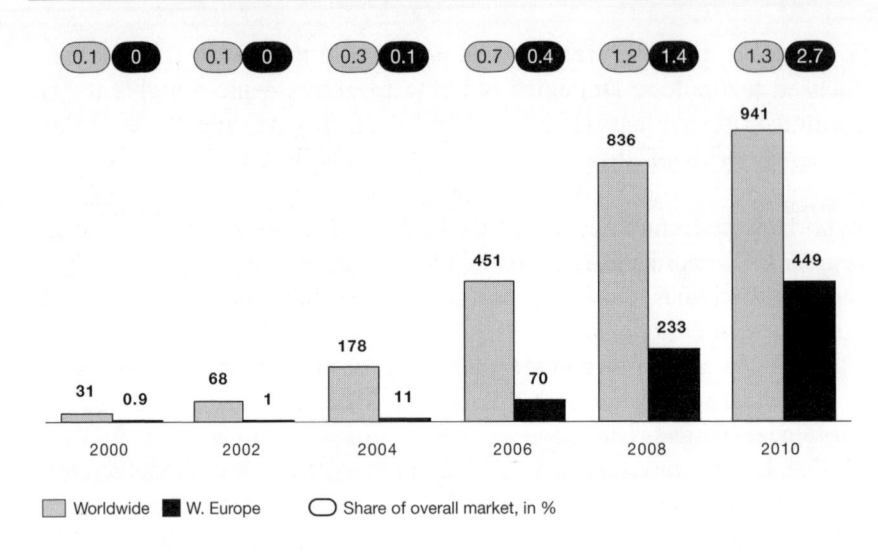

Figure 5.10 *Market forecast for hybrid vehicles (in thousands of units)*
Sources: Automobil-Produktion (publication), Freedonia Group, Global Insight

Honda Insight Hybrid effectively shared top billing with John Travolta and Uma Thurman in their movie *Be Cool*, it is obvious who Toyota has identified as 'key customer opinion leaders'. The Japanese car maker also manifestly has a clear strategic focus on leadership in this technology segment, and stringently manages its technology development programme. Toyota has, in other words, seized this opportunity with both hands.

Just when Europe's incumbent premium brands such as Mercedes were indulging in a spot of navel-gazing regarding quality and product portfolio issues, Toyota launched an assault on the Old Continent with its Lexus brand. Armed with a powerful arsenal – a more attractive, European-style design, new technology (with hybrid technology positioned as core competence for the Lexus brand) and top rankings on quality and service – the Lexus is gunning to narrow the gap on Europe's home-grown premium brands. Within the space of five years, all top-of-the-range Lexus models are to be fitted with hybrid technology.

From bitter past experience with the Lexus brand in Europe, Toyota knows full well that the climb to premium peaks will be a long and arduous one. Its only chance is to beat the European premium car makers in the arena of leading-edge technology. Accordingly, the group pumped over €5.5 billion into new technologies in 2005. Hybrid technology is a central tenet of Toyota's overall strategy, which aims for market leadership by 2010. And so far, the Japanese company has achieved every goal it set itself. That is why the automotive world has to sit up and take notice. Now that exciting, innovative cars are no longer necessarily 'made in

Europe', Toyota definitely has the potential to rearrange the existing pecking order.

European and US car makers are making impressive efforts to catch up. A series of new models have already been announced for the years ahead. Ford has fitted a hybrid engine in the Escape and four more models will hit the market within the next three years. General Motors (GM) and DaimlerChrysler – neither of which could, until recently, be described as ardent believers in hybrid engines – are working together to develop an even more efficient technology which is due out in 2007. BMW is also in on this collaborative venture. Audi is working flat out on a hybrid engine for its new Q7 SUV, and even Porsche is considering the option of a hybrid solution for its Cayenne SUV.

Hybrid technology is not the only field where the battle for customers is heating up, however. European – and especially German – manufacturers, keen to roll up the American market with diesel technology, are even now preparing to launch stage two of their 'diesel assault'. Still plagued by a negative environmental image, diesel is as yet only a footnote to the US's automotive success story and accounts for just 3.2 per cent of the market. But not for much longer, the Europeans hope. Over 40 per cent growth in sales of diesel vehicles in the past six years has spurred them on, as did the prospect of diesel fuel with significantly lower sulphur content, due out in autumn 2005. Accordingly, vendors such as VW, Audi, BMW, Nissan, Ford and – leading the charge – DaimlerChrysler are thinking hard about how to increase market share with diesel cars.

The sophisticated exhaust gas treatment in DaimlerChrysler's brand-new 'BlueTec' technology reduces nitrogen oxide emissions by as much as 80 per cent, bringing them well below even California's ultra-strict specifications. BlueTec technology depends on the availability of low-sulphur diesel fuels. It also requires AdBlue, a urea solution, to be topped up at regular service intervals. Yet despite these limitations, the technology now presents serious competition to hybrid engines on two counts: fuel consumption and environment-friendly properties. DaimlerChrysler has thus announced its intention to hit the US market with four new models armed with BlueTec technology. The first will be the E320, whose roll-out is timed to coincide with the launch of low-sulphur diesel. More ammunition for the diesel assault could also come from GM, the number one car company in the United States and the world. Combining technology derived from the GM-Fiat powertrain joint venture with completely new developments, GM is planning a diesel offensive of its own in 2008.

Optimistic market forecasts assume that diesel cars will raise their market share to as much as 7.5 per cent – or 1.3 million vehicles – by

2012. It will therefore be exciting to see which of the two technologies, hybrid or diesel, makes the running in the medium term. In the light of pent-up customer demand for greener autos, both alternatives exhibit plenty of upside potential.

All these examples emphasize the importance of rigorous technology management that focuses on the real needs and wants of customers – a strategy that will gain further ground in the future. The introduction of Euro-NCAP crash tests first caused a stir in the 'safety' arena. Then Toyota brought hybrid technology into the ring – and threw established technology leaders back on the ropes. One thing thus becomes abundantly clear: companies that swiftly and accurately interpret new trends can significantly improve both their market positioning and their brand image. Conversely, if trends are anticipated wrongly or too late, targeted revenue potential can be squandered while complexity and costs go through the roof. Any attempt to use high technology as a differentiator without taking into account customer benefits is doomed to failure. This is another lesson we can learn from the above examples, such as the trajectory of the 42V vehicle power system. Current debate surrounding environmental issues confirms the point: innovative engine technology and environment-friendly fuels alone will not get cars out of the showroom. Customers expect a coherent all-round package demonstrating the vehicle's driving dynamics, whether it is fun to drive, its image, safety and environmental friendliness.

For car manufacturers, the key success factor in the future will be 'customer-oriented technology management'. Manufacturers must ask themselves whether their inherited approach to technology management is up to the challenges that the future holds. Is the customer genuinely the focus of attention on every level? The examples we have seen clearly show that, even within one and the same company, the line between success and failure, between dream results and disastrous performance, can be very fine indeed. This being the case, it is fair to assume that, while car makers have in principle understood the need to focus all technological development squarely on the customer, they have not yet put this principle into practice systematically throughout their entire organization.

OUTLOOK: THREE CORE ELEMENTS OF CUSTOMER-ORIENTED TECHNOLOGY MANAGEMENT

Many manufacturers will have to review the technology strategies they have already approved, and possibly even rewrite them to focus them more strongly on the customer. Strategy is not the only thing that needs to be examined, however. Companies must also query whether their existing organizational structure and processes are conducive to realizing the stated focus of their technological development across all new vehicle projects, levels and regions. The stated technological focus must be applied stringently but it must also be adaptable to the specific requirements of different model series, for example. Nor is it enough for manufacturers to revector only their internal organization. They must also reconfigure the changing structure of their supply network.

Car makers must not make the mistake of applying their technology management strategy to actual technology development alone. To successfully master the challenges of the future, companies must introduce an integrated, customer-oriented system of technology management that is made up of three key building blocks (Figure 5.11).

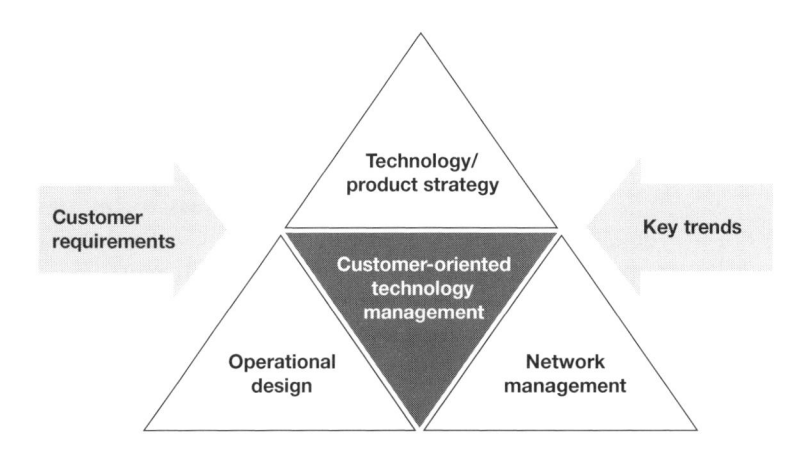

Figure 5.11 *Key building blocks of customer-oriented technology management*
Source: Roland Berger

The **technology or product strategy** ensures agreement with overall strategy and market positioning. It transforms trends and customer requirements into vehicle attributes and technologies that shape the brand.

This strategy also defines the precise technologies and innovations that can and should be used to differentiate a brand and product from rival brands and products. The target value chain structure is then mapped out on this basis. The secret of successful transformation is to focus development rigorously on the value to the customer – and to verify this value orientation for every detail and on every level.

The **operational design phase** aims to systematically implant or embed a customer's-eye view of the car maker's development organization across every level, division and vehicle project. Traditional, function-oriented value chain structures must be reoriented to focus on the brand-shaping vehicle attributes and customer needs. These structures must be enabled to recognize and respond quickly to emerging trends. Change must also come to the development process. In the past, the development approval process was focused on individual components. Now, specifications of defined vehicle attributes must be added. Also, the development organization must have the skills and resources it needs to rise to future challenges and cope with the ever faster pace of innovation. Critical knowledge must be available within the organization.

Network management will play a very prominent role in the future. More and more links in the value chain will be outsourced to suppliers and service providers. This will leave the manufacturers free to concentrate on the brand-shaping elements of the value chain. But it is also a pragmatic way for OEMs to maximize productivity and exploit cost advantages despite their own limited resources and lack of expertise in innovative technologies. In the future, however, this process will slow down noticeably, and will not go as far as was expected until recently (Figure 5.12). The flood of new models has already passed its high-water mark. With productivity gains now being eroded to some degree by higher coordination overheads, manufacturers face considerable overcapacity and strive to build up critical knowledge resources in their own organizations.

Even so, the shift in the value chain between manufacturers and suppliers will still be significant. New business models will result that establish car makers and their external suppliers as strategic partners within tightly meshed networks. For the car makers, the main success factors will be choosing the right partners and managing the resultant network effectively as a virtual company. The individual partners will operate different business models, have different levels of vertical integration, possess different competences and be responsible for different areas. Ensuring that such a network focuses consistently on one and the same customer-oriented strategy is a highly complex task. Efficient network management will be crucial to keep auto makers competitive while constantly adapting to current and anticipated market changes.

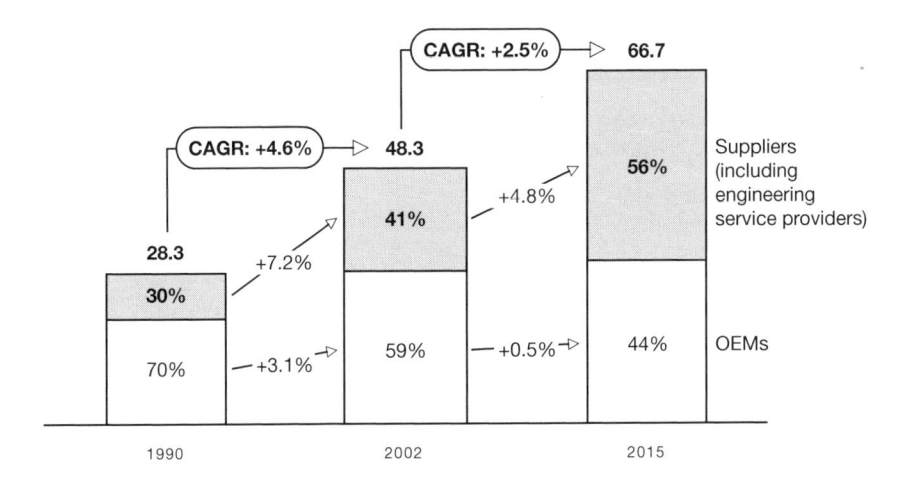

Figure 5.12 *Trend in value chain structures (in € bn)*
Sources: Interviews, Roland Berger Engineering Study

Customer-focused technology and product strategies

It will take a completely new strategic approach to enable automotive firms to concentrate strictly on customer value. Traditionally, their development organizations have been focused on technical components. As a consequence, approaches designed to differentiate themselves from the competition have enabled companies to design and market precisely these components in innovative ways. The problem is that customers do not buy technical components. They buy vehicle attributes such as driving dynamics, performance, comfort and safety. To succeed in the future, development must line up with customer perceptions and focus on concrete vehicle attributes (Figure 5.13).

This focus on vehicle attributes is at the very core of the technology and product strategy. All other aspects of the strategy build on this foundation. Generally speaking, an integrated, customer-oriented technology and product strategy will break down into four distinct levels (Figure 5.14):

1 Spot changes in customer requirements at an early stage

In the future, it will be vitally important to monitor changes in customers' requirements and keep a close watch on emerging core trends. Most car makers know the needs of their target customers and have positioned their brands and products accordingly. Any such positioning is by nature static, however. It works fine as long as no fundamental changes occur, for example in the value system of the customers, and hence in customers' perceived requirements.

130 *Major challenges*

Past/present
Component-oriented

- Air-conditioning system
- Heated rearview mirrors
- Four-cylinder engine
- ABS
- 5-gear automatic transmission
- Aluminum radiator hood
- etc.

Differentiation →

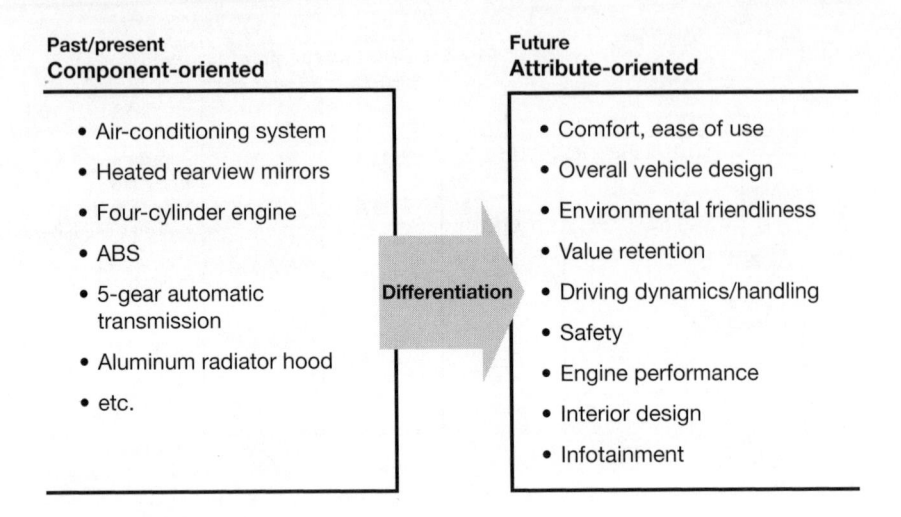

Future
Attribute-oriented

- Comfort, ease of use
- Overall vehicle design
- Environmental friendliness
- Value retention
- Driving dynamics/handling
- Safety
- Engine performance
- Interior design
- Infotainment

Figure 5.13 *Focus of development – shifting from a component orientation to a focus on vehicle attributes*
Source: Roland Berger Engineering Study

Spot changes in customer requirements at an early stage
- *New core trends*
- *Factors that influence trends*

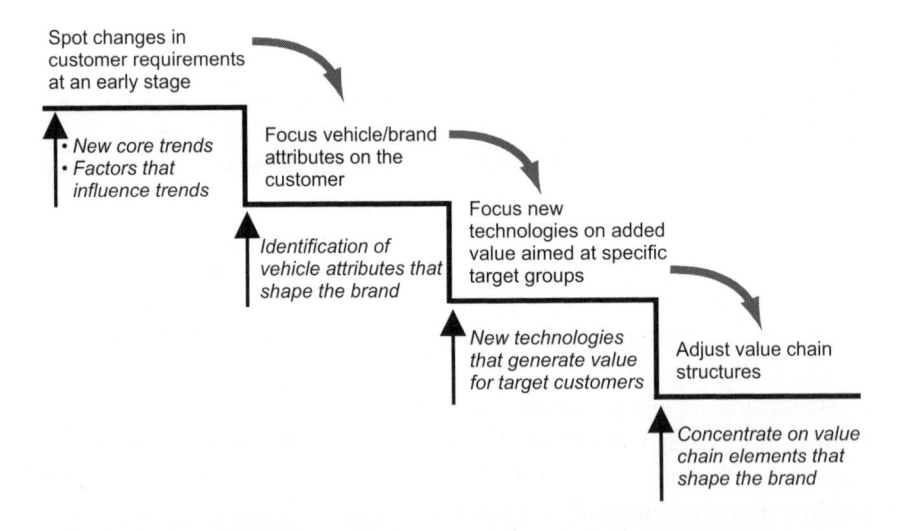

Focus vehicle/brand attributes on the customer
Identification of vehicle attributes that shape the brand

Focus new technologies on added value aimed at specific target groups
New technologies that generate value for target customers

Adjust value chain structures
Concentrate on value chain elements that shape the brand

Figure 5.14 *Steps in technology and product strategy development*
Source: Roland Berger

When new trends begin to impact the market, change comes about. Established market players nevertheless often lack the systematic 'sensors' that would allow them to detect such shifts early on. That is why many of them often respond very late. Manufacturers who are intent on transforming their image generally adopt a much more aggressive stance. As soon as a new blip on their radar screens signals a change in customer requirements, they seize the opportunity and rigorously focus their technology strategy on this trend – witness the examples of Euro-NCAP and hybrid engines.

All car makers essentially face the same challenge: to wade through the flood of short-lived trends and filter out those ones that will have a lasting impact. This requires transparency and a systematic approach. Transparency is needed in respect of **macroeconomic trends** that suddenly begin to drive technology and so affect the activities of the market. But manufacturers also need a clear overview of **opinion leaders**, such as newly emerging **technology institutes** (like Euro-NCAP) and **market research institutes** (like JD Power, whose analyses of customer satisfaction are gaining more and more importance). Transparency is equally essential with regard to the **media**, such as journals whose regional influence is growing (*Auto Motor Sport* is a good example in Europe), and concerning **multipliers**, such as the Oscar awards scenario in the case of Toyota's hybrid vehicle.

A systematic approach is necessary to wean firms off the kind of ad hoc, 'gut feeling' models that have been prevalent in the past. Car makers must instead learn to regularly track familiar and new drivers and trends. In many cases, organizational deficiencies are one of the reasons that information that could have a critical influence on key decisions never makes it from Marketing to Development – or that the latter often rejects any such input. Again, the reason for these deficiencies is mostly that customer orientation has not been implanted in technology management at a strategic and organizational level, or that customer orientation has not yet become the sole focus of the development process across all levels and all relevant divisions. The fact that one and the same manufacturer can deliver both glowing successes and abject failures of technology management substantiates this hypothesis: the ability to realize a customer-oriented technology management strategy is obviously there. It just isn't everywhere – yet.

2 Transform customer demand into brand-shaping vehicle attributes

Once a car maker knows what its customers need and want and has positioned its brand values in line with this data, the requirements placed on the product – the vehicle – can be defined in a systematic 'cascade' process. The first step is to nail down exactly what customers expect of the brand, what vehicle attributes will shape the brand in accordance with defined brand values, and what will set the brand apart from its competitors. To this end, vehicle attributes must be grouped into logical clusters and then analysed and prioritized to determine their relative importance to the brand profile and their emotional or rational nature (Figure 5.15). This exercise must be conducted on the basis of a clearly defined target group for each model series.

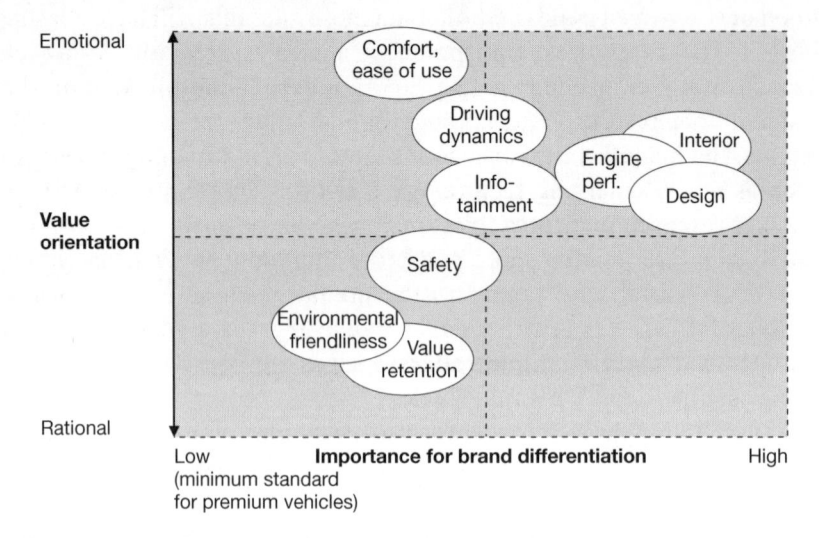

Figure 5.15 *Positioning of vehicle attributes*
Source: Roland Berger

The next step is to transform brand values into sets of vehicle attributes. The attributes themselves must be such that they can be experienced by the customers, generate value for them and clearly differentiate the vehicle from other vehicles. Once all vehicle attributes have been defined, it is time to decide which technologies and innovations are best suited to realizing them. The technologies selected must be clearly assigned to the corresponding vehicle systems. Based on these defined guidelines and their intended mode of functioning, the final step is to translate the requirements placed on these systems into the language of development: that is, into technical specifications. This is the crux of the whole process: the conversion of customers' wishes into technical specifications. After all, not every abstract customer perception can be mapped one-to-one onto a detailed technical description and measured in terms of physical units.

A concrete example helps illustrate this four-step process (Figure 5.16). The figure shows how a premium manufacturer converts the brand value of 'sportiness' into a vehicle attribute that drivers can experience, namely 'excellent handling through superior traction in all weathers'. Translated into the language of development, this attribute is realized in part through 'optimal load distribution and superb grip'. The innovative technology 'electrohydraulic suspension control' is selected to achieve this objective. Once this technology has been pinpointed, it is then possible to draw up the specifications for the 'suspension and damping' systems.

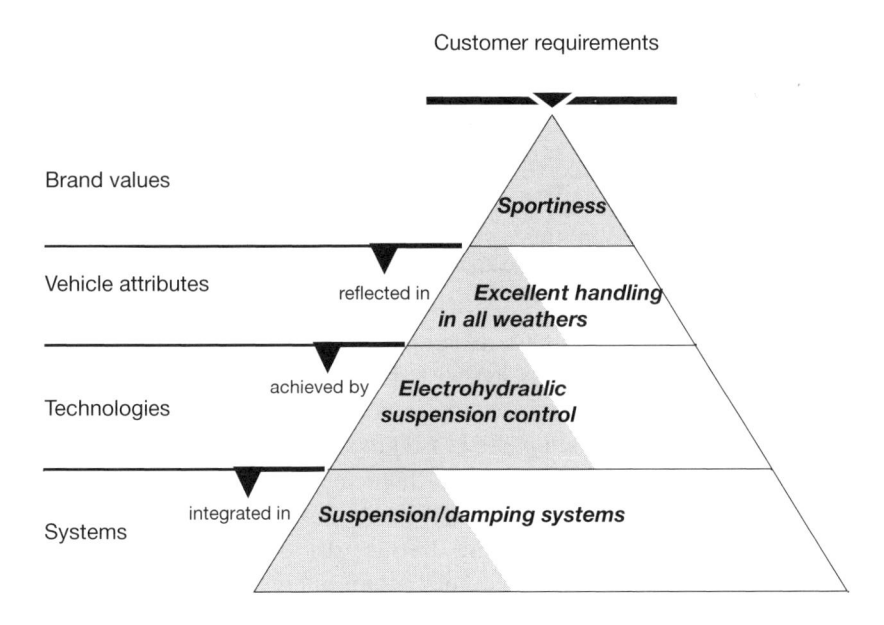

Figure 5.16 *Translating what customers want into product specifications*
Source: Roland Berger

The extent to which marketing requirements are translated smoothly and coherently into the language of development varies considerably from manufacturer to manufacturer. Glitches in the process lead to situations where vehicle attributes do not turn out the way they were intended. In such cases, they may then fail to satisfy customer expectations.

3 Systematically generate customer-focused innovations

As we have consistently argued in this chapter, new technologies and innovations will be well received by the market only if they fit the relevant brand image and line up with customer requirements. They must also sharpen the contours of the brand profile and distinguish it from rival brands. These fundamental principles dictate a number of consequences if a company systematically wants to generate innovations that will meet with customer acceptance. One consequence is that a selective approach to innovation is imperative. Not every new technology will fit a car maker's brand profile. It should also be obvious that technology strategies must also vary as a function of manufacturers' differing brand values. If technology strategies are too similar, the differentiation potential diminishes. This erodes customer loyalty, causing pressure to be exerted via the lever of price. Another consequence is that innovations and technologies must be developed with a strong focus on customer requirements, customer value and customer acceptance. The third aspect in the process of generating innovation is the manufacturer's own view. In order to be profitable, car makers must be able to persuade customers to pay a premium that covers the considerable expense incurred in developing an incessant stream of new innovations. Taken together, these three aspects – the brand fit, the benefit to the customer and the benefit to the maker – are the core filters to determine whether or not particular innovations align with a given brand.

Appropriate innovations can, of course, only be generated systematically if a systematic process is in place. This process consists essentially of three steps in which innovations are pooled, evaluated and selected (Figure 5.17). The innovation pool, a repository for all of a company's innovative ideas, receives input from three sources. First, it serves as a store of all existing innovative ideas. Second, it is fed by the systematic analysis of factors such as core trends, drivers, opinion leaders, competitors and changes in customer requirements, as well as by the resultant identification of future innovation deficits. Third, input is derived from technology roadmaps, which indicate when what technology will probably hit the market. As we saw earlier, these roadmaps themselves require upstream filters to detect changes in customers' value systems. They must never be the product of an obsession with technology for technology's sake.

To filter suitable potential technology projects out of the innovation pool, the brand fit, the value to the customer and benefits to the maker are evaluated in the second step. The third step is to prioritize the attractiveness and technological positioning of the candidate projects identified in step two. At this stage, potential projects are either rejected or selected and cleared for development. This systematic approach ensures that the new technologies and innovations selected for implementation will indeed generate value in a way that customers can understand and are willing to pay for. Also, this process will ensure that each selected development contributes to the sharpening of the brand profile. The internal impact in terms of technical optimization, cost, quality and internal processes, for example, is also rendered transparent at this point.

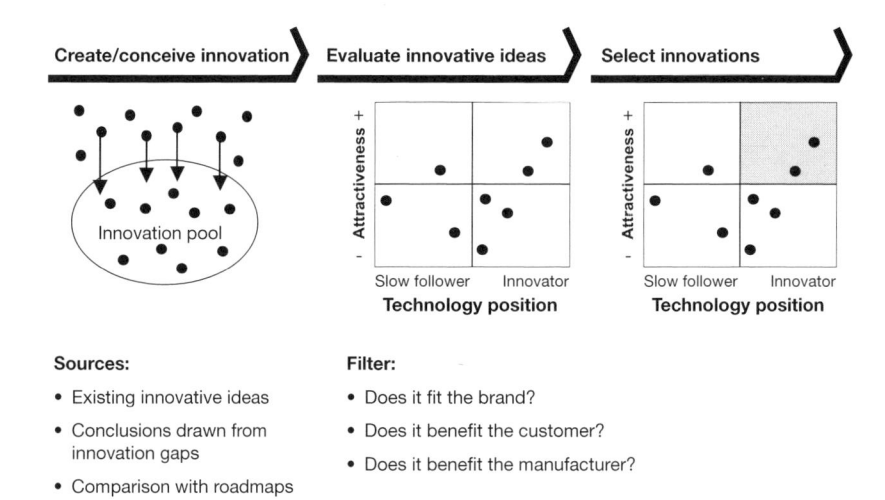

```
Create/conceive innovation    Evaluate innovative ideas    Select innovations
```

Sources:
- Existing innovative ideas
- Conclusions drawn from innovation gaps
- Comparison with roadmaps

Filter:
- Does it fit the brand?
- Does it benefit the customer?
- Does it benefit the manufacturer?

Figure 5.17 *Customer-focused innovation process*
Source: Roland Berger

4 Align the value chain with the technology strategy

Once initiated, the customer-oriented technology and product strategy must be applied consistently across the entire value chain. It is the OEM's responsibility to ensure customers will perceive the brand-shaping and differentiating vehicle attributes in line with the brand promise. For this reason, it is important to identify those elements of the value chain that have an impact on shaping and differentiating the brand, and those that do not. The former are part of the car maker's core competence and should therefore be kept in-house. Activities that make little or no contribution to the distinctive brand perception are generally ideal candidates for outsourcing to suppliers. In the latter cases, the car companies can benefit from more efficient processes, focused product portfolios, lower complexity and structural cost benefits often enjoyed by external specialists. Essentially, every system and every component must be examined to determine the extent to which it influences the characteristics of the brand. This exercise results in the manufacturer's target value chain structure (Figure 5.18).

During implementation of this strategy, two processes run in opposite directions at the same time. On the one hand, the car maker outsources large chunks of the value chain – those elements that do not influence the brand perception – to suppliers. On the other hand, core competencies and critical expertise are insourced. This trend is born of many car makers' painful experience that external suppliers often dominate areas of expertise that are crucial to those attributes that make a brand so

136 Major challenges

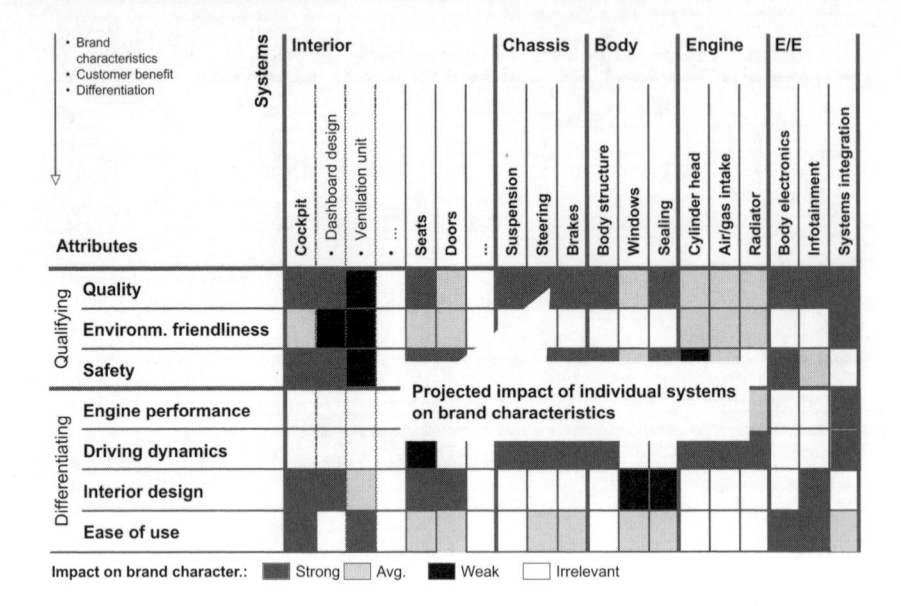

Figure 5.18 *Impact of vehicle components on brand characteristics (example)*
Source: Roland Berger Engineering Study

distinctive. Today, the brand-shaping attributes of products and technologies in the various systems and components are often generated by electronics and software. Chassis control systems, powertrain and motor management systems are just three examples, and the knowledge behind these systems and components often lies with outside suppliers. Moreover, since little progress has been made in standardizing hardware and software platforms, such suppliers are far from interchangeable. This situation highlights how important it is to brand image for manufacturers and suppliers to collaborate closely in tightly woven networks.

Forms of operational design

Once core competencies have been defined and the value chain structure has been designed to match, the next challenge is to ensure that the company's technology and product strategy can generate the expected benefits in practice. To make sure that vehicle attributes defined on the basis of customer requirements and brand values will realize in models as expected, car makers have begun to give their development activities a functionality focus. Depending on their individual philosophy or the degree to which they apply this strategy, manufacturers adopt a number of different approaches to operational design. There are, however, three organizational forms that are most common (Figure 5.19).

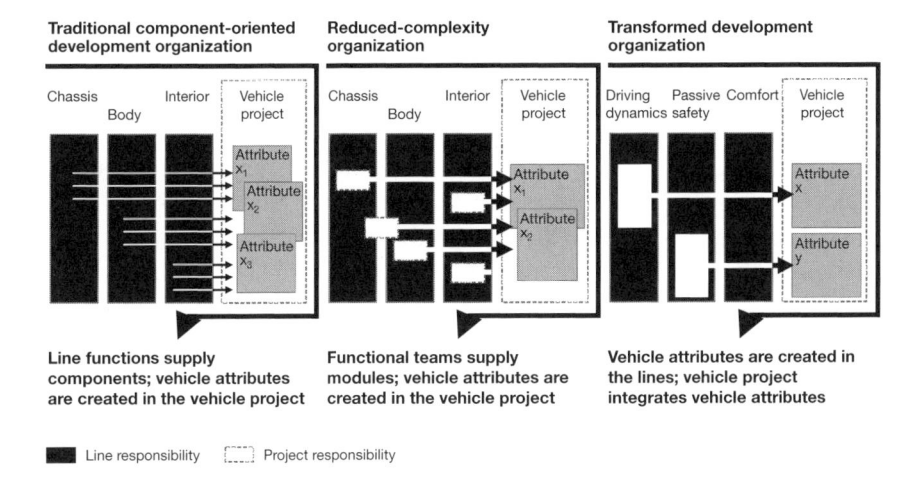

Figure 5.19 *Different organizational approaches to integrating vehicle attributes*
Source: Roland Berger Engineering Study

1 Component-oriented development organizations drive complexity

Vehicle attributes that customers actually perceive – such as 'sportiness' – are produced not by just one component, but by the smooth interplay of several components. In a traditional development organization, which is component-oriented, each line function supplies isolated components as its contribution to the vehicle project. The project team then has to try to put all the systems and components together in a way that produces the desired vehicle attributes. Given the multitude of systems (especially electronic systems) that have to dovetail perfectly in today's vehicles, delaying integration until this late stage often causes problems and makes projects unmanageably complex. Since each individual project is unique and therefore has its own learning curve, it becomes difficult to realize the brand-shaping vehicle attributes consistently across all product lines. It is not unusual for different projects to end up reinventing already defined attributes.

2 Functional teams reduce complexity

Although this model seeks to sharply reduce the complexity of a vehicle project, it is still based on the traditional 'geometric' development organization. Line functions team up to build functional subteams that hand over finished modules or submodules to the vehicle project. Subteams are responsible for bringing the components contained in modules in line with desired vehicle attributes. The approval of the functional attributes of the module is also placed in their hands. The attribute 'excellent handling', for example, could mean that the electronics unit gets together with the powertrain unit to test and fine-tune the interplay between ESP sensors and the motor management system. The finished module is then handed over to the vehicle project, which integrates it with the other modules. Though this model certainly does reduce the effort within the vehicle project itself, interfaces remain a problem and complexity remains high. The main benefit is that it can often be applied within the confines of traditional organizational forms, in effect giving employees a 'soft' introduction to new ways of working and new challenges. The residual threat remains, however, that failure to coordinate up-front on the integration of individual modules in higher-level systems may cause the intended vehicle attributes to be missed.

3   Function-oriented development organizations guarantee customer focus

The more important it becomes to carve out a distinctive brand profile – and hence to focus rigorously on customer requirements, brand values and vehicle attributes – the more carefully companies must think about how to transform their development organization into a function-oriented structure (Figure 5.20). It follows that premium manufacturers in particular must tackle this approach head on.

Wherever a function-oriented development organization exists, all aspects of the integration needed to create specific vehicle attributes can be performed within the line and then handed over to the vehicle project as a ready-made system. The driving dynamics unit, for example, might develop and integrate everything needed to deliver the attribute 'excellent handling' from start to finish. This approach makes vehicle projects markedly less complex, while ensuring that every unit that develops a new vehicle model builds on a common understanding of customer requirements, brand values and vehicle attributes. At the same time, the use of this approach on different vehicle projects over time helps the company accumulate a wealth of experience – all of which enables the technology in question to permanently improve and mature.

Development processes must, of course, be adapted at the same time as the development organization. These processes should be focused on the vehicle attributes from the earliest phases of development, and must then retain this focus from beginning to end (Figure 5.21).

Example 1

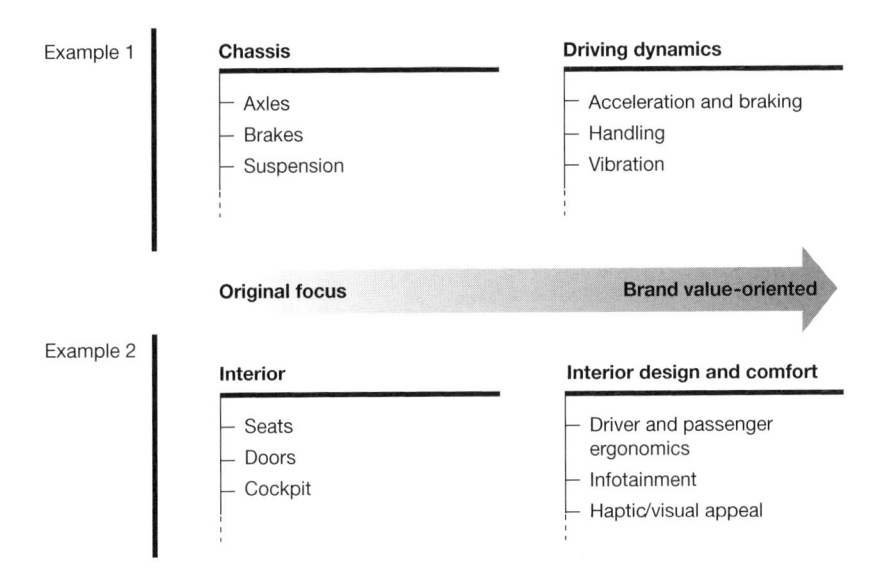

Chassis
- Axles
- Brakes
- Suspension

Driving dynamics
- Acceleration and braking
- Handling
- Vibration

Original focus → Brand value-oriented

Example 2

Interior
- Seats
- Doors
- Cockpit

Interior design and comfort
- Driver and passenger ergonomics
- Infotainment
- Haptic/visual appeal

Figure 5.20 *Focusing the development organization on brand-shaping vehicle attributes*
Source: Roland Berger

Focus on the specification of vehicle attributes instead of component attributes

Component-specific approval process, complemented by approval of vehicle attributes

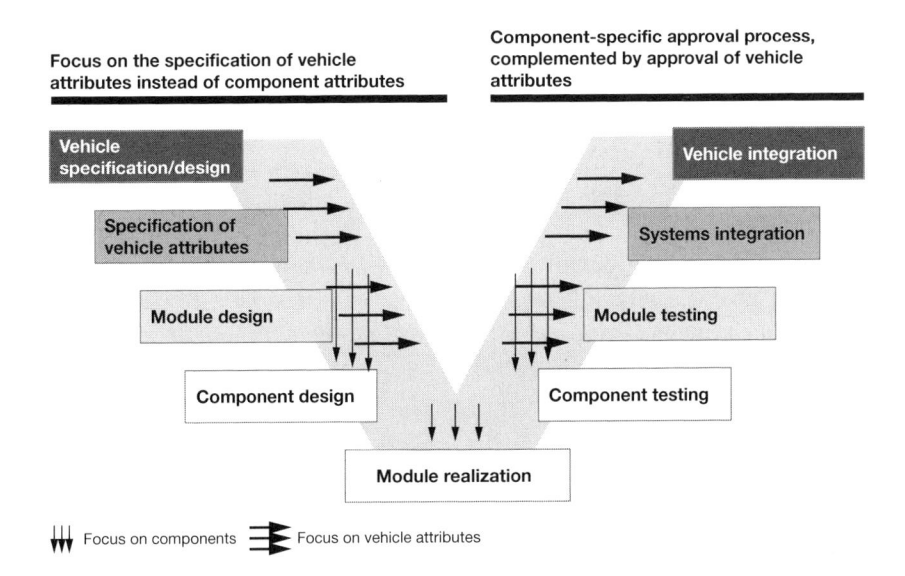

- Vehicle specification/design
- Specification of vehicle attributes
- Module design
- Component design
- Module realization
- Component testing
- Module testing
- Systems integration
- Vehicle integration

Focus on components | Focus on vehicle attributes

Figure 5.21 *Focusing the development process on vehicle attributes*
Source: Roland Berger

At present, the development approval process is usually still carried out at the level of specific components. To achieve the desired focus, however, approvals must also be granted for complete vehicle attributes. These attributes must be clearly defined in advance. And that is no easy task, bearing in mind that customers' perceptions must be translated into the language of development on such a detailed level that they ultimately deliver precisely the desired attributes – and leave no room for subjective interpretation.

Yet another challenge stems from the fact that vehicle attributes should not merely embody a car maker's general brand values in the same way across all product lines. They must also reinforce the individual 'personality' of each and every product line. This requirement is usually accommodated by setting up a core strategy unit in the development department. In close collaboration with marketing, this unit prescribes the technology and product strategy and determines exactly which innovations fit the brand in general, and which fit the individual product lines in particular. It also defines the brand-shaping and differentiating vehicle attributes, so that core competencies can be staked out and the value chain strategy drawn up for the development process. To strengthen the unique identity of the individual product lines, today's rather case-by-case project organizations should be transformed into more formal units within the development organization. If a company goes a step further and merges related product lines in a sensible way into such units, it also becomes easier to harmonize vehicle architectures and to introduce modularization and standardization strategies.

BMW is regarded as a pioneer in designing brand-shaping value chain strategies, and in focusing its development organization on vehicle attributes. BMW assesses the importance to the brand of every module in every vehicle. It then focuses its value chain strategy accordingly. The way in which development is organized has likewise experienced far-reaching changes. Having singled out the 'interior' as a brand-shaping vehicle attribute that is crucial to the BMW brand, the company extricated this unit from its body unit and further transformed its chassis unit into a new driving dynamics unit.

Networking closely with external partners

Changes in the supply network can be linked to three main drivers that affect the network concurrently but in different directions.

1 Value chain elements that do not contribute to brand characteristics are increasingly being outsourced

One obvious driver is manufacturers' stated aim of concentrating on the brand-shaping and differentiating elements of the value chain. This is their core competence. As a consequence, elements that do not contribute to the brand characteristics are increasingly outsourced to suppliers. Indeed, entire modules or systems encompassing extensive content all the way along the value chain are being farmed out, involving for example purchasing, production, assembly, logistics and integration tasks. As a result, various forms of collaboration are emerging depending on the individual module or system, and depending on the individual scope of responsibility assumed by the supplier.

2 Brand-shaping value chain elements demand fair partnerships

The second driver is rooted in many manufacturers' belated realization that they have little or no core expertise in-house to cope with electronic and software functions and the integration of them. In theory, car makers can quickly find a solution in the discipline known as 'insourcing'. In practice, however, the road to effective insourcing is a long and difficult one. Suppliers are naturally reluctant to hand over their module or system-specific expertise, precisely the expertise that has often given them a dominant role in innovation and in creating the brand characteristics. Close networking on both sides offers a way out of this dilemma.

OEMs depend on suppliers to realize defined brand characteristics, for instance by programming brand-specific attributes into the motor management system. Conversely, suppliers are obliged to align their modules and systems with the brand-specific vehicle attributes dictated by the OEM. They must therefore engage in fine-tuning and any number of minor coordination loops involving other systems in order to produce brand-compliant vehicle attributes. Both parties are thus forced to open up to each other. OEMs must disclose their brand and differentiation strategies and information on targeted vehicle attributes to their suppliers. The latter must in turn contribute their intellectual capital – that is, their technological and innovation competence. It is thus vital for both sides to commit to a fair, trusting partnership that offers a long-term strategic perspective.

The third driver derives from the fact that vehicle model lifecycles are 'out of synch' with electronic and software development cycles, as we saw earlier (Figure 5.5). Electronic components and software are developed at such a fast pace that certain modules and systems – such as navigation systems, telephones and entertainment systems – will need to be upgraded within a vehicle model lifecycle, and integrated in existing vehicle systems without disrupting functionality. OEMs lack some of the competencies needed to handle this challenge and would therefore be unable to cope. Again, therefore, they have little choice but to network closely with suppliers, nurturing long-term partnerships in order to ensure that upgrades and updates go ahead smoothly.

3   Competences and competitive capabilities demand tight networking

Since it makes sense for the owner of the know-how to also play the role of process leader, suppliers have to shoulder extra integration work, for which they too must build up expertise. To meet this challenge, Bosch, for example, launched Bosch Engineering as a subsidiary company. Bosch used to supply ready-made control systems and associated software for engines, transmissions and braking systems as separate modules. Now, Bosch Engineering pools the expertise needed to integrate these systems, and sells this service to OEMs. The Bosch subsidiary brings together the engine, brake and transmission controllers and hands them over as a self-contained system to the customer.

The need for access to innovative skills and the need to remain competitive compel OEMs to compete with each other to find the best partners. It is therefore necessary for OEMs to cement the long-term loyalty of top-flight suppliers. Depending on the precise value chain links that have been assumed by the supplier and their importance in shaping the car makers' brands, a variety of business models emerge as a result. 'Little OEMs' handle everything from the development to the production of derivative products. System suppliers develop extensive functionality groups in the context of long-term partnerships, while independently managing second and third-tier suppliers. Spin-offs ensure that value chain elements that are not critical to the characteristics of the brand remain competitive in the long run. Direct equity investments safeguard access to the skills and capacity needed for strategically important components. Joint ventures develop new technologies, and OEMs serve as incubators to foster innovation in collaboration with small, thinly financed firms. All of this points to a future in which business relationships will become more variegated and more important than ever for car makers (Figure 5.22).

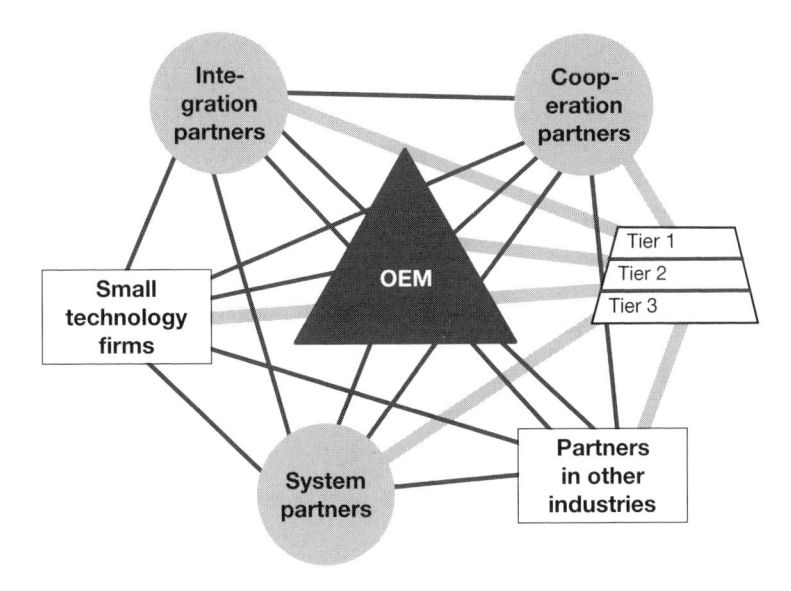

Figure 5.22 *Networking all kinds of business relationships*
Source: Roland Berger

From hierarchies to genuine partnerships in tightly meshed networks

Traditional functional and hierarchic structures can no longer cope with these many and varied challenges. Collaboration must now take on new forms that focus on customer requirements and brand values. Ultimately, this will lead to efficient partnerships that operate in tightly meshed networks. Something akin to virtual companies will emerge that contribute specific modules and/or systems to sharpen the brand profile or raise competitiveness (Figure 5.23).

The opportunities afforded by such networks can only be realized if network management is institutionalized, however. Network managers need to synchronize the various business models. All the parties involved should share the same understanding of customer requirements, brand characteristics and defined vehicle attributes. Legacy structures inherited by OEMs and their network partners alike must systematically be transformed to accommodate the new forms of collaboration we have discussed. Network partners must bring their organizations into line with their defined focus on vehicle attributes. Their workflows and procedures must be synchronized to create stable, reliable development processes that release functionalities rather than just components. Network managers must define a set of systematic criteria by which to select suitable partners and permanently monitor the network configuration. Collaboration in an atmosphere of trust demands partnership agreements on issues such as intellectual capital and exclusivity arrangements, but also on matters such as how potential conflicts between the partners are to be resolved. In the long run, partners will only remain in the network if they possess strategic core competencies or improve competitiveness.

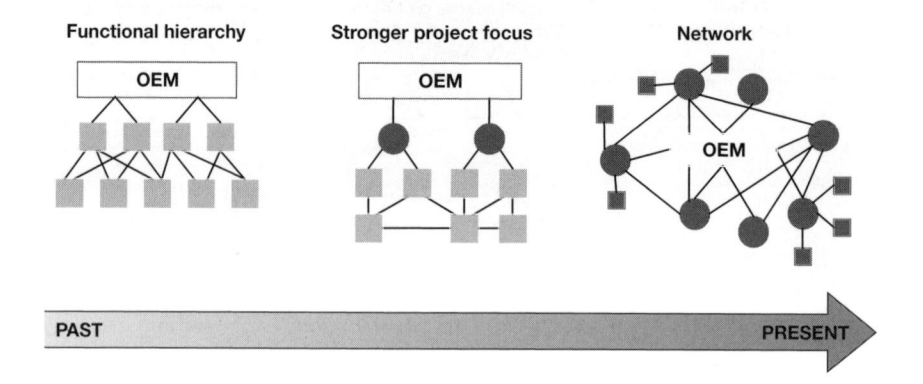

Figure 5.23 *From heirarchies to networks*
Source: Roland Berger

SUMMARY

The technology challenge: does it constitute progress, or is it a pitfall? The conditions and constraints surrounding technological development have changed. Whereas innovation proceeded at a comparatively modest pace until the early 1990s, technological advances – especially in the field of electronics – have since triggered dramatic acceleration. This trend, coupled with the fact that new technologies now spread ever more quickly to other brands and lower classes of car, is making it hard for car manufacturers to differentiate themselves from their competitors. Even premium brands are becoming more interchangeable. The pressure to innovate, the competition that exists between alternative technologies and the crushing burden of R&D expenditure are threatening to catch premium manufacturers in a cost and complexity trap.

The way to avoid this trap is to focus on those technologies that are critical – that is, those technologies that distinguish a manufacturer from its competitors, sharpen its brand profile and, no less important, bring in more revenues. Premium car makers must abandon their 'technology creates demand' mantra in favour of a development rationale based on the understanding that 'technology generates value'. They must know what their customers want and need, and quickly identify trends that will alter customers' system of values. At the same time, they must keep a watchful eye on the importance and development of opinion leaders. Together with the need for technology to match the brand profile, all of these factors will be crucial to car makers' future success.

Some manufacturers have already spotted the potential inherent in technology strategies that focus on the customer. By achieving top grades in the Euro-NCAP crash tests, Renault, for instance, moved up to a leading position in passive safety. Toyota's current drive to establish hybrid technology as an innovative core competence of the Lexus brand is another example.

Evidently, the process of rethinking is well under way. Many car makers are nevertheless still adopting a piecemeal approach: technological development is not focusing on the needs and wants of target customers across the board. If they are to master the challenges that lie ahead, manufacturers will need to apply a customer-oriented technology strategy that centres around three core elements. First, the technology and product strategy must establish benefits to the customer as the focal point of all technological development, defining those technologies that are to differentiate a brand and product from rival brands and products. Second, a suitable operational design must foster this mentality and ensure that a customers'-eye view is implemented across all levels, divisions and vehicle projects. To this end, traditional development organizations and processes must be transformed into functionality-oriented structures. The third key element is network management. Role splitting between OEMs and suppliers along the value chain is creating a need for new forms of collaboration. All kinds of different business models will in the future coexist within tightly woven networks, and cooperation will take place in what amounts to a virtual company. Efficient network management will safeguard access to the knowledge and capacity held by key partners. It will ensure that customer-oriented technology strategies are implemented uniformly across all external partners in the network. It will also enable network partners to closely integrate their activities, and will continually adapt the overall structure to current and future changes in the market.

Advances in technology are a decisive factor in giving premium vehicles a distinctive brand profile. This has been true in the past and it will be true also in the future. It is therefore imperative for car makers to focus strictly on the requirements of their target customers. Only then can they escape the cost and complexity trap and successfully position their brands. The more accurately a manufacturer anticipates customer requirements and responds to these in its product and technology offerings, the more leverage it will gain to exploit strategic opportunities.

6

The market challenge: who will gain strategic control?

Jürgen Reers, Partner, Roland Berger Strategy Consultants

CHALLENGES IN AUTOMOTIVE SALES

'Premium segment now also hit by price-cutting war.' 'Car makers' long struggle with stagnant sales in core markets.' 'Margins nowhere near adequate at many companies.' These are the kind of depressing headlines that are currently being seen in the media. For all market players – manufacturers, component suppliers and dealers – today's automotive industry is becoming an ever more challenging arena. And for all of them, what is already hard-fought competition is set to become even tougher.

The industry's key markets are stagnating. Growth can be achieved only by either broadening the product or service portfolio, or expanding into emerging markets. At the same time, worldwide overcapacity and the ambitious entries by newcomers from the Far East are making competition fiercer than ever.

Changed behaviour? Change the way you think!

In this climate of flat demand and ruthless competition, customers' expectations and behaviour too have changed significantly. For many buyers, cars have long since graduated from being just a way to get from A to B and are increasingly becoming an expression of a lifestyle. The traditional forecast models that used to segment target groups by income, social background and age alone are no longer sufficient to accurately predict how people will behave. For instance a growing section of the affluent population like to understate their prosperity. So buyers in this segment opt for small, modern autos in place of the traditional high-end sedans and saloon cars. In doing so, they are making a statement about their post-materialist lifestyle. To take another example, new value systems often breed hybrid consumption patterns. The same buyer might head for the luxury segment when satisfying special requirements while consciously looking for rock-bottom price offerings in other categories.

Smart shopping appears unstoppable – and will heat up market competition further still. In consumer goods, the trend is already well established. Customers have a detailed knowledge of where they can get the best price for products and services. They also have a perceived need to settle for nothing less. This combination has nourished the dominance of discount formats in food and consumer electronics retail. Even stores that sell luxury items are now having to accommodate this development. As a result, 30 to 50 per cent markdowns are bringing luxury fashion wear into the same price bracket as no-name products.

The same harsh wind is also blowing in the face of car dealers. In the past, would-be buyers would stroll down to the nearest dealer to ask for an offer for the brand of their choice. Today, an array of channels allows them to find out for themselves about the products and prices available from a variety of vendors. In Germany, 56 per cent of car buyers now use the internet to gather information on possible configurations and prices, before weighing up and taking their decision (source: TNS Emnid/Autoscout 24). They then leverage information about incentives and discounts to haggle over prices with the dealer. The attractiveness of the brand and the product is still important, but decisions to buy autos is now increasingly being linked to price (see Figure 6.1).

In the automotive industry, intensified competition and price pressure have driven a fast rate of innovation that has affected both product portfolios and core values.

Manufacturers' response: a varied approach to products and costs

On the product front, car manufacturers have responded by extending their model ranges. Mercedes-Benz and BMW typify auto makers' efforts to move into new segments. The former's A class and the latter's 1 Series have given both companies a foothold in the less profitable compact class. Conversely, Volkswagen has added the Touareg and the Phaeton to the top

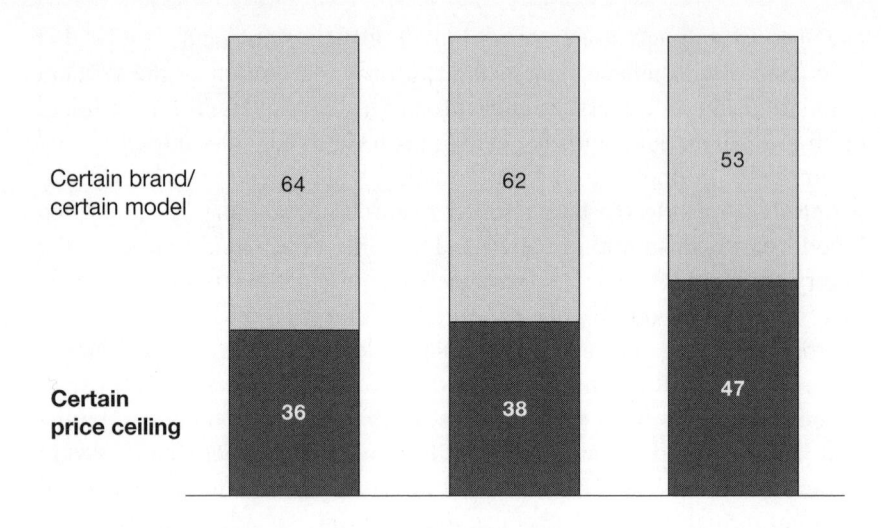

Certain brand/ certain model	64	62	53
Certain price ceiling	36	38	47

Figure 6.1 *Key criterion in decisions to buy autos in Germany, 2000–04 (per cent)*
Source: Roland Berger Market Research survey conducted in Germany

end of its traditional portfolio. The growing trend for vendors to set themselves apart by developing innovative niche vehicles is constantly spawning new subsegments. Twenty years or so ago, model segments were clearly defined. Recent years have seen an explosion in niche segments, however. Cross-over models that combine elements of different segments have been introduced and have shaken up inherited product categories. Innovative roof models, for instance, have blended elements of the coupé, the convertible and the saloon car. Fresh models combine features of sports utility vehicles (SUVs) and large saloon cars, adding the comfort of the luxury segment and using sleek roof lines to give a sports car-like flair reminiscent of a coupé. Current concept cars even cross coupés and convertibles with SUVs.

Mercedes-Benz is an excellent case study illustrating the entire trend toward the expansion of model ranges. Having produced just seven model series in 1980, the company was rolling out 20 by the end of 2005 (see Figure 6.2).

While spreading the range of models on offer, manufacturers have also shortened vehicle lifecycles. Volkswagen's first Golf had a rated lifecycle of nine years. With the Golf IV, that figure diminished to six years.

On the cost side, moves to optimize development, sourcing and production processes have yielded substantial gains in efficiency. Extensive standardization based on a common platform, and identical parts strategies, have enabled firms to tap vast potential all along the value chain (see Figure 6.3).

	No. of model series
7 8 8 9 14 20	Passenger cars

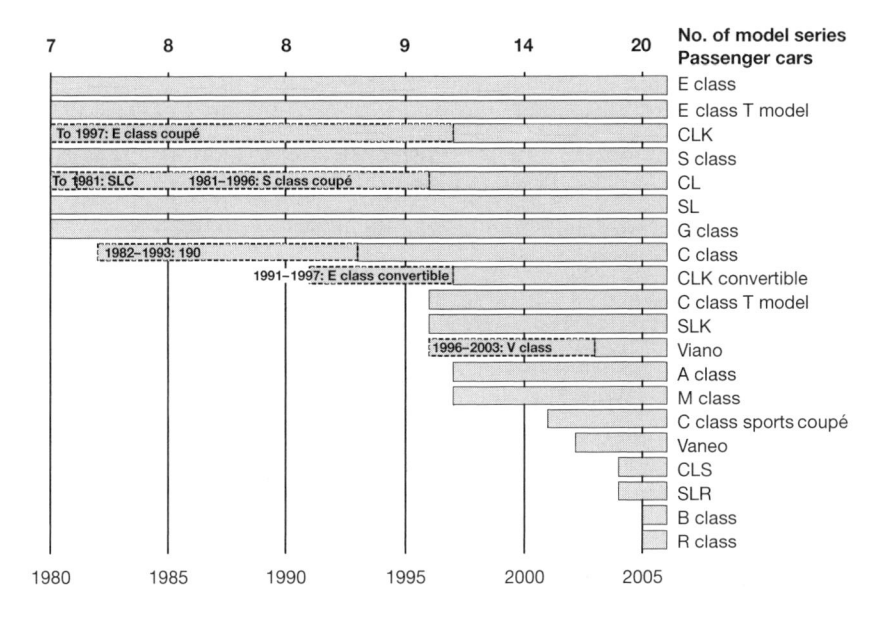

Period	Model
	E class
	E class T model
To 1997: E class coupé	CLK
	S class
To 1981: SLC 1981–1996: S class coupé	CL
	SL
	G class
1982–1993: 190	C class
1991–1997: E class convertible	CLK convertible
	C class T model
	SLK
1996–2003: V class	Viano
	A class
	M class
	C class sports coupé
	Vaneo
	CLS
	SLR
	B class
	R class

1980   1985   1990   1995   2000   2005

Figure 6.2 *Expansion of model series at Mercedes-Benz, 1980–2005*
Sources: Roland Berger Strategy Consultants, Global Insight, DaimlerChrysler website

Close collaboration between auto makers and their suppliers, with both sides acting as partners, has delivered huge successes in this area. The early involvement of component suppliers in the product development process and the spread of networking thanks to open CAx data models can

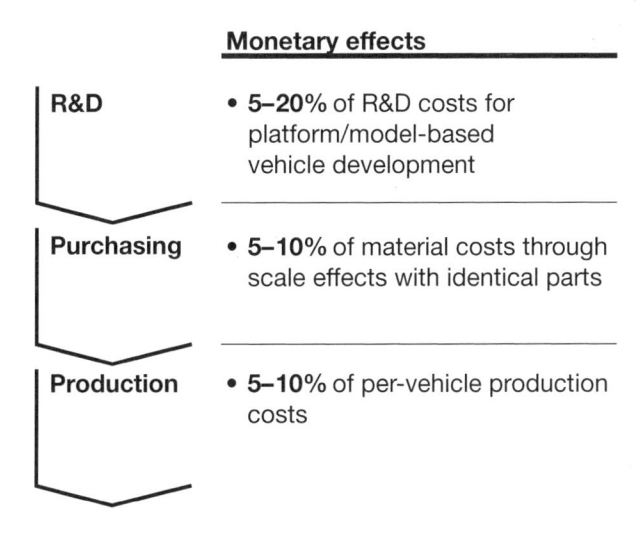

Monetary effects

R&D	• **5–20%** of R&D costs for platform/model-based vehicle development
Purchasing	• **5–10%** of material costs through scale effects with identical parts
Production	• **5–10%** of per-vehicle production costs

Figure 6.3 *How standardized technology can boost efficiency*
Source: Roland Berger Strategy Consultants

save both time and money. Platform strategies and the outsourcing of the development and production of entire systems to first-tier suppliers enable economies of scale to be realized across corporate brands and even across multiple manufacturers. In a similar strategy, heavily integrated production processes (where suppliers deliver parts just in time or just in sequence) reduce complexity and speed up assembly on the line.

Competitive pressure remains severe

However, as all car makers focused their efforts on product and cost aspects, cost advantages and unique selling propositions cancelled each other out over time. In addition, the expansion of product ranges has made product development, manufacturing and marketing more complex in many cases. Consequently, the automotive market found itself in an even more difficult situation.

The volume segment, in particular, is likely to face similar problems. By 2010, this segment will see its share of the total market decline to around 70 per cent, from nearly 80 per cent in 1980 (see Figure 6.4). The consumer goods market has already experienced this trend. In Germany, the volume segment has lost considerable market share to the premium and discount segments over the past five years. A market share of 65 per cent in 1999 has now shrunk to just 54 per cent (source: GfK).

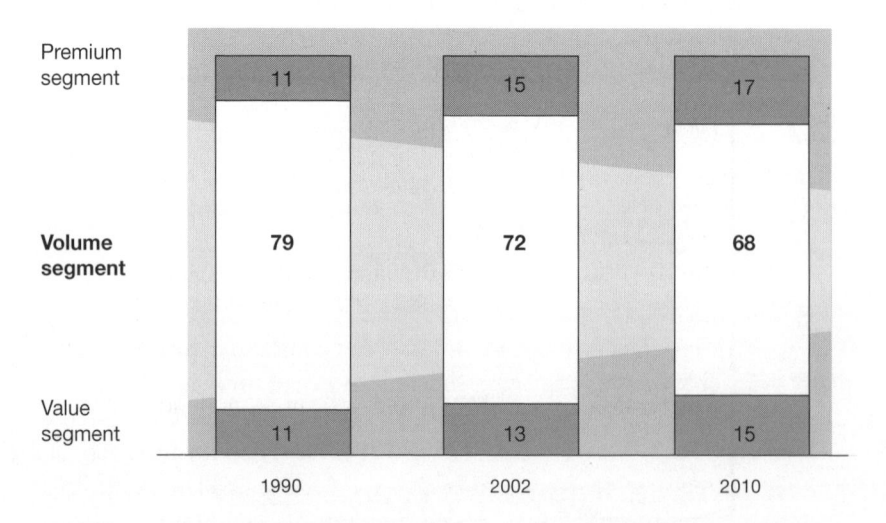

	1990	2002	2010
Premium segment	11	15	17
Volume segment	79	72	68
Value segment	11	13	15

Figure 6.4 *Trend in segments in Western Europe, 1990 versus 2010 (percentage shares of new car sales)*
Source: Roland Berger Strategy Consultants

In the automotive industry, the battle for the growing premium segment is intensifying. For some considerable time, manufacturers have been conceding sizeable discounts on premium models in order to gain or defend market share. In the German market, for example, price reductions of 10 per cent, 15 per cent and more are commonplace in this segment.

At the bottom end of the price range, low-cost offerings are facing even more intense competition. One pioneer in focusing on cost efficiency and minimal features and fittings has been Renault/Nissan, the company that developed the Dacia Logan. Volkswagen's announcement that it intends to pursue a similar market strategy clearly shows that other players cannot escape from this pressure. Volkswagen is looking to the 3-K, whose production costs should come to about €3,000, to improve its competitive position in emerging markets in particular. Further low-cost Asian vehicles will also penetrate the market. The Koreans and Chinese are expanding aggressively. Indian makers also are working on vehicle strategies that would take production costs down below €2,000.

Harsher competition outside the new car market

New vehicles are not the only source of earnings that is coming under pressure in the automotive business. New market players, new delivery channels and the deregulation of automotive sales are adding to competition throughout the vehicle lifecycle.

Non-captive financial service providers and regular commercial banks are increasing the competition to finance auto purchases. Manufacturers' banks have already lost some ground, even in Germany where growth prospects for vehicle financing are decidedly positive, and where the market share of loans and leasing-based financing is expected to rise from 70 to 76 per cent by 2010. In 2004, 38 per cent of all new cars sold were financed by loans or leasing arrangements with the car makers' banks, compared with 40 per cent two years earlier.

In vehicle insurance, the deregulation of contractual provisions and wider tariff spreads have led to a sharp drop in premiums. According to information from GDV, the German Insurance Association, the average car insurance premium stood at €475 in 1995. Adjusted for inflation, this figure had already slipped to €375 by 2003, a decline of 21 per cent.

In vehicle maintenance too, the elimination of quantitative selection pursuant to the new Block Exemption Regulation has fuelled stiffer competition. Moreover, professional sourcing logistics and service models are transforming non-captive repair shops into ever more serious competitors.

As the technological complexity of vehicles increases, both authorized dealers and non-captive repair shops are having to invest heavily in diagnostics tools, technical support and ongoing employee training.

In the replacement parts business, non-captive wholesalers are gaining new significance now that the Block Exemption Regulation has loosened conditions surrounding the sale of original parts. Expectations that the Design Protection Regulation will be eased throughout Europe are also strengthening the position of this channel. At the same time, the pan-European consolidation of parts wholesalers is only adding to the pressure to provide competitive services (in terms of the breadth of offerings, punctual and accurate delivery and professional logistics) while still offering attractive discount rates.

In the used car market, new information and delivery channels are creating more transparency, which makes it more difficult for dealers to realize attractive prices. In addition, the internet makes it easier for private individuals to trade directly.

New providers with aggressive pricing policies are likewise fuelling greater competition in other areas, such as car rental and other service segments.

Sales activities: an additional key to success

In light of all these challenges, it is increasingly important to pay more attention to sales as well as to costs and product offerings. Here, there is room for improvement on both the dealers' and the manufacturers' sides. Much of the existing sales system remains rigid and multi-tiered. Relationships between car makers and dealers have remained largely unchanged for a long time. Accordingly, there is plenty of potential for optimization.

Returns on investment in the car selling business are below the norm, trailing behind all other links in the automotive value chain. Whereas car makers' banks earned an average return on equity (ROE) of 16 per cent from financial services in 2004, the car makers themselves posted an ROE of 12 per cent. Even large component suppliers managed an average of 10 per cent, far more than the 4 per cent averaged by German dealers (sources: Autohaus, Bloomberg, Roland Berger's own analysis).

The return on sales in the automobile trade has been in constant decline since the 1970s. The average return on sales netted by authorized dealers in Germany is now down to about 1 per cent. Nearly 30 per cent of dealers post losses (see Figure 6.5). Nevertheless, Roland Berger Strategy Consultants' project experience shows that greater professionalism and structural improvements can add at least one or two percentage points to dealers' operating profits (relative to sales).

Percentage of dealers [%]

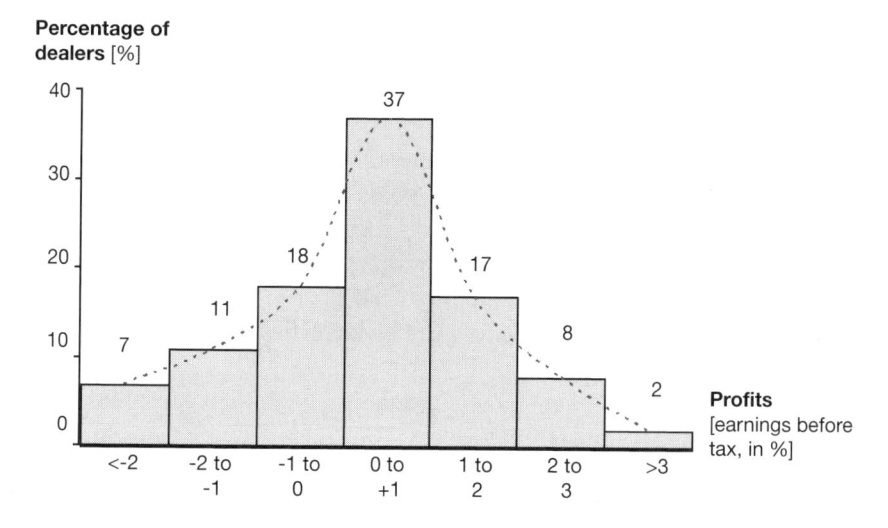

Bracket	%
<-2	7
-2 to -1	11
-1 to 0	18
0 to +1	37
1 to 2	17
2 to 3	8
>3	2

Profits [earnings before tax, in %]

Figure 6.5 *Distribution of dealers' profits based on the example of Germany, 2004 (percentage of dealers in each bracket)*
Source: Autohaus

Significant potential also remains to be tapped within manufacturers' own sales activities. Numerous projects performed by Roland Berger Strategy Consultants have improved per-vehicle earnings by €300 to €500. These gains can be achieved primarily by boosting administrative efficiency on the wholesale level, and by providing better support to authorized dealers in order to optimize market penetration.

The sections that follow analyse key levers to tap these potential improvements in sales activities. To begin with, we shall examine the principal success factors in **systematically identifying and addressing customers' needs**. The next step is to find ways to **break down the barriers inherent in the traditional sales system**. Once we have discussed the issue of who gains strategic control of the sales channel, the final section looks ahead to **future trends and developments in sales**.

UNDERSTANDING THE CUSTOMER: A KEY SUCCESS FACTOR

As customer behaviour changes and competition intensifies, understanding customers and the structure of their needs becomes an ever more vital ingredient in business success.

In this context, companies must accurately define their target groups, the value propositions linked to their brands and the positioning of those brands. Only then can they consistently focus their product and service offerings to the specific needs of their target groups throughout the entire sales trajectory, right down to the point of sale.

The following key success factors can be identified:

- detailed knowledge of customers' needs;
- exact definition of the target group;
- clear definition of the brand's value proposition and positioning;
- sharp focus on the value proposition of, and target group for, product and service offerings;
- consistent implementation at all stages in the selling process;
- professional communication with customers throughout, down to the point of sale in the car showroom.

Traditional forecasting models are out; value-based strategies are in

With all these success factors identified, one major challenge is to operationalize customers' needs and the brand's value proposition. Since traditional customer segmentation is breaking up and customer behaviour is becoming more difficult to predict, a value-based strategy is now required. Conventional models that forecast consumer behaviour solely on the basis of social background and income no longer give accurate guidance.

That is why Roland Berger Strategy Consultants developed 'RB Profiler', a tool that models the structure of needs and values in a clear, understandable way. Using 19 key values, it is possible to segment customers on the basis of their preferences and aversions, but also based on their perception of brand positioning (see Figure 6.6).

The Mini is a good example of the benefits of this kind of value-based strategy. A clear notion of the specific target group to which this car would appeal was critical to its market success. Accordingly, both brand and product had to be positioned very precisely.

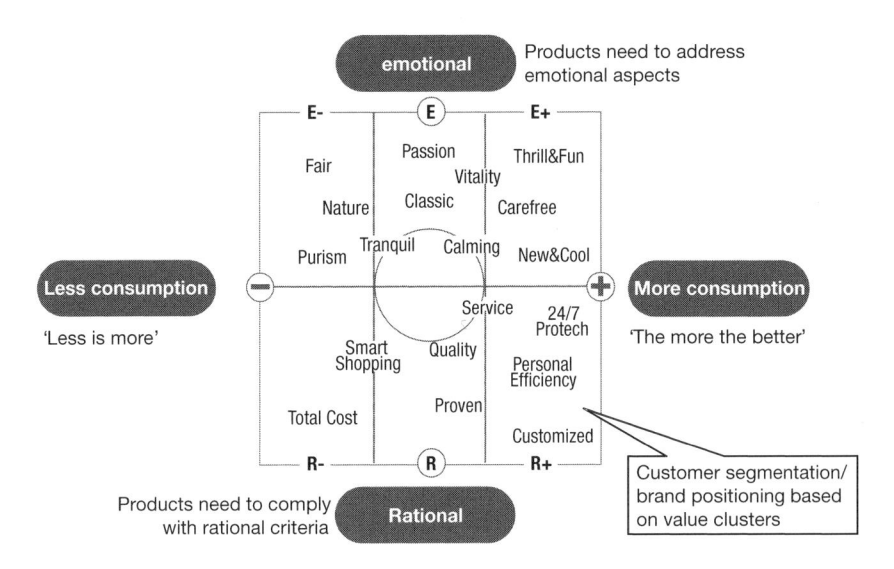

```
                        emotional        Products need to address
                                         emotional aspects
              E-           E            E+
                    Passion      Thrill&Fun
              Fair         Vitality
                  Nature  Classic  Carefree
                      Tranquil  Calming
                  Purism              New&Cool
Less consumption  ─               ─  + More consumption
                            Service   24/7
'Less is more'              Quality   Protech   'The more the better'
                      Smart            Personal
                      Shopping         Efficiency
                              Proven
                    Total Cost
                                    Customized
              R-           R            R+
     Products need to comply   Rational        Customer segmentation/
     with rational criteria                    brand positioning based
                                                on value clusters
```

Figure 6.6 *Key values in the RB Profiler model*
Source: Roland Berger Strategy Consultants

Based on such a clear-cut definition, manufacturers can collaborate with dealers to set the direction of their product and service strategy. This approach ensures that customers' needs are addressed consistently at all levels including to the point of sale, a strategy designed to attract and retain potential buyers (see Figure 6.7).

For premium manufacturers, for example, it is important to create an exclusive setting that lines up perfectly with the brand values the company wishes to communicate. This includes elegant rooms in which customers can talk privately with well-trained staff. It involves high-class presentations of seat covers and wood panelling, evocative of a quality tailor cutting a suit to measure. It means presenting maintenance work in an atmosphere reminiscent of hand-made production, caring for vehicles in specially designed car wash systems, and so on. Similarly, car dealers that sell low-cost ('value') automobiles can powerfully underscore their profile as price leaders precisely by crafting a rigorously purist ambiance that eliminates gimmicks and peripheral elements. Another crucial aspect is that the behaviour and communication of the entire sales and service team must fully match the image presented at the point of sale.

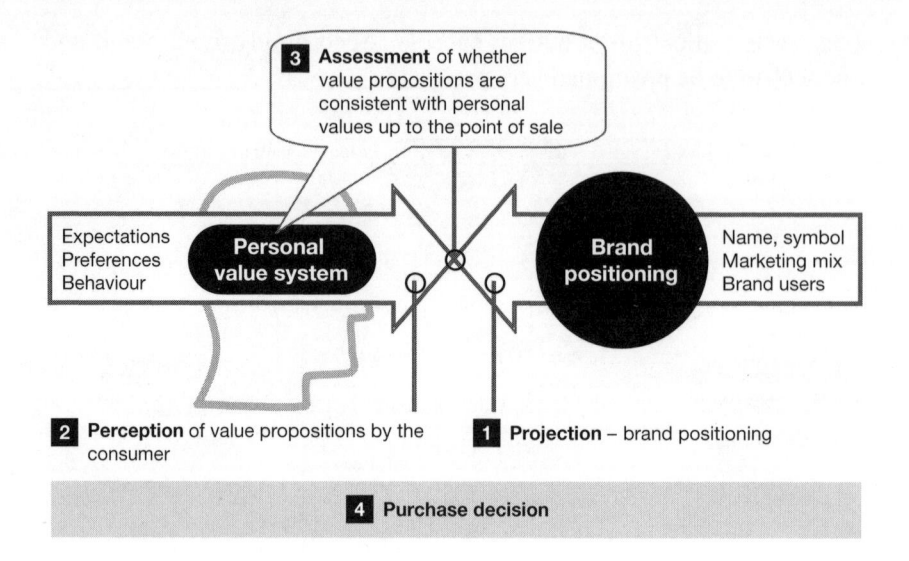

Figure 6.7 *Value assessment and consistent brand positioning*
Source: Roland Berger Strategy Consultants

End-to-end CRM systems: an important success factor

Another important tool to help translate an understanding of customer needs into new business or more loyal customers is a powerful customer relationship management (CRM) system. Careful customer targeting that consistently 'fulfills customer needs' can open up vast reserves of acquisition and cross-selling potential throughout the customer and vehicle lifecycle. Especially in the automotive industry, customer loyalty is rated as one of the most vital success factors.

From the vendor's point of view, the main functions of CRM programmes are to facilitate long-term customer loyalty across multi-year purchase cycles, and to reinforce the brand image.

Customer loyalty programmes are becoming increasingly widespread in the automotive industry. Bonus programmes, customer cards and customer clubs are frequently used as elements of CRM strategies. Compared with other sectors such as airlines, hotels, service stations and department stores, however, the use of these programmes is still at a relatively early stage.

Alongside these programmes, car makers have already invested substantial amounts of money in CRM systems and customer care centres, yet the results have so far failed to live up to expectations. One main reason for this failure is that neither information nor processes flow seamlessly between manufacturers and dealers. The rigid structures of today's sales systems still prevent market players from truly understanding their customers, identifying them systematically, winning their custom and retaining it in the long term. These limitations must be recognized and overcome.

OVERCOMING THE LIMITATIONS OF TODAY'S SALES SYSTEMS

Existing sales systems still contain glaring structural deficits and effectively prevent manufacturers and dealers from tapping the full market potential. The core problem is the rigid, multi-tiered sales structure that involves manufacturers, wholesalers, dealers and in some cases subsidiary dealers or service companies. This structure makes it difficult for delivery, service and information processes to flow smoothly from end to end. Improvements can be made on all three levels: the manufacturers' level, the wholesale level and the dealers' level.

Potential for improvement on all levels of the existing sales system

Many auto makers still focus too narrowly on production and model portfolios. Rather than rigorously aligning everything they do with customer needs and current demand, they run expensive special offer campaigns to encourage the market to soak up overcapacity. Offers launched in the context of employee discount campaigns on the US market in the summer of 2005 provide a graphic illustration. In early summer 2005, GM rolled out an extremely aggressive programme in the United States, offering every potential car buyer the chance to buy a broad selection of the model range at GM-internal rates. Rivals were forced to respond in kind. When GM's sales leapt 47 per cent in June, Ford and Chrysler followed suit in early July and also made their internal-rate discounts available to all customers. These two vendors also saw their July sales surge by 25 per cent. It is, however, extremely questionable whether people were actually buying more rather than just buying earlier. Promotions of this kind often adversely impact brand image. Perhaps worse still, customers' higher expectations with regard to realizable discounts can erode the profitability of current and future models for a long time to come.

Although many auto makers have integrated the wholesale level in the larger markets, the traditional principle of 'one country, one company' remains generally valid. Hub models, in which geographically and socio-culturally related countries merge to form a single organization, are still few and far between in the car industry. Many smaller markets are still served by importers, who tend to use either the same elaborate processes and systems as are operated in larger markets, or very rudimentary solutions. Cost disadvantages result, and managing these systems is difficult because of substandard support functions. Cross-border synergies and opportunities to run a more professional operation are often squandered.

Like the manufacturers' level and the wholesale level, the dealers' level too still exhibits structural deficits. Especially in Europe, countless efforts to restructure networks have left the market as fragmented as ever, as is shown by a comparison with the United States (see Figure 6.8). Failure to reach critical mass thus prevents companies from pursuing professional marketing strategies and reaping economies of scale.

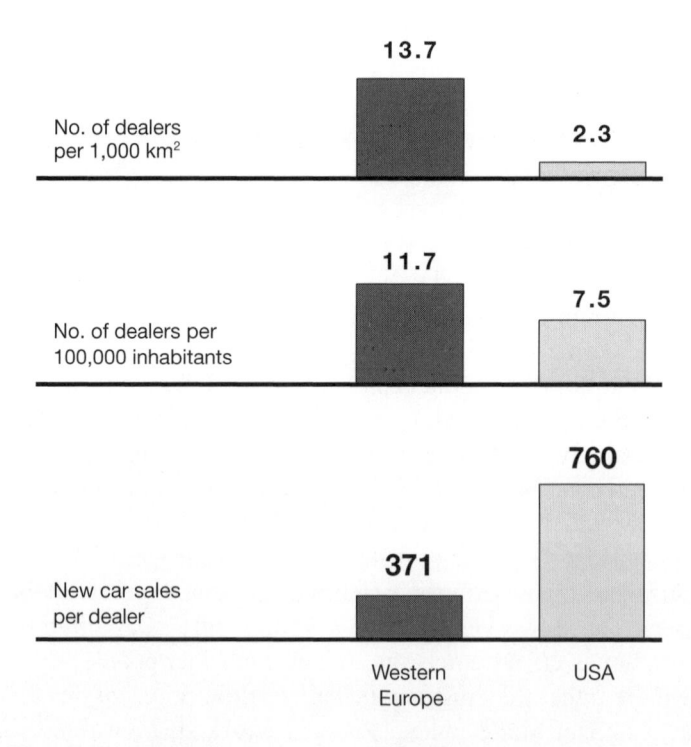

	Western Europe	USA
No. of dealers per 1,000 km²	13.7	2.3
No. of dealers per 100,000 inhabitants	11.7	7.5
New car sales per dealer	371	760

Figure 6.8 *Structure of dealer networks in Western Europe and the United States, 2003*
Sources: Roland Berger Strategy Consultants; HWB; Automotive News, Ipeadata; IBGE; Fenabrave

Unsatisfactory earnings often inhibit necessary investments both in point-of-sale presentations that do justice to the brand and in technical infrastructure. Many dealers thus find themselves trapped in a vicious circle. All manufacturers' margin systems naturally include fixed margins and volume bonuses, but they also include significant spreads for compliance with defined quantitative and qualitative standards. Standards to ensure that a company supports the brand image are one example. Other criteria include the availability of demonstrators, specifications for sales workplaces, participation in dealer benchmarking exercises, the size and nature of showroom space, and attendance on mandatory training courses. Depending on the particular car maker, authorized dealers can increase their margins by up to seven percentage points by meeting these standards. However, if meagre earnings prevent them from investing what can be substantial sums of money, they forfeit a significant share of their margin. Earnings deteriorate further, leaving even less room for investment. This negative feedback system leads to further inadequacies.

The bottom line is that the sales systems often in place today need to become much more effective and much more efficient – despite the fact that car makers and dealers alike have already done a lot to overcome the limitations of these systems.

Limited success for optimization programmes to date

Manufacturers have indeed pumped huge sums into sales and dealerships. First and foremost, they have set up their own outlets to reinforce brand identity. They have restructured sales networks to improve dealer quality, and they have integrated wholesale activities in order to improve market access.

Auto makers invest hundreds of millions in their own outlets and brand experiences to give a lift to the presence of their brand in metropolitan areas. According to press reports, BMW, for instance, is spending some €100 million on BMW World, the new delivery centre at its headquarters in Munich. Meanwhile, DaimlerChrysler is spending €250 million on new premises in Stuttgart which feature an adjacent automobile museum.

Practically all car companies have been restructuring their sales networks for years. In 2000, 53,000 main dealers ran a total of 106,000 sales outlets in Western Europe. By 2004, the numbers had shrunk to 43,000 dealers (a decline of almost 20 per cent) and 74,000 outlets (a decline of 30 per cent; source: HWB). Such adjustments cost manufacturers a great deal of money, most of which goes on taking back vehicles and parts, and especially in Germany, on compensating now-redundant dealers (pursuant to Section 89b of the German Civil Code (HGB)). In addition, where network adjustment involves recruiting new, more professional dealers, the car makers also have to pay investment support and increase their marketing budgets to launch the new dealerships. A Roland Berger project illustrates just how much investment is needed: in one European market, a car maker spent over €150 million to cut 20 per cent of its 600 sites, while enrolling new dealers to enable the leaner network to increase its market share.

In the wake of the Block Exemption Regulation, manufacturers have also invested in integrating independent importers to maximize their access to core European markets. These firms have spent considerable sums to buy outright or acquire a majority interest in previously independent importers.

These realignment programmes call for substantial resources, but still usually happen within the boundaries of traditional sales systems. Genuine innovations – strategies that break the rules, that optimize sales from top to bottom by reshuffling roles and improving the integration of dealers, wholesalers/importers and auto makers – have so far been the very rare exception. Brand values are not communicated and transformed consistently all along the line to the point of sale. In many cases, products and services simply do not harmonize. Nor is it unusual for poorly coordinated strategies to cultivate contradictory perceptions among customers. Actions taken by different sales partners do not complement each other, but actually tend to cancel each other out – or even have a negative impact.

If companies spend huge sums on spectacular showrooms but then populate these with ill-qualified sales and service staff at the point of sale, customers perceive this dissonance and begin to see where processes are not really working. A brand claim loses its credibility the moment the salesperson fails to embody the brand values or inadequately explains the products and services. The same thing happens when Customer Service misses a fault because it uses obsolete diagnostic systems, or when repair shop customers have to wait for replacement parts that are out of stock.

Ultimately, even the redeployment of resources in sales has not yielded the improvements that are still possible. Inefficient processes and structures hinder smooth collaboration between partners at different points in the sales trajectory. Yet considerably more potential could be tapped if the sales system was remodelled from the ground up. The question is, how should the various market players go about driving the change process? There are inevitably conflicts of interest between auto companies, wholesalers/importers and dealers. The crucial issue will therefore be who gains strategic control as the 'sales power play' unfolds.

POWER PLAY IN SALES: WHO WILL GAIN CONTROL?

Manufacturers have traditionally exercised significant control over sales in the automotive industry. Although the majority of sales partner organizations were independent, the Block Exemption Regulation laid the foundations for this control for a protracted period. For a long time, the large number of small partners in the market prevented dealers from becoming a strong counterweight, and thus from taking control of the delivery channel. Now, however, deregulation and increasing concentration among dealers is rewriting the rules.

Sales operations must therefore ask themselves a number of key questions about the future:

- Can dealers gain control of the delivery channel?
- What steps will car makers take to defend or even improve their position?
- Will new players gain a foothold in automotive sales in future?

Dealer power

The process of concentration among dealerships raises the question whether car dealers are poised to gain more power and follow a similar path to the one already travelled by, for example, the consumer goods industry. Concentration in the German food retail industry, for example, has been extreme in recent decades. The five largest food chains have increased their share of total sales nearly threefold, to almost 70 per cent, over the past 25 years. By comparison, concentration in the automotive retail industry is very much weaker, in all European markets. While the UK's top five car dealer groups can at least boast a 14 per cent market share, the corresponding figure is 6 per cent in France and 4 per cent in Spain. In Germany, the five largest dealer chains account for a mere 3 per cent of the total new vehicle market.

Concentration will nevertheless continue in this industry. Indeed, it is likely to accelerate to enable companies to realize economies of scale. At present, the car-selling industry is consolidating in two directions: towards internationalization and towards multi-brand sales.

Large dealer groups are enlarging their footprint by acquiring companies at home and abroad. Some, like the Weller Group in Germany, are focusing on national and regional purchases. Pan-European and even global acquisitions are becoming increasingly widespread, however.

Pendragon, a retail group of British origin, has bought on a massive scale in its home market, and has also been acquiring dealerships in Germany and the United States since 1990. By the end of 2004, the company had acquired 12 US and 10 German operations on top of its 244 UK-based dealers.

Porsche's Austrian holding company has been pursuing a similar internationalization strategy, and today operates in 15 European countries. When Eastern Europe opened up, the Porsche holding company became a wholesaler (importer) in Hungary, Slovakia, Slovenia, Croatia, Romania, Serbia-Montenegro, Bulgaria, and more recently in Albania and Macedonia. In these countries, as in the Czech Republic, Germany and Italy, the Porsche holding company also runs sales outlets exclusively for brands belonging to the VW Group. Its involvement in Western Europe dates back to wholesale activities with niche brands that began in France in the mid-1970s. The move into retail sales came when an equity stake in France's PGA was acquired in 1999. This was followed by acquisition of an interest in the Nefkens Group in 2001 and the purchase of CICA, a French company, a year later. One PGA subsidiary also runs an operation in Poland. The story does not end there, however. In mid-2005, the company also entered the Chinese market, where it is now selling vehicles in a pilot project.

This kind of strategy can yield scale advantages in all parts of the business. In the new vehicle segment, higher sales strengthen the company's demand position in relation to auto makers. Bundling inventories and centralizing vehicle preparation harbour huge potential for new cars and demonstrators, and even more so for used cars. These practices also make it possible to standardize the valuation and pricing of used cars. After-sales operations can leverage higher volume target agreements and realize substantial potential by centralizing capacity for coachwork and paintwork repairs, as well as for parts logistics. Indirect savings can also be achieved by bundling corporate functions such as management, accounting and human resources.

Alongside regional expansion, a discernible trend toward multi-brand sales is being driven by customers and dealers alike. A study by Roland Berger Market Research found that 69 per cent of auto buyers prefer to be able to compare different brands under one roof. Dealers are equally enthusiastic about multi-brand sales: 47 per cent of single-brand dealers intend to add at least one more brand to their portfolio. A further 24 per cent are still undecided, but are considering a similar course of action.

Multi-brand strategies can enable dealers to exploit a wide range of synergies. In the new car business, broader market coverage and a more balanced spread of end-customer risk are the key market-side advantages. The option of offering and managing mixed fleets is a further source of potential in relation to small and mid-sized corporate customers. Bundling used car business across a number of brands likewise lets dealers offer a wider choice and opens substantial potential to improve inventory management. Earnings can be further optimized by bundling demand for identical parts across brands, and by making better use of repair shop capacity. Finally, overheads can be lowered by organizing management, accounting and other administrative tasks across brands too.

Larger multi-brand groups are generally able to translate economies of scale into higher earnings, as can be seen from comparisons of large, publicly traded mega-retailers with the average of retailers in the UK.

Multi-brand groups do not restrict their business models solely to traditional retail sales, however. The example of the Dutch-based Kroymans Group is indicative of their innovative expansion strategies. This auto dealer group now has a presence in 27 European countries, in which it sells 17 brands. Kroymans' focus is on GM and Ford. Its total new car sales volume came to 60,000 units in 2005. Besides expanding its array of retail outlets, the company is also making inroads into the financial services sector. It has set up its own leasing companies in Belgium, the Netherlands and Luxembourg, and is currently launching internet-based leasing service providers in Germany.

Furthermore, the Dutch group is now the sole European wholesale distributor for GM's Cadillac, Corvette and Hummer brands. In return, GM is injecting some US $25 million into Kroymans to help fund its planned growth. This is the first time that an auto maker has outsourced its entire European sales operation for a given brand – and the result is a classic win–win situation. Kroymans now has the chance to expand further and add to its market muscle. For its part, GM now has a powerful partner with a professional market image, but can also reduce its management costs and contain its financial risks. Not content to commit only to GM, Kroymans is also collaborating with Alfa Romeo, and secured the distribution rights for this brand too in the Netherlands in mid-2005.

As we have seen, the process of concentration will continue in the car selling business in the years ahead. Even taking a medium-term horizon of 5 to 10 years, however, car dealers will not attain the strength that their peers in the consumer goods industry have achieved. There are several reasons for this. The investment bill will be very high indeed. Multi-brand sales runs the risk of diverting rather than growing business. In addition, the product, service and process levels will all become more complex. For concentration to progress to the stage we have seen in consumer goods retail, each of the five largest German dealer groups would, for example, have to increase its new car sales from 20,000 or so today to an annual average of 400,000. Growth by a factor of 20 does not appear realistic.

The auto makers strike back

The car makers are also doing their utmost to consolidate their strategic competitive position in sales. Almost all manufacturers have already taken steps to launch their own outlets. Premium providers in particular, but also French volume producers have applied themselves to making this strategy work. Their primary objectives are to gain more control over end customers at the point of sale and to improve the way they present their brands. Especially in the larger cities, exorbitant land and rental charges often prevent non-captive dealers from running a profitable business.

However, not all manufacturers will successfully build up the core competencies they would need in the retail discipline. High start-up costs and heavy capital tie-up will probably cause the number of car makers' own outlets to stagnate or dwindle (see Figure 6.9).

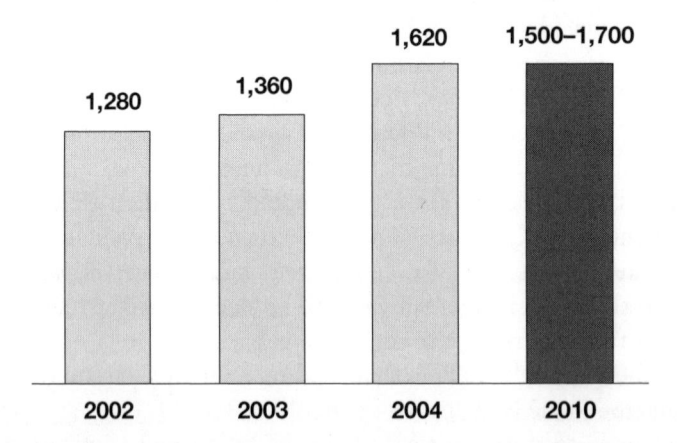

2002	2003	2004	2010
1,280	1,360	1,620	1,500–1,700

Figure 6.9 *Trend in the number of car makers' own outlets, 2002–10 in Western Europe (number of sites)*
Sources: Roland Berger Strategy Consultants, HWB

Auto companies are trying to use CRM activities (building call centres, for example, and establishing customer clubs and cards) to strengthen their direct contact with end customers. They are pursuing exactly the same goal in expanding their range of financial services to include credit cards, savings deposits, investment funds, savings plans for new vehicles, and even non-vehicle insurance. Volkswagen is going so far that it wants to become its customers' main bank. In keeping with this objective, it is marketing the entire spectrum of banking products, from current accounts to mortgages. BMW also recently announced its intention to systematically expand its portfolio of financial services.

At the same time, seizing the opportunity afforded in Europe by the new Block Exemption Regulation, car makers are seeking to gain greater control over sales by setting high standards for dealers.

New players in the market

In the past, new players have repeatedly emerged in the car sales business. The pioneers have mostly been consumer goods retail chains such as EDEKA, KarstadtQuelle and Tchibo in Germany, and Tesco in the UK. However, no dealers from outside the car industry have yet made a lasting success of such ventures. The examples we have seen suggest that customers are not enamoured by such providers and sales formats. Most of these players are unable to foster sufficient trust in their after-sales support capabilities in the event of warranty claims, or of goodwill claims when warranty expires. This is because most of these formats revolve around brokering models or pure sales promotions. Limited sales success and the one-off nature of the campaigns held by EDEKA and Tchibo, for example, paint a clear picture. Mastering the vast complexities of this business – ensuring that car sales, maintenance, replacement parts services, other services, and the return and marketing of used cars work smoothly together – demands a huge investment. Accordingly, players from outside the industry tend to shy away. Low margins, sizeable investments, heavy capital tie-up and the cyclical nature of the automotive business should be enough to keep new rivals from the door in future.

To summarize, we can expect that both dealers and auto makers will step up their efforts to tap new veins of value potential in the sales process. New competitors from outside the industry will remain a peripheral phenomenon.

Partnership promises greater success than running battles to control sales

When pondering whether dealers or manufacturers will come out of this power play on top, it is worth thinking back to the key success factors with which we started out. Understanding what customers need and translating brand values into unmistakable products and services are fundamental core competencies for car makers, but they are equally vital to successful sales. Applying such product and service competence consistently throughout the sales chain demands an uncompromising commitment to customer, sales and service orientation – all of which are the traditional strengths of dealers. If the complementary competencies of dealers and auto makers can be interlocked smoothly, considerable value can be added as a result. This development is likely to be accelerated if car makers concentrate on their core competencies while dealers expand and become increasingly professional at what they do. In other words, there are compelling arguments to abandon the rivalry model and instead build the relationship between manufacturers and dealers on partnership and collaboration.

Toyota's activities on the German market illustrate this approach. In Germany, Toyota has a two-tiered sales network in which 140 main dealers operate 290 out of a total of 630 sales centres nationwide. The network also includes 70 dedicated service centres (figures valid at year-end 2005). The car company focuses on large, professional dealerships with which it works together as a partner. In 2004, for example, Toyota invested in a large-scale dealer coaching programme involving external support. Conducted for the 120 biggest dealers, this project applied a specially developed action list with the aim of improving dealers' performance.

The principle of having only one dealer in one city lines up with the strategy of minimizing intrabrand competition. In large metropolitan areas, Toyota's stated aim is to increase collaboration with large dealers and dealer groups.

Going a step further, Toyota also worked with the dealers' association to draw up a fair play charter in order to involve its B dealers to a greater extent. The charter makes recommendations on collaboration between A and B dealers. It covers such themes as passing on discounts, splitting the cost of marketing activities and agreeing volume targets. Both parties' behaviour is monitored in an ongoing evaluation process.

These and other elements are helping Toyota to translate its strategy into visible market success. In recent years, the company has continually enlarged its market share, which grew from 2.4 per cent in 1996 to 3.9 per cent in 2004. Since JD Power first published its CSI study in 2002, the

Japanese brand has consistently topped the customer satisfaction table. In 2005, Toyota models won the top slot in five of seven segments. Among dealers too, Toyota is the most popular brand in the large imported brands category and ranks fourth among all manufacturers (source: MarkenMonitor study, 2005).

Looking ahead to what the future holds for automotive sales, the key question is, what concrete implications can and must be drawn from the need for a stronger focus on partnership?

THE FUTURE FOR AUTO SALES: FROM SEPARATE TIERS TO INTEGRATED NETWORK

Critical examination of the sales system as it stands leads us to the following conclusion: rigid, multi-tiered structures and the charged atmosphere of conflict between car makers and dealers are two of the main causes of inefficiencies. Examples such as Toyota's professional collaboration with its dealers and the partnership that exists between Kroymans and GM lend considerable credibility to the claim that partnership can make both sides more effective and more efficient.

To return to our point of departure, it is useful to enquire whether, and to what extent, the insights gained from revectored manufacturer–supplier relationships can also be transposed onto sales dealerships. Interestingly, there are a number of obvious parallels between the manufacturer–component supplier interface and the manufacturer–dealer interface.

At both of these value chain interfaces, the large number of external partners is one important driver of complexity. Today, the average auto maker has something like 650 direct suppliers – down by almost half from 1,200 in the early 1990s. In the same period, manufacturers have likewise almost halved the number of interfaces to individual dealers. The absolute figure, however, is still significantly higher. In 2004, every brand still had an average of 1,300 main dealers throughout Europe. For the leading brands, this figure rises to just under 2,000 (source: HWB).

Heavy demands are placed on logistical processes at both interfaces. At the interface to component suppliers, the complete value chain has to be coordinated, from raw materials supplier through first-tier supplier to production by the manufacturer. Innovation, quality and cost targets and deadlines likewise have to be reconciled. At the interface to dealers, the main challenge derives from the multiplicity of new car, used car and parts/accessories processes. Owing to the large number of parts, storage, transportation and order processing in relation to vehicles and replacement parts are just as error-prone as the production process itself. Deficiencies in the logistical chain can thus have a devastating impact at either interface. One missing part can bring production of an entire vehicle to a standstill. Similarly, one replacement part that is out of stock can leave a defective car standing in the repair shop for an unacceptable period.

Innovation and technological advances present major challenges on both sides. Electronics is not only revolutionizing the component supply industry, its impact is also being experienced in after-sales service. In-vehicle electronic content is increasing all the time. According to a study by Roland Berger, electronic content accounted for 12 per cent of the value of a vehicle in 1995 and will rise to 32 per cent by 2015. This means that both manufacturers and suppliers must develop and expand their software expertise in this field. Their development processes must dovetail more exactly, and standardization must be advanced in order to overcome quality problems in the electronics sector. In after-sales, dealers must invest substantial amounts in modern diagnostic systems and in the expertise of their service staff, if electronic defects are to be remedied quickly and reliably. This investment is balanced out by additional sales potential, however, as standardized system architectures allow the latest electronic innovations to be installed in plug-and-play mode by dealers themselves during the vehicle lifecycle.

Both suppliers and dealers have an important part to play in communicating and fostering customers' perception of brand values. Suppliers contribute modules whose attributes are instrumental in shaping brand perception. They must therefore develop an in-depth understanding of how to translate abstract brand values into concrete products. Dealers are crucial to the way products and services are perceived at the point of sale. They thus play a pivotal role in ensuring that brand values are communicated consistently across all channels.

Applying lessons learnt in collaboration with suppliers to collaboration with dealers

It therefore makes sense to look at how manufacturers' relationships with the supply industry have been improved and successfully realigned, and to consider how the same might be done in relation to dealers. Larger, more professional dealerships could in future increasingly assume the role of systems integrators on behalf of manufacturers. Such first-tier dealers would shoulder development and management tasks for an entire economic area, and integrate smaller downstream sales and service centres (tiers 2 and 3).

A wide range of functions could be entrusted to dealers in this way. Physical distribution (parts shipments, vehicle stocks), aspects of dealer support (training, business management advice), a variety of control functions (enforcement/monitoring of standards) and the coordination of regional marketing efforts are all possible candidates. Such arrangements would ease the burden on car makers by reducing the number of interfaces to direct partners. Quality could be improved by collaborating more closely with system partners. This structure should also yield tangible cost benefits. Since systems integrators in the dealer network could handle various functions from a position of closer proximity to the market, auto makers could reduce their own capital tie-up. This would allow them to concentrate on developing innovative sales and service strategies, improving the communication of brand values at the point of sale, and raising the quality of sales and service. To optimize the management and care of larger and increasingly international dealerships, the sales organization too should be reviewed. An international key account organization to serve dealer groups could effectively complement – or even replace – the heavily decentralized field service organizations that exist today.

From static multi-tiered model to dynamic network

Closer collaboration with a smaller number of better-quality partners is one way forward. Another is to dissolve rigid sales tiers and transform them into more flexible networks. In strategic sales regions, this would permit dealers to assume a more prominent role, while systems integrators could play a greater part in providing comprehensive geographic coverage.

At the wholesale level, the one-dimensional tradition of having one sales company per country can be overcome by centralizing functions or distributing them across regional hubs. Only those functions that genuinely constitute local unique selling points (USPs) would have to be based on site in the relevant countries or regions. Many industries already think along these lines. Leading players in the consumer goods industry have revectored their European wholesale stratum into multi-country hubs scattered across three to seven regions. These hubs mostly centralize administrative tasks such as finance, control and IT, alongside key account management, marketing strategy, business development, sales support and logistics. By contrast, decentralized organizations are set up for front-line activities such as sales operations and operational marketing activities. Sufficient proximity to the market and superior process quality are the key drivers for such models, which must also optimize cost efficiency. Introducing this kind of hub model can cut overhead costs by up to 40 per cent.

The model is not yet widely represented in the automotive industry, yet the first tentative beginnings are already discernible. One leading German car maker began building a hub in northern Europe in 2004 and soon plans to apply the same model to an Eastern European region. A Japanese OEM implemented the model as far back as 1999 and now has three regional hub organizations that run its European wholesale operations. A number of crucial criteria must be borne in mind when forming such clusters or hubs. Homogeneous customer preferences, regional proximity, cultural and/or language barriers, the level of local economic development, market size and competitive position must all be taken into account. Intelligently designed hub strategies will have similar effects to those in other industries. Process quality will improve on the wholesale level. Internal knowledge will grow as expertise is bundled across multiple countries. Wholesale costs will be cut, and dealers will enjoy a better quality of support.

Outlook

So who will gain control in this new constellation of partnerships and networks? When competitive conflict gives way to constructive collaboration, control is no longer the focal issue. The result is a win–win situation. Like the process that the component supply industry has already experienced, it will take at least a decade before new business models take shape that adequately accommodate new requirements and share out benefits and burdens in an equitable manner. As the spider at the centre of the web, manufacturers have the chance to actively guide processes on the sales side too. However, if they fail to take action in the areas we have discussed, powerful dealer groups will take matters into their own hands and rewrite the rules of the game. In sales, as in other disciplines, size and market power merely create potential. Lasting success demands entrepreneurial creativity and fast execution, by either the car maker or the dealer.

7

The sales and after-sales challenge: capturing value along the car lifecycle

*Max Blanchet, Partner, and Jacques Rade, Principal,
Roland Berger Strategy Consultants*

In the automotive industry, the car is not the only automotive activity that generates revenues. Various activities related to the vehicle along its lifecycle, such as vehicle financing, maintenance and repair, used car buy-back and reselling activities, wholesale spare parts, as well as services, provide quite substantial revenues.

These activities do in fact generate higher profits than manufacturing vehicles. It is no secret that vehicle manufacturers, or original equipment manufacturers (OEMs), make almost 50 per cent of their profits from the spare parts business. A study, which could perhaps sound too simplistic, estimated the price of a car built from spare parts at roughly four times its new price. These additional sources of profit are of utmost importance for OEMs because they are linked to the pool of cars in use and not to new car sales, which are always subject to cycles or dependent on the success of new models. The cars in use provide greater financial stability, which is especially appreciated by the financial community and rating agencies. In a similar fashion, financial services are also highly profitable, driven more and more by the used car business and less by the sale of new cars.

172 *Major challenges*

THE AUTOMOTIVE VALUE CHAIN DURING THE CAR LIFECYCLE

The average return on capital (ROCE) employed in automotive-related activities throughout the lifecycle of a vehicle is 6 per cent, which is rather low compared with other industries manufacturing similar high-tech products. This is especially true when we consider that activities not related to new car sales contribute more strongly to the ROCE.

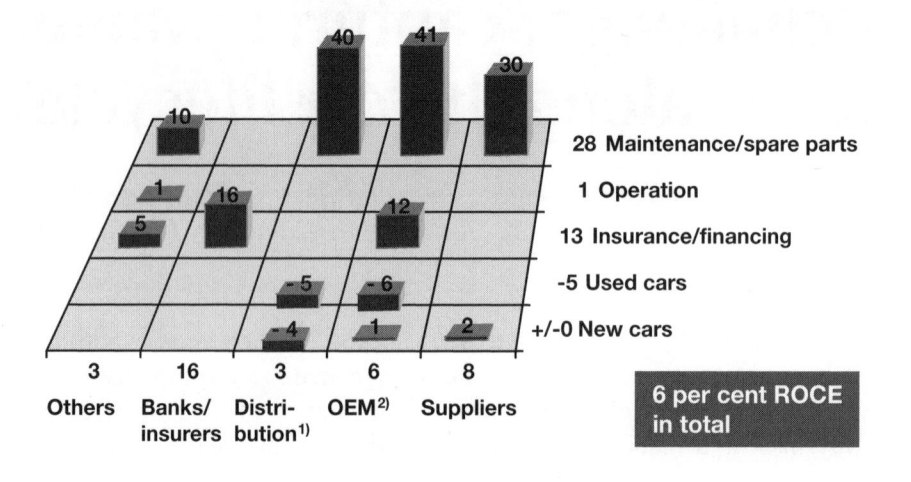

	Others	Banks/insurers	Distribution[1]	OEM[2]	Suppliers	
28 Maintenance/spare parts	10		40	41	30	
1 Operation	5	1 16		12		
13 Insurance/financing			-5	-6		
-5 Used cars			-4	1	2	
+/-0 New cars	3	16	3	6	8	

6 per cent ROCE in total

1) Including importers/distributors   2) Including subsidiaries

Figure 7.1 *Return on capital employed per vehicle in Europe (per cent)*
Source: Roland Berger Strategy Consultants

Profitability is somewhat unbalanced across activities and among players (Figure 7.1). The ROCE is high in all financing activities, in service and repair, and has been growing more recently in the used car business. These activities contribute strongly to the profitability of the overall market, and help compensate for the considerable capital required for developing new car models. Parts suppliers of products with high replacement volumes such as makers of wipers, tyres, filters and radiators benefit from this situation. This is not always true of original equipment suppliers (OES) that manufacture seats, roofs or dashboards, for instance.

In our analysis, the closer the activity is to the end-user, the higher the profitability. As a general trend, players that want to capture more value in the market are pursuing strategies aiming at involves moving closer to the final customers and strengthening ties with them.

For decades, this business model has operated in the European automotive market. As a result, the playing field has progressively reached a sort of equilibrium, with entrenched beliefs such as:

- 'Original parts are found in the OES channel, non-original parts in the independent aftermarket (IAM) channel.'
- 'Parts prices are set up by OEMs and are the indisputable reference in the market.'
- 'Recent vehicles are repaired in the OES channel, old vehicles in the IAM channel.'
- 'Used cars are cars with more than 30,000 kilometres on the clock.'
- 'Dealers are 100 per cent dependent on OEMs.'

When compared with other consumer goods sectors such as luxury goods and food, it becomes apparent how unique this situation is to the automotive market. Automotive sales and after-sales activities have historically been organized and managed using an 'offer-push' approach rather than 'customer-pull', because the customer's primary need is not driven by an emotional demand but rather by a necessity, namely to repair, maintain or get rid of a used car. In addition, the automotive product is unquestionably the most complex object sold in a mass production system.

A MARKET IN FLUX: MULTIPLE FACTORS ACCELERATE CHANGE

Profound changes have altered the contours of the market over the past five to eight years. In this changing environment, new rules have been introduced. While the new block exemption regulation (BER) has grabbed everyone's attention, partly because of the media spotlight on it, the actual impact of the BER has been rather limited. It is only one factor in a long list of issues changing the rules of the game. Other important factors include:

- Product technology and diversity: the increase in advanced technology, for example electronics, electromechanical systems and systems integration, together with the large diversity of models and brands, creates far greater complexity when it comes to managing after-sales activities.

- Car market evolution: the growing and ageing pool of cars that has emerged because of longer car lifecycles, third family cars and high adoption rates is changing the picture. For instance, the number of cars over 10 years old in Germany is growing at 3 per cent annually, and the number of seven to nine-year-old cars is growing at an annual 4 per cent in France and 10 per cent in Spain.
- Evolution of customer needs: customers' expectations regarding service quality, reliability and relationships are growing, largely encouraged by the experiences customers have gained with other services (banks, consumer goods and so on).
- Changes in consumer behaviour: the increase in professional vehicles (for example company cars and long-term rental), combined with the much wider and professional used car offer, is changing consumer behaviour.
- Regulatory changes: the BER is altering the automotive landscape especially for spare parts, but so too is Eurodesign, which threatens design-proprietary parts.
- 'Specialized prescriber groups': the growing influence of insurance companies and associations such as Thatcham, and rating institutes like Euro NCAP and JD Power, also affects the market.
- Europeanization: the creation of the EU-25 raises questions about how to address the additional countries with the leanest distribution costs, how to avoid grey markets, and so on.
- Channel consolidation: large dealer groups (especially in the UK and France) are garnering a huge market share; consolidated IAM wholesalers, large affiliated and networked repairers and large fleet management companies now command clout.
- New entrants: retail store chains have been viewed as potential new entrants, but entry barriers are too high. The real new entrants are banks and financial institutions, leasing and fleet management companies. These players are keen to acquire a share of this attractive market.

In this chapter, the OES channel stands for the brand distribution channels of OEMs. This includes for instance OEMs' affiliates, dealers and agents. The IAM channel stands for the independent after-market, which includes wholesalers, fast-fitters, repairers and body-shop networks.

THREATS AND OPPORTUNITIES INCREASE FOR MARKET PLAYERS

In this changing environment, all automotive players face risks relating to their current business model, but opportunities also abound. The risks faced by OEMs include losing a sizeable chunk of their spare parts business to distribution partners, and having financial services revenues fall into the hands of non-automotive players, especially in the used cars business. Technology is one area where opportunities exist for OEMs to capture and retain customers.

IAM wholesalers and repairers are in danger of missing the technological turning. For these players, opportunities exist in capturing the growth within the old car market, and by sourcing parts in low-cost countries. Fast fitters also face the difficulty of adapting their fast-fit business model to keep pace with the leaps and bounds taking place in technology, and to sidestep competition from OEMs.

The opportunities for large dealer groups stem from sourcing parts outside the OES channel, and acquiring new customers in the IAM channel.

Suppliers are confronted with threats arising from low-cost and non-OE suppliers, which offload so-called 'adaptable' products. They also face the risk of being locked out by OEMs and losing market access as a result of channel consolidation.

When insurers become more greatly involved in the spare parts business, profitability comes under threat, as insurers are looking to reduce the end-user part price.

Market players will have to adapt and redefine their business strategies as well as reshape their organization if they are to master these challenges. Should suppliers move downward in the distribution chain? Should large dealer groups step more expansively into the IAM wholesale business? Should insurers enter the wholesale parts business? Should fleet management companies increase their role in the repair and service business? These are just some of the most pressing questions market players have to consider.

Battles are being fought between various market players in the automotive sector to capture value along the vehicle lifecycle. The remainder of this chapter aims to show which players are likely to capture value and which are likely to lose out. The most important question concerns the captive (for example, OEM-owned) versus non-captive business model (for example, independent players), which is omnipresent along the value chain. All activities ranging from used cars and parts to general and financial services are sources of value from the

OEMs' captive solution, but also from alternative solutions provided by independent players.

Before we plot the key trends dominating the European market, the different activities related to vehicles such as fleet management, the used car business, repair and service, spare parts and financial services will be investigated.

DEMAND EVOLVES: PROFOUND SHIFTS REDEFINE THE MARKET RULES

New cars: from product to mobility

Fleets: a growing intermediary between OEMs and the final customer

The professional car segment, the so-called fleet market, has developed significantly in Europe. The segment saw an average annual growth rate of 2.7 per cent between 1997 and 2001, and is likely to continue to grow at 3.2 per cent each year through 2007 (Figure 7.2).

Fleet market penetration

Country	2001	2007 estimate
Germany	57	48
UK	65	60
France	36	30
Italy	36	30
Spain	48	40

Fleet market development in Western Europe

Year	Value
1997	14.4
1998	14.8
1999	15.1
2000	15.4
2001	16.0
2002	16.5
2007e	19.3

CAGR +2.7% (1997–2001); CAGR +3.2% (2002–2007e)

CAGR = compound annual growth rate

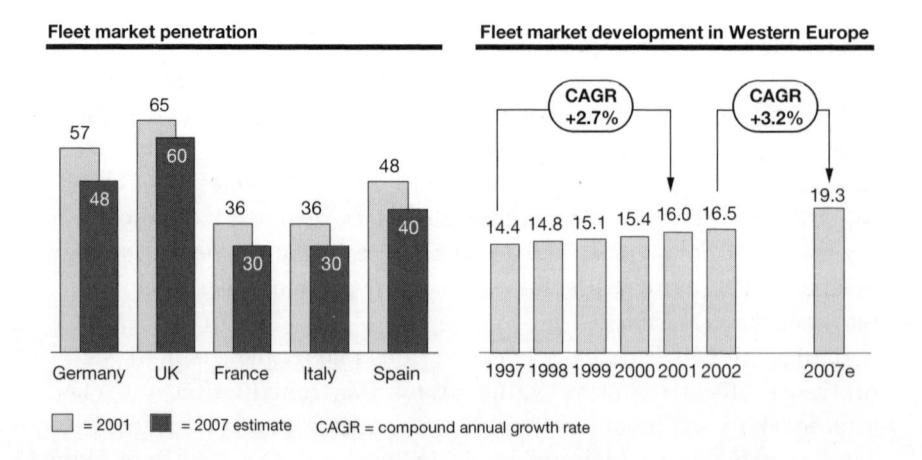

Figure 7.2 *Fleet market penetration and development in Europe (per cent)*
Source: Roland Berger Strategy Consultants

This development is powered by various factors including tax-related incentives. Vehicles increasingly form part of employees' salaries, company cars are being used more and more as an instrument to motivate employees, costs of mobility are rising, and customer attitudes towards leasing are changing.

The fleet segment is driven by traditional rental companies (short-term duration rental, or STD), administrative bodies and private companies, but also by long-term rental fleets (long-term duration contracts, or LTD).

New car sales can be split among different channels – direct sales, branches and dealers – and among various customer types – private, demo cars, STDs such as Hertz and Avis, companies' own fleets and leasers for LTD. The demo car segment, which consists of all vehicles purchased by OEMs for showrooms and dealers' services, accounts for a sizeable share of registrations (Figure 7.3).

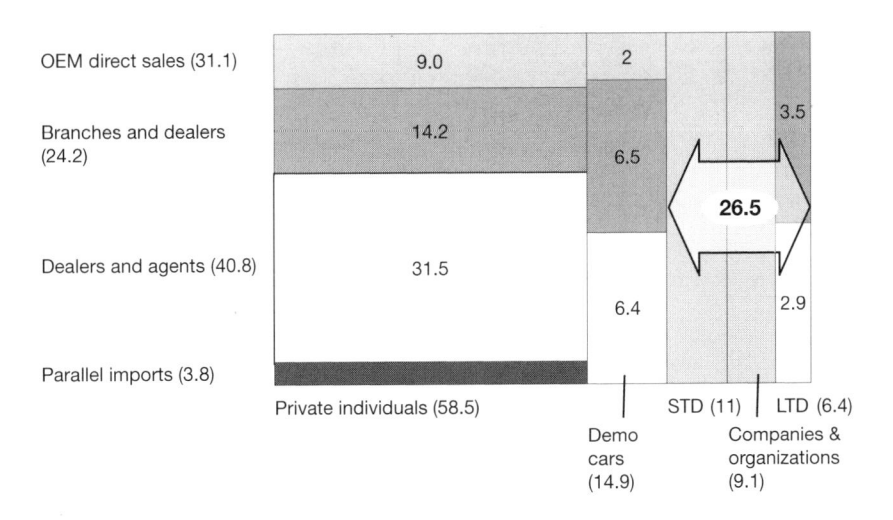

OEM direct sales (31.1)	9.0	2		
Branches and dealers (24.2)	14.2	6.5	26.5	3.5
Dealers and agents (40.8)	31.5	6.4		2.9
Parallel imports (3.8)				
	Private individuals (58.5)	Demo cars (14.9)	STD (11)	LTD (6.4)
			Companies & organizations (9.1)	

Figure 7.3 *Car registration mapping in France (per cent)*
Sources: Roland Berger Strategy Consultants, registration data 2003

This means that the share of professional customers among car buyers is expanding, creating a new type of intermediary between end users and car makers. The bargaining power of these intermediaries is intensifying. Professional customers are using their new-found clout to negotiate additional specifications and lower prices.

Full mobility service solutions tailored to specific needs

Compared with the private sector, the demands of fleet customers are becoming more specific, particularly when it comes to services expected, fleet management and maintenance.

This development is particularly true in the fast-growing LTD segment. The penetration of LTD rental among fleet customers is growing at between 8 and 10 per cent annually, with growth rates especially strong in the small and mid-sized fleet segment (Figure 7.4). LTD contracts often contain more services than their STD equivalents. Maintenance services are included in 90 per cent of long-term rental contracts, and tyre services are to be found in 80 per cent, for instance.

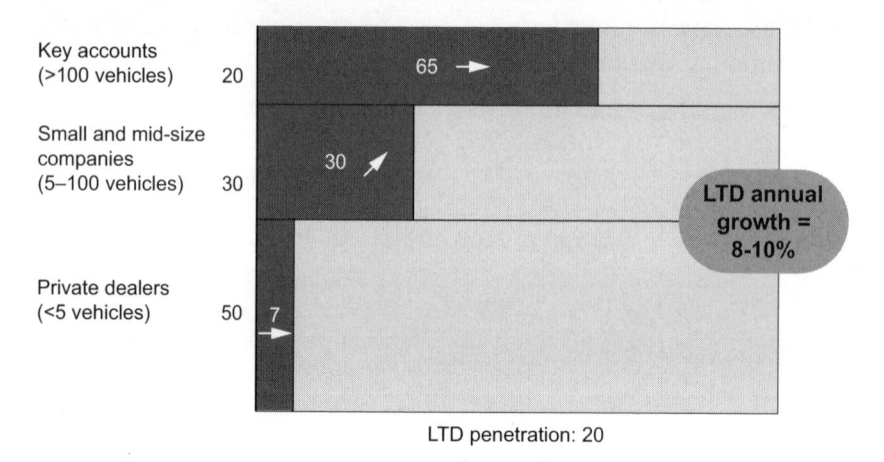

Segment	Share	LTD penetration
Key accounts (>100 vehicles)	20	65
Small and mid-size companies (5–100 vehicles)	30	30
Private dealers (<5 vehicles)	50	7

LTD annual growth = 8–10%

LTD penetration: 20

x% Penetration rate of LTD within each fleet segment in percent

Figure 7.4 *Penetration of LTD within each fleet segment (per cent)*
Source: Roland Berger Strategy Consultants

End-customers want greater freedom and mobility. Fleet management companies increasingly tend to demand *à la carte* services from OEMs and dealers to be able to meet customers' expectations and to stand out from the competition. These services include maintenance, insurance, flow management (buying, delivery, reselling) and fleet management. Leasing and fleet management companies are hunting out OEMs that can support them in their strategic development. They expect support, for example, in optimizing their geographical coverage, managing their spare parts and service contracts, and outsourcing technical support.

The 'user chooser' business model

Fleet management companies are also becoming more and more demanding when it comes to selecting the vehicles they want. In the UK, 34 per cent of fleets – the so-called 'user choosers' – give their customers total freedom when it comes to choice of vehicle. They do not keep to the standard practice of proposing a panel selection.

The 'user chooser' business model is radically changing the fleet business and transforming the relationship between fleet management companies and OEMs. Fleet management companies are no longer signing contracts with one or two OEMs with whom they have preferred conditions, but are behaving more like private customers, with much greater bargaining power.

In our opinion, fleet management companies will become a large customer segment, capturing a significant share of value along the automotive lifecycle. Fleet management companies are in a strong position to gain better services and more sophisticated offers from OEMs.

Fleet management companies are contributing to the development of new car sales, especially for expensive vehicles. Some high-range models are almost 100 per cent purchased by fleet management companies and no longer by private customers.

Used cars: a lever to regulate overcapacities

The 'nearly new car' system

A used car is by definition a car resold after a certain period of time or a certain mileage. Recent-model used cars are becoming increasingly important. Sales of used cars less than one year old have been growing at 6.2 per cent annually since 1998. This is almost twice as fast as the used car market as a whole, which at 3.9 per cent annually is already growing much faster than the new car market.

This trend is partly explained by the growing number of fleet management companies that resell recent vehicles, but a common practice called 'zero mileage vehicles' or 'nearly new cars' is also responsible for this development. Nearly new cars are registered by the dealers themselves and sold as used cars. This helps boost the dealers' official market share, and it enables them to sell new cars at a used car price, which is at 20 per cent discount, without making an apparent discount on new car prices. OEMs have encouraged this practice by giving STD fleets special deals. STD fleets are given incentives such as margins of 1 to 2 per cent to purchase vehicles for a period of six months, after which the vehicle is bought back by the OEM and resold as a used car.

A common practice among dealers and car makers is to purchase vehicles for showroom purposes and internal use, before reselling the vehicles with very limited mileage to customers. This is also pushing up the number of sales in the recent used car segment. These vehicles accounted for 11 per cent of new car registrations in Europe in 1999, and 15 per cent in 2003. This practice is especially prevalent in Germany, where 'zero mileage vehicles' have at times accounted for 25 to 30 per cent of new car registrations. This is facilitated by specific regulations that allow vehicles to be registered for an interim period of time, such as six months.

These 'flow regulation' levers have been used widely by many OEMs to boost their market share, which is measured by the number of car registrations. OEMs also use this mechanism to regulate the structural problem endemic in the European market, namely the overcapacity of new cars.

Professionalism increases in used car management

The used car business was once dominated by the private-to-private segment, helped along by various intermediaries such as specialized newspapers and the internet. In recent years, professional players have taken over this business activity. The OEMs and dealers especially understand that buying back old cars is necessary in order to sell new cars to customers. On average, 60 per cent of used cars are bought back from private customers and 40 per cent from fleet management companies or from OEMs (zero mileage). The share of the private-to-private segment is expected to decrease from 56 per cent in 1999 to 44 per cent in 2007, while OEMs' own subsidiaries and licensed dealers are likely to have captured 38 per cent of the market by this time (Figure 7.5).

The profitability of the used car business has risen significantly for distributors, and it is now making a real financial contribution to the overall profit and loss statements of distribution groups. What is also noticeable is the fast-growing share of used car brokers (+8.5 per cent annually) who buy used cars from dealers and/or agents and resell them to private customers.

'Nearly new cars' create a vicious circle

The professional management of the used car business – especially the 'nearly new car' practice – represents a risk for the overall industry. In short, it creates a vicious circle. The emergence of nearly new cars in the market with a discount of 20 per cent on the new car price creates unfair

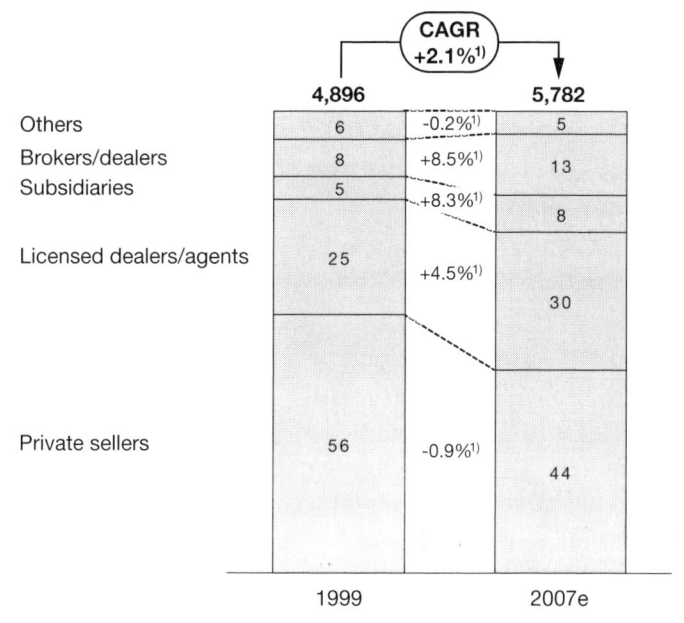

	4,896	CAGR +2.1%[1]	5,782
Others	6	−0.2%[1]	5
Brokers/dealers	8	+8.5%[1]	13
Subsidiaries	5	+8.3%[1]	8
Licensed dealers/agents	25	+4.5%[1]	30
Private sellers	56	−0.9%[1]	44
	1999		2007e

1) Based on underlying absolute figures

Figure 7.5 *Breakdown of used car sales by distribution channel (per cent)*
Sources: Observatoire de l'Automobile, CCFA, Roland Berger Strategy Consultants

competition for 'real recent used cars', which are also discounted by 20 to 25 per cent on new cars but have a mileage of 15,000 to 30,000 kilometres. This pulls down prices along the lifecycle and lowers the buy-back value. Since buy-back values are negotiated up-front by OEMs when selling to fleet management companies (that is, at the beginning of the period), this price reduction creates a depreciation trap for OEMs.

Several OEMs have been hamstrung by this vicious circle. To avoid falling into this trap, OEMs have to secure and control this activity better than before. OEMs especially have to control the way used cars flow into the market. They must leverage their Europe-wide network against regional and local distributors to create scale effect and synergies in the management of used car flows across Europe. A two-pronged approach is required: they should provide better service to customers while taking into account the used car price gap that exists across countries – for instance, a used Clio has a higher market price in Germany than in France. Renault, for instance, has managed to implement a European used car database to quickly check used car availability across different European countries.

Players active in the used car segment are capturing value. New cars are losing out as a result. The value captured by used cars is shared among more players than ever before. Dealers, agents, fleet management companies and brokers all take their share.

Repair and service: technology threat for the pool of six-to-nine-year-old cars

Customers demand greater reliability and better satisfaction

Customers have grown accustomed to increasing service quality, from booking flights to purchasing goods at a retail store, calling a telecoms operator or buying a service from a bank. Service quality can be expressed in manifold ways, including immediate availability, rapid response to requests, limited waiting time, special allowance for delays, high customer attention and fidelity tools. It has become a weapon in the arsenal of tools companies use to differentiate themselves from competitors. Service quality has become firmly embedded in the communication strategies of companies in various sectors. This can be witnessed by their clear commitments: a rail transportation company guarantees 'reimbursement after a one hour delay'; an appliance hard discounter commits itself by stating that 'we pay the price difference if you find it cheaper elsewhere'; and fast-food outlets guarantee a 'waiting time under 10 minutes'.

Improving customer experience is the underlying concept behind all these marketing campaigns. Every contact with the company must be an enjoyable experience for the customer. His or her satisfaction is what counts. Many companies, including state-owned enterprises and even government bodies, have sought out ways to improve customer experience for the services they provide.

Despite efforts made in the automotive distribution sector, service quality is still lacking compared with other industries, and customers' experiences could be improved. The nature of car distribution makes it difficult to monitor and improve interfaces with the customer: this is one reason that car distribution trails other sectors.

Customers' experiences with car distributors are rather complex, ranging from buying a new car to having it maintained and repaired. And the encounters are quite emotional. The buzz of repairing a car might be overshadowed by anxiety, and customers are never in a good mood when they have to leave their car at the repair shop. Additionally, the frequency of interactions with the customer is rather low. Customers do not go to their dealer every week. Furthermore, the fragmentation of distribution, which comprises OEM-owned dealers, contract dealers and agents, makes it difficult to implement the sort of standardized service quality procedures that have become standard at airlines and banks, for example.

However, customer experience is essential in improving the perceived value of the OEM's brand. Customers' purchasing intentions grow exponentially with the perceived value of the brand, meaning that a marginal increase in perceived value significantly increases the purchasing intent (Figure 7.6).

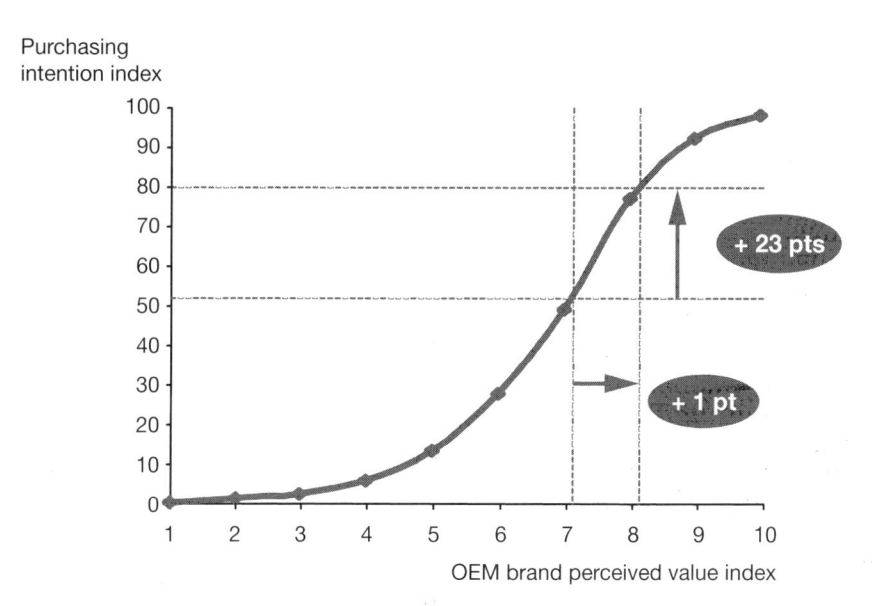

Figure 7.6 *Customers' purchasing intentions in relation to the perceived value of the brand*
Sources: Renault, Roland Berger Strategy Consultants

Once the product, the brand image and the costs are in line with customer needs, the quality of service received at the dealer or garage outlet strongly influences how the customer perceives the value of the OEM. It weighs in at around 40 per cent for customers who have already purchased a vehicle of the particular brand (Figure 7.7).

How can players in the automotive sector improve customers' experience? They must make the customer feel welcome, answer the phone quickly, inform the customer about what has been done to the car, give advice. They must ensure, for example, that the person who has checked out the vehicle after a repair is briefed and informed by the person who checked the car in. This enables consistent feedback about how the service has or has not met the client's expectations.

184 Major challenges

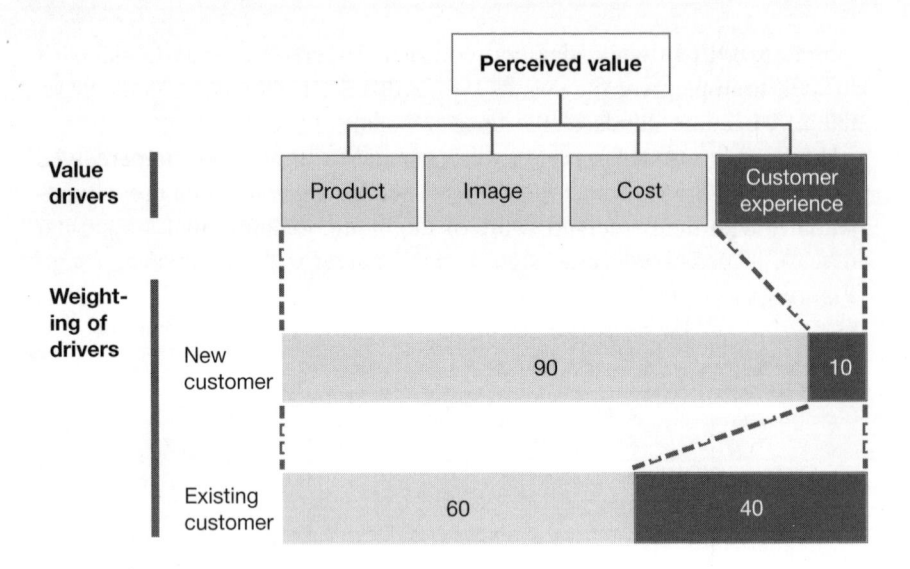

Figure 7.7 *Importance of customer experience in OEM perceived brand value (weighting of drivers in percentages)*
Sources: Renault, Roland Berger Strategy Consultants

What customers expect from repairers in terms of quality of service has increased in past years. Reliability and trust is the number one issue for customers. The importance of reliability has jumped considerably over the past decade, and it is now even more important than price (Figure 7.8).

Customers' repairer expectations (per cent)

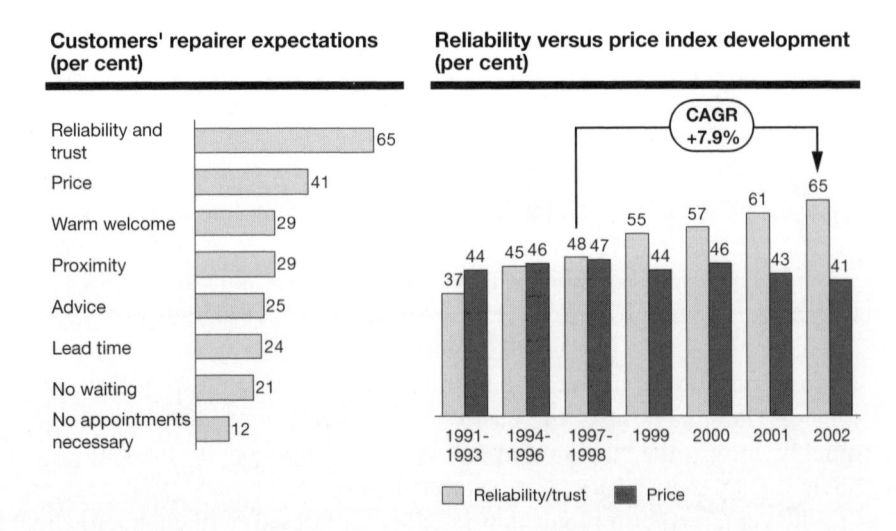

Expectation	%
Reliability and trust	65
Price	41
Warm welcome	29
Proximity	29
Advice	25
Lead time	24
No waiting	21
No appointments necessary	12

Reliability versus price index development (per cent)

CAGR +7.9%

Period	Reliability/trust	Price
1991–1993	37	44
1994–1996	45	46
1997–1998	48	47
1999	55	44
2000	57	46
2001	61	43
2002	65	41

Figure 7.8 *Importance of repairers' reliability and prices for customers*
Source: Roland Berger Strategy Consultants

This means that repair and maintenance players need to display greater professionalism if they are to capture and retain customers. Against this backdrop, it is likely that the OES channel and large branded repair networks will succeed, clawing market share away from independent outlets. The success of the fast-fitters can be attributed to their excellent service quality, standard procedures and codes of conduct – including dress code, clear commitments – 'no appointments' and quick service delivery.

The car market: the focus turns to the six-to-nine-year-old segment

The car repair and service expenditures profile is shifting along the car lifecycle. Expenditures on services including labour and spare parts are decreasing (Figure 7.9). More importantly, expenditures are shifting toward older vehicles. In the past, the maximum expenditure was spent on three-to-eight-year-old vehicles. Now, it is spent on six-to-nine-year-old vehicles.

Car service expenditure is decreasing and the maximum expenditure has shifted to six- to-nine-year-old vehicles

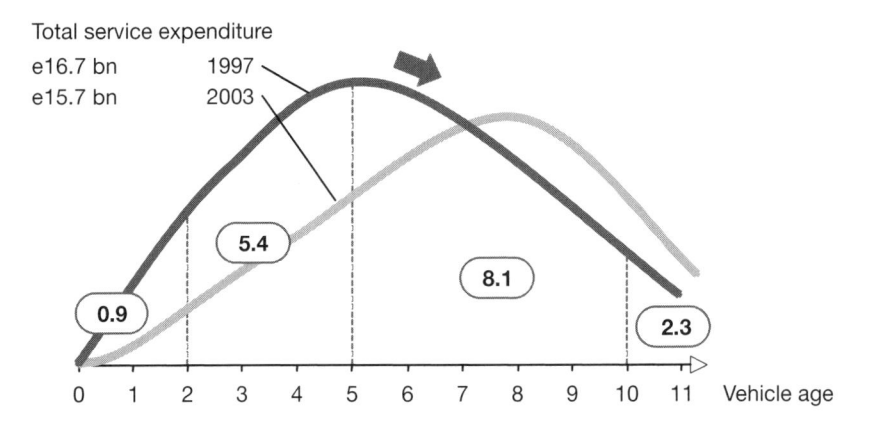

Total service expenditure
e16.7 bn   1997
e15.7 bn   2003

Figure 7.9 *Car service expenditures by vehicle age in France in 1997 and 2003 (in € billion, excluding tyres and lubricants)*
Source: Roland Berger Strategy Consultants

Several factors explain this trend. These include the increase in mean time between maintenance services or oil filter changes (even for older cars); the longer lifecycle stemming from anti-rust metal protection; fewer accidents owing to government action and also because of increased safety equipment such as antilock braking systems (ABS); fewer broken parts due to optimized vehicle architecture, more resistant parts such as plastic lights instead of glass, and more robust shock absorbers.

This trend is creating ground for battle between the OES and IAM channels. The OES channel is traditionally very active with recent cars – that is with cars less than five years old, and new cars under warranty – and enjoys high end-user loyalty. The shift of revenues to older cars directly impacts the OES channel as it increases the likelihood of revenues being diverted into another channel. The IAM channel, which generally addresses older cars, welcomes this trend, viewing it as an opportunity to invest in facilities to repair more recent cars (up to 10 years old).

Car technology: a threat or an opportunity?

The growing share of technology in vehicles is creating barriers that could shake up the market. The penetration of technology in the car pool has jumped considerably in the recent past (Figure 7.10).

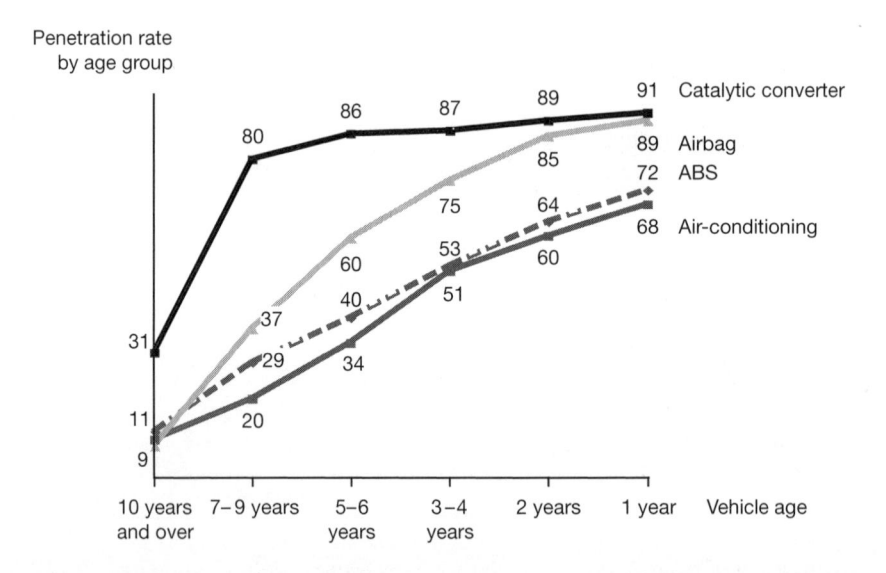

Figure 7.10 *Technology penetration in the car pool in Europe, 2003 (per cent)*
Sources: CCFA, Marketline, Roland Berger Strategy Consultants

With the rise of technology in cars, especially electronic hardware and software, much better skills are required these days to perform a car diagnosis. Although the BER forces OEMs to supply their repairers with appropriate diagnosis tools, a barrier is created because the tools are extremely OEM-specific and expensive. This prevents IAM repairers from gaining relevant experience.

The improvement of car technology directly impacts fast-fitters, who are now experiencing a reduction of their addressable market size, and have no possibility of completing more complex repairs.

The market for service and repairs is turning into a battlefield. New threats are emerging for all players from increasingly professional service quality expectations, shifts in car age, and from technology. But these threats also create opportunities for players capable of adapting their business model.

Spare parts: from a replacement to a retail approach

Captive spare parts are no longer immune from competition

Repairers and body shops are an important customer segment for IAM wholesalers, which supply them with 'competitive' parts. They are also important for OEMs via the OES channel. OEMs supply repairers and body shops with 'captive' parts and OEM-proprietary parts for the body and chassis. They also supply them with 'competitive' parts that they purchase from the tier 1 supplier panel and later resell under their own brand name and packaging.

Parts are replaced for three basic reasons: after accidents or crashes, when they fail to work or are damaged, and because of wear and tear. Accidents and crashes mostly concern body parts such as bumpers, side panels and front panels. Four to five parts are broken in 60 per cent of car accidents. Radiators, scratched bumpers, air-conditioning, windscreen and lighting are the parts that require replacing because of failure or damage. And finally tyres, oil filters, brake pads and shoes, as well as exhausts, are often replaced because of wear. Technical improvements mean that these wear-and-tear parts need to be replaced less frequently than in the past. Tyres, however, are an exception. Most drivers believe that tyres have to be changed every 40,000 kilometres, but tyres that need replacing after 15,000 kilometres' wear are becoming increasingly common: the new Laguna is just one example among many. Improved braking distance and vehicle stability has seen tyre size and adherence increase (from 14-inches to 17–18-inches). This pushes up the costs of tyres and increases wear and tear. Tyre makers benefit from this development, as do other players such as fast-fitters, which are jumping at this potentially life-saving opportunity. The wear-driven spare parts market is already highly competitive, with a specific distribution channel comprising fast-fitters, tyre specialists and the like, and will not be described in this chapter.

The accident-driven spare parts market has been largely immune from competition because it mostly comprises captive spare parts (eg OEM proprietary), which are replaced at the body shop. An examination of the spare parts volume purchased by body shops to repair cars after an accident shows that OEM captive parts represent around 77 per cent of total volume. This means that 23 per cent of parts could potentially be purchased in the IAM channel. This ratio is very likely to change in the coming years with the introduction of the Eurodesign regulation, since this allows other suppliers to develop captive parts without manufacturer agreement. Eurodesign already operates in some countries including Spain and the UK, but not yet in France or Germany. The introduction of Eurodesign could potentially reduce the share of captive parts from 77 to 25 per cent in the long term (Figure 7.11). This development would change the battlefield in favour of supply repairers and body shops by potentially allowing them to supply significantly more parts from the IAM channel or from low-cost countries.

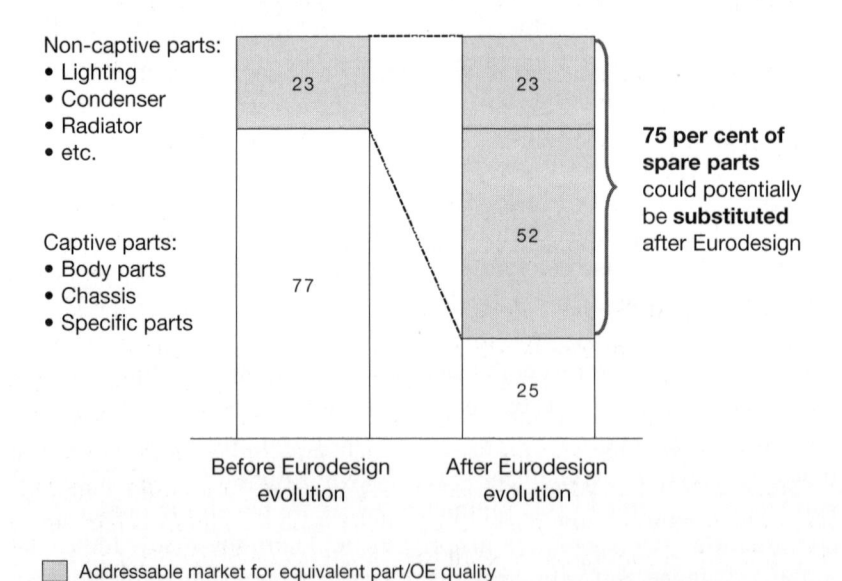

Figure 7.11 *Impact of Eurodesign on accident spare parts (per cent)*
Sources: Insurer databases, Roland Berger Strategy Consultants

Eurodesign covers OEMs' proprietary parts. It also encompasses all parts with proprietary design that may have been developed by tier 1 suppliers such as lighting, rear lamps and seats. Low-cost suppliers are emerging as a threat. Spare parts that already fall outside of Eurodesign, such as radiators, filters and spark plugs, are also being threatened by low-cost suppliers. Non-OE suppliers have captured a 40 per cent market share of the IAM channel with these sorts of parts.

The degree of impact low-cost suppliers have in various countries depends on whether or not Eurodesign is applied. The penetration rate of low-cost adaptable parts suppliers is most striking with old vehicles because the end-user is extremely cost-sensitive. The owner will likely not resell the vehicle and often receives no insurance reimbursement. That is why end-users try to have repairs done at minimum cost. When it comes to the older vehicle segment, end-users search for the cheapest solutions themselves, even down to spending time at the scrap yard to find a reused part.

Reused parts are also capturing a sizeable market share. In some countries, including France and Germany, Eurodesign prohibits adaptable products, and the reused segment is much more developed as a result. Reused parts account for almost 20 per cent of the lighting IAM in France, for example. Once adaptable products are allowed to be sold, however, the low-cost adaptable category grows very fast. This has been the case in Spain, Italy and Eastern Europe. Players such as the Taiwanese headlamp manufacturer TYC have already captured a strong market share in Spain and Italy, and particularly in Eastern Europe.

Spare parts wholesaling: competition heats up for repairers and body shops

If we break down the cost of repairing a car, we see that spare parts account for more than 40 per cent and labour costs make up more than 50 per cent (Figure 7.12).

When it comes to the level of service and quality of supply, body shops are becoming increasingly sophisticated. With the implementation of large-scale facilities (for example body shop factory concepts) that are capable of repairing 200 cars each week compared with the average-sized body shop that manages to repair 20 cars a week, it is clear that body shops are becoming better organized and more professional. One of the most effective ways to improve the profitability of body shops is to reduce the time a car spends on the premises during a repair. The immobilization time directly increases the cost of repair and reduces the vehicle slot turnover. Missing parts or parts that do not exactly fit the car and need to be adjusted are the most frequent reasons for increased immobilization time. A large diversity of parts need repairing after an accident (Figure 7.13). Even though only six parts on average are wrecked in an accident,

Typical cost of repair

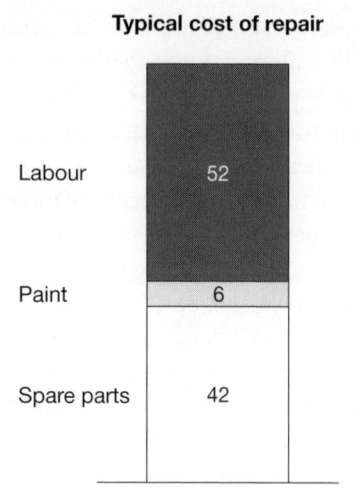

Labour	52
Paint	6
Spare parts	42

Figure 7.12 *Breakdown of typical repair costs (per cent)*
Sources: Rechange Automobile, Roland Berger Strategy Consultants

the 10 parts that most frequently need replacing represent only 22 per cent of the total crash parts volume.

Ranking of the parts most frequently damaged (volume per cent)

Total	Other	51st–90th	21st–50th	11th–20th	Top 10
	39	8	18	13	22

50 parts cover only 60% of crash parts volume

Top 10 crash parts (volume per cent)

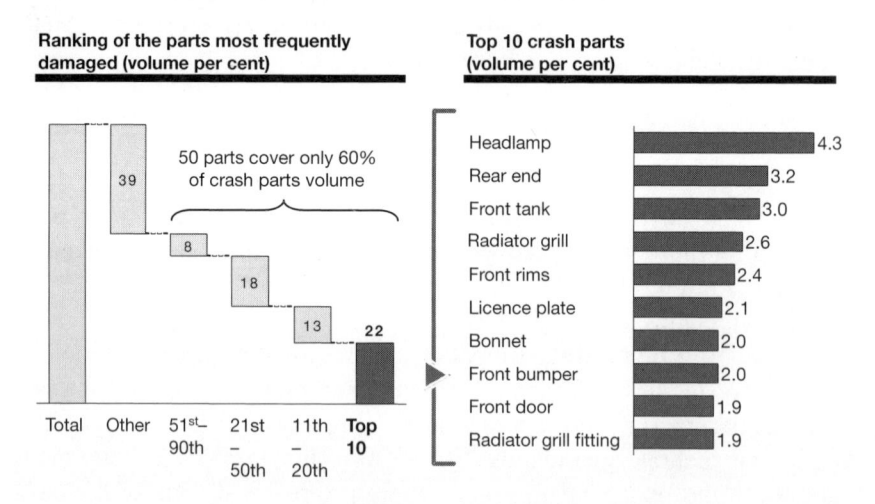

Headlamp	4.3
Rear end	3.2
Front tank	3.0
Radiator grill	2.6
Front rims	2.4
Licence plate	2.1
Bonnet	2.0
Front bumper	2.0
Front door	1.9
Radiator grill fitting	1.9

Figure 7.13 *Parts most frequently damaged in accidents*
Source: Roland Berger Strategy Consultants (analysis based on database of 166,000 accidents)

As soon as body shops and/or repairers become more professional, their needs from parts suppliers – OES, OEM dealers, wholesalers – rank as follows: first, efficient tools to identify the correct part number; second, relevant technical support and documentation; third, availability of the original part and/or a part that fits perfectly; fourth, the commercial rebate. Interestingly, the rebate criterion is becoming less and less important, because the price difference is largely cancelled out by the additional work-hours required if the part does not fit.

Body shops are stepping up their efforts to purchase the exact set of accident parts for a given model, under the 'accident part offer' idea. Multi-make wholesalers are unable to implement this offer because of the huge complexity involved in cataloguing, logistics, IT and so on, and the difficulty of covering the entire spectrum of parts: the likelihood of having all parts damaged by accidents in stock or in catalogue for a given model exponentially diminishes with the number of parts involved. The only players that can supply such accident part offers are the OEMs. This gives them a significant competitive advantage.

While it is much more convenient for body shops to bundle the supply of all the parts they need to the OES channel, the IAM channel actually offers more aggressive discounts, provided its referencing system is reliable and user-friendly, allowing correct parts to be easily identified.

A battle is being waged between the IAM and the OES channels for orders from body shops and repairers. The intensity of this battle differs between countries. In France and the UK, most body shops bundle their spare parts in the OES channel because OES dealers are strong and can offer discounts similar to those given in the IAM channel. Additionally, they have significantly improved the efficiency of referencing and/or ordering tools. These days, the body shop finds the parts it needs simply by entering the vehicle plate number.

In Germany, most body shops do not bundle their orders. Instead, they purchase competitive parts in the IAM channel from players such as Temot and ATR because they offer more aggressive discounts (15 per cent or more), and provide efficient referencing tools as well as technical support. In Spain, the situation is balanced. Neither of the channels has yet won against the other.

The spare parts wholesale activity will also be subject to major changes in the future, driven by the introduction of adaptable and low-cost suppliers, and by a more open market. Some OEMs are intensifying their efforts to win a share of the spare parts wholesale market. Renault, for instance, has implemented a huge dedicated sales force of around 500 people to sell spare parts, which should improve its chances when competing with traditional IAM wholesalers. Some IAM wholesalers, such as Temot and ATR, have also made significant progress by offering repairers efficient referencing tools and technical support.

The financial services challenge

A highly attractive segment coveted by non-automotive players

Slowly but surely, Europeans are increasingly using credit to finance purchases. Credit use is highest in the UK and Germany and lowest in southern European countries, thus reflecting typical consumer habits in Europe (Figure 7.14).

Development of outstanding credit in five European countries (€ billion)

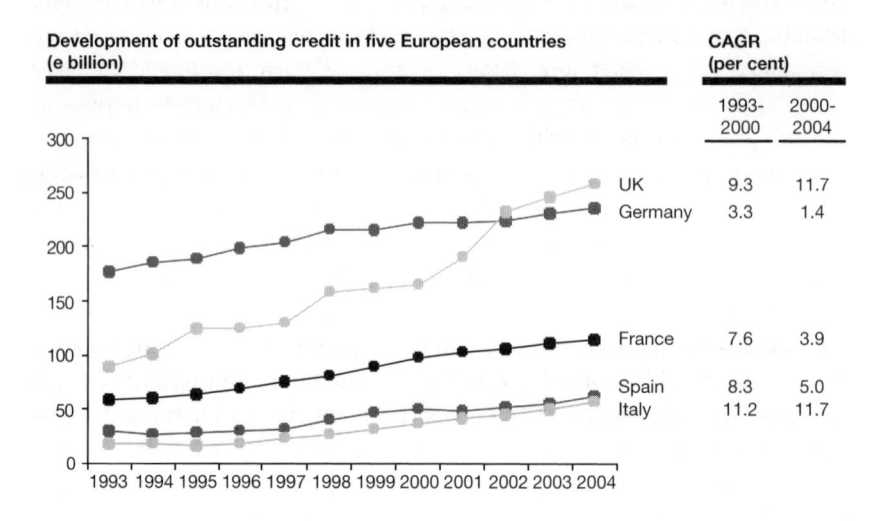

	CAGR (per cent) 1993–2000	CAGR (per cent) 2000–2004
UK	9.3	11.7
Germany	3.3	1.4
France	7.6	3.9
Spain	8.3	5.0
Italy	11.2	11.7

Figure 7.14 *Outstanding credit in five European countries*
Sources: Observateur Cetelem, Roland Berger Strategy Consultants

The automotive credit market is attractive to financial institutions because it provides them with a lever to penetrate consumer segments with high potential including youth, family (more than one car), rural areas or small cities, and income potential. Given its attractiveness, it is understandable that many players are interested in securing a share of this market. These players can be grouped into two segments: captive financial institutions and non-captive financial institutions. Captive financial institutions consist of OEMs' own financial services providers, operating under either private labels or the OEM brand. Private labels are generally financial services providers that were previously independent and have since been bought by an OEM. Non-captive financial institutions are either independent financial institutions or the leasing subsidiaries of commercial banks (Figure 7.15).

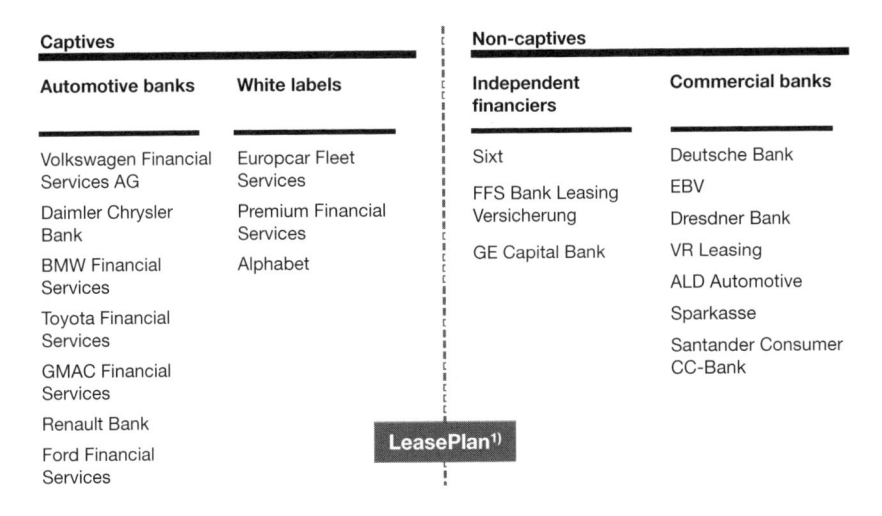

Captives			Non-captives	
Automotive banks	**White labels**		**Independent financiers**	**Commercial banks**
Volkswagen Financial Services AG	Europcar Fleet Services		Sixt	Deutsche Bank
Daimler Chrysler Bank	Premium Financial Services		FFS Bank Leasing Versicherung	EBV Dresdner Bank
BMW Financial Services	Alphabet		GE Capital Bank	VR Leasing ALD Automotive
Toyota Financial Services				Sparkasse
GMAC Financial Services				Santander Consumer CC-Bank
Renault Bank			**LeasePlan**[1]	
Ford Financial Services				

1) LeasePlan is considered to be 'non-captive' in this chapter

Figure 7.15 *Categorization of automotive financial service providers*
Source: Roland Berger Strategy Consultants

Although the financial services business is not a core activity for car makers it is highly profitable. Since captive financial institutions have access to the customer at the point of sale they have developed rapidly. Finance and insurance activities generally have higher ROCE than car sales. As well as providing higher profitability, these activities also provide more stable profits and sales when the core car business is languishing. Financial services activities also help car makers in the war for customers and in bolstering customer loyalty. Customer retention is boosted through effective customer relationship management or by influencing repurchase behaviour, by providing customers with financial offers that enable them to make a purchase sooner. New customer acquisition arising from complementary financial services cross-over is an additional advantage.

If we look at the overall expenditure related to a car throughout its lifecycle, financial services account for 24 per cent, with straight financing accounting for 9 per cent of this (including leasing) and insurance accounting for 15 per cent. OEMs increasingly rely on their financial subsidiaries to contribute to profit. As well as being able to boost sales and earn extra profit, financial subsidiaries also help OEMs stabilize their profits in times of crisis.

Automotive trends are changing the credit battlefield

Two trends in the automotive sector strongly influence how automotive credit is purchased. First, the growing share of fleets and the rental business model drive the share of automotive credit not purchased at the dealer point of sale. Thus it does not necessarily fall into the hands of captive financial services providers. Second, the growing share of the used car segment creates a new attractive segment for financial services, since more and more used cars are being purchased with credit (Figure 7.16).

Penetration rate of car credit in 2003
(Used and new cars purchased by private customers, per cent)

	New car (25)	Used car (75)
No credit	25	35
Credit purchased outside point of sale	39	53
Credit purchased at the point of sale	36	12
Total outside point of sale		32.5
Total at point of sale		49.5
		18

Major automotive credit players in France

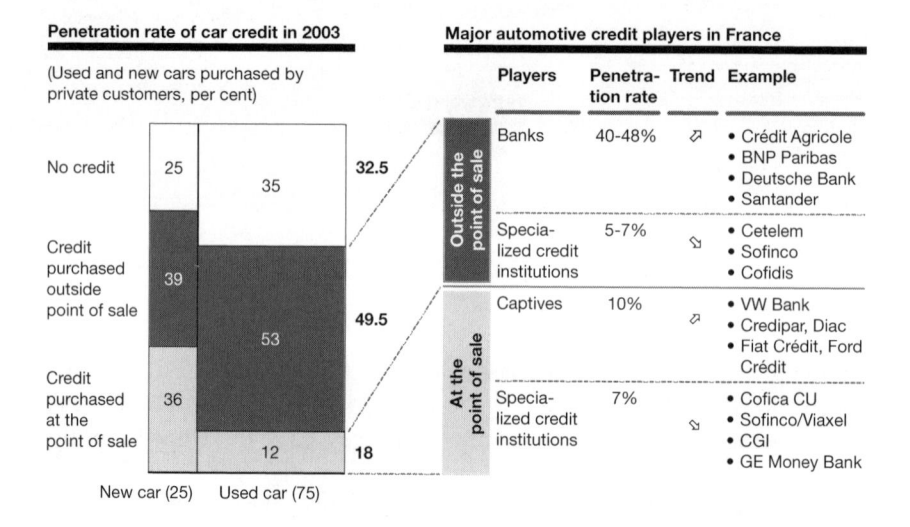

	Players	Penetration rate	Trend	Example
Outside the point of sale	Banks	40–48%	↗	• Crédit Agricole • BNP Paribas • Deutsche Bank • Santander
	Specialized credit institutions	5–7%	↘	• Cetelem • Sofinco • Cofidis
At the point of sale	Captives	10%	↗	• VW Bank • Credipar, Diac • Fiat Crédit, Ford Crédit
	Specialized credit institutions	7%	↘	• Cofica CU • Sofinco/Viaxel • CGI • GE Money Bank

Figure 7.16 *Major automotive credit players in France and the penetration rate of car credit*
Sources: Observatoire de l'Automobile, Crédiscope, Roland Berger Strategy Consultants

Each player's strategy differs according to whether the credit is purchased at the point of sale or outside the point of sale. The 'outside point of sale' segment is increasingly dominated by non-captive financial institutions such as banks that are directly contracted by fleet management companies and intermediaries, whereas the 'point of sale' segment is largely dominated by the captive and specialized credit institutions of OEMs. Without the presence of OEMs' in-house fleet management companies, non-captive financial institutions would completely command the fleet management market (Figure 7.17).

The attractiveness of the fleet management segment means that players are pursuing various strategies in an attempt to garner market share. Captives are focusing on fleet management and full-service leasing solutions, establishing additional 'white label brands' to serve multi-brand

Company	Country	Size of fleet (000 vehicles)	Owned by
Leaseplan Corporation	NL	650[1]	Volkswagen AG, 50%; Olayan Group, 25%; Mubadala, 25%
PHH Arval	F	600	BNP Paribas
ALD International	D/F	545	Société Générale
Volkswagen/Europcar	D	315	Volkswagen AG
Athlon/Fleet Synergy	NL	310	N/A
DaimlerChrysler Services	D	310	DaimlerChrysler
Overlease	F	278	RCI Bank
GE Fleet Services	US	220	General Electric
Masterlease	UK	170	General Motors
ING Car Lease	D	155	ING

1) Europe only, 1.1 million worldwide

Figure 7.17 *Leading European providers of fleet management services*
Sources: Fleet Europe, Datamonitor, Roland Berger Strategy Consultants

customers, and offering complementary bank services such as that offered by Volkswagen Financial Services. Independent non-captives, usually active in large fleets, are progressively extending their offers to small fleets and even private customers with new concepts such as 'leasing under a different name' (Figure 7.18). Non-captive commercial banks are setting up or acquiring leasing subsidiaries to extend their financial services portfolio. ALD is a good example in this respect. Non-captive commercial banks are also approaching dealers more aggressively with more attractive financing offers, and sometimes even approaching private customers. Sixt immediately springs to mind in this context.

Automotive credit is a tantalizing segment. Used car credit is the growth driver compensating for stagnation in new car sales. Traditional captive financial services providers are being challenged by non-captive financial institutions that take advantage not only of the 'outside point of sale' segment, such as fleet management companies and large dealers, but also of used car intermediaries.

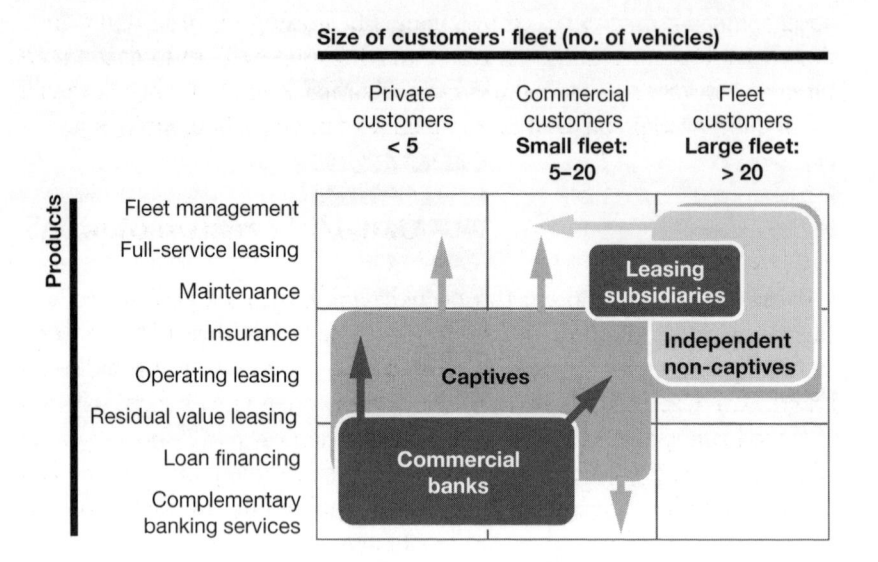

Figure 7.18 *Strategies taken by leading financial services providers*
Sources: Fleet Europe, Datamonitor, Roland Berger Strategy Consultants

THREATS AND OPPORTUNITIES CREATE NEW CHALLENGES

Dealer groups: the relationship challenge

Dealer groups have consolidated in recent years. They have become increasingly important players, with dominant positions in certain regions and areas within the national landscape. In the UK, large dealer groups such as Dixon, Arnold Clark and Reg Vardy have been established for some time. These players sometimes have a local market share of more than 50 per cent within their customer areas (Figure 7.19).

In France, for example, the top 100 distribution groups account for 46 per cent of the market and are particularly well developed. Although Germany has a few large players, dealer groups there are still highly fragmented. French dealer groups have grown mainly by acquiring multiple franchises. Between 1999 and 2002, the share of the French market controlled by the top 100 distributors grew faster than the total market (a compound annual growth rate (CAGR) of 4.8 per cent versus 0.3 per cent) (Figure 7.20).

The sales and after-sales challenge 197

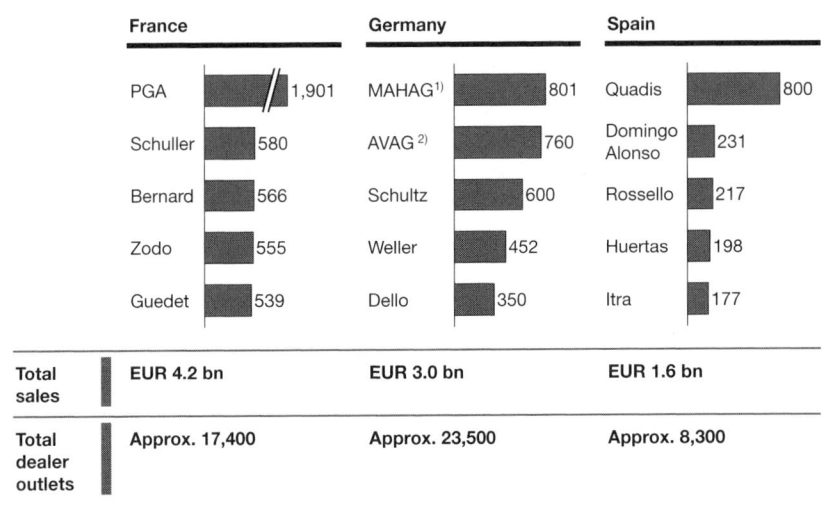

	France		Germany		Spain	
	PGA	1,901	MAHAG[1]	801	Quadis	800
	Schuller	580	AVAG[2]	760	Domingo Alonso	231
	Bernard	566	Schultz	600	Rossello	217
	Zodo	555	Weller	452	Huertas	198
	Guedet	539	Dello	350	Itra	177
Total sales	EUR 4.2 bn		EUR 3.0 bn		EUR 1.6 bn	
Total dealer outlets	Approx. 17,400		Approx. 23,500		Approx. 8,300	

1) 2002 figures   2) Including international activities

Figure 7.19 *Top five automotive dealer groups, 2003 (sales in € million, total dealer outlets with service contracts)*
Source: Roland Berger Strategy Consultants

Top 100 automotive distribution groups grow faster than the market (number of new cars sold in France: Index 100 in 1999)

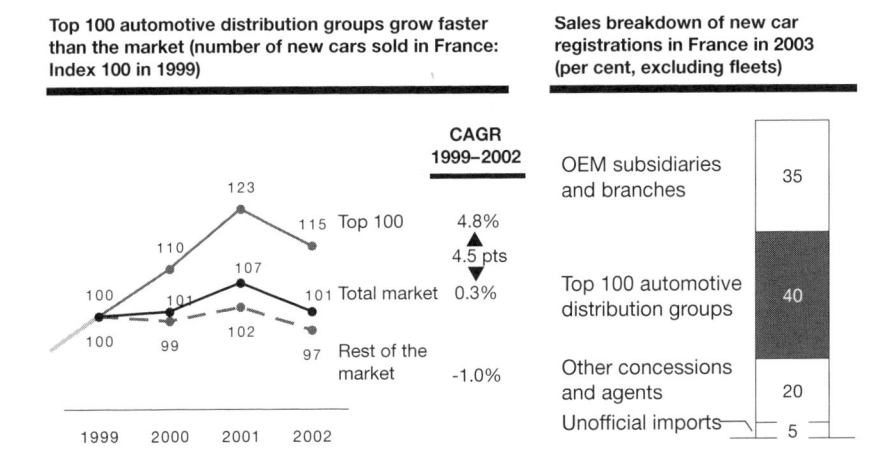

	CAGR 1999–2002
Top 100	4.8% ▲
	4.5 pts ▼
Total market	0.3%
Rest of the market	-1.0%

Sales breakdown of new car registrations in France in 2003 (per cent, excluding fleets)

OEM subsidiaries and branches	35
Top 100 automotive distribution groups	40
Other concessions and agents	20
Unofficial imports	5

Figure 7.20 *Growth and market shares of the top 100 automotive distribution groups*
Sources: Résoscopie supplement 2001–2002–2003, Roland Berger Strategy Consultants

Dealer groups are generally positioned with the following characteristics. They often have a multi-mono-make portfolio, meaning they have separate contracts with several OEMs; they display a strong concentration in one geographic area; they leverage local scale effects; they boast a

198   Major challenges

strong relationship with end-customers; and they have the financial power to invest in other related businesses such as rental and mobility services.

Dealer groups are currently heavily reliant on OEMs, especially with regard to spare parts, which they purchase from the OEMs' parts and accessories (P&A) department. However, given their size and potential bargaining power, dealer groups are becoming attractive targets for spare parts suppliers or even IAM wholesalers from whom they could potentially get better rebates. In the medium term, we believe that dealer groups will source many parts directly from suppliers instead of buying from OEMs. Recent acquisitions of IAM wholesalers by dealer groups support this. It is a clever tactical move that allows dealer groups to have a foot in the IAM market while avoiding breaking the sacred rules with OEMs.

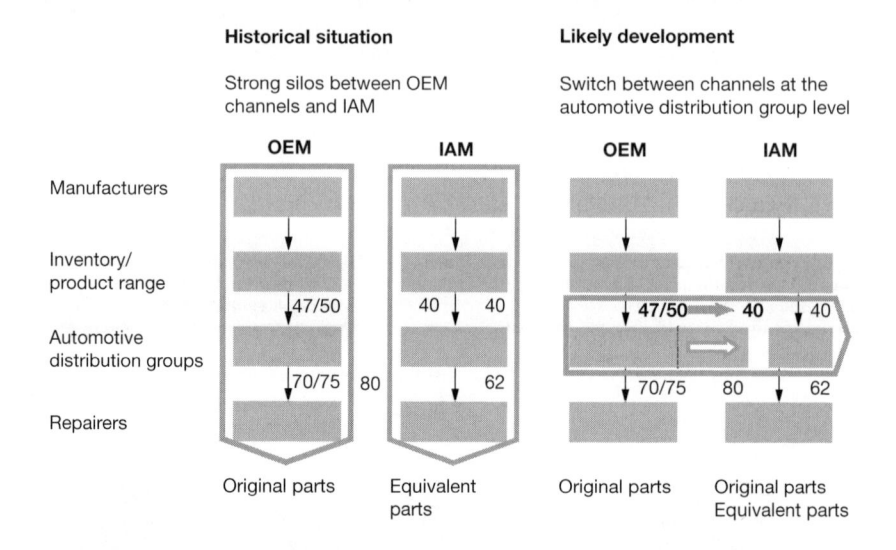

Figure 7.21 *Automotive distribution groups are closing the OEM and IAM channel silo (figures represent the average discount rate)*
Source: Roland Berger Strategy Consultants

The structure of the market is likely to change significantly in the coming years, especially because of the shift made by automotive distribution groups (Figure 7.21). The figures above represent the average discount rate. Today, quite a large silo exists between the IAM and OES channels because of so-called OE parts. These parts were once in the domain of the OES channel. Following BER, an OE part can be sold in any channel. The implication is that the IAM and OES channels will become more porous and develop into a more traditional supplier–distributor model.

Aside from P&A, the sheer size of dealer groups will also enable them to better leverage their strong multi-make regional position. They have the size to optimize the used car process across different car makes and to develop services with greater outreach, for instance loans, leasing and renting, as well as to develop relationships with customers at the local level.

The challenge for dealer groups is to master the transformation from a multi-make dealers' network into a regional integrated player. This challenge is multifaceted and requires well thought out actions. Dealer groups need to improve customer relationships throughout the lifecycle. This involves making better use of their multi-make portfolio to provide customers with appropriate mobility solutions. Dealer groups are also widening their services offer by launching new services such as car rental and financial services. Repair and service activities are improved by developing the multi-make body shop factory concept and developing parts sourcing directly from suppliers, for instance. Under the revised BER, dealer groups are theoretically allowed to source parts directly from the equipment and/or parts supplier. By skipping over one rebate level, they could get better price rebates. Such action is best suited for older cars less than 10 years of age because these vehicles appear less frequently on the radar screens of OEMs. Dealer groups also face the challenge of developing the wholesale parts business. Their size enables them to provide competitive wholesale offers to repairers with similar high-performance logistics and services levels to those offered by large IAM wholesalers.

Of course, these challenges will not be surmounted without OEMs. The relationship between dealer groups and OEMs will become increasingly critical. The impressive size of both players creates a mutual dependency. The challenge is to develop a win–win situation with OEMs, while progressively increasing the level of independence.

IAM repairer and wholesalers: the technology challenge

At repair level: consolidation toward affiliated networks

IAM repairers will face significant challenges in the future. They will have to cope with increasingly sophisticated vehicle technology, and get better at diagnosing problems, as well as serve more demanding customers. IAM repairers will have to improve their skills and change their repair practices in the light of these factors.

IAM repairers' affiliation with networks is growing. IAM repairers are taking this step to benefit from greater training support and access to tools, which enables them to tackle more sophisticated car technology. The number of affiliated repairers has grown constantly in past years, much to the detriment of independent repairers (Figure 7.22).

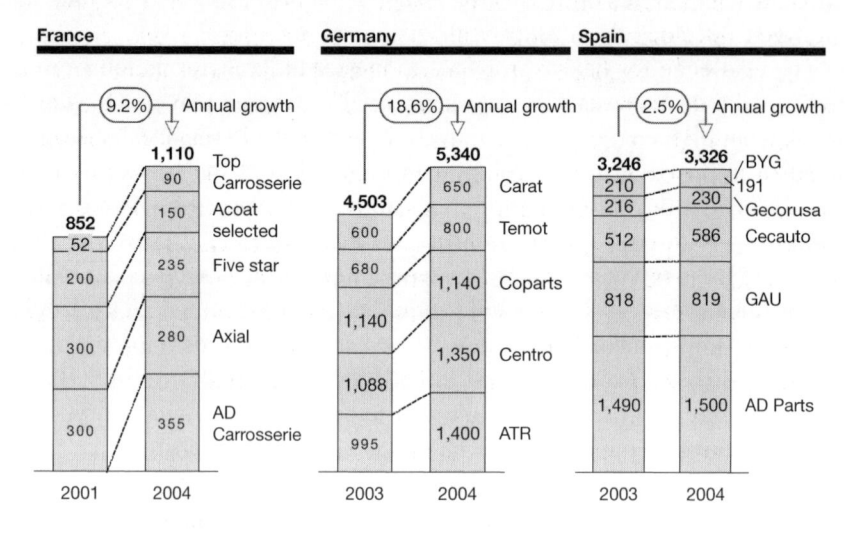

France		Germany		Spain		
9.2% Annual growth		18.6% Annual growth		2.5% Annual growth		
1,110	Top Carrosserie	5,340		3,246	3,326	BYG
90		650	Carat	210	191	
150	Acoat selected	4,503		216	230	Gecorusa
852		600	800 Temot	512	586	Cecauto
52		680				
200	235		1,140 Coparts			
		1,140		818	819	GAU
300	280	Axial	1,350 Centro			
		1,088		1,490	1,500	AD Parts
300	355	AD Carrosserie	995	1,400 ATR		
2001	2004	2003	2004	2003	2004	

Figure 7.22 *Number of repair and/or body shops affiliated to a network in France, Germany and Spain*
Source: Roland Berger Strategy Consultants

Large affiliated repairer and body shop networks have emerged which specialize in different areas: these include body shop repairers (mainly sharing painting and body expertise), insurer networks, and parts wholesaler networks. By joining forces, these networks could better leverage their size. This would mean that they could share diagnostic abilities and better develop partnerships to complete the multi-brand offer. Branded networks would also help further improve the customer experience, but the most critical issue for repairers is changing their repair habits. The way to identify the root cause of a problem with a vehicle is changing. The empirical approach to repairing cars – deducing the cause of a breakdown from a set of symptoms – will soon no longer be applicable. With all the various electronic systems built into vehicles, the same symptoms can have many different root causes. New methodologies, for example root cause analysis and AMDEC, will have to be acquired by the repairer to properly diagnose vehicle problems. Repairers today are hardly trained to deal with this new environment.

At wholesale level: consolidation toward large buying groups

IAM wholesalers are consolidating into large-scale purchasing associations, with strong technical support and a large network of in-house or affiliated wholesalers and repairers. Independent wholesalers and repairers are the losers in this development, since they are unable to compete against the consolidated groups with their better price conditions, modern technical support and order flows.

Large IAM wholesalers are now present in three major countries, and have significant clout in the market (Figure 7.23). In Germany, networks such as Carat, ATR and Temot (which includes MAHAG) are extremely powerful and high-performance players. Large IAM wholesalers are diversifying into more service activities, taking advantage of the decline of independent players.

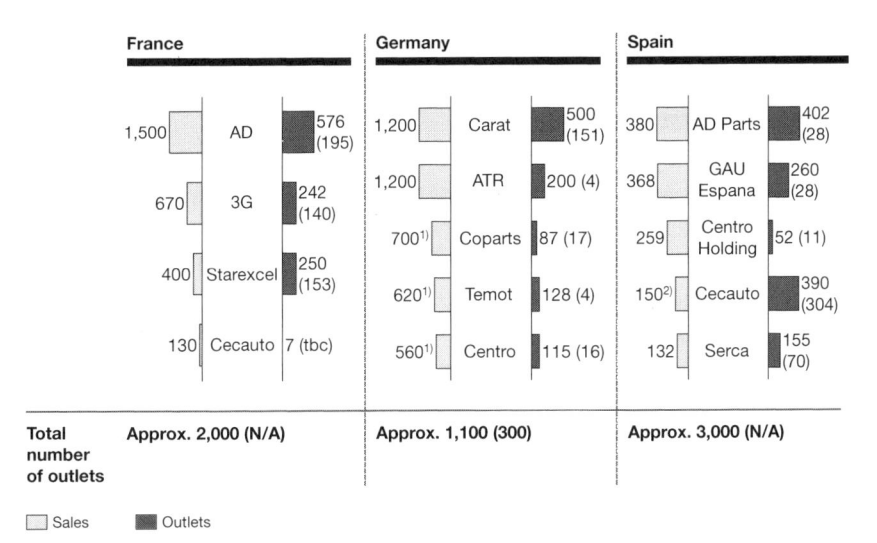

France			Germany			Spain		
1,500	AD	576 (195)	1,200	Carat	500 (151)	380	AD Parts	402 (28)
670	3G	242 (140)	1,200	ATR	200 (4)	368	GAU Espana	260 (28)
400	Starexcel	250 (153)	700¹⁾	Coparts	87 (17)	259	Centro Holding	52 (11)
130	Cecauto	7 (tbc)	620¹⁾	Temot	128 (4)	150²⁾	Cecauto	390 (304)
			560¹⁾	Centro	115 (16)	132	Serca	155 (70)

| Total number of outlets | Approx. 2,000 (N/A) | Approx. 1,100 (300) | Approx. 3,000 (N/A) |

☐ Sales   ■ Outlets

Note: a minority of wholesale outlets belong to more than one cooperation

Figure 7.23 *Top wholesale cooperative groups in France, Germany and Spain, 2004 (sales in € million, and number of outlets)*
Sources: Company websites, specialized press, Roland Berger Strategy Consultants

The large IAM wholesaler Auto Distribution, for instance, covers all levels in France, from purchasing associations to end-customers. Its activities encompass a parts purchasing association with sales of around €1,044 million and over 700,000 parts numbers, a network of distributors with around 200 companies and 680 points of sales, seven specialist service and repair networks and an internet portal with databases (products and services) and information regarding prices and supplies available online.

IAM wholesalers face a handful of key challenges. Leveraging their clout across Europe will become an important factor. These corporations are driven too much on a national level, even when international coordination exists. This is because of the ownership structure, which is often not consolidated or frequently structured in the form of associations. To compete with the large dealer groups and OEMs which are increasingly capturing market share and channelling it into body shops, IAM wholesalers would be wise to improve their technical support, parts referencing and coverage, and to deliver excellence in logistics. Technical support must also be efficient. This will mean implementing in-house and centralized testing and diagnostic skills, and offering online tools. Getting a grip of expanding sourcing capabilities to low-cost countries with OE-quality products is also important. By taking a retail approach to product collection, they could also broaden their product offering. This could mean going beyond OE products.

Fast-fitters are a specific subsegment of IAM players. Their business model in the long term appears risky for the following reasons. First, they face strong competition from incumbent players – that is from OEMs and dealers – who propose similar services bundled with car maintenance. Renault Minute is a pertinent example here. The market is also shrinking because of the decrease in failure parts that need replacing such as exhausts and filters. Fast-fitters are also neither equipped to tackle the technology challenge nor able to diversify into other areas. One short-term opportunity they are all grabbing is the tyre aftermarket, which in contrast to other fast-fit parts is growing.

To maintain their position, fast-fitters will have to expand geographically, requiring strong financial backing. Developing alliances or partnerships with potential prescribers such as fleet management companies or insurers would also be helpful. In view of the growing competition, fast-fitters must be vigilant in providing excellent service quality.

Insurers: the influential challenge

The influence and role of insurers in the automotive aftermarket is growing. Aside from the end-user, insurers are the only market player with a strong interest in lowering the price of spare parts. The influence insurers have on the price of parts starts well before the vehicle is launched on the market. The Allianz Danner test, for instance, carries particular authority for OEMs. It consists of a low-speed crash test and a measure of the cost of the basket of spare parts needed to repair the vehicle. This famous test is used by all insurers, and forms the basis for defining insurance fees for any given car model.

Nearly all insurance companies have adopted the Danner test as the basis for claims, and it greatly influences the product development strategies taken by OEMs. There are valid reasons for this. End-users who have access to the test results, which are available in most automotive newspapers and magazines, are becoming increasingly sensitive to total costs, especially in Germany where repair costs are much higher than in other European countries. Furthermore, it is essential to have good scores in order to be referenced by fleet customers, as fleet customers represent a significant share of the market volume for OEMs.

As a consequence, most OEMs are improving their products at the vehicle development stage to reduce the number of broken parts that end up in the basket. Repair costs have dropped significantly in recent years because of technical improvements. For the same test conditions, the cost to repair an Audi 80 produced in 1978 was €5,200. In contrast, an Audi A4 produced in 2001 cost €3,900 to repair taking inflation into account.

Beyond technical improvements, the pricing strategy of OEMs regarding spare parts is also influenced by insurance test results. OEMs currently optimize the price of spare parts to meet the 'Danner basket' by lowering the price of certain parts found in the basket and increasing the price of others. Spare parts pricing is a complex mechanism, the logic of which is very difficult for external observers to understand. The pricing of spare parts is not only influenced by the results of insurers' tests, but also by various other criteria. OEMs are the only players that have managed to master this game.

The criteria for pricing parts include vehicle range. Even if a part is exactly the same across models, which is often the case due to the platform strategy followed by many OEMs, prices of parts are not identical and can show substantial differences, for instance between a VW and an Audi. The country's competitive environment is also a criterion. Here several factors need to be taken into consideration, such as the presence of low costs, the existence of Eurodesign, and the weight of IAM wholesalers. Whether or not parts are captive is another consideration. Trade-offs are made on purpose, as the example of Renault shows. Renault recently modified its prices by pushing through higher rebates on competitive parts and lower rebates on body parts. As a result, the price of spare parts can become fairly disconnected from industrial costs.

Taking this into consideration, it is understandable that insurance companies want to increase their level of control over the price of spare parts. Three basic strategies or models are being developed by insurance companies: 'sell', 'select' and 'buy'.

- The 'sell' strategy consists of focusing volumes to selected body shops and negotiating prices with the wholesalers. This approach requires large-scale communication to body shops as well as incentives, including pick up, delivery and replacement cars. It provides reach to around 60 per cent of customers.
- The 'select' strategy consists of referencing a reduced number of body shop partners by developing multiple partnerships with body shop networks. This implies a new distribution of roles between body shops, the insurance company and the expert.
- The 'buy' strategy goes even further and consists of creating a purchasing structure to negotiate contracts with spare parts suppliers. Some cost reductions are shared with body shops.

'Sell' and 'select' approaches are a prerequisite for the 'buy' strategy. The UK is the country that is the most advanced in the latter practice. In France, the 'sell' and 'select' models are developing quite fast. Taking on this approach requires insurers to steer clients towards a selected network of body shops to achieve volume commitments made with the body shop network. Volumes stemming from guidance given by insurers can be significant for body shops, and can represent up to 35 to 40 per cent of their activity. As shown in the example of France, the level of guidance from insurers has increased markedly in recent years (Figure 7.24).

The influence of insurers varies significantly across countries in Europe. It is the most influential in the UK, and is becoming progressively more so in France. But the situation is very different in Germany, where the insured customer has the freedom to choose between a direct cash payment and vehicle repair. The customer is also free to select the location where the repair work should be conducted. Repair and body shops always make use of one-time agreements with insurers to regulate payment flows. This explains why the level of guidance of insurers to customers is much lower in Germany than it is in France (10 per cent versus 40 to 60 per cent).

Insurers can play an even more important role, as the example of the UK shows. UK insurers have achieved a 75 per cent guidance rate and are increasingly becoming purchasers. This has a substantial impact on labour rates and on the cost of parts. For example, Direct Line and Norwich Union covered 50 per cent of the private market in 2003 and achieved huge guidance rates: 85 per cent for Direct Line and 65 per cent for Norwich Union. Moreover, some OE-equivalent or adaptable parts are also referenced

The sales and after-sales challenge 205

Weight of insurers (per cent)

- Mutuals, no brokers, eg Macif
- Insurance company branches — 50

- General insurance agents (36%)
- Brokers (4%)
- Bank insurance, eg CA, Crédit Mutuel — 40
- Direct sales, eg direct assurance (AXA) — 7
  — 3

€ 5.8 billion
Repair costs in 2003

Change in guidance rate (per cent)[1]

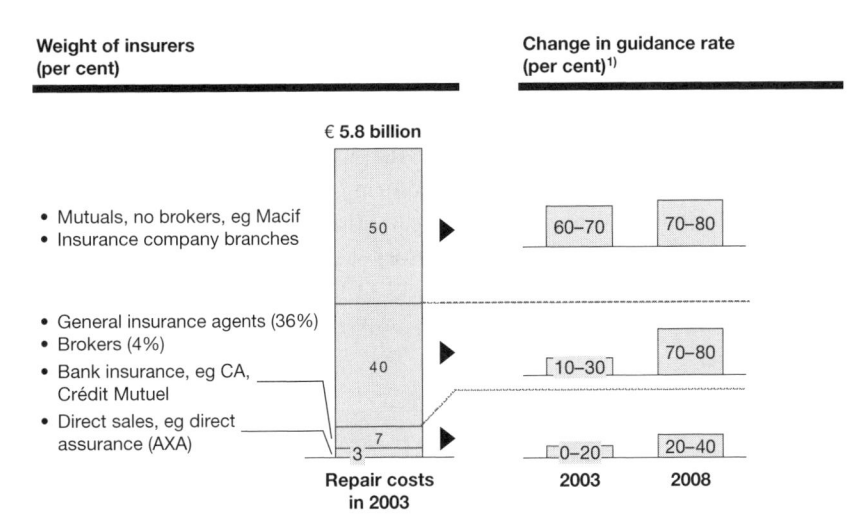

	2003	2008
	60–70	70–80
	10–30	70–80
	0–20	20–40

1) The guidance rate measures how many clients go to the garage or body shop recommended by the insurer after an accident

Figure 7.24 *Insurance guidance rate development in France – insurers' guidance level likely to exceed 70 per cent by 2008*
Sources: DRI 2002, Sidexa, Roland Berger Strategy Consultants

by approval bodies such as Thatcham, and are prescribed to repair a car. In France, insurers only prescribe OE parts because the expert becomes liable if a problem occurs as a result of replacement by a non-OE part.

Parts suppliers: the market access challenge

Parts suppliers basically sell products using the OEMs' network and under the OEMs' brand or via the IAM channel with a private brand such as Hella, Valeo or Bosch. Although BER has theoretically made it more favourable for suppliers to sell more OE products in the IAM channel, this has not translated into practice. Parts suppliers are increasingly being squeezed on several fronts. They face substantial and growing price pressure from the OEM channel. In the IAM channel, they are confronted with larger buying groups, progressively looking for alternative products. Regulation trends also do not make life easier for parts suppliers. Non-OE parts are gradually being allowed to be sourced from low-cost countries. The growing OES channel and the subsequent shrinkage of the IAM channel in several markets increases pressure on parts suppliers, as it reduces market access for suppliers' private brands. Price pressure from insurers is also a considerable factor.

Parts suppliers would most likely benefit from taking a more proactive strategy toward the market. This could include marketing at the repair and wholesale levels, introducing a pricing and brand positioning that enables differentiation according to the level of competition for individual parts, addressing large dealer groups, and exploring all potential growth opportunities, including accessories, niches and other countries.

Market changes offer parts suppliers new ways to capture value (Figure 7.25).

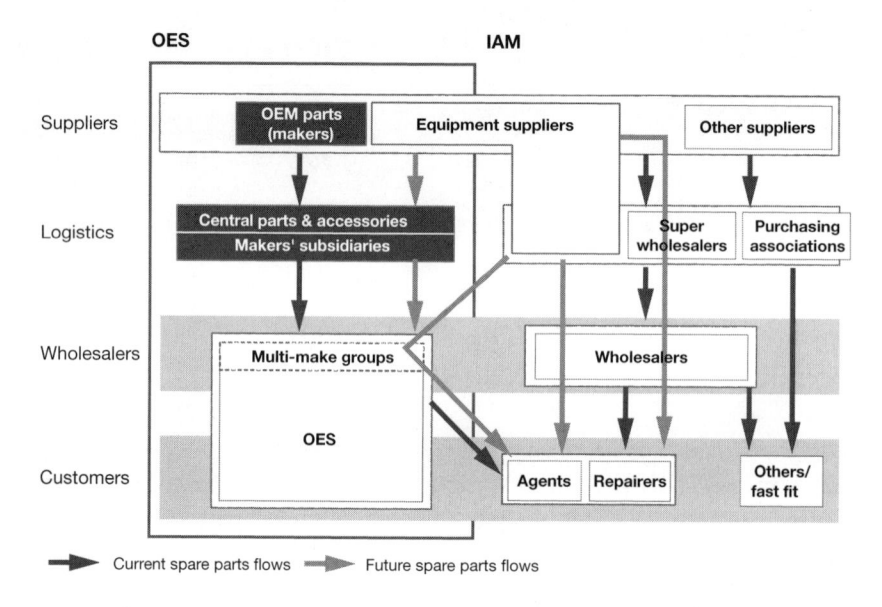

Figure 7.25 *Potential changes in spare parts flows*
Source: Roland Berger Strategy Consultants

Captive and non-captive financial institutions

Captive and non-captive financial institutions have very different market positions. At the point of sale, captive financial institutions have a dominant position, with clear competitive advantages achieved by leveraging integrated offers such as buying back a used car, selling a new car, financing the vehicle and providing services. This allows OEMs to make trade-offs between the level of credit granted, the rate applied, the used car buy-back price and the rebate on the new car. Credit provided by captive financial institutions at a 0 per cent rate is commonplace. The reason is simple: the OEM has already negotiated a cheaper buy-back price for the used car.

Captive financial institutions have to tackle a number of issues. Their lack of financial expertise would suggest that improving scoring capabilities should be a priority. Developing the used car financial services model as well as offering additional financial services for customers, such as retail banking services, would help them improve their standing. This last strategy is especially favoured by German OEMs, which excel in this area. The next subsegment of the chapter is dedicated to exploring this model.

Captive banks: the German exception

Volkswagen, DaimlerChrysler and BMW are the only OEMs to offer retail banking services in their domestic market. Although OEMs' financing activities are maturing, retail banking follows a steady and regular growth pattern. The bank deposits of VW Financial Services have increased by 26 per cent each year since 1998, amounting to €8.7 billion (Figure 7.26). VW Financial Services is among the top 10 Visa card providers, one of the leading direct banks and the eighth largest insurance company in Germany. The bank deposits of BMW Bank have also developed significantly since 1998 (at around 31 per cent annual growth) and totalled around €3.8 billion in 2003. Bank deposits at DaimlerChrysler Bank, which was created in 2002, grew from €0.8 billion to €3.1 billion between 2003 and 2004.

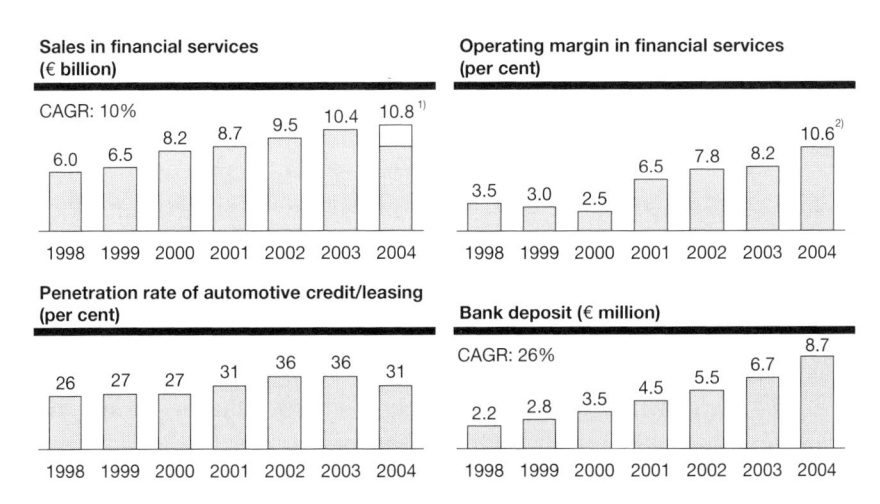

Sales in financial services (€ billion)
CAGR: 10%
1998	1999	2000	2001	2002	2003	2004
6.0	6.5	8.2	8.7	9.5	10.4	10.8 [1]

Operating margin in financial services (per cent)
1998	1999	2000	2001	2002	2003	2004
3.5	3.0	2.5	6.5	7.8	8.2	10.6 [2]

Penetration rate of automotive credit/leasing (per cent)
1998	1999	2000	2001	2002	2003	2004
26	27	27	31	36	36	31

Bank deposit (€ million)
CAGR: 26%
1998	1999	2000	2001	2002	2003	2004
2.2	2.8	3.5	4.5	5.5	6.7	8.7

1) Published data not consistent with previous years because of changes in underlying accounting – number shown has been extrapolated based on 2003 figures
2) Based on new accounting

Figure 7.26 *Development of Volkswagen Financial Services*
Sources: VW financial reports, broker reports, press

These banks provide a complete product and service portfolio. VW Financial Services sells a large product range including accounts, credit, loans, insurance policies and leasing. The range of products on offer at DaimlerChrysler Bank and BMW Bank is less broad, but covers all of the customers' basic needs. Such retail banking activity has been developed by leveraging partnerships with specialized suppliers. VW, for instance, has signed dozens of contracts with companies including Neue Leben, HDI, Allianz and SEB Invest for insurance and investment products. VW and BMW have also signed agreements with some of the very same companies.

The development of OEMs' retail banking activities has been progressive and is set to continue across Europe. VW Financial Services, created in 1990, has progressively broadened its scope in Germany by introducing private accounts and investment management services. VW wants to expand these activities by winning non-VW brand customers, and intends to extend its financial product range to other European countries. DaimlerChrysler Bank, which has expanded the scope of its specialized financial services and cites cementing customer relationships as its primary objective, is now planning to extend its activities to other countries. The same expansion objectives also apply to BMW when it comes to direct banking.

Is this model unique to Germany? Given the enormous success of this activity, could other OEMs apply the model? Is retail banking a growth opportunity, and does it support OEMs in further developing their brand and position? Surely it does, but we also believe that certain characteristics specific to the German banking sector have contributed to the success experienced by German OEMs.

First of all, the banking sector in Germany is highly fragmented, comprising large private banks including Deutsche Bank and Dresdner Bank, as well as many local banks and savings banks. The current players are often relatively weak. Second, automotive distributors already have a strong advisory role. The OES channel, for instance, is the most developed for insurance products. Third, the awareness of OEMs' brands in Germany is extremely high. Strong value is attached when a customer has a BMW credit card in his pocket because it reveals that he or she owns a BMW vehicle. A fourth factor is the banking habits of German customers, who tend to hold accounts at more than just one bank. This is not the case in many other countries including France. A fifth factor is the specific weight of funds compared with a National Savings Bank passbook, and the specific usage of checking accounts (Girokonto).

Those characteristics are very specific to Germany and do not necessarily exist in the UK, France or Spain. We believe that OEMs in other European countries would have difficulties employing this sort of model.

Non-captives: the challenge of capturing market share in new growth areas

For non-captives, the major opportunity resides in capturing market share in new growth areas such as the fleet segment and the used car segment. A number of challenges also exist, however. Non-captives would likely improve their situation if they leveraged cross-selling potential with the existing product portfolio and defined target sales channels in line with future developments in automotive retailing (multi-brand dealers, large dealer groups, large fleet management companies and so on). Forming partnerships with the captive financial services providers of importers or manufacturers in unexplored markets, and expanding regionally in currently immature automotive financing markets such as CEE, may help non-captives capture market share.

OEMs: the captive business model challenge

OEMs are obviously the only players to master all business models described above: new car sales, used car buy-back and resale, car repair and maintenance, spare parts wholesale, and financial services. OEMs are also the first player encountered by the final customer, and while loyalty to the dealer network may differ from one country to another, it is generally high. According to the analysis below, customer loyalty does not depend solely on the age of the vehicle, it also depends on where the customer has purchased the car and whether it is a new or a used car. For a used car purchased at the dealer, the loyalty to the dealer is still high even if the car is already old. This curve is extremely important for OEMs, and is a key indicator to monitor the retention of their customer base (Figure 7.27).

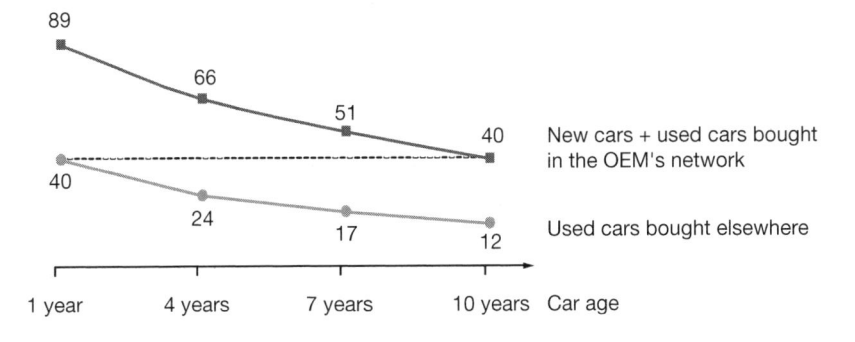

Figure 7.27 *Customer loyalty to dealers for service (per cent)*
Source: Roland Berger Strategy Consultants

OEMs face threats on many fronts. Eurodesign and the impact of BER, consolidation of dealer groups and IAM wholesalers, the increasing penetration of adaptable parts, the growing influence of insurers, and the number of ageing cars in use are just a few of the threats. But OEMs have the upper hand when it comes to technology; they also own original parts and specifications, are able to monitor the used car buy-back process, and have firm control over financial credit.

All the same, the key success factor for OEMs is to develop an even more integrated business model, leveraging their 'bundling' competitive advantage across several dimensions. The first step could be to leverage trade-offs between new and used cars by further monitoring car flows and the buy-back process through maximizing their European scale. In a second step, the trade-offs between captive and competitive spare parts wholesale could be optimized by further expanding wholesale activities, better controlling spare parts flows, and by optimizing pricing and logistics. A third step could involve improving repair and service control. This could be achieved by further consolidating their own repairer and body shop networks, and by maintaining competitive advantage and entry barriers in diagnosis capability. Further development of the customer experience and service quality could also be achieved at this stage. In a fourth step, OEMs could try to develop captive financial services beyond new cars at the point of sale through leveraging bundled offers and proposing creative solutions to the customer to beat the competition. A fifth step could involve developing strategies to retain the final customer in the OES channel, by bundling warranty extensions, mobility services, roadside assistance and other services.

Facing those challenges will also require adapting the distribution organization. This must be done at several levels. Many sales and marketing processes could be managed on an even more European basis, especially with respect to used and new car pricing and marketing. An increased level of integration will be required to better control the distribution, implying the reduction of independent national sales companies, or to develop more entrenched alliances and to increase the weight of affiliates. Distribution costs can be further optimized by adapting the traditional country organization into leaner structures, especially to cope with small countries within the newly formed EU-25. In this context, leaner structures could mean clustering business into regions with shared activities at the regional level. Many activities, from call centres to HR payroll processes, can also be outsourced.

CONCLUSION: WHICH PLAYERS WILL MANAGE TO CAPTURE VALUE ALONG THE CAR LIFECYCLE?

The automotive sales and after-sales landscape will continue to evolve over the next few years. Market players will have to adapt their business models to survive in this new environment. New threats will develop, but automotive market participants will also gain opportunities to capture additional value throughout the car lifecycle.

Despite the strong acceleration over the past five to eight years, the pace of evolution in this sector is rather slow. This is a result of industry fragmentation, the evolution of the car market (a model lifecycle is between 10 and 15 years!), and the regulation spread. Another factor contributing to the slow pace of evolution is specific to Europe. No single market in Europe is completely identical to another owing to different regulatory environments, different car market profiles, different types of players and different customers' habits.

Projecting the winners and losers that will emerge in 10 to 15 years time is difficult given the complexity of the different markets and drivers. Irrespective of the market, one key strategic issue is how the relationship between captive and non-captive players will pan out. Despite the difficulty of projecting winners and losers in the near future, we have sketched out three potential scenarios for 2015 to 2025 to illustrate how the sector could develop.

Although the sketched scenarios are perhaps a little exaggerated, they are based on our trend analysis. We have also taken into account the contrasting situation that already exists between European countries today, for example between the UK and Germany, and Spain or Italy and France.

Let's assume we are in 2020.

The 'fully captive' scenario

Given the new technologies that have been introduced over the past 10 to 20 years such as X-by-wire or multiplexing, cars have become so complex and repairs so specific that it is near-impossible to have them repaired anywhere else but at the OEM. Car maintenance these days has more to do with providing updates for the different software inside the car than with changing tyres. As a consequence, multi-brand repairers have either vanished or are restricted to repairing very old vehicles. Only OEMs have the ability to maintain and repair new cars.

Remote maintenance tools and assistance warnings that oblige the customer to bring the vehicle back to where it was purchased also directly bind the vehicle and the place of purchase. A similar situation exists in the used car market. Used car customers are offered such attractive financial services and insurance conditions as well as other services that they become tied to the place of purchase. The IAM has shrunk because cars cannot be repaired there, suppliers – unable to sell many parts in this market – are firmly locked in by OEMs, and easy-to-fit parts such as some spark plugs, wipers and tyres are sold by retail store chains. OEMs are vertically integrated, with subsidiaries in most critical geographical areas. They have developed fleet management services, either internally or via partnerships, to offer LTD solutions to private companies.

The 'fully non-captive' scenario

Cars have become too expensive to purchase, too expensive to repair, too polluting, and not safe enough, according to the European Commission. Various major independent players and 'specialized prescriber groups' are increasingly defining the rules of the market owing to their influence on customer choice. Customers are more frequently choosing vehicles based on ratings from specialized agencies and institutions. These favour certain criteria such as fuel consumption, safety, quality, ergonomics, contribution to sustainable development, buy-back value, total maintenance cost, and body shape selection flexibility. These specialized agencies have even developed their own official label.

The sales channel is driven by various non-captive and independent players such as banks, financial institutions, insurance firms and fleet management companies, all of which offer their customers bundled solutions. For instance favourable credit is offered for real estate investments, which is bundled with the LTD rental of a fully-serviced family car, and a full insurance package covering both vehicle and house is thrown into the deal as well. The package also enables customers to change their car model throughout the year, when it suits their needs. The customer can drive, for instance, a monospace vehicle over the weekend, a 4-wheel drive on vacation, and a coupe for work. The customer can choose not only between different types of vehicle but also between different brands.

These independent players have partnered with selected, referenced fleet management companies with whom they have negotiated specific rates for new and used cars. Repair and maintenance is fully managed by the independent company, which provides such services as roadside assistance, pick up, and repair at referenced repairers. The end-user does not know what parts have been replaced in the car because everything is covered in the contract. OE parts, matching quality parts, adaptable or reused parts are not visible to the end-user. Customers simply purchase a completely tailored contract providing full mobility service.

The 'retail' scenario

Distribution is controlled by powerful automotive distribution groups that not only sell cars but also provide all related services, including financial services, leasing and LTD. These players were once dependent on OEMs, but their size and multi-make contracts have granted them greater independence over the past years. Automotive distribution groups are also deeply involved in wholesale and repair activities, made possible through their own pan-European structure. Some have even developed a global structure. This situation arose following mergers between large multi-make dealer groups and previous IAM wholesalers and repair networks. It was also spurred along by organic growth in emerging countries such as China and India, and by alliances with distributors in the United States and Japan.

The distinction that once existed between the captive OES channel and the non-captive IAM channel is no longer in place. Automotive distribution groups are capturing customers and are in charge of defining sourcing policy for new cars, used cars, spare parts and financial services providers. They are starting to impose product and service specifications (car range, options and specific equipment) and are even selling cars and services under their own brand. Spare parts are sourced from an assortment of offers from their global footprint based on the best cost and rebates. Distribution groups also offer their customers innovative solutions such as multi-brand showrooms, one month's car trial, and bundled services. The market is divided between producers, OEMs, suppliers and distributors in a retail logic set-up.

Striking the balance

The future will likely contain elements of all three scenarios. Germany is the European country that already most closely fits the captive scenario, while the non-captive scenario can best be seen in the UK, and the retail scenario is best demonstrated in France. The balance that is struck between the players will be the determining factor in any scenario that develops. That balance will not be easy to find, since the bargaining power of many players is almost equal and a mutual dependency connects them. The equilibrium reached in each European market will depend on various factors.

One important factor is the country and market structure within any particular country. What will be critical in this context is the level of concentration among the different players, whether it is the OEM's home market, how integrated the banking and insurance system is, and how developed the OEM's brand equity is.

A second important factor is the maturity of the market. Whether the market is emerging or is already mature is a key question in this context. The maturity of the market also takes into account such factors as the transformation of the pool of cars and changing consumer habits.

Customer groups are also a factor that will affect the relationship between the players. Here a balance needs to be reached between the premium versus the volume segment, family versus youth, and even urban versus rural. The specific strategy taken by individual players, including brand and international development, will also be a critical factor.

The winners of this battle for value will likely be the players with the most financial power, the closest relationships with customers, and those that can best bundle opportunities. Independently financed players with only one business activity, brand and geographic area will lose this battle. To a large degree, the winners in terms of capturing value along the automotive lifecycle are already visible. It is easy to imagine an automotive landscape composed of four types of players: OEMs, large distribution groups, financial and insurance groups, and large professional customer groups.

Yet the mutual dependency between these players will become too strong to allow any one player to dominate the others along the value chain, as we depicted in each of the three scenarios. This powerful mutual dependency between the players with strong bargaining power will create the need for alliances or partnership structures. Based on predefined strategies, these partnership structures will be developed to address a specific market or customer segment.

In the premium car segment in emerging countries, for instance, a strategy that could be taken by an OEM would be to maximize vertical integration (as depicted in the captive scenario) but to simultaneously develop alliances with large fleet groups and financial companies. A volume OEM not operating in its home market could favour a strategy that involves partnering with key distribution groups and the development of a differentiated offer to compete with incumbent players (as we sketched out in the retail scenario).

The objective pursued will always be the same: to offer increasingly broad but tailored mobility solutions to the end-customer at lower and lower total cost. The automotive distribution value chain in Europe is far from optimum. Significant improvements can be made. Like other industry experts, we believe that 30 per cent of distribution costs could be eliminated or replaced by providing more added value to the final customer.

Part II

Case studies

8

Partnership as a model for success

Franz Fehrenbach, Chairman, Robert Bosch GmbH

This chapter considers cooperation between automobile manufacturers and their suppliers.

INTRODUCTORY REMARKS

In the course of many decades, German and European automobile manufacturers and their suppliers have worked hard to achieve their leading position in the world. A key factor in this success is the tradition of close cooperation, which has proven its worth and is just as valuable today as it has always been. This partnership was and is the prerequisite for the state-of-the-art technology with which the German car industry has made a name for itself across the globe. However, manufacturers and suppliers must now come to grips with profound changes of various kinds.

One of the main drivers behind these changes is the shifting of weights in the global automotive market. Asia continues to gain momentum as the world's most dynamic growth region. On the one hand, the emerging markets of Asia present enormous sales opportunities; on the other, international competition is becoming increasingly stiff. New contenders are coming of age in China and in India. Their goal is to establish themselves as major players, not only domestically, but also in international markets.

In addition, new market segments are developing: in the emerging markets of Asia and Eastern Europe, the demand for economy cars is growing. Despite their low price, these vehicles must comply with key consumption and emission standards, since the need to conserve resources and protect the climate is also growing, and this on a global scale. Such cars are also attracting the interest of buyers in established markets. If it wants to participate in global growth, then it is especially the German automobile industry, with its strong focus on advanced technology, that must find appropriate responses to these changes.

The sharp upswing in the price of oil poses a further challenge, and has rekindled the debate about future drive systems. If the automobile is to remain the favoured means of transportation, the car industry must find a suitable response to this debate. Moreover, with more and more cars on the road worldwide and with an increasing density of traffic, heightened demands will also be placed on safety.

At the same time, the automotive sector is marked by growing complexity. One reason for this is the growing diversity of models; another is the industry's increasing international spread. Among other things, this is leading to a change in the way automotive partners co-operate. Suppliers are assuming more and more tasks in development and production, tasks involving entire vehicle systems.

These numerous changes raise some important questions. Is the idea of partnership viable under these new conditions? What form will cooperation between automobile manufacturers and suppliers take in the future? What factors will be most important for successful cooperation between partners down the line?

THE EXAMPLE OF ESP: THE STORY OF A SUCCESSFUL PARTNERSHIP

When considering how partnerships can function successfully in the automotive industry and what factors come into play, one example that readily springs to mind is the development of ESP. Technologically, ESP was based on ABS, also developed as a joint effort between today's DaimlerChrysler AG and the Bosch Group. When it came to further developing the ABS system, the two companies initially took separate paths. The challenge they shared was to stabilize the vehicle against lateral forces; stabilizing it in a longitudinal direction was no longer enough. A Bosch engineer came up with the idea of a lateral slip control utilizing two lateral-acceleration sensors. At the same time, Bosch was in the process of developing a more economical single-channel ABS, which in the end proved not to be viable. The need for an additional sensor, a yaw-rate sensor, became apparent. Consequently, a decision was reached to develop a vehicle dynamics control system based on high-quality four-way hydraulics. In winter trials, engineers from Bosch and DaimlerChrysler demonstrated their differing solutions to each other. All involved agreed to cooperate even more closely in the future, and to use the concept developed by Bosch as the basis for continuing the project.

This marked the start of a joint project. Both sides established project organizations, each comprising nine teams of experts in the relevant disciplines: sensor technology, hydraulics, control unit engineering, controller and software application, measuring and test engineering, simulation, as well as purchasing and sales. The advantage of this mirror-image approach was that each of the specialists could contact his or her counterpart at the other company directly, without resorting to time-consuming official channels. In software development, where especially close co-operation was required, a core team of experts from both companies was assembled and assigned its own project facilities. This organizational structure alone meant that development took a good year less than originally planned. As a result, ESP was ready for its market launch as early as the mid-1990s.

Many obstacles along the way

The path to ESP was strewn with numerous technological challenges, notably in the area of software. For example, testing revealed that the initial prototypes were unable to distinguish between cornering on a steeply banked surface and spinning out on ice, since both situations involve only minimal lateral acceleration forces. Consequently, algorithms had to be developed to identify both the traction properties of the road surface and the banking angle of the vehicle. Such detailed work requires not only intensive communication with the customer, but also a willingness by both parties to carry out projects with uncompromising commitment. It also requires the ability to endure setbacks.

One key task was to adapt the yaw-rate sensor, the heart of the ESP system, to the requirements of the automobile. This kind of sensor was developed for space travel. In a rocket, such a sensor must function under extreme conditions, though here it is generally designed for one flight only. In an automotive application, on the other hand, it is expected to remain intact throughout the entire service life of the vehicle. But the task was not only one of developing the sensor itself. If the system was to achieve success in all segments of the market, then a solution had to be found that was suitable for large-scale series production and thus cost-effective. And today, a sensor that once required a bulky housing is contained in a micromechanical chip no larger than a fingernail. It is also now available for a hundredth of its original cost.

What can be learnt from the example of ESP

ESP has been a success story for years now. The legendary 'elk test' triggered a major surge in demand. At the time, Bosch managed to ramp up large-scale series production of ESP for the Mercedes A class within just a few weeks. This would have been impossible without the teamwork and coordinated project work with the manufacturer that had become routine during the development phase.

By the end of 2005, Bosch had delivered more than 15 million systems. Almost three-quarters of new cars currently sold in Germany are equipped with ESP; the total figure for Western Europe is 40 per cent. All manufacturers here support initiatives like the EU e-Safety programme, which aims to halve the number of road deaths by 2010. This requires that an increasing percentage of cars and trucks be equipped with ESP. This percentage will also grow in the United States, as independent studies have confirmed that the significant safety benefits of ESP apply equally to American road traffic.

This example of the joint development of ESP touches on virtually all the factors that make for successful cooperation and partnership between car makers and suppliers. These include:

- the independence and responsibility of both parties;
- the common goal of technological leadership;
- cost-effective structures and processes;
- international cooperation;
- a shared long-term perspective.

FACTORS IN PARTNERSHIP

The first factor in partnership: independence and responsibility

In the automotive industry, a key international sector, major successes have many sources. One of the main reasons for the technological leadership of the German and European automotive industry is undoubtedly the close cooperation of car manufacturers with independent suppliers acting on their own responsibility. Close cooperation is characterized by common goals: both partners work to achieve overriding common objectives to their mutual benefit. Manufacturers and suppliers see themselves in many respects as being in the same boat, but especially when it comes to ensuring that the automobile remains appealing to consumers on a long-term basis, while at the same time remaining geared to changing demands on environmental compatibility, safety and economy.

Entrepreneurial independence and responsibility means that each party involved is responsible for its own business success, and therefore retains the authority to decide whether or not to enter into contractual relationships. The other side of the coin is, of course, loyalty to the terms of a contract, which leads to a complex web of economic interdependencies. In this regard, business always involves a system of dependencies. However, this system must be designed for the benefit of all concerned. A one-sided advantage is generally possible for the short term only, and even then it poses a threat to the long-term success of the parties involved, including the supposed 'winner'.

The independence that allows companies to enter into contractual relationships brings with it all the fundamental advantages of the division of labour. Each partner company specializes in its strengths, concentrating its competence on the further development of those areas in which its specialization holds particular advantages. And since both sides must also compete in the marketplace, both feel the pressure to drive innovation and efficiency with great creativity, as well as to adapt flexibly and consistently to changing requirements. Based on this proven division of labour, the ideas and developments of suppliers contribute significantly to technological progress throughout the entire sector. At the same time, they must make every effort to produce systems and components as cost-effectively as possible. And in cooperation with manufacturers, they must ensure that the various systems in a vehicle are perfectly compatible with each other.

Inequality of power

The independence of suppliers results in tangible benefits for all concerned, yet working relationships often suffer when there is a disparity in power between the partners. The fact is that concentration has sharply increased in the industry. Automobile manufacturers have grown into worldwide conglomerates that consistently utilize their strong positions, especially when it comes to purchasing. In principle, what serves to check this increase in manufacturers' market power is the proportion of value added contributed to the automobile by suppliers in general, which has now grown to between 60 and 70 per cent. To counter this, manufacturers pursue a strategy of breaking down systems into components, to enable them to purchase interchangeable parts at lower prices.

Purchasing prices are not all that is under pressure today. There is a growing trend towards transferring a greater share of quality risks and the associated guarantee costs to suppliers, often in full awareness of the risk of adversely affecting their capacity for innovation. Especially for small and medium-size suppliers, an individual order can be critical to the survival of the entire company. For this reason, they are extremely limited in their freedom to say 'no', and often agree to accept risks that carry with them a potential threat to their very existence. Appealing here to the manufacturer's sense of fairness may be an honest approach, but in light of today's gruelling competition on all sides, it holds little promise of success. The consequences are only logical: shake-out and increasing concentration also in the supplier camp.

Competence and a broad footing support independence

Having the strength to maintain an independent position means that a supplier must have a strong and reliable capacity for innovation, quality and cost-effectiveness. Also of key importance is the ability to draw on a broad portfolio of customers and products, as well as to utilize a global presence. Ever since Bosch was founded, it has been working systematically to fulfil these requirements. The company has gone even further by entering into markets beyond the area of automotive technology, with good business success.

Bosch has achieved presentable results with this strategic orientation: sustainable, positive growth over the course of many decades, coupled with a stable financial position. This in turn puts Bosch in a position to make major up-front investments in new technologies, while offering its customers long-term, stable cooperation that is successful for both sides.

Our observation is that this approach of achieving and consistently defending a position of independence is in the best interests of the entire automotive industry, an observation which is clearly borne out by the many negative examples of other companies that had for a long time pursued a different approach. This is especially apparent today in North America, where domestic manufacturers and suppliers alike are struggling with major economic problems. In the cultural contexts of Japan and South Korea, there has long been a tradition of close ties between manufacturers and suppliers, even to the point of cross-investments and holdings. Such a relationship affords the supplier comparatively little decisional autonomy. For the most part, responsibility for technological development here is also in the hands of the manufacturer, with suppliers taking on a largely in-house role.

But here too the situation is beginning to change, as the automotive industry can no longer take part in the global market on the basis of export activities alone. The impetus to change is coming from both sides: from manufacturers, who cannot simply take their suppliers with them when expanding into other regions, and from suppliers, who either seek cooperation with leading international systems suppliers with specific know-how or wish to establish a worldwide customer base themselves. Generally speaking, Bosch has already achieved what these companies are working towards: independence based on competence and a broad international footprint.

The second factor in partnership: the common goal of technological leadership

The purpose of a partnership is to bring each party's specific skills and capacities to bear on common challenges and goals. If the European and German automotive industry is to prevail in global competition, manufacturers and suppliers alike will have to master three main tasks: to maintain technological leadership by means of innovation, continue to improve quality standards, and offer products at competitive prices.

Especially over the past 10 years, a wide range of innovations have played a crucial role in the success of the European and German automotive sector. These advances have helped boost vehicles' performance dramatically, in terms of fuel consumption and emissions as well as in terms of safety, comfort, and driver support.

Bosch has also participated in this positive development, even though expanded activities outside Europe have accounted for a major portion of the substantial sales growth recorded in its automotive technology business sector, a growth in sales from 10.5 billion euros in 1995 to some 26 billion euros in 2005. The greatest contribution Bosch has made to the innovation drive over the past 10 years is to be found in the development of ABS and ESP, in direct-injection systems for diesel and gasoline engines, and in navigation and driver assistance systems. To achieve this, the Bosch Group has continuously increased its research and development expenditures in its automotive technology sector over the same period. Today, these expenditures represent more than 9 per cent of sales in this sector, considerably above the industry average.

Suppliers assume more and more responsibilities

Such exceptionally high research and development expenditures of Bosch and other automotive suppliers clearly reflect the fact that suppliers are taking on a growing share of vehicle development tasks. The trend among car makers is to concentrate more on overall vehicle architecture, specific model features and design, as well as on assembly, marketing and service, in order to prevail in today's globally merging markets.

In this context, suppliers are playing an ever more important role in driving innovations, becoming more active in the development and production of systems and special components. In the end, this is also absolutely necessary to ensure that innovations remain economically viable. Provided suppliers are independent and work with different customers, they can stay in a position to manufacture in the large production runs required to amortize their high R&D costs. Ultimately, it was this ability that allowed Bosch to carry out such developments as ESP and high-pressure diesel injection.

Forward-looking cooperation: AUTOSAR

Future developments in automotive technology will be driven by electronics even more than has been the case up to now. The share of electronics in vehicles will thus continue to rise in the years to come. Yet electronics, alongside the greater diversity of models and variants, today's significantly shorter model cycles, and the enormous range of subsystems used, is a major driver of complexity and cost. Generating viable solutions for the future under these circumstances places exceptionally high demands on partnerships between manufacturers and suppliers.

In 2003 Bosch was one of the founding members of the industry alliance AUTOSAR, together with other German suppliers and manufacturers. This acronym stands for 'Automotive Open Systems Architecture', and accordingly the partnership is dedicated to developing a concept for a common, standardized electrics/electronics architecture. The concept is to be introduced to the market as a way of replacing a number of conventional company-specific solutions. Nearly all major manufacturers and suppliers worldwide have now joined the initiative. AUTOSAR is thus not only an example of how partnership allows growing systems complexity to be brought financially under control to the benefit of all involved; it also takes account of the increasing levels of global interdependence. The initiative gives each partner the freedom to differentiate in order to secure a competitive advantage. At the same time, it will be possible to develop uniform basic software functions which have no immediate bearing on competitive position.

The common goal of quality

Along with reducing the development costs of electronic systems, a key objective of AUTOSAR is to master the complexity of such systems, which results from the proliferation of control units in the car. Many cars today have as many as 70 control units. For the future, it is planned that a network of some 20 control units will regulate all vehicle functions. This complexity is by no means arbitrary, but for the most part the logical consequence of current demands with respect to emissions and fuel consumption, as well as safety and comfort. However, malfunctions as a result of complexity have given rise to a new quality debate among customers. Breakdown statistics in recent years have shown that quality leadership no longer resides with German premium car makes. On occasion, manufacturers and suppliers have even publicly blamed one another for quality deficits. Such a debate is damaging to the entire industry, regardless of where responsibility for the shortcomings may lie. The situation has now improved considerably, and statistics reflect initial positive trends. And German cars are regaining lost ground in quality rankings.

An important milestone was reached on 22 June 2005: the agreement 'Quality, the Foundation for Joint Success' between manufacturers and suppliers on the managing board of the German Association of the Automotive Industry (VDA), an agreement which also regulates communications. The focus of this agreement is on partnerships between manufacturers and suppliers, not only in terms of external communications, but also in terms of sharing knowledge and taking rapid, coordinated action when the necessity arises.

Partnership is built on trust and transparency. Trust means that critical and difficult issues as well as outright bad news are discussed openly and without delay. Problems are solved by working together. This applies to all corporate levels, internal as well as external. As a systems supplier,

Bosch must act as both transmitter and receiver of such information in communications with its customers and suppliers.

Transparency means that each partner must be aware of the other partner's current projects, what modifications are planned, and how the products will later be deployed, even if a system or component is to be deployed in a model not originally planned. However, should this benefit a product, partnership also means adopting quality tools that have been used successfully by a partner. For instance, Bosch has adopted a number of quality tools from Toyota.

In the future, Bosch will review its own processes and those of its suppliers more intensively than ever before for ways of optimizing quality. As tier 1 automotive suppliers become fewer in number, we have a greater responsibility for tracking the high-quality demands of car makers throughout the entire supply chain. In doing so, it will be essential for us to extend the spirit of partnership to include every supply level.

Innovative products for new market segments

The German automobile industry has experienced most of its international success over the last 10 years with premium vehicles. In many areas, German suppliers have stood for high-tech systems and products. In the 10 years to come, however, the most significant growth can be expected with cars selling for under 10,000 euros net, or even less than 7,000 euros net in some cases. And this applies not only to emerging markets in Asia, but to Eastern Europe as well. New responses are called for.

These markets are demanding low-cost vehicles that can still meet minimum standards with respect to fuel consumption, emissions and safety. For example, for the meantime the Euro 3 emissions standard for diesel engines applies to Beijing and Shanghai. Only with modern electronic injection systems is compliance with this standard possible. At the same time, new local manufacturers are maturing in emerging markets such as India and China. These new contenders have set their sights on precisely this target group, and are also looking to succeed worldwide with such cars. But it is not only German suppliers who need to answer the all-important question, whether they are able to deliver the right products in order to do business with these new manufacturers. It would help if both German manufacturers and suppliers were to work together on technological solutions to exploit these market opportunities.

Shared market interests

One example of shared market interests, which more than anything brought Bosch and manufacturers closer together, resulted from the debate on particulate matter in 2005. In Germany, the controversy was focused almost exclusively on diesel engines. With its undisputed benefits for fuel consumption and climate protection, diesel technology has significantly strengthened the competitive position of the European and German automotive industry in recent years. Germany has profited considerably as a business and industry location. In 2005, roughly half of all new passenger vehicles sold in Europe were equipped with diesel engines.

A heated debate threatened to end this success story, particularly in Germany, after a strict EU directive on particulate matter came into effect in early 2005. It remains undisputed that diesel emissions from local passenger vehicle traffic constitute as little as 3 per cent of particulate-matter pollution in our cities. Yet the German public perceived diesel engines as the sole culprit, even though the image of diesel-powered cars as sluggish polluters should be a thing of the past. Diesel engines have become not only more fuel-efficient and agile, but also significantly cleaner: internal engine improvements alone have reduced particulate emissions by a good 90 per cent since 1990.

The Euro 5 standard, planned for 2010, foresees particulate emission levels close to zero for new cars. In addition, early replacement of older vehicles would further reduce these emissions by almost 20 per cent in five years, and this applies to all diesel-powered passenger cars on the road. Not least thanks to a persistent information campaign by the automotive industry, more objectivity was brought to the debate. This is also necessary if the diesel is to exploit its potential beyond Europe.

The 'globalization of diesel' is in the interest of the entire European automotive industry. It has a technological advantage in this area which it should utilize on a global scale. Diesel acceptance in North America is crucial, and accomplishing this will require a joint marketing strategy for the European automotive industry. Bosch has already made a large-scale commitment, with measures including 'Diesel Days' and a test-drive fleet. Initial success can be seen: approximately two out of every three drivers in the United States plan to at least consider a diesel when buying a new car. Were its proportion of diesel-powered light utility vehicles at the European level today, the United States would be largely independent of oil imports.

In 2005, the US Congress agreed on measures to promote fuel-efficient vehicles. Fortunately, this applies to diesel-powered cars as well as hybrid models. The addition of the particle filter further improves the chances for 'dieselization' on the other side of the Atlantic. Bosch is also working on control concepts and metering systems aimed at reducing nitrous oxides to comply with US07 limits in all states. Development projects involving American and European manufacturers are in progress.

A further challenge for the European automotive industry is the simultaneous development of hybrid solutions. Hybrid drive concepts are mainly suitable for stop-and-go traffic, and thus offer most of their benefits in urban areas. Accordingly, the market share of hybrid passenger cars and light utility vehicles in Japan could reach 10 per cent by 2015. More modest changes are predicted in the American market, despite notable initial successes scored mainly by Toyota. The United States is a nation of long distances, heavy cars and powerful engines. This situation cries out for partnerships between manufacturers and suppliers, partnerships that will allow them to shoulder the costs of developing this technology together. Bosch is working intensively on various hybrid concepts, and has established a 'Competence Centre for Hybrid Systems' dedicated to this purpose.

The third factor in partnership: cost-effective structures and processes

Structures and processes in the automotive sector must reflect the changing demands of the market. Along with technological leadership, this is a fundamental prerequisite for the future joint success of manufacturers and suppliers. As already mentioned, an ever larger proportion of value added is being shifted from manufacturers to suppliers. The associated changes in the division of labour necessitate further structural adjustments in the cooperation between manufacturers and suppliers, as do abbreviated product lifecycles and expanding product variant ranges. Moreover, the growing number of production sites maintained by manufacturers and suppliers at locations all around the world results in heightened demands on all business processes.

These challenges cannot be mastered by individual companies alone, nor can they be mastered through individual measures. The entire value added chain, beginning with the product-creation process, must be looked at. Here, more than at any other stage, close cooperation in the spirit of partnership is required. In a very early phase of product development, engineers must begin to work in a close-knit network. This is the only way to avoid unfortunate product design constellations that result in unnecessary additional costs or even quality risks for the manufacturer or supplier.

It is not only in development, however, that customer and supplier must closely coordinate their processes at an early stage. A logistics concept must be defined almost equally early on. The same goes for a quality and inspection concept for the supplier's products. The goal must always be to optimize the competitive position of both partners by avoiding the waste of resources in any form, while at the same time developing reliable manufacturing methods that allow inspection processes to be minimized at the end of the assembly line. This applies to the entire supply chain.

Geographical proximity remains important

The proximity of manufacturers and suppliers is becoming increasingly important for the application stage. While new communications technology renders face-to-face meetings unnecessary in some cases during the design and development phase, it is essential that engineers and technicians are able to practically get behind the wheel together during application. In order to provide this hands-on service to customers in as many countries as possible, Bosch is significantly expanding the number of its application centres worldwide.

Once a component or system has gone into production, fast and effective communications between supplier and manufacturer become a top priority. Both parties must be in a position to take rapid and decisive action in the event of a critical situation, be it a supply bottleneck or a quality-related incident. This was illustrated by the example of diesel pumps in early 2005: during production, ongoing endurance tests conducted by Bosch indicated that a number of pumps failed to perform for the length of the defined service life. Bosch swiftly relayed this unpleasant and unwelcome finding to the automobile manufacturers affected, and it was possible to halt delivery of vehicles with potentially defective pumps to buyers. Furthermore, in cooperation with the manufacturers' materials specialists, expert teams from Bosch were able to isolate and evaluate the defect, and reach a decision together with their partners on measures to correct it. The incident gave rise to a new discussion on partnership in quality issues at the VDA, with fruitful results. As mentioned above, the entire VDA managing board signed the accord 'Quality, the Foundation for Joint Success'.

Balancing innovation and cost leadership

Throughout the value added chain, each company in our sector is reliant on the cost-effectiveness of its partners. First and foremost, however, each is of course responsible for optimizing the cost-effectiveness of its own operations.

As the world's largest automotive supplier, Bosch faces the twofold challenge of maintaining its leadership in technological development while at the same time offering its products at competitive prices. Which of these challenges outweighs the other depends on the maturity and age of a given product. Bosch will continue to introduce pioneering developments such as

ABS, ESP and high-pressure diesel injection in order to set itself apart from the price competition. Yet it has become increasingly difficult to retain a technological edge for any length of time, with the result that innovations must now face stiff cost competition soon after they are launched. At that point, if not earlier, it becomes crucial to optimize processes for cost-effectiveness and to consider alternative production sites. For this reason, some 50 per cent of our R&D expenditures today are dedicated to product and process innovations whose purpose is to reduce costs. At the same time, a worldwide production network that includes low-cost sites in emerging markets must be established at an early stage, even for high-tech products. In the case of the highly innovative common-rail diesel-injection system, nearly two-thirds of its value added is already created outside Germany. In this way, Bosch not only meets the demand of producing locally within its markets, but also reduces total manufacturing costs.

To realize the maximum earnings potential in a given area of business, it is essential to recognize at an early stage the point at which the competitive advantage of technological differentiation is superseded by price. Business in systems is typically displaced by business in components as a technology matures. Today, classic gasoline-injection technology is rarely delivered as a complete system. However, it is considerably more difficult to achieve technological differentiation with individual components, such as injection valves or fuel pumps, than with complete systems. In this case, the focus is on keeping costs as low as possible, and thus on optimum processes.

Process optimization is called for

This demands a new, and above all self-critical, approach to processes. Whether they involve development, purchasing, production or sales, many processes on all levels of the value added chain are often still too complex and thus too costly. In order to exploit the potential of greater efficiencies, it is necessary to part with a number of traditional yet often superfluous procedures. For example, in some cases Bosch had taken complexity a step too far in automating its production. The Bosch Production System, designed after a Japanese model, represents at least a partial return to more straightforward processes and procedures.

A mix of high-cost and low-cost countries

Bosch, like other companies, must exploit the value-added potential of the world's low-cost regions in order to stay competitive. However, its principles remain unchanged: for Bosch, there is more to intelligent locational planning than cost management. Now, more than ever, skilled leveraging of an international development and production network is the key to success. Each region of the triad requires a mix of locations, those offering special cost advantages as well as those that benefit from proximity to major customers or research centres. And it is still the case today that Bosch plants in Germany have enormous strengths when it comes to new product launches, not least thanks to their experience in handling complex systems. On the other hand, their competitive position must be ensured by integrating low-cost locations into the network.

The number of Bosch associates working in automotive technology in Germany has risen to more than 65,000 over the past 10 years. However, the automotive workforce outside Germany has doubled during the same period, growing to more than 90,000. For the future, the question that arises for us is how these jobs can be retained at today's locations. And this applies not only to Germany, but also to the rest of the world. It is impossible to bring about wage parity between industrialized and emerging countries. In essence, what we are after is an intelligent weighting of all locational factors in order to create a balance between locations with advantages in terms of know-how or of political and social stability on the one hand, and locations in emerging countries with especially pronounced cost advantages on the other. Such weighting cannot be a one-off action, but must be continuously adapted in step with global changes.

The fourth factor in partnership: international presence

A further factor is becoming increasingly important for the success of the industry, as well as in cooperation between car makers and their suppliers: their international spread. The German automotive sector is now a global business. This is especially true of Bosch. Some 75 per cent of our sales in automotive technology are generated outside Germany, including non-German production. Europe, with roughly two-thirds of sales, still accounts for the lion's share. Yet the two other regions in the triad, the Americas and Asia Pacific, continue to grow in importance. In 2005, the Bosch Group had around 110 production sites in 34 countries in automotive technology alone.

Internationalization began early at Bosch

Bosch is an international company by tradition. As early as 1898, the company's founder Robert Bosch established his first sales office outside Germany in London, just 12 years after his 'Workshop for Precision Mechanics and Electrical Engineering' opened for business in Stuttgart. In

1913, the last year of peace before the First World War, Bosch generated nearly 90 per cent of its sales abroad. The key product in this early internationalization was the magneto ignition device. It made Bosch an automotive supplier and established the company's global presence, even at that early stage. Following each of the world wars, however, Bosch had to go though the difficult process of becoming re-established in international markets. It was especially difficult to regain a foothold in the aftermath of the Second World War, as by then the markets were firmly in the hands of competitors. Moreover, unlike at the beginning of the 20th century, Bosch was not in a position to offer a product with the same unique appeal as the high-voltage magneto ignition device.

Like other suppliers, Bosch carried out its new internationalization initiative in three steps. The company began by supplying original replacement parts for exported German cars, including Volkswagen and Mercedes, in the United States. The second phase began after German car makers had established plants in countries such as Brazil, Argentina, Mexico and Australia, as early as the 1950s and 1960s. To supply them, Bosch built its own local production facilities, an especially important move, as high import duties coupled with local content regulations would have rendered delivery from German plants impossible. These facilities continue to exist today, although now following the liberalization of markets their main advantage is that they allow Bosch to be close to the customer and to utilize generally lower wage costs. In a third phase, Bosch succeeded in winning over non-German car makers as original equipment customers. In the 1990s, important milestones in internationalization included the acquisition of the brake business of the American manufacturer AlliedSignal and the assumption of industrial leadership at the Japanese supplier Zexel.

Shifting growth regions

German manufacturers and suppliers must learn to accept that globalization of the automotive industry will continue. Most importantly, the strongest growth will occur in Asia and Eastern Europe in coming years. If German car makers and German suppliers wish to participate in this growth, they must make an even greater commitment to internationalization. This holds in equal measure for the Bosch Group. In the long term, we aim to increase the proportion of our automotive technology sales in the Americas and Asia from the present level of approximately 36 per cent to roughly 50 per cent. It is worth mentioning that internationalization is by no means a one-way street. This is evident in the moves of Japanese and Korean manufacturers to establish plants in the United

States and Europe, as well as in the redoubled efforts of American and Asian suppliers to expand their presence in the European market.

Global responses to local requirements

International presence is thus a key factor in partnership between manufacturers and suppliers. It is not just for cost reasons that Bosch has established an international development and manufacturing network for its core products. More importantly, a successful supplier must act at least as globally as its customers. This also means being able to develop local solutions for specific needs in each country. For VW and GM in Brazil, for example, Bosch has produced a fuel-injection system that functions with sugar cane ethanol in addition to gasoline. Such new ideas can only be anticipated and carried through on the basis of a strong local presence.

However, local solutions alone are not enough. The first 'global ABS', which was introduced to the market in the mid-1990s, represented a milestone for Bosch. It was shaped by the needs of Japanese car makers with plants in Asia as well as in Europe, which wanted to be supplied with the same system at all locations, yet with as much local content as possible. In other words, the system had to be manufactured regionally or at least on the same continent. A global ABS was the only solution that would allow this to be achieved in combination with high production volumes. Only in this way was it possible to minimize initial costs for development and process technology.

Yet this did not necessarily mean that special customer wishes would be neglected. Indeed, standardized key technologies provided the basis for modifications. This approach even shortened release procedures. Once an automobile manufacturer had approved an ABS component at one production facility, there was no need to carry out another time-consuming analysis on the other side of the globe. If this was to work, there had to be identical manufacturing processes and machine tools at all sites involved, in Germany, the United States and Japan just as in Australia and South Korea. This coordination encouraged greater flexibility. Despite local content requirements, case to case capacity bottlenecks could be compensated for with deliveries from other plants. The worldwide manufacturing network was backed up by a worldwide development network. Accordingly, the design of the hydraulic modulator for the global ABS emerged from a competition held within the company. American, German and Japanese engineers participated, and the design chosen to be manufactured included ideas from all sides. The process led to a sustained intensification of cooperation on a global scale.

Bosch has a broad international footprint

Today, Bosch operates more than 50 engineering and application centres around the world. One out of three R&D associates works outside Germany. Of these associates, some 2,000 are located in the Americas, and roughly a further 2,000 in Asia. In Japan alone, Bosch employs nearly 1,000 automotive engineers. Development capacities have been concentrated there for good reason: automobile production may be growing only modestly within Japan itself, yet as far as technical concepts for international business are concerned, Japanese manufacturers continue to reach important decisions in Japan.

The capacity to adapt locally to the individual needs of each manufacturer is therefore critically important if automotive suppliers are to be successful globally. Accordingly, it was no coincidence that in 2004 Bosch decided to establish a new engineering centre with 2,000 engineers in Abstatt, near Heilbronn in south-west Germany. A supplier wishing to present itself and its know-how to the world side by side with German manufacturers must be near the car makers' development centres. At the same time, Bosch set up further engineering centres in the Chinese cities of Suzhou and Wuxi. Again, our software development centre in Bangalore, India, provides valuable support for all our automotive technology divisions. For example, the Bosch subsidiary Blaupunkt also utilizes the know-how of Indian software specialists in the development of its navigation systems.

The fifth factor in partnership: a long-term perspective

The increasingly complex and international structures of the global automotive industry are not the only factors influencing cooperation between manufacturers and suppliers. Not only the hard, but also the ostensibly soft factors play a role. Along with independence, these include a long-term perspective.

In these hectic times of quarterly reporting, dictated by the finance markets, there is no denying that the ownership structure of Bosch, with a charitable foundation as its principal shareholder, makes it easier to take such a long-term perspective. Bosch is in a position to commit itself to major up-front investments over the long term without having to justify the short-term financial consequences to the outside world. Especially for fundamental innovations, perseverance is an asset.

The example of ESP demonstrates the extent to which the development of electronic systems can become an obstacle course. Again and again, the path to success in innovation is fraught with difficulty, and can also be long and hard. Even the development of ABS was certainly on the brink of failure more than once. During the first winter trial of ABS in 1972, nearly one in three control units broke down under gruelling conditions. The electronic systems were prone to failure because they were made up of over a thousand analogue components. When today's DaimlerChrysler AG and Bosch introduced ABS to the market in the Mercedes S class in the summer of 1978, this marked the first application of a digital LSI circuit in a series-produced car: the breakthrough that put electronics on the road.

The need for stamina and perseverance

Nor was the current diesel boom a matter of course. It began in 1989 with the Audi 100 TDI, the first passenger car with electronically controlled direct injection. Bosch had worked tenaciously for 15 years to get this technology up and running. No less demanding was the development of the common-rail system to the point of maturity for series production in the mid-1990s. For example, the nozzle needle play in the injectors had to be manufactured to a level of accuracy measured in fractions of micrometres, and initial yields of the pilot series were not even half of what was expected. It was not easy to maintain faith in success in this phase of development and preparation for series production.

Innovation drives alone are not enough to bring about innovations, nor do they mean that good ideas will prevail in the global marketplace. Stamina is called for, especially in the face of setbacks. The German automotive industry's strong international position is also the result of long-term thought and action. In other words, technological advances are also rooted in culture. The ability to be spurred on by setbacks along the way and to defiantly face down temporary failures is the basis of the great innovative strength that has characterized the German automotive industry in recent years.

PARTNERSHIP IN THE CONTEXT OF GLOBAL CHANGE

What does the future hold? How will the coming changes affect future cooperation? Will today's factors remain significant?

The automotive sector stands a good chance of maintaining its position as one of the world's key industries also over the next 10 years. The undiminished desire for individual mobility, which is no less strong in today's developing countries and emerging markets than it is in wealthy industrialized nations, speaks in favour of this optimism. Mobility forms the basis of modern society and also of a flourishing economy. As a flexible means of transportation, the automobile plays a decisive role in this mobility.

At the same time, the automotive industry undeniably faces major changes. One of the biggest challenges is the shift in the focal points of global growth. By 2015, Asia will overtake both Europe and North America to become by far the world's highest-volume car manufacturing region. And this is more than a purely regional development: it will also bring with it structural changes in the automotive markets. What is more, tough competition awaits established manufacturers, whether in Europe, North America or Japan, from new players in today's emerging countries. The same can be expected for suppliers. This development is already taking shape in China and India, further intensifying global competition in the automotive sector among manufacturers as well as suppliers. In this context, innovative products and processes will remain key factors, as these alone can generate true progress in the industry.

Pressure of competition, increasing demands on innovative strength and international presence, as well as the greater share of value added assumed by suppliers (resulting in ever higher amounts of capital employed): all these factors will lead to higher levels of concentration among automotive suppliers. This prospect is not without its problems. After all, amid growing concentration among manufacturers over the past decade, it was the suppliers who provided much of the necessary flexibility, and thus generated crucial impetus for the further development of the automotive industry as one of the world's most innovative sectors.

Considering this development, it will be even more important for the individual supplier to hone an unmistakable and individual profile in the future. Those who succeed in adapting to the process of change, systematically enhancing their innovative strength and international presence, will be rewarded by considerable market opportunities.

How will this influence cooperation between manufacturers and suppliers? The global market entry of new manufacturers and suppliers from developing and emerging countries will reshuffle the cards: that much is certain. The question is, however, whether the rules of the game in international cooperation will also be redefined.

Joint responses to future challenges

If the individual mobility that only the automobile can provide is to continue growing on a worldwide scale, solutions to fundamental future challenges are required. As was touched on at the beginning of this chapter, these include the necessity to further reduce consumption and develop alternative drive concepts, especially in light of finite oil reserves. Equal importance must be attached to heightened demands on vehicle emissions derived from increasingly strict legal regulations in all countries, intended to counter global climate change. Furthermore, rising traffic density will not only lead to even greater demands on vehicle safety; it will also necessitate improvements in traffic guidance. And the fact that populations are ageing means there will be more demand for additional comfort and driver assistance, not only in today's industrialized nations.

Finding responses to these fundamental future challenges calls for considerable research and development expenditures involving the entire industry. This calls for a concerted effort on the part of manufacturers and suppliers. It requires not only bilateral partnerships between individual companies, but also cooperation on a global scale. AUTOSAR is a good example of what such a partnership might look like.

It is precisely here that significant future opportunities for the German and European automotive industry lie, provided it can make its development cooperation model viable for the 21st century. Its successes are based on networks of close ties which have grown over a long period. These represent a decisive competitive advantage, as business relationships of this calibre are virtually impossible to establish artificially and on a short-term basis. Alongside manufacturers and suppliers, these 'clusters' include an outstanding toolmaking and mechanical engineering industry, a highly developed training system, as well as reputed colleges of applied sciences, universities and research institutes. In addition, awareness of the need to reduce consumption and protect the climate is already strongly pronounced in Germany and the rest of Europe. For ideal test markets, the industry needs to look no further than its own backyard.

However, the essential prerequisite for mastering these major challenges for the future of the automotive industry is cooperation built on shared long-term perspectives, trust and partnership. This by no means excludes intense competition between manufacturers and among suppliers. On the contrary: healthy competition is the only guarantee of processes that are cost-effective over the long term. Consistently working to establish and fine-tune such processes is the responsibility of each individual company, for manufacturers and suppliers alike. However, shared objectives and fair rules are also a must. Each party involved must be able to profit from such joint efforts in proportion to its contribution, allowing it to continue investing in the future and in its innovative capacity. Anything else would endanger the long-term competitiveness of manufacturers and suppliers, indeed of the automotive industry as a whole.

Trust as a basis

Such relationships, as well as trust, will only survive if all those involved feel they have been treated fairly and openly. Only then will partners agree to join forces in long-term, capital-intensive (and risk-oriented) innovation projects. It is on projects such as these that the future viability of the entire automotive industry depends.

In light of the increasingly interdependent nature of the global automotive industry, it is important to establish such a culture of trust on a worldwide scale. That means agreeing on shared values or basic principles. In some cases it also means returning to neglected or forgotten approaches. Once established, the advantage of such shared principles is that, despite cultural differences, they obviate the need for rigid rules. From a business standpoint, they reduce risks, lower costs, and create the basis for long-term relationships. To achieve this, it is essential that all those involved recognize the fact that close cooperation based on partnership offers both manufacturers and suppliers decisive advantages in confronting the common challenges they face, and thus a solid basis for successfully taking the automotive industry into the future.

9

Brand differentiation on the basis of platform and module strategies

Dr Bernd Pischetrieder, Chairman, Volkswagen AG

FRAGMENTATION

The global automobile market has been undergoing an intensive process of change for some time now, with the borderlines between national markets becoming increasingly blurred and the tempo of information gathering pace at a tremendous rate. Technical developments are increasingly speeding up, and at the same time the competitive environment in the automobile markets is becoming progressively tougher.

The growing fragmentation of the markets has become one of the biggest challenges facing the automobile industry. Recent analyses show that in 1987, customers discerned nine different vehicle segments, the perceived dimensions of this segmentation being in particular driving pleasure, prestige, usefulness and versatility as well as price. By 1997 this number had already risen from 9 to 26 different vehicle segments, while this year our customers are perceiving no less than 40 (Figure 9.1). From the automobile manufacturers' point of view this means that each vehicle project requires the production of an ever decreasing number of units. On the other hand, however, our aim has to be to offer each customer precisely the car that reflects his or her own individual tastes and lifestyle.

The continuing market fragmentation is reinforcing the already existing trend in which the number of models and model families on offer will

242   *Case studies*

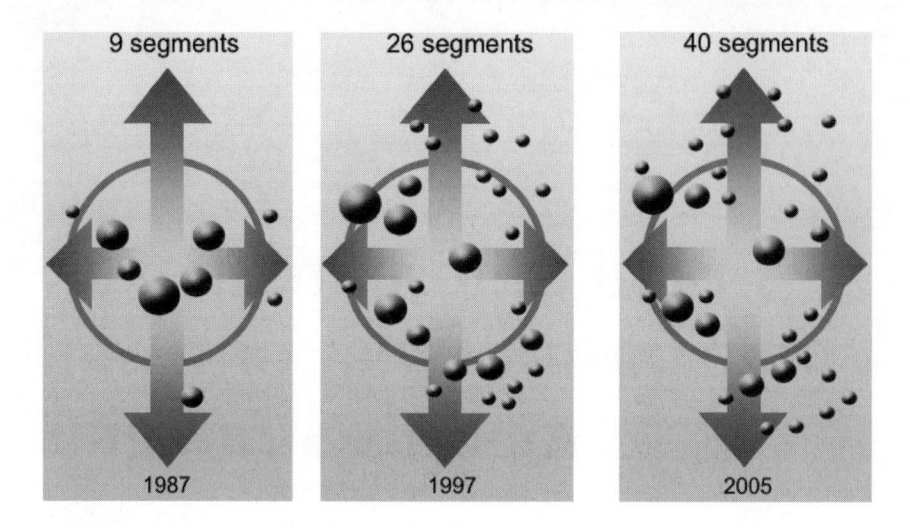

Figure 9.1 *Fragmentation of the markets*

grow further in the future. Moreover, the rising degree of competitive pressure will make for a reduction in the number of car producers as well. The upshot of this general situation is an increasingly declining number of manufacturers producing a significantly broader diversity of models while building fewer units per model (see Figure 9.2). The decisive challenge here lies in also being able to carry out each project successfully in economic terms, and secure the company's success in the long term.

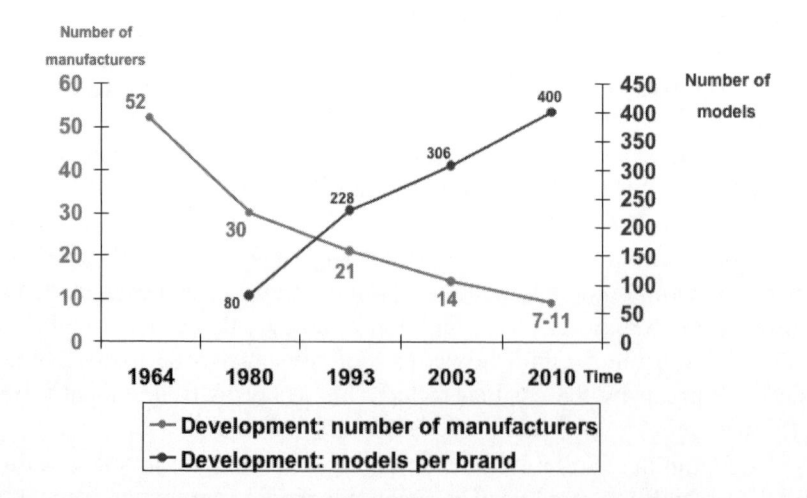

Figure 9.2 *High competitive pressure caused by a continously diminishing number of manufacturers while the spectrum of models on offer grows*

In many sectors the products are increasingly becoming more homogeneous. Technical innovations are only decisive in the decision to purchase up to a point, and only to a limited extent are they suitable for setting a product apart from those of competitors. An empirical survey examined the relevance of brands in different industry sectors. The analysis of the results showed that their importance varies significantly (see Figure 9.3). For example, brand names are of little significance for energy providers but occupy a very high level of importance where automobile manufacturers are concerned. In this automobiles are comparable to other luxury goods such as expensive watches. This means that from the point of view of our customers – automobile buyers – the car represents a special opportunity to set off their own individual personality in an individual manner. The choice of brand is thus also linked with a certain attitude to life, or set of values.

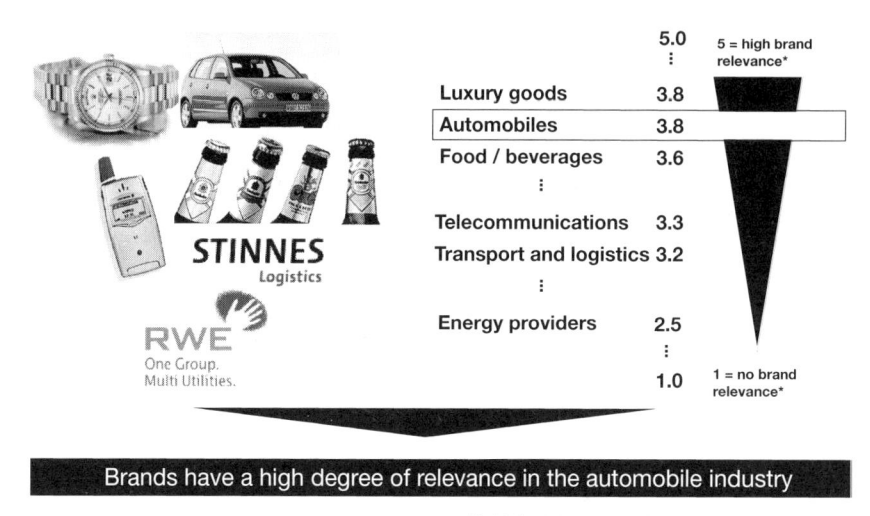

Luxury goods	3.8
Automobiles	3.8
Food / beverages	3.6
Telecommunications	3.3
Transport and logistics	3.2
Energy providers	2.5

5.0 = high brand relevance*
1.0 = no brand relevance*

Brands have a high degree of relevance in the automobile industry

*Empirically calculated on a scale from 1–5

Figure 9.3 *Relevance of brands in different industrial sectors*
Sources: McKinsey/MCM, 2002

Seen against this background, the importance becomes particularly clear of the various brands and the multi-brand strategy as an integral whole, together with the associated processes. Having established this, we now move on the individual backgrounds and the essential steps and process phases of the multi-brand strategy.

In step one the brands are lastingly positioned in the customers' perception. The next step involves the definition of a brand core for each brand and the logical derivation of the brand values. The third step involves determining brand-typical product and design characteristics for each individual brand. Brand-typical segments and body styles are then selected in the fourth phase. The strategy for each individual brand then has to be put into long-term practice at the operational level by way of an optimal marketing mix (Figure 9.4).

Positioning of the brands in customer segments

Definition of brand core, derivation of brand values

Definition of brand-typical product and design characteristics

Definition of brand-typical segments and body styles

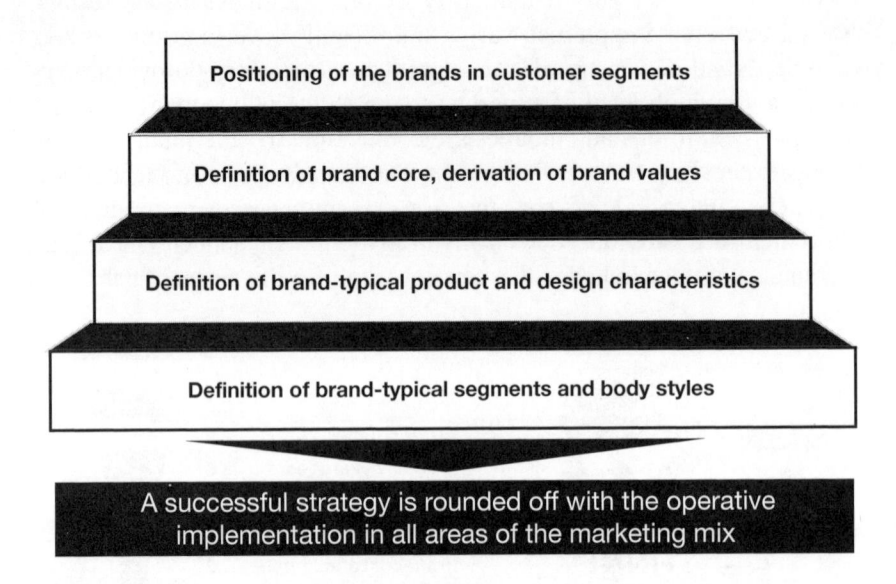

A successful strategy is rounded off with the operative implementation in all areas of the marketing mix

Figure 9.4 *Multi-brand strategy process*

Now we have looked at these aspects, it is necessary to take a look at a few of the strategy's fundamental approaches. The process of brand positioning requires effective account to be taken of both current and future demographic trends. In the past, the society in which we live was largely middle class, but this middle class will become smaller in the future, and this too has consequences for the strategic orientation of a large number of brands. This trend is already becoming very apparent.

Demographic trends could in the future have an even greater impact on the growth rates achieved by various automobile producers, and brand positioning orientated accordingly is already in evidence today. Producers that, for example, positioned their brands in Western Europe as base brands or premium brands showed the highest growth rates between 1994 and 2003. This goes hand in hand with an orientation as cost or quality leader. However, it should be emphasized that even against the background of this insight, unambiguous positioning of each and every brand is nevertheless an absolute necessity and makes sense.

A further fundamental element of brand differentiation comes in the form of brand values derived from the rather abstract brand cores. The brand values are intended to firm up the brand cores and provide effective and lasting expression of explicit brand associations. All activities relating to a brand have to be consistent with these brand values. Similarly, the defined mission is orientated to the brand image and has to be authentic. A failure of the substance of products to live up to the claims made for them, and thus also failure to satisfy the customers' wishes and requirements in terms of the brand, means that the brand lacks 'grounding' and comes over on the whole as lacking credibility. These insights apply to a far greater degree in the automotive industry than in many other sectors. In addition, manufacturers with several brands are faced particularly with the necessity to clearly demarcate their brands and models in the product segments, in order to avoid any overlapping of product ranges and thus any risk of cannibalization (see Figure 9.5).

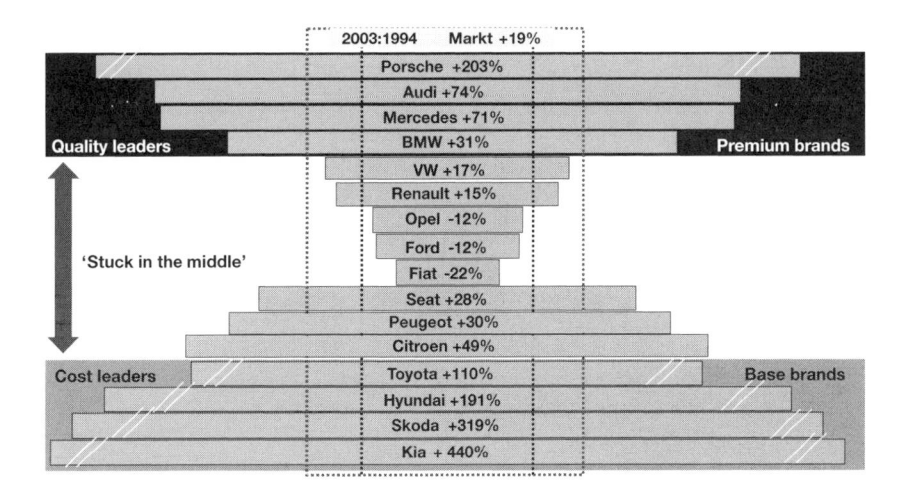

	2003:1994 Markt +19%	
	Porsche +203%	
	Audi +74%	
	Mercedes +71%	
Quality leaders	BMW +31%	Premium brands
	VW +17%	
	Renault +15%	
	Opel -12%	
'Stuck in the middle'	Ford -12%	
	Fiat -22%	
	Seat +28%	
	Peugeot +30%	
	Citroen +49%	
Cost leaders	Toyota +110%	Base brands
	Hyundai +191%	
	Skoda +319%	
	Kia +440%	

Figure 9.5 *'Companies without unambiguous positioning lose!' Comparison of growth rates 1994–2003 in Western Europe*
Source: Newreg 2004, comparison of growth rates 1994–2003 Western Europe, units without vans

The basis of achieving this lies in a clear definition of the brand-typical segments and the unambiguous allocation of the bodywork designs. Recent years have seen an increasingly sharp downward trend where customers' brand loyalty is concerned, with new offers constantly and to a growing extent encouraging them to abandon their accustomed brand in favour of a new one. However, in some cases it is possible to retain them as customers of the company by way of a broad product spectrum and a choice of several brands.

It should nevertheless be pointed out that it is not nearly enough to simply have an extensive portfolio of brands. Of far more crucial importance is taking long-term account of essential components when implementing the multi-brand strategy. Two decisive aspects are a global orientation for the brand product policy, aimed at blanket coverage of the markets, and at the same the creation of a largely overlap-free product range. A further essential factor to this end is an unambiguously clear positioning of the brands through the creation of brand personalities with emotional consistency, and effective implementation and deployment of the brand images. In addition, ensuring long-term consistency and high-level credibility of the brand experiences is a priority, starting with the product itself and going right through to the marketing process (see Figure 9.6).

- Global orientation of product policy
- Unambiguous positioning / Differentiation of the brands
- Consistency and credibility of the brand experiences

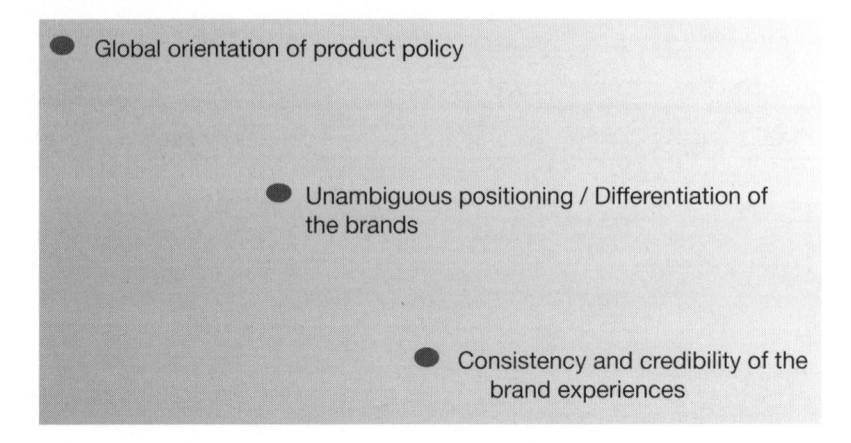

Figure 9.6 *Success factors of a multi-brand strategy*

Accordingly, offering a multiplicity of products and bundling brands within the company framework are possible responses to the growing fragmentation of markets. On the other hand, the platform strategy as part of the multi-brand strategy is aimed at enabling ongoing expansion of the growing range of models and series on a sound economic basis, and at the same time offering a higher level of quality at competitive prices. The platform strategy involves using identical components – which the customer neither sees nor perceives – in several vehicle models and even in whole model families produced by various Group brands. What the platform does not include are the individual product variants, which incorporate components that the customer does see or perceive.

The platform strategy has a number of advantages from our point of view. For example the use of platform components in various models and series reduces vehicle development times, and this in turn enables a swifter response to changing market requirements. The creation of identical parts in high unit quantities has cut the costs of developing and manufacturing individual models, as well as entire series and model families. This has also opened up the possibilities of better development of niche potential by way of enhanced product diversity, and at the same time of responding to the growing degree of market fragmentation. The platform strategy has also enabled expansion of the individual brands' product ranges, and we have enhanced the quality of our products by simplifying and standardizing the manufacturing processes.

It remains to be emphasized that it is hardly possible to introduce an extensive new-model campaign and include various brands, at a high tempo and based on a relatively moderate input of resources, without using identical platforms for several models or model families and series (see Figure 9.7).

- Reduced development times
- Reduced development and manufacturing costs
- Expanded product range
- Simplified production processes

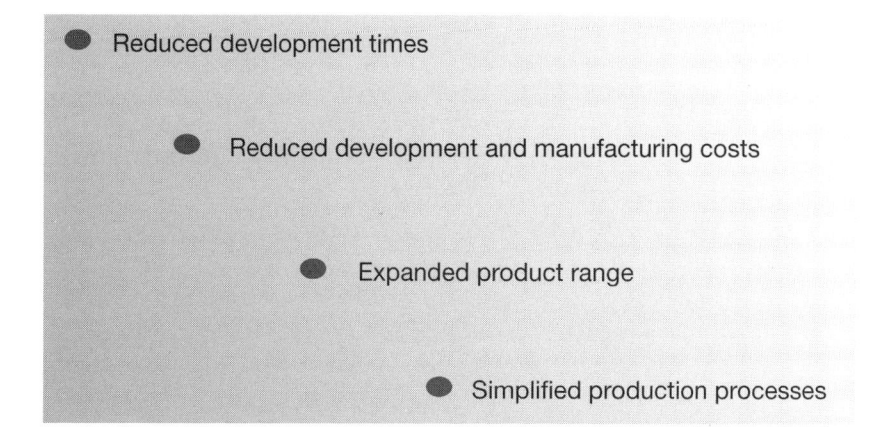

Figure 9.7 *Advantages of a platform strategy*

The platform strategy does however harbour risks as well, and these are not to be underestimated. Alongside the synergy effects, it is necessary to keep an eye on and take account of the erosion effects in terms of brand policy. It is essential to ensure that the attractiveness and keen positioning of individual products and entire brands are not watered down as result of employing the platform strategy. It is safe to say that the greatest temptation, and the one that carries the most risk, lies in the possibility of continuously developing similar variants on one single platform and positioning them in similar or identical market segments.

The platform strategy's variant-driven cost reduction effect leads to the risk of an ever growing number of variants being offered on a common platform and 'thrown' onto the market. These products then compete with each other in similar or the same market segments, resulting in a cannibalization of the products within the company's brands. This effect can also be described as 'segment saturation'. Besides the effects on product and brand strength, the decisive risk generated by a development of this nature lies in the possible impact on earning power. An uncoordinated multiplicity of increasingly similar products generally leads to rising costs and a downward revenue trend. Negative cost effects in particular result from the inevitably arising type-specific development, production, marketing and distribution costs.

A further critical aspect lies in the cost spread, and the difficulty of asserting a clearly defined price hierarchy when there are platform-similar products in a segment. The possible effects of product positioning that is platform-driven and no longer market-driven should therefore on no account be left out of consideration (see Figure 9.8).

- The attractiveness and positioning of individual products might become watered down
- Similar product variants can be developed and positioned in similar market segments
- Platform-driven diversity of variants and 'segment saturation' can negatively impact earning power
- No longer possible to assert price hierarchies

Figure 9.8 *Risks entailed in a platform strategy*

On the contrary, the positioning of new products should have been closely checked in the definition phase. At this point any and all chances and risks should be analysed and evaluated in detail. When taking each relevant decision it is therefore essential to balance the advantages of the platform strategy with the values of the brand in question, and to evaluate them. As a matter of general policy, all product-related decisions should be analysed meticulously and taken on a purposeful and selective basis, taking account of the chances and risks involved.

Besides the possible weak points to which attention has been drawn, there is a further fundamental deficit to be drawn into the discussion. The platform strategy in its known form is too strongly orientated to segments and vehicle categories, since it is there that the focus is on the development of similar models. Development on a cross-segment and cross-vehicle-category basis is hardly possible with the platform strategy alone. For this reason, among others, combining the platform strategy with the module strategy appears to be a line of action that makes real sense.

Under the module strategy, components and sub-assemblies are no longer developed just for one particular model or platform. Instead, modules are generated on a cross-platform basis for use in various model types. For example, an axle is developed that provides for various track widths and wheel sizes, and can therefore be used for a number of different models rather than one specific type or series.

If it is systematically applied and implemented, this strategy can enable faster production of greater differentiations and new variants. This makes for new flexibility, which better allows the use of new products in a segment to be extended, and thus, from the company's viewpoint, enables economic objectives to be brought into an acceptable accord with those on the marketing front. This is the basis for economic and thus entrepreneurial success.

Combining the platform and module strategies makes for considerable advantages in the long term. The platforms comprise modules which it turn come from the module building blocks, and a situation should be created in which various modules can also be used in different series. The use of some modules is bound to be restricted to one single series or model family in the future as well, and this applies especially in cases where these modules are of a specific nature.

Ongoing checks need to be carried out for whether an existing module might possibly be used in a further series or model family, perhaps by differentiating it, reducing its complexity or upgrading it. Constant checking on all modules enables the existing platforms to be kept at a permanently and consistently high technical standard, and simultaneously ensures an even better realization of economic priorities.

A further advantage of the module strategy is that it facilitates the identification of synergy potential in the module's development phase, and hence leads to a reduction in existing complexities. Against this background, the basic objectives behind the module strategy can be defined as securing more rapid and flexible market orientation, continuous cost reduction, a smoothing of investment and expenditure, as well as an easier and more cost-effective derivation of an expanded number of niche models. Further possibilities accorded by the module strategy lie in the saving of time between vehicle project kick-off and market launch – in other words the 'time to market' – as well as a significantly optimized useful life in terms of technologies. Another fundamental objective to be underlined is the achievement of enhanced quality, and all in all a solid competitive edge (see Figure 9.9).

- Components and sub-assemblies can be used on a cross-platform basis in significantly higher unit quantities

- Differentiations and new variants can be produced faster with the aid of modules

- Platforms can be permanently and rapidly updated by way of new modules

Figure 9.9 *Advantages of a modular strategy*

A broad portfolio of brands offers companies the unique opportunity to offer a diversified and comprehensive product range and to successfully and lastingly establish their profile in the market. Multi-brand strategies, brand images and an individual marketing concept are decisive elements, and at the same time they form a basic prerequisite for successful operation and consistent development of a broad product portfolio.

The platform strategy is a crucial prerequisite for enabling the speedy and effective implementation of a new-model campaign while meeting the relevant economic requirements. The module strategy constitutes the logical and intelligent advancement of the platform strategy, above all offering vertical development possibilities from the technical point of view. It affords the platform strategy an evolutionary stage and enhances its overall efficiency. All in all, these building blocks offer the company the opportunity to continue to develop its range of products on an ongoing and selective basis, and to respond to the increasingly more specific customer demands and wishes and market conditions even more rapidly than before.

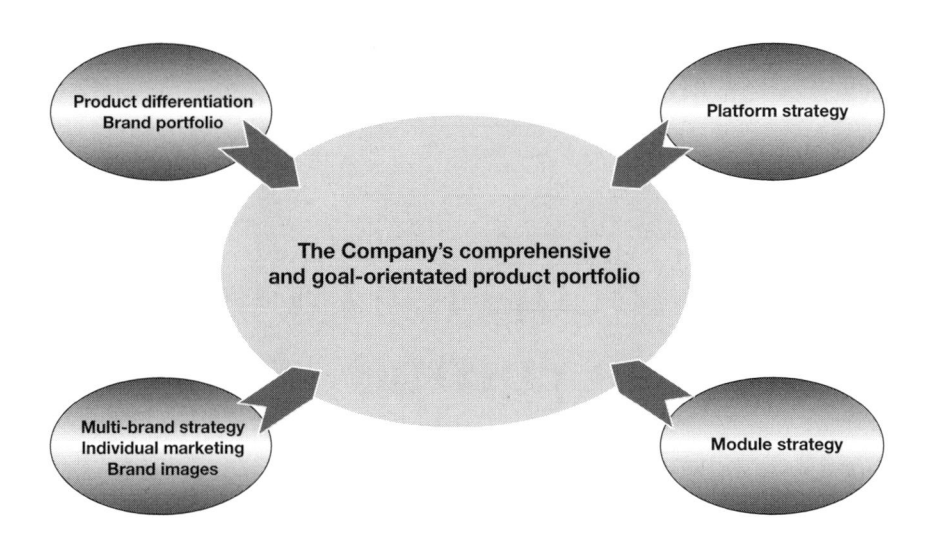

Figure 9.10 *Summary*

10

New impetus for General Motors in Europe

Carl-Peter Forster, President, General Motors Europe, Europe GM

Eighty world premieres and millions of visitors eager to see Europe's latest highlights: the 61st International Motor Show (IAA) in 2005 offered manufacturers a large and spectacular stage on which to showcase their new models and forward-looking solutions. And that was not the only reason for optimism: ahead of the IAA, a significant rise in new passenger car registrations was recorded in Germany and elsewhere in Europe. After five difficult years, there is light at the end of the tunnel, reaffirming belief in a turn for the better.

This positive development is for the most part owed to new models and buying incentives. German automakers – and especially Opel – have performed better than average in this area, with Opel's success based on a major model initiative. New cars including the retractable roof Astra TwinTop, the new Antara off-roader and the Opel GT (to be launched in spring 2007), to name just a few models, demonstrate the brand's potential in important market niches. Opel has also raised the bar even higher in terms of versatility, innovation and emotion with its most important new edition in 2006, the completely newly developed fourth-generation Corsa. Other GM brands are also tailoring their new version to European customers. With the BLS, the luxury brand Cadillac launched a distinctively styled sedan developed specifically for Europe, where it is also produced in Trollhättan, Sweden. Saab is also making waves with its 9–3 SportCombi and completely restyled 9–5 range.

However, the positive mood among European automakers is not as strong in all areas. While much of the long-standing resignation has all but disappeared, intense price wars and fierce competition are forcing the automobile industry to constantly take action. So, despite the strong upturn in West European markets in 2005, most automakers feel obliged to consider closing down plants and cutting their workforce. At the same time, increasing market segmentation demands constant innovation to meet changing customer needs and preferences. Automotive corporations are well aware that the fledgling recovery in sales figures alone is not enough to help them survive the cut-throat price war and intensified international competition.

For this reason, we at General Motors (GM) Europe are concentrating our efforts on optimizing the competitive strength of Europe as a production location, and on setting the stage for more growth. To accomplish this, we must further develop the increases in efficiency we have achieved thus far.

GM has made tremendous progress in its European operations with its efficiency optimization programme. The region is now considered a model for restructuring the company's US business units. However, even GM Europe has a lot of work ahead of it.

WORLD-CLASS CARS WITH OUR QUALITY AND PRODUCT INITIATIVE

Our initiative to augment our product development and improve quality gives us the best chances possible to succeed in the face of tough competition. In one comparison test after another, vehicles like the Vectra, Astra and Meriva continue to take home trophies. And with the new Zafira, the best-seller enters its second generation. According to a recent study conducted by the highly respected institute JD Power & Associates, GM has a decisive lead on all competitors in the United States when it comes to building test-winners in the category 'Most dependable'. The company also took the top spot worldwide in initial quality, with five test-winners in 18 vehicle segments.

In Europe, the quality turnaround is also progressing at a similar pace, which is especially well demonstrated by the impressive figures of our core brand Opel. Since the JD Power institute began conducting its studies in 2002, Opel has shown the strongest improvement of all German high-volume car manufacturers in the Customer Satisfaction Index (CSI). The Signum achieved the greatest single success: in each of the four categories Quality/reliability, Appeal, Dealerships/service centres and Running costs, the spacious and versatile vehicle was awarded the highest scores of any European car model. With regard to customer satisfaction, we at GM can confidently say that we are in the passing lane. And the Opel brand is in the driver's seat: in comparison with competitors' products, its new cars boast the lowest operating costs of all. These are the findings of a comparison test carried out by the German Automobile Club (ADAC).

Europe's largest automobile club is not alone in giving our Opel brand top marks. Two of the most reputed research institutes in the automobile industry, the Automotive Research Center at the University of Bamberg (FAW) and the Institute for Automotive Research at the University of Applied Sciences Nürtingen (IFA), examined the satisfaction of car dealers: outstanding scores confirmed Opel's upward quality trend.

COMPLETE SATISFACTION AMONG CUSTOMERS AND CAR DEALERS

Proof of the quality advances in Europe can also be found in reliable, key internal figures. For example, Opel succeeded in reducing the number of guarantee claims by 65 per cent between 1999 and 2004. The costs of guarantee claims and services carried out on a goodwill basis dropped by 20 per cent within the same period. A new awareness for defect prevention, involving our entire workforce throughout the GM organization, made these results possible. The time required by our employees to completely rectify a problem is now just a quarter of what it was as recently as the mid-1990s.

GM plants are masters of product launch management. Our European production facilities are extremely well equipped to manufacture new models. This too is the result of a comparison study that examined car manufacturers and automotive suppliers, published jointly by the University of St Gallen and the Aachen University of Technology (RWTH). One of the main consequences of this expertise is that the risk of costly and – for the customer – inconvenient recall measures is minimized. While the vast majority of new-model production launches by European car makers in recent years failed to achieve their goals, Opel and two suppliers, along with one other manufacturer, represent the commendable exception. Praised for its quality by customers and the trade press, the new Astra is a prime example of a successful launch.

Opel appoints a support team for each new-vehicle production launch. This interdisciplinary group of experts supports the plants and assumes responsibility for the development, implementation and continuous optimization of manufacturing processes. Depending on the complexity of the project, the team becomes active as early as 30 months prior to the production launch, to begin setting the stage for trouble-free processes. The conclusion of the reputed chair of production engineering at the RWTH and director of the Fraunhofer Institute for Production Technology in Aachen, Prof Dr Günther Schuh was, 'Successful production-launch management can eliminate recall measures.'

SPECIALISTS AND INTERNATIONAL KNOWLEDGE-SHARING

Not only the support teams are responsible for this success. All employees in every European plant are integrated into the implementation of uniform manufacturing processes, a key aspect of GM's holistic quality philosophy. Along with staff involvement, four other principles apply: standardization, quality from the very beginning, short processing times and continuous improvement. Every employee has an obligation to pull the Andon cord, whenever he or she encounters a problem that cannot be solved within the defined cycle time. This sends a signal to the group foreman, who provides immediate support. In addition, clearly defined 'quality gates' must be passed successfully during the production process.

An integral component of this process is an exchange of information on the international level between GM plants. The Rüsselsheim Opel factory pioneered the implementation of a standardized water test, which every single vehicle must undergo. After the car has spent two minutes in a water tank, quality controllers check for leakages with special electronic moisture sensors. This test procedure proved so effective that it will now become standard at GM plants worldwide. Knowledge-sharing functions in both directions: the European GM facilities have adopted a squeak and rattle test from their American counterparts. Each vehicle must move through a standardized test track during final inspection by specialists, who detect and eliminate bothersome noises.

At GM it is not always the high-tech systems that advance quality: small details often make a big difference. One of the day-to-day problems at car manufacturing plants all over the world is that workers accidentally damage the paintwork with their tools during final assembly. Employees at the Opel plant in Rüsselsheim have developed protective plastic sleeves for the tips of electric screwdrivers. This idea too, however unspectacular, has an excellent chance of becoming standard practice at GM on a worldwide scale.

The key to sustainable quality improvement at GM is not just to treat symptoms, but rather to thoroughly analyse and get to the root of the problem. At all European GM plants, this is the responsibility of a task force consisting of around 275 engineers and technicians, the 'Red X Team'. This task force makes a significant contribution to the acceleration of problem-solving processes. The experts work in close cooperation with the Current Engineering department. The automotive engineers and designers no longer consider their task completed the moment a new model goes into production. For each model line, a core team of engineers assumes responsibility for continuously optimizing 'its' model. The European GM production facilities maintain a staff of more than 4,000 in Quality Promotion & Assurance in the manufacturing process.

MOTIVATED EMPLOYEES PLAY A DECISIVE ROLE IN SUCCESS

In 2005, 20 Opel teams were nominated for the GM Chairman's Honors Award for their creativity and teamwork. The projects selected by GM are model examples of corporate culture, which show the way to a future of even more intensive global cooperation. Each of the teams has already delivered outstanding performance in its area – and the nomination alone is recognition of their excellent work. At GM Europe, team spirit elevates business to new heights. The creative ideas of employees boost efficiency and lead to better products.

Due to the increasingly important role suppliers play in car manufacturing, supplier quality is more and more in the spotlight. The fundamental prerequisite for top-quality components from suppliers is close cooperation between suppliers and General Motors. A prime example is the precisely defined process that establishes the stage at which GM can make final design modifications to a new model, and how even marginally involved suppliers are to be informed.

GM Europe gives its suppliers extensive support in maintaining quality standards. A team of more than 100 specialized engineers is charged with the sole responsibility of solving any problems that arise with partners at their source. And they perform this task with remarkable success: the quota of substandard parts from suppliers has dropped by 80 per cent in recent years.

EXPERIENCE AND FEEL THE QUALITY

When it comes to quality, monitoring is especially indispensable, no matter how good the ideas and stable the processes are. At GM, pan-European 'quality controllers' ensure consistently high standards by appearing unannounced at the individual plants and looking over the quality auditors' shoulders.

To regard quality as limited to manufacturing quality would be far too narrow. We at GM Europe are well aware that our products can only achieve true excellence in all aspects of quality if customers are also thoroughly convinced by the perceived quality and overall image of our cars.

Quality must be something the customer can feel and experience. For this reason, we have appointed more than 40 specialists at the International Technical Development Center (ITDC) in Rüsselsheim to represent customers. Their job is not to judge new developments primarily from an engineer's point of view, but rather to systematically represent the preferences and interests of the customer during the development stage. This cross-functional team, which covers a broad scope of expertise including market research, design and product development, is supported by an internal team of assistants. Eight hundred GM employees in Rüsselsheim act as a representative focus group. For example, when the engineers design a new folding mechanism for rear seats or a new child's seat fixture, they know within a few hours whether their solutions are really as practical as they had thought.

There is a great deal more to quality than producing defect-free cars. At GM, we have learnt that positive results can only be achieved with the involvement of all employees at all times. The fact that we do not accept faulty results – regardless of where they occur – is an integral part of our corporate culture.

THE CUSTOMER BUYS BEAUTY – DESIGN EXPERTISE

The look and feel of quality is not the only crucial factor in the decision to buy a car. The design of the vehicle is also a key component, because the customer buys beauty first. And design is a central element in GM's product philosophy.

In keeping with this exceptional emphasis, GM opened a new European Design Center in Rüsselsheim, in the spring of 2006. Along with ongoing styling updates of models currently in production, the design of future models (advanced design) will take place there. The direct connection between forward-looking development and product planning as well as brand management teams will allow better utilization of synergies. This will also strengthen ties to the ITDC in Rüsselsheim.

The European Design Center is integrated in the Group's global design organization. All around the world, the multinational GM design team operates at 11 networked facilities. Thanks to virtual reality technology, all studios are able to work on all products. The new European Design Center is an important addition to this international collaboration. It is also helpful in securing the worldwide design leadership of GM.

The decision to locate the Design Center in Rüsselsheim also secures jobs in Germany, and at the same time reflects the confidence GM has in the performance of the Opel organization. The GM engineers and designers in Rüsselsheim will play a key role in the worldwide GM network in coming years. In its capacity as development location for the compact and mid-size classes, Rüsselsheim will deliver the technical basis for a major proportion of the GM range throughout the Group. Our Rüsselsheim employees are more than up to the task: the Opel Vectra has clearly proven that they are among the best in their profession. And when it comes to flexibility, hardly another automobile production facility in the world can compare with the state-of-the-art plant in Rüsselsheim. With the four- and five-door Vectra sedan, Vectra station wagon and Signum, GM is currently building four body variants on a single production line – and doing so in outstanding quality. In the future, we will further increase this flexibility and continue to expand the potential of the plant.

One reason for these ambitious plans is that Rüsselsheim has been chosen to build a number of future vehicle architectures beginning in 2008. Selected Opel and Saab models based on a shared architecture will be produced at this location. A comprehensive analysis of numerous factors, including capacity, required investment, wage costs, plant efficiency, flexibility, logistics and models of working hours, as well as currency exchange considerations, led to the decision. The Rüsselsheim and Trollhättan plants both presented convincing studies. In the end, however, Rüsselsheim demonstrated slight advantages, and was more cost-effective than Trollhättan measured over the entire production period.

At the same time, we at GM Europe also have great confidence in our competitive production location in Sweden, as well as in the Saab brand, whose core products will remain the models 9–3 and 9–5. And we stand by Trollhättan, where we will open a Saab Brand Center. A strong expression of the Saab brand character, it will be home to a design team mainly responsible for Saab-specific styling. In terms of design, Saab looks back on an exceptionally rich history. This must be preserved and developed further, to ensure that future Saabs maintain this DNA, accentuating the elements the individualist brand Saab continues to stand for after almost 60 years of swimming against the mainstream: sporty driving characteristics, convincing functional attributes and vehicle safety.

A core team of engineers and marketing specialists will work in close cooperation with the designers at the Saab Brand Center. This team is to shape, further develop and cultivate the Saab-specific elements on all levels – from conceptualizing future products to uniform communications on a global scale. The main task of the Saab Brand Center will be to answer a single question: what makes Saab so special? The Saab qualities should be reflected in design, development, marketing, communications and many other areas.

In Trollhättan GM is also opening a new Science Office that will expand our advanced technical work portfolio in the areas of vehicle safety, emissions and advanced manufacturing. The new Science Office will establish centres of expertise in Sweden and coordinate all GM activities and projects related to research and development. In Sweden, GM profits from an extensive network of partners, including the Royal Institute of Technology (KTH) in Stockholm and Chalmers University in Göteborg, as well as research institutes and suppliers throughout the country. This is the result of the extraordinarily successful work of Saab in fostering cooperation.

The Science Office represents a natural evolution of existing collaborative partnerships. The Swedish government is affording GM an outstanding opportunity to further expand its global network of partners.

PORTFOLIO POSITIONING

Opel and Vauxhall, Saab, Chevrolet and Cadillac – as the world's largest car manufacturer, we must position each of these brands unambiguously in order to precisely address the needs of a broad market spectrum. This does not mean reinventing our brand, but rather sharpening its profile in the context of our multi-brand strategy. Cadillac is our luxury brand in the high-end segment, while Saab is our classic, distinctive premium brand; Opel and Vauxhall represent the innovative, high-quality core brands of our volume business, and Chevrolet offers significant growth potential as the foundation brand in volume business. With each model General Motors introduces to the market, the positioning becomes more sharply defined.

The success of the new Zafira and Astra clearly shows that the brand definition focusing on dynamics, versatility and quality is extremely well received. Further models, like an SUV, will afford Opel an even broader base. In the case of Saab, GM initiated an important product portfolio expansion this year with the 9–3 SportCombi; additional models will follow. And Chevrolet puts GM in an excellent position to react to current market trends with models like the economical entry-level Matiz.

An automobile manufacturer operating on a global scale requires a broad market base in Europe. This is not something we can afford to take for granted: GM must detect trends and adapt the model portfolio accordingly. Even highly successful models like the Opel Vectra, Europe's best-selling mid-size class sedan, must be updated continuously. Customers expect innovation – in terms of both technical features and interior comfort – in these models too.

Our decision to market the vehicles produced by GM's Korean business unit Daewoo specifically for sale in Europe as Chevrolets has proven correct. This is confirmed by our sales figures: in the first half of 2005, GM Europe sold around 117,000 Chevrolets throughout Europe, 25 per cent more than in the same period of the previous year. The objective is an annual sales volume of 200,000 cars. Chevrolets are entry-level GM models, in Europe and worldwide. The brand is positioned below Opel, yet it offers not only outstanding value for money, but also – perhaps most importantly – quality, cost-effectiveness, appealing design and a long service life. GM remains extremely active in this segment, with competitively priced entry-level models that look back on years of market success, such as the Matiz.

A global corporation must also be strong in the premium sector. Customers looking for a luxury automobile with an individual character can find the answer in the Cadillac BLS. Built in Trollhättan, Sweden, the BLS offers high-quality equipment at an attractive price. This is also the first Cadillac with a diesel engine, and the first to be developed especially for the European market. GM Europe sees a pan-European annual sales potential of up to 10,000 units for the BLS. From a business standpoint, these are substantial figures. With dynamic cars, a state-of-the-art engine range and innovative, distinctive design, the Cadillac brand has enhanced its luxury image with forward-looking technology.

A DRIVING FORCE FOR THE FUTURE

Innovations first become relevant to the market when they generate consumer interest and satisfy specific customer needs. This applies equally to propulsion technology.

In the context of fuel prices soaring to record heights, economic alternative propulsion concepts have become the centre of attention. The average fuel consumption of passenger cars in Europe has dropped by almost 15 per cent since 1998. The development in oil prices shows the importance of investing in energy efficiency and renewable energy sources. For this reason, we continue to expand our range of low-consumption and environmentally compatible engines. Our research and development in the area of propulsion is focused on hydrogen fuel cell technology as a long-term solution, along with hybrid technology in the short to mid-term. At the same time, we remain concentrated on developing the future-oriented classic internal combustion engine – in terms of efficiency, consumption and emissions. In this context, the development of an advanced diesel engine technology is a focal point of our efforts. GM will cooperate with Bosch and Stanford University in the United States to further optimize the HCCI engine, which burns a highly compressed fuel-air mixture without ignition. This technology will be significantly more efficient than today's engines. In addition, we will develop a hybrid engine in cooperation with BMW and DaimlerChrysler. GM has set the ambitious goal of equipping its next generation of full-size off-road vehicles with hybrid propulsion systems, which consume 25 per cent less fuel, beginning in 2007.

Along with the selective activation of electrical or internal combustion propulsion depending on the situation, further technologies such as cylinder deactivation will be used. At the IAA in Frankfurt, GM presented the GMC brand's SUV concept vehicle Graphyte. Thanks to its bimodal full-hybrid system, this automobile already achieves the stated objective for efficient consumption. Knowledge gained from the Graphyte will also benefit other GM brands. The premium marque Saab has introduced the first flexible-fuel vehicle (FFH) to the market. It can be operated on bioethanol or on pure gasoline in every imaginable constellation. The model BioPower, offered as a sedan or SportCombi, is based on the 2.0-t version of the 9–5. The BioPower variant generates an output of 132 kW/180 hp. In line with the Saab philosophy, a single unique vehicle unites various advantages: environmental compatibility and sporty performance. The BioPower engine was developed by Swedish engineers in collaboration with GM-Powertrain experts in Brazil. This location was no coincidence: Brazil uses pure ethanol from sugar cane to produce its most widespread fuel, E100.

With the world premiere of the new Zafira 1.6 CNG (compressed natural gas) at the IAA in Frankfurt, Opel presented the new generation of Germany's best-selling natural gas vehicle. As the market leader in natural gas propulsion, Opel has made these vehicles popular – one in three natural gas vehicles sold is an Opel Zafira. Outstanding results in crash tests have done a great deal to help dispel fears and prejudices concerning natural gas cars. The Zafira 1.6 CNG boasts superb economic efficiency.

Taking average fuel consumption of approximately 5.3 kg of natural gas per 100 km and the current price of around €0.78 per kilo of natural gas, fuel costs can be reduced by approximately 30 per cent compared with diesel variants, or even around 50 per cent compared to gasoline models. Taxes and insurance ratings are on the same level as those of its 1.6 litre gasoline counterpart. The Zafira CNG with an output of 71 kW/97 hp also offers distinct advantages in terms of environmental compatibility: this type of propulsion generates 80 per cent less nitrogen oxide than a diesel and around 25 per cent lower CO_2 emissions than a gasoline engine (diesel: minus 10 per cent). In addition, the emissions are free from soot particles, ensuring that the Zafira CNG is not affected by potential driving bans in large cities.

SMART USE OF ELECTRONICS

Electronics and software are the major driving forces behind today's technological innovations. The amount of software in vehicle control units doubles every two to three years, and we expect around 90 per cent of future advances in passenger cars to be based on electronic engineering. Currently, electrical and electronic components account for approximately 22 per cent of the manufacturing costs of a passenger car. In 2010, this figure will probably reach 35 per cent. As the technologies and electronic innovations continue to grow in number and scope, car makers must exercise great discretion in selecting which ones to implement. Every manufacturer should question whether the available innovations are also marketable. In this regard, GM Europe pursues a very clear strategy, focusing solely on new features that are purposeful and practical. In concrete terms, this can be summed up in three points: new technologies and innovations must make a substantial contribution to customer satisfaction; their cost–benefit ratio must be favourable; and the balance between technological progress, costs, quality and customer benefits must be the focus. New developments should not be dictated by what is technically feasible. Ultimately, our job as manufacturers is to deliver a cost–benefit ratio in healthy balance. This is why GM Europe sees further potential primarily in the area of active and passive safety.

Engineers at the GM European Development Center are currently developing a driver assistance system with innovative sensor technology for series production. The objective of this system is to further support the driver and increase safety and comfort in road traffic. An integral part of the GM philosophy is to make useful innovations affordable for as many drivers as possible. This trend-setting driver assistance system with adaptive distance and speed control automatically maintains a constant safety zone to the vehicle ahead in all driving situations, from stop-and-go traffic to high-speed highway driving. Integrated in an Opel Vectra GTS, this technology is ideal for everyday use. It employs road data, along with specially developed enhanced power steering, to stay on track – in other words, the vehicle steers automatically to correct deviations from the centre of the lane.

GM develops new technologies within the framework of the global GM Group, which are then made available to each of our brands. This applies to everything from future drive systems to advances in vehicle electronics. Drivers in Europe have always associated new propulsion concepts such as fuel cells or natural gas with the Opel brand. These technologies must be affordable to yield real benefits, which is only possible in combination with high-volume production.

GROWTH ABOVE INDUSTRY TRENDS

Maintaining a position as a key player in the automotive industry means initiating new technological trends and delivering technology to a broad consumer base at the right time. GM Europe is dedicated to fulfilling this task, now and in the future. Of course this requires extensive investment, but we are convinced that the benefits more than justify the costs and efforts. A prime example is the Opel brand's rapid rise in quality rankings – an unbeatable sales argument at the retail level. GM also offers customers a winning range of state-of-the-art engines. The Group's advances in diesel units and the particulate filter set standards. Our increase in market share clearly shows that quality pays off: in the first half of 2005, GM sold more than 1,063,000 cars in Europe, an increase of more than 23,000 cars or 2.3 per cent over the same period of the previous year. GM's share of the generally stagnating European market grew from 9.5 to 9.7 per cent.

Particularly in their home markets, the GM volume brands Opel and Vauxhall developed positively, in both cases outstripping the general market trend. Chevrolet continued its strong growth in Europe in the first half of 2005. Saab sales varied in Europe during this period. Sales in the United Kingdom increased by 41 per cent, reaching an all-time high of nearly 14,000 cars. Although Saab also achieved substantial growth in a number of its smaller markets, including Ireland (up 12 per cent), and Germany (up 5 per cent), this was offset by decreasing sales in other regions. The GM premium brands Cadillac, Corvette and Hummer made good progress in their respective niche markets in 2005. Corvette sales were three times as high as the previous year, while sales of Cadillac in Europe doubled. Hummer sales remained stable at just under 200 units. The new Hummer 3 is now being launched in Europe.

OVERCOMING A WEAK ECONOMY

Auto makers around the world face enormous pressure. Over the past five years, car registrations in Europe have been declining. All Western European plants must be examined critically, as structural problems in many countries are surprisingly similar. GM sees five major challenges facing the automotive industry: stagnating demand, overcapacity and inadequate productivity in manufacturing, growing competition, falling prices, and the offensive by countries with low labour costs, particularly China.

Considering the developments in the market in recent years, no company in the industry can afford to lose any time. The negative developments demand quick and resolute action. Since the beginning of 2005, GM has been implementing extensive restructuring measures, with the objective of achieving a cost reduction of at least €500 million by the end of 2006. In order to accomplish this, the company has reduced its workforce by 12,000 employees throughout Europe. At the same time, the GM brands will continue their product and quality initiative. In this context, the Group places central importance on safeguarding all of its competitive facilities in Europe.

Design and engineering are further focal points of the restructuring programme. GM made great strides with the decision to locate the European Design Center and the development of future vehicle architectures in Rüsselsheim. Duplicated operations will be eliminated, thanks to the alignment of engineering activities in Sweden, the United Kingdom and Germany. At the same time, these synergies will strengthen each of our brands. For instance, Saab was simply not large enough to develop its own engineering capacity, which is necessary to build up a large premium segment portfolio. For this reason, GM is fully integrating the International Technical Development Center in Rüsselsheim and Saab's Technical Development Center in Trollhättan into the Group's worldwide engineering organization.

This creates additional economies of scale for GM, and frees up resources by developing global components and vehicle architectures for a number of brands. The strategy also supports the development of new niche models like SUVs and roadsters. In addition, it yields customer benefits: GM can offer more new models, variants and technologies in shorter periods of time. A successful turnaround starts with high quality and attractive products. In this regard, GM has clearly taken charge of the situation.

Everyone involved in the restructuring programme at General Motors knows that it is not possible without painful cuts, yet the goal of implementing the plan without dismissals or plant closures has been achieved.

NEW MARKET CHALLENGES

The economic situation is not expected to improve substantially in the immediate future. In addition, demand in different car segments has fundamentally changed, and completely new segments have been created in response to evolving customer preferences. The market in Western and Central Europe is changing fundamentally. The mid-size segment has decreased dramatically since 1999, from a share of 17.2 to 13.1 per cent of the total market. The compact class has met a similar fate, losing over six percentage points of its market share during this period. At the same time, new segments and niche markets have been established. A good example of this is the development of the monocab or van segment, where Opel/Vauxhall already enjoys great success with the Zafira in the compact van class and Meriva in the minivan segment. GM Europe will continue to build on these successes. The clear trend toward new segments and niche models will continue in the future. In this respect, one of our most important strategic and competitive advantages is the ability to detect and cover new niche markets.

Despite the current challenges, we are by no means bemoaning developments in recent years, simply objectively analysing evolving customer preferences toward more dynamics, versatility, flexibility and comfort. GM has successfully responded to this change with a number of models. The most recent examples are successful niche models like the Opel Speedster and Tigra TwinTop. The Astra TwinTop will continue this success. The restructuring measures of GM Europe make allowances for this segmentation, as they pave the way for more innovations. We are developing future-oriented cars and niche models with new concepts for flexibility and versatility. GM is planning a total of 45 attractive new models and variants in the next five years. The reorganization of GM Europe is a key component in creating ideal conditions for its brands to realize this model initiative. At the same time, the Group is significantly improving the effectiveness of its investments.

ONE COMPANY

The key to success for our European business lies in thinking and acting as one single company. GM has traditionally been a multi-brand organization, comprised of largely independent brands that were managed separately. There are advantages to this approach, such as the benefit of strong regional brands that adapt to and meet specific regional market needs. However, we cannot overlook the disadvantages. These include the fact that the considerable potential GM offers by virtue of its sheer size was not realized sufficiently. The opportunities presented by the joint vehicle architectures, components and processes throughout the Group were exploited on a limited basis only.

Yet the concept of a global car, at times favoured by other car makers, is no recipe for success either. In fact this approach has never worked, nor will it work in the future. For this reason, GM pursues a strategy of balance. We strive to achieve a perfect equilibrium between centralized management and coordination on the one hand, and decentralized responsibility for local market needs on the other. In other words, GM is aiming for the best of both worlds – autonomous brand responsibility hand in hand with strategic management from a single source. This is of crucial importance for the future success of the GM Group, GM Europe and each of the Group brands.

GM will continue to develop and build cars for national and regional markets, supporting brand identities in becoming recognizable and tangible to customers. At the same time, shared development processes, development of new technologies, vehicle architectures and components will be further exploited. But the basic principle remains: GM cars are adapted to the regional markets.

In this context, GM enjoys a decisive advantage due to its size, provided this size is leveraged efficiently. All of the resources that a global player like GM has must be utilized, while redundant processes and duplicated developments within General Motors Europe and the Group as a whole must be eliminated.

All Group brands and divisions in Europe will be steered on a uniform course in the same direction, under the umbrella of GM Europe. GM is following the clear objective of further cultivating its brands. To this end, GM determines the positioning of each brand in its market.

The strength of a multi-brand organization like GM Europe is not only of key importance in terms of leveraging size advantages: the proportions and performance output of a company are also decisive in mastering the increasingly rapid developments in technology. Here, the automotive industry as a whole faces enormous challenges.

As the world's largest automobile manufacturer, GM is in a position to capitalize on the benefits of its size in this area as well. Complex and cost-intensive research, development and engineering efforts can be carried out a single time, yet the benefits are reaped by all Group brands. Business risks are minimized, as the expenditures for innovations can be shared by a number of brands. Moreover, the strategic innovation management of GM looks at new technologies critically. The decisive factor is always whether or not an innovation delivers tangible benefits to the customer. Ultimately, the key question is, is the customer willing to pay for this added value? This makes early and close cooperation between marketing and development crucial, in order to successfully transform market needs and preferences into concrete technological developments.

Of course we consider all available technologies in vehicle development. They are integrated in the technology portfolio, but only if and when a sensible balance between progress, costs, quality and real customer value can be achieved. Although new technologies can play an important role for the customer, this is not necessarily the case. The best example of smart handling of technological innovations is the chassis of the new Opel/Vauxhall Astra. GM used an enhanced McPherson strut front suspension and a specially adapted torsion-beam rear axle in the Astra, utilizing proven, top-quality solutions. The Group also offers the optional IDSPlus chassis (interactive driving system) with electronic continuous damping control (CDC) and networking of all driving dynamics systems in an integrated chassis control (ICC) system.

This technology ensures balance between driving dynamics and comfort with increased active safety on an even higher level. The networking of ABS, CDC and ESPPlus is an innovation not only in the compact class, but in the entire automotive industry. This is precisely the type of innovation customers are willing to pay for.

The focus of a company of the size and standing of GM must not be only on the short and mid-term cycles of technological progress. That is why the Group is already actively working on long-term perspectives of individual automotive mobility. For example, the company has thus far invested US $1 billion in the development of fuel cell vehicles. The result of this investment is the HydroGen3, a close-to-production prototype based on the Opel Zafira, which has already proven itself in everyday use. The HydroGen3 has successfully passed another endurance test, emerging as victor among fuel cell cars at the first 'Rallye Monte Carlo Fuel Cell and Hybrids'.

GM's European and global resources are a decisive factor in bringing fuel cell technology to volume production maturity. All GM brands will benefit from this, but no one brand alone could carry the burden of developing and introducing to market such a groundbreaking technology.

DESIGN TREND-SETTER EUROPE

Just as a new, highly efficient production system was decisive for the reorganization of GM plants in the United States, Europe is the role model for design of passenger cars. We have fundamentally changed our philosophy, and boring draft designs or superfluous ornaments do not stand a chance at GM Europe. A major purchasing factor is the emotional currency of a car design. Accordingly, GM Europe has introduced a new design language and new vehicle formats, leading the way into a stylistically new future. The new models must reflect the character, history and cultural background of the brands and successfully carry on their line of ancestry. It has always been the objective of GM Europe to build cars for individualists wishing to express their passion for cars outwardly. A perfect example of this is the legendary Opel GT. The Rüsselsheim car maker has always understood how to interpret the French coupé – cut-off – in a car with sporty lines and a flowing rear form. Opel coupés were crosses between low-cost volume production technology and powerful engines. A successful line of predecessors testifies to this, from Commodore A, B and C to Monza and Calibra. This successful tradition of sporty and affordable cars will be continued with the OPC (Opel Performance Center) models. The high-performance variants of the Astra, Vectra and Zafira are more powerful, faster and more dynamic. Further OPC models will follow. With exciting niche models like the Tigra and Astra TwinTop, the GM brand Opel is putting more focus on emotional appeal and dynamics.

Our premium brand Saab is also very successful with cars that evoke emotion. The 9–3 Cabrio and 9–3 SportCombi meet the individual tastes of customers in a special way. The latest JD Power Institute study confirms that Saab brand cars have markedly improved in reliability, quality and cost-efficiency.

WELL EQUIPPED FOR A SUCCESSFUL FUTURE

Decisive factors in mastering the challenges the European automotive industry faces will be competitive strength and a heightened focus on growth. Key measures include increased work flexibility, a reform of the social security system and renouncing any further increases in the cost of mobility. Those who act in a timely and consistent fashion have the best chance of retaining a healthy work environment. Auto makers have to find new ways of adapting to the changing global competitive situation, such as diversifying product portfolios. The speed of innovation is very fast, particularly in the electronics area. New technologies such as fuel cell propulsion must be developed to market maturity. This all has to happen at the same time, under constantly mounting cost and competitive pressure, and this pressure has not even reached its peak in Western Europe. The market is almost saturated and substantial growth is not in sight. The result of stagnation and shrinking markets is massive overcapacity, as is the case in Germany. Experts calculate that the average utilization of automobile plants in Europe is currently less than 80 per cent, while the break-even point is at around 85 per cent. At the same time, some manufacturers have announced they will increase their production capacity in Europe, which will introduce an additional 1 million units to the market.

Analysts predict a crisis along the lines of that in North America. In order to keep plants operating at full capacity, more and more cars are offered with rebates. This increases price pressure and reduces profitability. And the long-term picture does not look any prettier: competitors from China and India are entering the European market. The latest IAA in Frankfurt gave us a small taste of where this will lead.

Initial exports to Europe and the United States have focused attention on cheap cars from China. These manufacturers, which presented themselves for the first time at the IAA in Frankfurt, have a long, rocky road ahead of them. So say Chinese experts, pointing to problems with quality and customer service. But their sights are firmly set on Europe.

GM Europe is ready for increasing competition in the coming years. The restructuring plan has put the brands and business processes on the right course. We have now positioned ourselves to meet our goals of a competitive employment environment in ultra-productive sites coupled with strong, profitable brands. We continue to look far ahead with confidence, and our model initiative is a visible expression of this future-oriented approach.

11

How electronics is changing the automotive industry: from component suppliers to system partners

Peter Bauer, Member of the Management Board, Infineon Technologies AG

THE EVOLUTION FROM COMPLEX MECHANICAL TO COMPLEX ELECTRONIC SYSTEMS

Since transistors were first fitted in cars in the 1970s, vehicles have advanced from being complex, predominantly mechanical systems to complex and increasingly electronic systems. Simple electrical systems were initially used to supply power to lighting and powertrain components. Today, however, very few mechanical functions are not influenced or improved by electronics. A plethora of new functions have also been added: we need only think of ABS, stability control, airbags, air-conditioning, rain sensors, distance warning systems, navigation systems, on-board troubleshooting, driver assistance and telematics services. A whole raft of power, safety, convenience and infotainment applications would be unthinkable without electronics (see Figure 12.1).

How electronics is changing the automotive industry 271

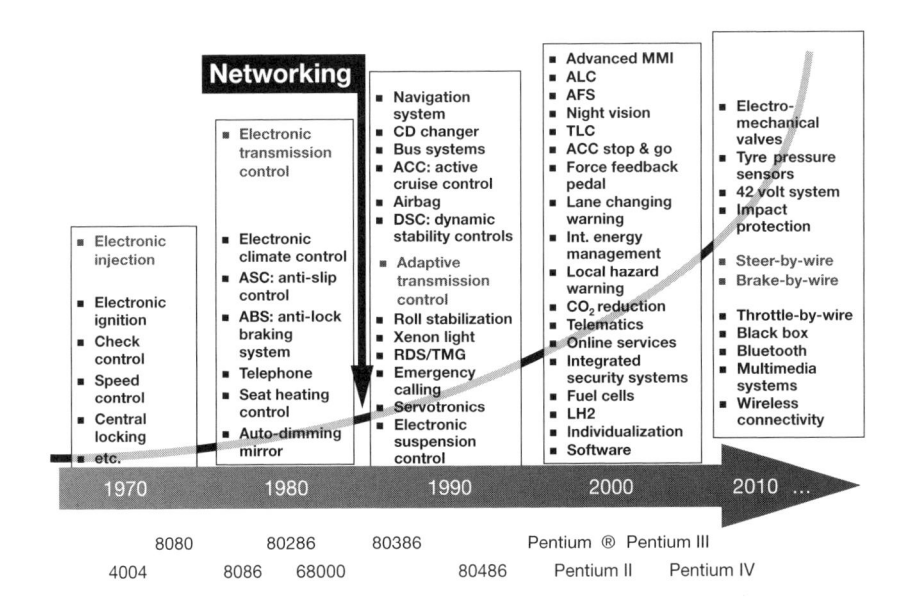

Figure 11.1 *Development in automotive electronics, 1970 to 2010*

Despite all this progress, the pervasiveness of automotive electronics is still in its fairly early stages. The potential for electronic innovation in convenience applications is nowhere near exhausted. And safety systems in particular – including driver assistance systems – are expected to post the strongest growth in the years ahead. Roland Berger estimates that, over the next 10 years, the electrical and electronic content of vehicles will increase from a good 22 per cent in 2005 to around 32 per cent in 2015 (see Figure 12.2).

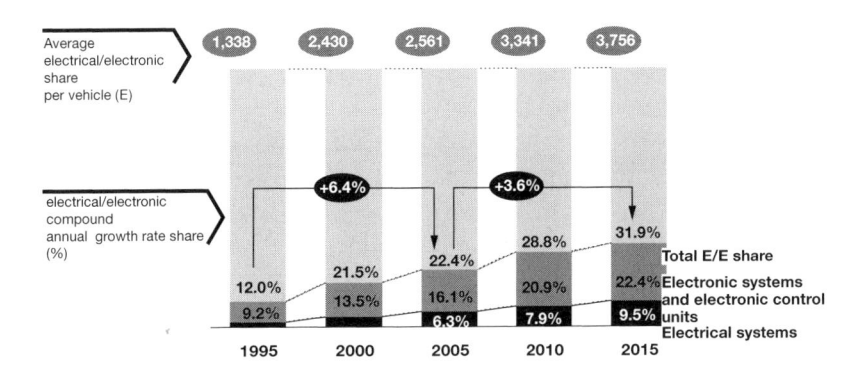

Figure 11.2 *Steadily increasing electronic content in vehicles*
Sources: Strategy Analytics, Roland Berger analysis

In future, scarcely any innovations in automotive engineering will not be based on electronics. For those component suppliers that specialize in this discipline, that is good news indeed. Semiconductor firms, for example, are benefiting from automotive electronics' voracious appetite for the whole spectrum of semiconductor products, ranging from sensors, microcontrollers and power semiconductors through memory products to chips for wireless communication. Between now and 2010, in-car semiconductor content is projected to leap by some 50 per cent.

The automotive industry – caught in the productivity vice

At the same time, rampant growth in the 'electronification' of automobiles is also confronting the supply industry and car makers alike with many and varied challenges. Technological advances (and the danger of falling behind) place the automotive industry under tremendous pressure to innovate. Statutory requirements relating to safety and environmental protection are having the same effect. So too are customers' demands for ever greater functionality. However, since consumers are generally unwilling to pay more for new technology, inflation-adjusted prices will stagnate in just about every vehicle class. Car manufacturers therefore have no choice but to consistently raise their productivity (see Figure 12.3).

The requirement for more innovation at lower cost, coupled with demands for top quality and absolute reliability, means that the pressure to become more productive is not restricted to car makers alone, however. Upstream links in the value chain are feeling the full force of this trend. Quality standards of the kind one would normally only expect in aerospace or military contexts, but at prices reminiscent of the entertainment industry: that neatly sums up what auto makers today expect of the supply industry. Under cost pressure themselves, auto companies are demanding that their suppliers cut prices by between 3 and 10 per cent per year. What some manufacturers evidently do not realize, however, is that there are limits to the ability to optimize the cost of existing systems or reap savings from economies of scale. They fail to grasp that the component supply industry alone will not be able to continue financing innovation in the long run. As a rule, first-tier suppliers tend to pass on this cost pressure to their own subcontractors. Semiconductor firms, for example, must therefore ask themselves to what extent they can make a contribution to innovation and quality in a market that is dominated by car makers and first-tier suppliers (see Figure 12.4).

This challenge can only be mastered by a paradigm shift in the automotive value chain. This paradigm shift is linked to a specific realization:

How electronics is changing the automotive industry 273

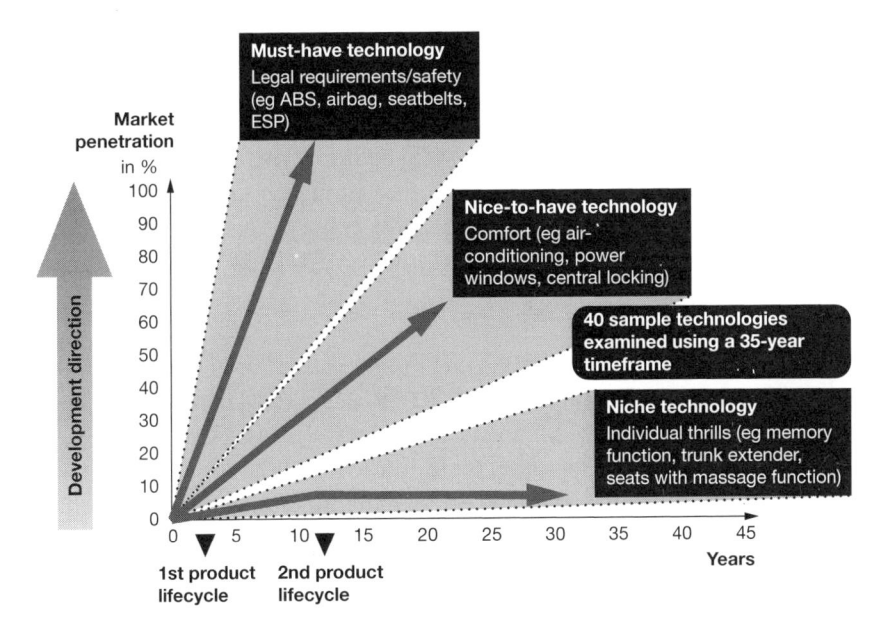

Figure 11.3 *The pace of innovation introductions*
Source: McKinsey/PTW-HAWK survey 2003

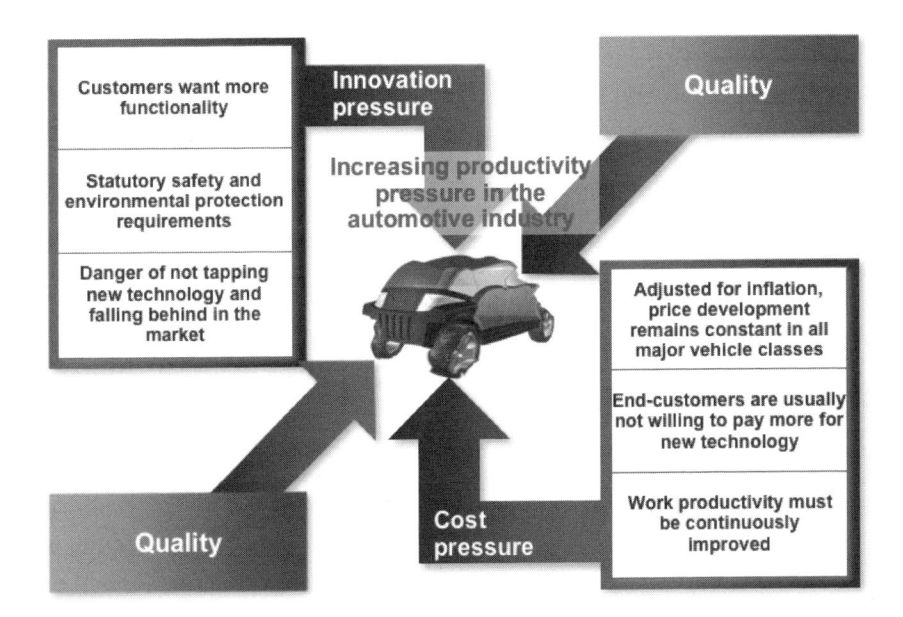

Figure 11.4 *The automotive industry is taking heat from all sides*
Sources: McKinsey/PTW-HAWK survey 2003, Infineon

it is not the number of extra features and fittings that will determine a company's lasting success. It is more important to develop appropriate business and profit models that shape the underlying cost structures, and also to establish a suitable position in the value chain. Finance is therefore the biggest issue facing the automotive industry. Given the growing complexity of automotive electronics, how can a constant stream of innovation be churned out reliably and affordably? And who is to bear the cost of this innovation?

The need to get a handle on growing complexity

The growing complexity of vehicle platforms is a subject intimately linked to the fast pace of innovation – and another subject with which car makers and suppliers must concern themselves as they examine financing issues. Loosely interconnected electronic control units (ECUs) have dominated this segment of the industry hitherto. Future innovation, however, will depend on deeply integrated and closely networked systems. As many as 80 electronic systems and components still coexist independently in today's cars. Forecasts nevertheless indicate that, by 2010, they will all be networked and will interact to a considerable extent (Figure 12.5).

This advanced level of networking is a fundamental precondition if new, cross-system functions – mostly to enhance safety – are to be implemented, and if synergies are to be tapped in order to reduce costs. However, precisely this development gives rise to complex functional interdependencies between the various electronic components. For auto makers, it is imperative to master these interdependencies. Why? Simply because every extra sub-system and every extra electronic control unit increases the statistical probability that different sub-systems could interfere with each other – and that the whole system could then fail.

There are all kinds of ways in which companies are trying to get a handle on this growing complexity and to square the circle that demands ever more functionality at ever lower cost. One method to which both the supply industry and the auto makers are giving their backing is to establish standards. Breaking down all in-car electronic systems into structured domains is another approach. Manufacturers such as BMW and suppliers such as Bosch are treading this path. The outsourcing of larger assemblies to a single supplier is likewise under discussion. However, although both suppliers and car makers are energetically exploring so many different avenues, the search for the ultimate solution will probably not be over for some considerable time, for a variety of reasons.

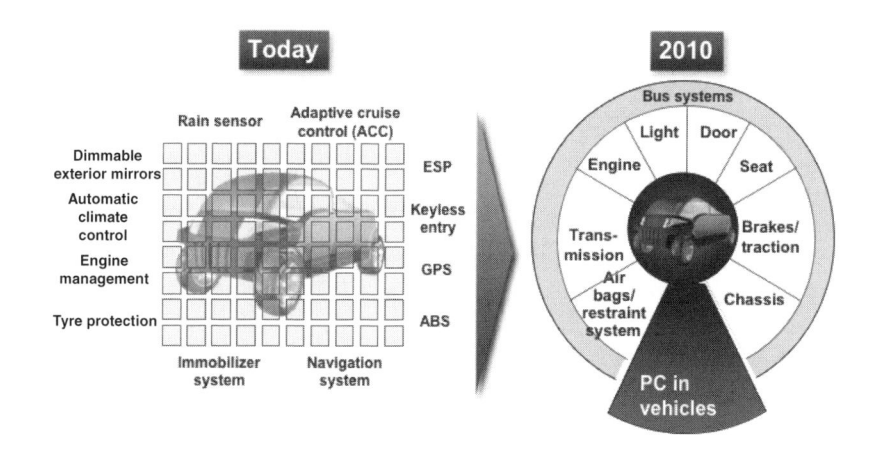

Figure 11.5 *Individual applications are developing into complex networks*
Sources: Mercer/Hypo Vereinsbank

Competence in electronics – a critical factor of competition

Rapid innovation and the spiralling complexity of in-car electronics are also increasing the potential for technical risks that, at worst, could lead to breakdowns, system failures and recall campaigns. Any of these possibilities would prove very expensive. It is therefore important to get a handle on the risks too, as on the technology itself. Problems can arise, for example, when car makers include innovative electronic developments in mass-produced models before the innovations are fully mature. Accumulating electronics expertise would be one way for auto companies to minimize these risks. Indeed, auto makers that see themselves as innovators have no choice but to build up competence in electronics in-house.

THE CONVERGENCE OF TWO VERY DIFFERENT INDUSTRIES

Historically, most car manufacturers have obviously leaned more towards mechanical skills. Unlike their traditional core competences – vehicle design, body construction and engine development – electronics expertise was for a long time the exclusive preserve of specialized electronic component suppliers. Since those days, most car makers have realized that they cannot get by without a command of electronics, and have taken steps to acquire skills in this field. One reason is that they do not want to fall behind their competitors. Another is to avoid becoming completely dependent on outside suppliers. Premium manufacturers in particular are spearheading this trend. For them, electronics is now clearly recognized as a core competence.

The trend is also reflected in the practice of launching subsidiaries (such as BMW Car IT, Audi Electronics Venture and the Porsche Engineering Group), in the establishing of competence centres (such as the Audi Electronics Center, which opened in mid-2005), in moves to ramp up in-house development departments, and in the introduction of specific electronics strategies. Auto makers are also recruiting more and more electronics engineers and IT experts.

It is, as we have seen, important for car makers to deepen their knowledge of electronics, but not only because of the technical risks mentioned above. Unless these companies fully understand what automotive electronics really involves, how will they ever be able to optimize the way they assign tasks to outside suppliers? How will they be able to judge and coordinate these efforts? The same principle applies to the commercial appraisal of suppliers' performance. Unless they acquire a suitably detailed technical understanding, car makers will be unable to reliably compare the components and services of different suppliers. By no means least, they will not be able to optimize the in-car integration of complete electronic systems unless they have the skills they need to do so.

As more and more electronic content finds its way into cars, the need for an in-depth knowledge of software will also grow in the next few years as this becomes a focal point in the value chain. Software lays the foundation for all kinds of new in-vehicle functions, over and above deeper integration and greater flexibility. For example, software can allow new applications to be built into a car during its lifecycle.

Car makers clearly see this as a new source of revenues. Consequently, they will increasingly use software as a unique selling proposition. Here again, however, specific knowledge is needed in order to find new business models with which to tap software's potential to the full. An example from the mobile communication industry illustrates just how important this factor is. Some mobile phone makers have tried to buy in entire platforms and outsource software expertise in the volume segment. However, their attempts have showed that market success is closely linked to a mastery of the technologies involved. In this industry, the successful players are those that have kept and cultivated in-depth, application-oriented software engineering competence in-house.

For many auto makers, software is a relatively new field. Especially in the area of software maintenance and updates, many questions remain

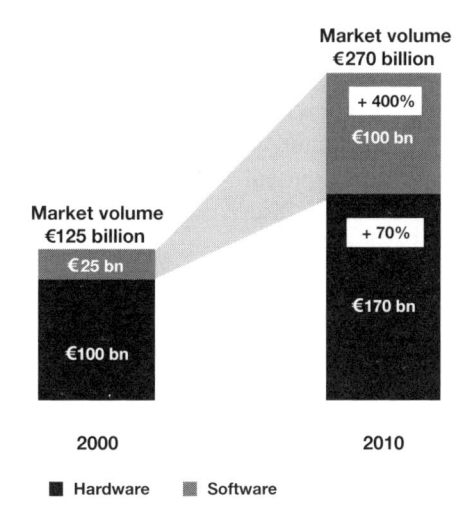

Figure 11.6 *The market volume of automotive electronics is going up*
Sources: Mercer/Hypo Vereinsbank

open and can only be resolved in close collaboration with suppliers. Software expertise will play an ever more important role in the specializations that emerge within the automotive value chain in future. As software accounts for an increasing share of automotive electronics, this will also change the processes involved. The automotive industry is therefore called on to learn lessons from the IT industry.

Electronics suppliers are growing in importance

Although they are building up their own electronics expertise, car makers do not seem desperately interested in expanding into the relevant supply links in the value chain. They rather seem to want to secure a position as 'informed customers'. A study by Mercer Management Consulting, for example, found that suppliers added 84 per cent of automotive electronic value and car makers only 16 per cent in 2002 – and that this ratio will not change significantly in the years ahead. In light of pressure to raise productivity and cut costs, not every car maker will readily have the resources to invest in ramping up electronic content in vehicles. Accordingly, many links in the chain will remain in the hands of outside suppliers.

If only because of widely varying innovation cycles and the problems to which this leads, suppliers will in fact assume an even more prominent role. As electronic content increases, electronic control components will rank as standard replacement parts. Auto makers will therefore have to ensure a steady supply of electronic components throughout the entire product lifecycle. This is problematic, however, because development and product lifecycles in the automotive and semiconductor industries are way out of sync. Whereas development lead times in semiconductors range from 9 to 24 months, it takes the auto industry three to five years to develop a new vehicle model. This model will then normally be manufactured for around seven years and used for a further 15 years or so after production stops (Figure 12.7). Obviously, then, car makers will depend heavily on their electronics suppliers to ensure that replacement part provisioning continues to run smoothly.

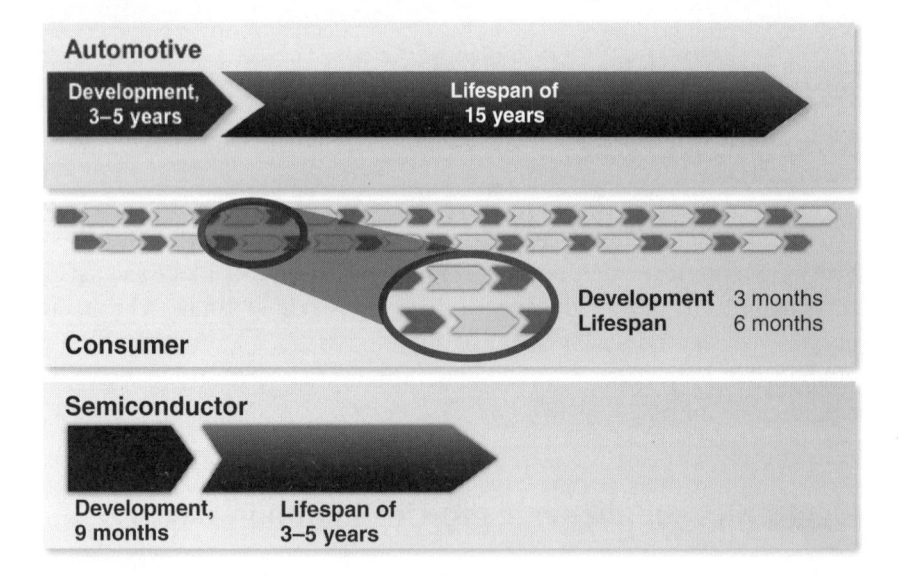

Figure 11.7 *Various technology cycles*

There is no easy way to bridge the gap between the pace of innovation in the automotive industry and that in the semiconductor industry. If car makers were to adapt to the dizzying speed of semiconductor development, in-car electronics would have to be redesigned every time a new semiconductor component came onto the market – even after production of a model had been discontinued. On the other hand, stockpiling electronic components for 20 years or so is extremely difficult and expensive, not only because of the sensitive nature of such components. Storage options are also hampered by the facts that only rough estimates of actual demand are possible – and that no one wants to bear the added risk (and associated cost) of maintaining such huge inventories.

ZVEI, the German electrical engineering and electronics industry association, has set up a workgroup to examine the 'long-term provisioning of electronic replacement parts for the automotive industry'. Car makers, suppliers and chip manufacturers (including Infineon) are collaborating in this group to formulate suitable models. Standardizing the components used and committing to the retro-development of components whose stocks are exhausted would be one possible option. In light of the huge costs involved, however, this possibility is of limited practical value. By improving storage capabilities, it would at least narrow the provisioning gap. The cost would nevertheless remain exorbitant.

The early exchange of information throughout the entire process chain could also solve some of the provisioning problems. This might even work when changes are made to semiconductor products while a vehicle model is still being produced. Clear communication and greater transparency would nevertheless be needed to ensure long-term provisioning and guarantee quality levels. Only then can the full potential of innovation in electronics be exploited and applied in the auto industry. Auto makers will depend on strategic partnerships with semiconductor manufacturers, which in turn must clearly commit to ensuring the long-term availability of the technologies needed by automotive electronics. In this context, car companies must nevertheless remember two important things. One is that maintaining ageing technologies necessarily incurs additional costs. The other is that long-term provisioning can only be guaranteed by semiconductor firms for which automotive electronics is part of their core business.

THE CHALLENGE OF SYSTEMS INTEGRATION

Automotive electronics is a fertile breeding ground for innovation. It is spawning a rich diversity of systems, modules, components, operating systems and software from a variety of manufacturers. Added to this variety are ever more complex development structures, multi-layer software models and increasingly extensive bus protocols. All of this pushes up the cost of integrating both hardware and software in vehicles. The relevant players in the automotive value chain must therefore ask themselves how systems integration can be simplified despite this growing complexity, and how they can at the same time ensure that functionality and quality are maximized.

We have already touched on one way to reduce complexity and thereby simplify systems integration, namely a model (operated by manufacturers such as BMW) that carves systems integration up into structured domains.

This model groups individual functions that exhibit similar requirements together with the related control units to form larger domains. Within these domains, central control units integrate a number of functions (as well as actors and sensors) that possess their own built-in intelligence. The separate domains can then be networked using proven bus systems such as CAN and LIN, or using new, deterministic systems (such as Flexray) that are currently being crafted by industry committees. To ensure that the whole construct works smoothly, the principles of this domain architecture must be reflected in the way systems are partitioned.

Many pundits see open, standardized solutions as the high road to seamless communication between the individual systems and control units. They also believe that this approach will simplify the task of networking systems from different suppliers. Consequently, numerous initiatives such as HIS (a manufacturers' software initiative) and development partnerships such as AUTOSAR (Automotive Open System Architecture) are striving to standardize software interfaces and software modules (Figure 12.8). AUTOSAR aims to develop an open standard for in-vehicle electronic architectures, and thereby to make it easier to reuse (and interchange) software modules across different types and classes of automobile.

A single, standard platform that defines the fundamental software architecture and basic functionality would slash costs in two ways. It would not only shorten development times, it would also vastly simplify the process of integrating new functions. When individual components needed to be replaced, it would no longer be necessary to redesign the entire system every time. Instead, the modules or add-on components concerned could simply be plugged into the appropriate software interfaces. This would sharply increase the proportion of fully tested and proven modules, which in turn would reduce system costs and improve quality in the long run.

Does standardization raise a barrier to competition?

Standardization is definitely one feasible way to master the complexities of automotive electronics and systems integration. Even so, it will still probably be some time before a uniform standard is in fact applied. This is only partly because standardization is a very protracted and laborious process. (It can take years to advance from verification to formal ratification.) Another reason is quite simply that the various market players attach different degrees of importance to this issue.

Cursory examination might lead us to the conclusion that the car makers are the only players who would benefit, because fiercer competition between suppliers would give them more flexibility to pick and choose

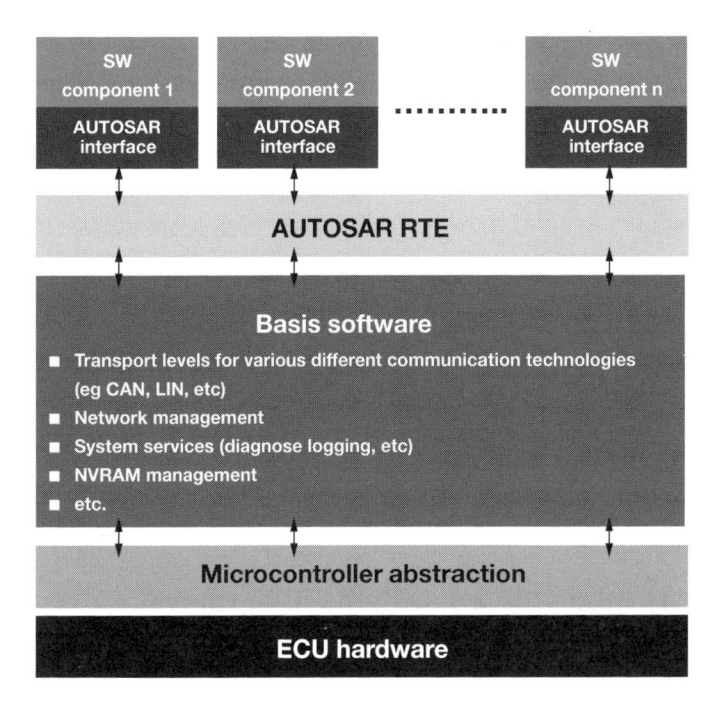

Figure 11.8 *AUTOSAR standardization initiative*

their partners. The fact is, however, that standardization would initially impose a much heavier burden of development expenditure on component suppliers in particular, especially in relation to software engineering. Yet the smaller suppliers especially will not be able to fund such development as things stand. In other words, contrary to the economic laws of standardization, we might see precisely the opposite effect occurring: competition – and hence the car makers' freedom to choose – might actually be further restricted as higher expenditure and lower margins drive a number of suppliers out of the market.

A ZVEI paper on standardization addresses the issue of whether standardization prevents competitors from distinguishing themselves from each other. One could take this question a step further and equate standardization with the interchangeability of products, systems, and ultimately of manufacturers themselves. In this case, one could conclude that, in committing to standardization initiatives such as AUTOSAR, suppliers are investing in making themselves replaceable. This obviously cannot be in their interests. Alongside the need to improve quality and safety, therefore, there must also be plausible economic reasons for semiconductor firms such as Infineon to take part in development partnerships such as AUTOSAR and actively advance the cause of standardization.

By sensibly standardizing basic electronic functions that do not constitute unique selling points, both car companies and suppliers can rid themselves of links in the value chain that are necessary, but that do not set them apart. This will leave them free to focus on activities that directly impact value creation. In the context of the standardization of automotive electronics, market players will set themselves apart – and thus compete – primarily by varying the way they use software and implement specific functions and operating models.

The important thing is that car makers must not see standardization as a way to squeeze the entire supply industry into a single mould. Instead, it must be grasped as a means to reduce complexity and to simplify systems integration. Standardization must leave room for differentiation. It must present no obstacles to deeper integration. Thus, if standardization were to go too far, that would ultimately put the brake on innovation.

Who is responsible for systems integration?

As more and more components and modules need to be integrated, a further question arises: who will be responsible for systems integration tomorrow? Is it conceivable that a partner in the supply industry will in future ensure that all the systems and modules fit together? Devolving full responsibility (or at least responsibility for large packages of activities) to a supplier would have two advantages. It would sharply reduce frictional losses at the interfaces between different systems, and it would vastly diminish the cost of cross-system harmonization. The downside is that only a very small number of hand-picked suppliers have the breadth of knowledge that such a complex assignment would necessitate.

Liability is another key issue in this context. Some auto makers are currently charting a rather 'schizophrenic' course. They want to delegate system responsibility, complete with liability, to their suppliers. At the same time, however, they want to retain control because they are afraid of becoming too dependent. Separate responsibility from competence, however, and it is only a matter of time before problems begin to arise. It is not unusual for deficient coordination to threaten entire projects. This kind of approach does not only place a burden on development: in many cases, the players involved seem to forget that a working, self-contained system can be less expensive than the sum of the costs of individual components if these then also have to be integrated.

Given the large number of players involved, overall project management is manifestly the key to successful systems integration, and this key must be in the hands of the car maker. Overall project management forges the link between different suppliers, each of which, in accordance with the car maker's specifications, delivers separate but networked sub-systems. If the companies involved are not brought together around the same table throughout the entire process, it is unlikely that a workable solution will be the outcome. Problems are bound to occur in the attempt to develop and coordinate so many sub-systems. Moreover, the car maker depends on transparency with regard to the suppliers' processes. A clear overview of all tributary processes is essential if all the different systems are finally to be blended together perfectly in the vehicle concerned.

KNOWLEDGE AND BUSINESS MODEL-RELATED DEPENDENCIES FOR AUTO MAKERS

Auto makers depend on the expertise of their suppliers, but they equally depend on their suppliers' business models. Automotive electronics is such a complex discipline that specialization within the supply industry is developing an ever narrower focus. As a result, only a limited number of suppliers can produce certain systems. Small and medium-sized suppliers might survive if they have a clear technology lead, but they will have great difficulty realizing the savings on which car manufacturers insist. Semiconductor firms, on the other hand, definitely need both a certain critical mass and a broad product portfolio if they are to rise to this challenge.

The scope of competence that stays in-house will largely be determined by the auto makers' sourcing strategy. In the United States and to some extent in Europe, a trend toward purchasing strategies that are purely cost-driven has been in evidence for some time. This practice has even reached the stage where many auto companies auction their orders over the internet. We must nevertheless query the extent to which this kind of sourcing strategy can foster the long-term collaboration from which everyone – not only the car makers and their suppliers, but also car buyers – will ultimately benefit.

Selecting suppliers purely on the basis of cost might let car manufacturers save money in the short term. In the long term, however, the drawbacks will doubtless weigh heavier. This kind of strategy promotes a narrow focus on price that can choke off innovation and can, at worst, also undermine quality and vehicle safety. This is surely not the road down which makers of automobiles wish to travel. Purchasing strategies that are concerned exclusively with costs are indeed the main hindrance to long-term strategic collaboration that aims to build win–win constellations across different links in the value chain. However, vehicle manufacturers cannot escape from the productivity vice unless they engage in precisely this kind of close, strategic partnership with a few hand-picked suppliers.

Large auto makers of the calibre of BMW and Toyota have long since committed to such strategies – and are now reaping the rewards. Positive collaboration with suppliers is reflected both in regular supplier appraisals and in the commercial success of these companies. Toyota, for instance, actively encourages collaboration between its suppliers. Rather than being content with a traditional stance right at the end of the value chain, it acts more like the conductor of a huge orchestra, ensuring that each player stays in harmony with all the others.

A new quality of collaboration

There is an urgent need to extend this kind of partnership along the whole value chain. This is because architectural decisions taken unilaterally by car makers, and the way system component suppliers choose to divide up their systems, can already have a major impact on the cost structure of semiconductor solutions. Technologically reliable products can be created only if auto makers and suppliers collaborate closely as partners. To avoid the effort and expense of having to cultivate lots of partnerships but to maintain an element of competition, many car companies today operate a 'second source' strategy. In this constellation, the manufacturer concentrates on one main supplier and one secondary supplier, to which a smaller volume of orders is awarded. For technologically less sophisticated components, system suppliers are free to choose their own component suppliers – a fact that leaves this procurement market highly fragmented. For technologically more sophisticated components, car makers usually restrict the system suppliers' choice of possible component suppliers. This short-listing practice is heavily influenced by component suppliers' technical expertise, quality and reliability.

Some auto makers also encourage additional component suppliers to develop proprietary solutions. This makes it increasingly difficult for individual semiconductor manufacturers to innovate, however. In this situation, many of them are unable to tap the economies of scale that are so vital to the semiconductor industry in particular. Consequently, only large semiconductor firms that bundle the demand that exists in a fragmented market, and demonstrate technical skills that go beyond their own products, will in future be able to deliver the necessary level of quality and innovation.

Both auto makers and suppliers that have not yet grasped the importance of working together as partners must rethink their positions. If they want to stay competitive, both must inject a new quality into their relationships with their suppliers. Ideally, collaboration between components suppliers, system suppliers and car makers will be very close. Semiconductor manufacturers must be involved as early as possible in the preliminary development and development projects run by first-tier suppliers and the car makers themselves.

For many years, Infineon has been working closely with both system suppliers and automobile companies in order to supply efficient and optimally tailored semiconductor solutions. To fully understand what an application requires at an early stage, and to ensure that its solutions genuinely meet these requirements, Infineon engages in in-depth dialogue with the car makers. This form of interaction also plays an important part in the early development of innovative products.

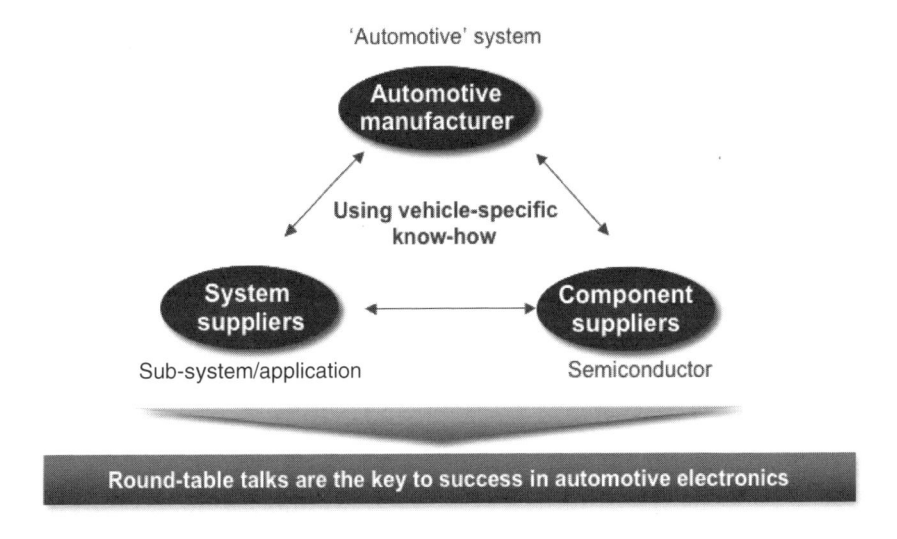

Figure 11.9 *Business model for a successful future*

When development contracts are awarded, finance is often treated more or less as a mere footnote to the 'real' issues. Yet low margins and fierce global competition have brought many suppliers – and not only the small and medium-sized enterprises (SMEs) – to the very limits of their financial capabilities. Working in a highly volatile industry whose capital-intensive nature places heavy demands on capital markets, semiconductor firms in particular rate financing as a singularly important matter. In other industries, low single-digit margins might be enough to satisfy investors and cover the cost of capital. Not so in semiconductors, however, where firms have to earn margins upward of 10 per cent. That is why any discussion of future collaboration and cost distribution along the value chain must also look closely at new business models.

THE NEED FOR NEW BUSINESS MODELS

Standardize and cut costs, yes, but make sure you innovate too. Delegate responsibility and liability, but make sure you stay in control. Avoid quality costs, but keep the supplier landscape fragmented to avoid unhealthy dependencies. The fact that many auto makers feel trapped in this area of conflict is primarily attributable to severe cost pressure. However, they cannot escape from this area of conflict simply by dumping all the burdens on the supply industry. The only way out is to engage in partnership and collaboration all along the value chain.

New business models are needed if car makers and suppliers (including semiconductor companies) are to master the challenges they currently face. These new business models must aim to translate innovation into volume production at reasonable system cost. But they must also seek to keep system complexity manageable, to master the art of developing new products under stiff time and cost pressure, and at the same time to uphold strict quality standards. Forward-looking models will forge value chains that are based on partnership. Performance and reward will be well balanced. Business models that focus solely on price should therefore soon be a thing of the past. After all, innovation is only affordable in the long run if the inherent costs are not always being passed along to the previous link in the chain.

This being the case, the central issue is to define who foots the development bill, especially for software projects. In future, software will be much more than just an extra bit tacked onto the hardware. It will increasingly establish itself as a separate product. Car makers have repeatedly called on the semiconductor industry to put more effort into this area. The growing importance of software and moves to define a standardized software architecture will naturally have consequences for semiconductor firms. The latter will thus have no choice but to tackle the issue of co-designing hardware and software head on. Even so, it is unlikely that semiconductor manufacturers will cultivate application-specific software expertise as a new core competence. For one thing, this would run counter to the interests of first-tier suppliers. For another, it would be difficult for semiconductor companies to market this competence in any sensible way. In the long term, these companies will therefore only contribute software in the form of hardware-related software (that is, firmware).

Innovation must nevertheless be made possible in future, despite the systemic differences in innovation and product lifecycles between the automotive and semiconductor industries. To make sure this happens, durable standards must be fashioned, components must be made available for longer periods, and the entire product lifecycle – from start-up through modification to discontinuation – must be accompanied by intensive communication. At the same time, new approaches to financing and risk management must be discussed and clarified. Networked organizations, mergers or collaborative ventures between selected partners would, for example, be conceivable options. The important thing is that every party to the automotive value chain must identify and concentrate on its own core competencies. For their part, car makers should advance the development of open standards, ramp up their in-house integration skills and provide the support that their partners need. In return, suppliers can position themselves as reliable system partners, contributing stable, scaleable and innovative solutions.

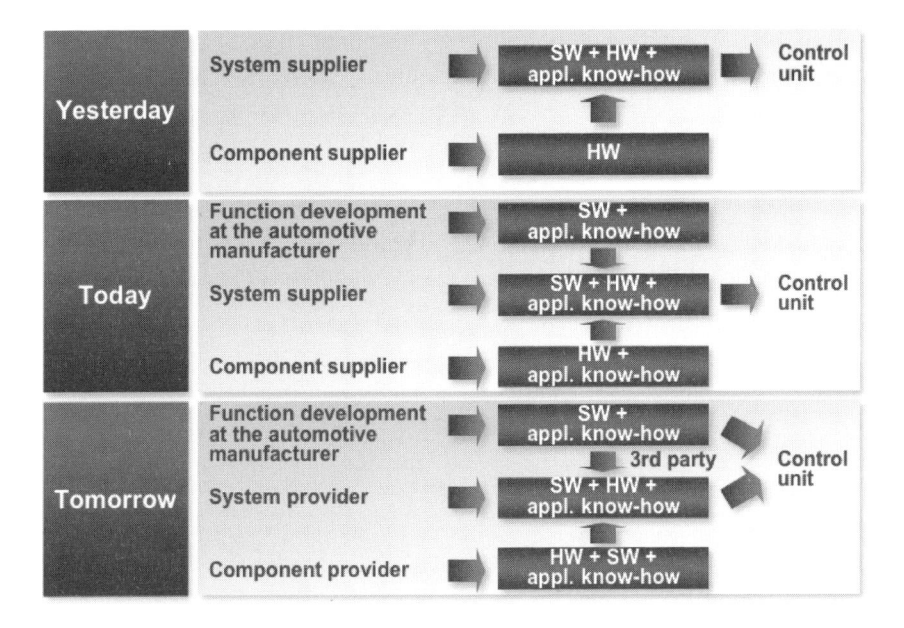

Figure 12.10 *Changes in the value chain*

Networked, strategic system and development partnerships with a long-term horizon are the key to future success. Within these partnerships, suppliers will do far more than merely deliver components at the lowest possible cost. They will rather be treated as equal partners who are involved from the earliest stages of the auto maker's entire development process. When these different players cooperate across the entire value chain, the car companies can assume responsibility for the system as a whole, for drawing up specifications and coordinating the various suppliers. System suppliers can shoulder responsibility for integrating the applications they deliver, while semiconductor firms such as Infineon can take care of integrating their chips. Substantial synergies can be derived from this approach to innovation – synergies from which everyone who plays a part in the value chain will benefit. Ultimately, the resultant savings will also help underwrite the cost of innovation.

For all the efforts already in progress, there are still far more questions than answers about how solutions that satisfy all players can be found to the challenges raised by automotive electronics. It is, for instance, interesting to ask why the automotive electronics market is so fiercely contested despite such immense challenges. System suppliers, component suppliers and semiconductor companies alike are all stepping up their activities in this market. Although the automobile market as a whole is unlikely to expand by more than a modest 3 per cent per year, one reason for such keen interest is undoubtedly the expectation of significantly stronger growth in automotive electronics. The market for automotive semiconductor applications, say, is forecast to grow by an average of around 7 per cent per year between 2005 and 2010 (see Figure 12.11).

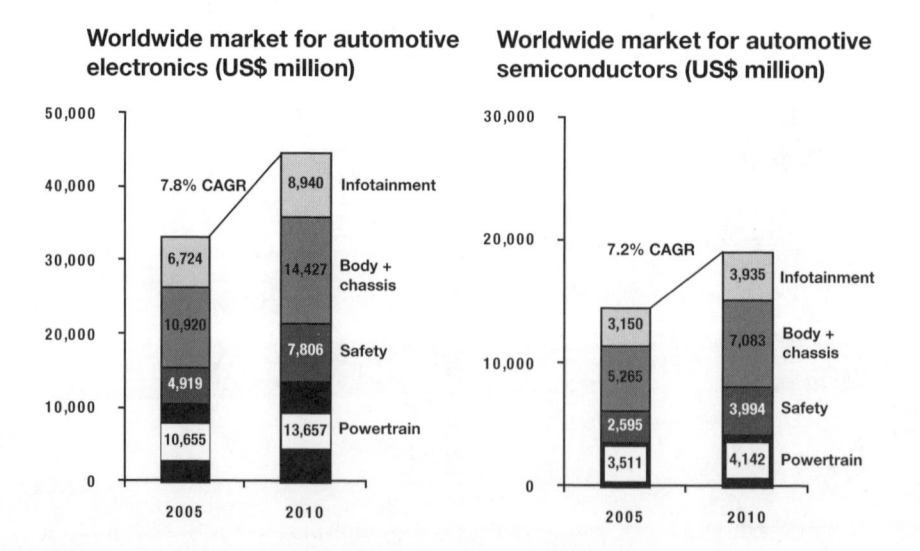

Figure 12.11 *Market developments in automotive electronics and semiconductors*
Source: Strategy Analytics, October 2004, August 2005

Thanks to its in-depth knowledge of applications, its broad product portfolio and an appropriate corporate structure, Infineon is well placed to rise to the challenges issued by car makers. It should therefore benefit from this growth as it draws on in-house knowledge in areas such as communications, safety/security and storage products.

Innovation remains the driving force behind the German automotive industry. The comparative competitive advantage enjoyed by German auto makers is in large measure attributable to their innovative prowess. It is also true that the whole world looks up to the German car industry as the 'most efficient innovator'. However, whilst striving to escape from the productivity vice, Germany must take great care not to forfeit its competitive advantage to emerging economies such as China and Korea. It can only defend – and capitalize on – its position if car makers, system suppliers and component manufacturers all pull together.

12

The next evolutionary step for the automotive industry is just around the corner: factors for sustainable success in the interplay of OEMs and suppliers

Siegfried Wolf, CEO, Magna International

INTRODUCTION

The automotive world is changing at a rapid speed. The demands of consumers are becoming ever more differentiated. Their demand for mobility is increasing, and development and production cycles are shortening dramatically. Globalization has intensified the speed of change even more. While auto makers open up new niche markets, new competitors are pushing into the market. In addition, record price levels for raw materials are driving up costs and demanding ever more efficient development and production practices. In parallel, hedge funds have discovered an industry traditionally of little attraction to them, probing acquisitions which only a few years ago would have been unthinkable.

Despite these far-reaching processes of change, the automotive industry is, without any qualifications, one of the key industries of the global economy. A high-tech industry with an enormous potential for innovation, it has fascinated people from childhood. The millions of people visiting automobile shows around the globe provide a glimpse of the fascination the automotive world exercises on humankind. Like hardly any other industry, the automotive industry is linked to strong emotions. Automobiles are an important part of our daily life. The continuously growing societal need for mobility becomes manifest in them, and they have increasingly come to reflect people's personality. Thus, automobiles epitomize the desire for individuality like hardly any other product. In a nutshell, car buyers like to create a 'home on four wheels' for themselves.

'The automobile' apparently has not lost any of its fascination over the years. Experts are saying that the automobile will remain the most important means of passenger transportation in the future. We can anticipate that the fascination for automobiles will not fade – quite the opposite.

The future of the automotive industry, though, is anything but clear. Over the first years of the new millennium, sales have been slow. As a result, the pressure for profitability has increased on all original equipment manufacturers (OEMs). The industry is faced with enormous structural changes which raise new questions about its value chain. The market entry of Japanese and Korean auto makers about 20 years ago has already led to fundamental changes in competitive and market conditions. More change is to be expected through the market entry of Chinese OEMs, especially in Europe. For the auto makers, at the beginning of the new century, new competition has set in which has already reached new levels, but has not yet reached its peak.

It is interesting to note that in the context of structural change processes, once again the impetus to define value chains anew has originated within the industry itself. The far-reaching restructuring processes of the 1990s were themselves initiated from within the automotive industry, so part of the automotive world's fascination is apparently in its nature to constantly challenge things, to always want to improve things, and to understand change as an opportunity for improvement. The quest for top performance is particularly strong within the automotive industry, as several examples in this volume demonstrate.

A ROLE MODEL FOR OTHER INDUSTRIES

There is hardly an industry that has influenced other branches of the economy more strongly than the automotive industry. Particularly for the production of consumer goods, auto makers have set benchmarks and established a new way of thinking. The restructuring of value chains that the automotive industry implemented over the 1990s – keywords being 'lean production' and 'kaizen' – is increasingly taking place in other industries as well. Mostly driven by globalization, many enterprises in very different industries see themselves forced to question their self-conception and to turn the organization of their processes on its head in order to be capable of a top-level performance in future. In the wake of these changes, vertical integration is often reduced, entire production chains are chopped off, and operations and workflows are designed completely anew to enable 'just-in-time' scenarios.

Take the banking industry as an example. The increased intensity of competition among financial service providers is forcing open the traditional value chains. To increase their profitability in international competition, more and more financial institutions – in cooperation with specialized service providers – are beginning to separate their primary (core) processes like sales and product development from secondary (non-core) processes like order fulfilment. According to industry experts, these secondary processes are especially characterized by fragmented workflows which can be made substantially more flexible. Thus, the thinking within the financial services industry strongly reminds us of the automotive industry of the 1990s. Even more: the auto industry has become a role model for other industries.

Look at retailing for another example where concepts from the auto industry are finding their way into another industry. According to a McKinsey study, the retail industry, particularly in Germany, aims to increase its profitability through more efficient process management. Under the keyword of 'lean retailing', the complete supply chain from the manufacturer to the shelf is being reconsidered. Simplified processes are being introduced to ensure that goods get to the customer more quickly, that expensive stock levels are lowered, and that retailers have more time for service activities.

CURRENT CHALLENGES IN THE INTERPLAY OF AUTO MAKERS AND THEIR SUPPLIERS

One way in which auto makers are increasingly dealing with the challenges briefly sketched out above is through alliances. Recently, Porsche's taking a financial stake in Volkswagen has received a lot of attention. On a more operational level, the two auto makers have been long cooperating, for example on the shared architecture of the Porsche Cayenne and Volkswagen Touareg. The list of strategic cooperations could easily be extended: Toyota and PSA Peugeot-Citroën have entered a manufacturing joint venture, and Ford and VW have been cooperating since the 1990s. General Motors, DaimlerChrysler, and BMW have formed an alliance to develop and build hybrid drive systems.

The rising number of strategic alliances, experts agree, is caused by the increasing fragmentation of markets. A smaller volume per model, and proliferation in the number of models, increase development and production cost per model. In addition, overcapacities have increased pressure on margins, while innovation and the integration of new technology into the production process is demanding ever more resources. OEMs accordingly use strategic alliances as well as modularization concepts to reduce one-off costs.

There is yet another reason that alliances have a positive effect: the willingness of OEMs to form alliances with their immediate competitors shows that – notwithstanding their competition with each other, which is good and necessary – a desire to do the best for the entire industry enters into their considerations. Behind this is the simple but accurate insight that the perspective of an individual OEM is improved if there are joint efforts to increase the global competitiveness of the entire industry.

Accelerated by globalization, the need to lower costs in general and development costs in particular, along with a need for higher flexibility, have long been influencing not only auto makers, but increasingly suppliers as well.

Many suppliers in North America and Europe, especially medium-sized ones, are therefore in a precarious situation. Besides pressure on their costs and margins, and development risks passed on to them by the OEMs, rising prices for raw materials burden the suppliers. They find themselves in what might be called a sandwich position: from above they experience the OEM cost pressure, and from below they are pushed by exploding raw material prices. What remains is the filling in this sandwich, which for many suppliers has become so thin that you can hardly see it any longer, only smell it at best.

Some experts forecast that another round of cost pressure would mean the end for many smaller companies.

Just how serious the situation of the supplier industry is can also be seen from the rising number of insolvencies, which does not spare large corporations. Even an industry giant like Delphi had to file for Chapter 11 protection for its North American operations in October 2005. Only the future can tell what this will mean for its 185,000 employees, and what the consequences are for the North American market. At the same time, the example of Delphi demonstrates the enormous dynamic of changes, and this leads to the question what factors lead to success in the market under these conditions.

MAGNA: AN EXAMPLE OF SUSTAINABLE GROWTH IN THE SUPPLIER SECTOR

The case of Magna International shows that those suppliers that have moved ahead of the competition, have recognized future challenges early on and have positioned themselves accordingly, can survive and even thrive in this environment. Suppliers that aligned themselves strategically along the requirements of 'lean management' during what some have referred to as 'the second automotive revolution' in the 1990s are nowadays profiting from the structural changes in the industry.

At the same time OEMs reduced their level of vertical integration, starting a strong trend of outsourcing. Those supplier companies that did not reduce their role to that of an 'extended workbench', but developed into real production and became engineering partners of the auto makers, have fared best under these circumstances. But these suppliers also had to understand the needs and problems of OEMs, and to have the know-how to proactively offer new products and services.

Generally, *a consistent focus on the needs and desires of customers* is a key factor for success in the supplier industry. At Magna, this thinking is deeply rooted and can easily be illustrated: when a customer says 'Jump!', the Magna response is not 'Why?', but 'How high?' Behind this is the simple but absolutely correct insight that a supplier company can ultimately only be as successful as the customers it is allowed to serve.

Another aspect is certainly *technological competence*. A company that has identified which technologies will prevail in the market, and that masters and further develops these technologies, can offer its customers solutions that put them in a particularly promising position compared with their competitors. Take all-wheel drive technology for an example, which Magna has developed to create a decisive competitive advantage for itself in drivetrain technology. Magna could offer its OEM customers a specific know-how which the final customers increasingly demanded. This ability to take extend its thinking to the final customer – or to put it differently, its customers' customers – distinguishes Magna from many of its competitors.

MAGNA TODAY

Over the past years, Magna has grown very dynamically in both quantitative and qualitative ways. In this context, the acquisition of Steyr-Daimler-Puch in 1998 was certainly a special milestone. Besides increasing sales, through this acquisition Magna entered a new dimension within the auto supplier industry. It added complete vehicle competence, which meant that Magna was now accepted by OEMs as a fully fledged engineering and manufacturing partner. Comprehensive know-how, in combination with a very broad and high-quality product portfolio, along with a global footprint, really do mark unique selling propositions.

Based on this, in 2004 Magna accomplished another jump in sales. Magna Steyr contributed substantially to this by increasing its complete vehicle production from 118,000 units in 2003 to 227,000 units in 2004, thereby doubling sales and almost tripling earnings before income and tax (EBIT).

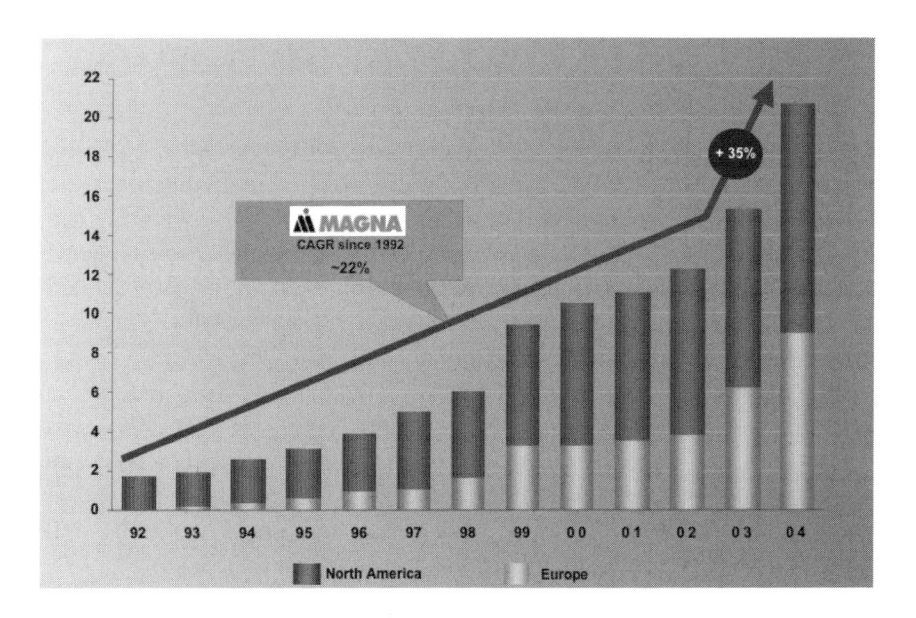

Figure 12.1 *Magna International: sales development*

With sales of US $20.7 billion, about 83,000 employees, and 279 facilities (223 manufacturing, 56 engineering) in 23 countries, Magna now is the world's third largest automotive supplier.

	Facilities					Employees	
	● 223 Production ● 56 Engineering, R&D					● 82,200	

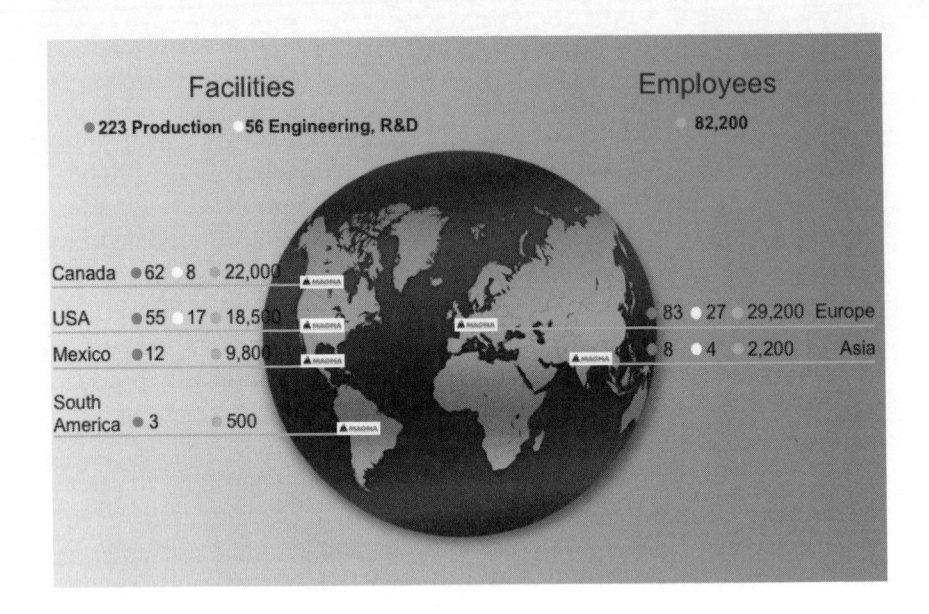

Canada	● 62	● 8	● 22,000		● 83	● 27	● 29,200 Europe
USA	● 55	● 17	● 18,500		● 8	● 4	● 2,200 Asia
Mexico	● 12		● 9,800				
South America	● 3		● 500				

Figure 12.2 *Magna's global presence*

MILESTONES OF CORPORATE DEVELOPMENT

The success of Magna over the past decades is closely linked to Frank Stronach's name. In 1957, Frank Stronach opened a one-man tool and die shop called Multimatic. In 1969, Multimatic merged with Magna Electronics Corporation Ltd, and in 1973 the company name was changed to Magna International Inc. In the years that followed, Frank Stronach led the rapidly growing company to the top and – partly through systematic acquisitions – built Magna into the global corporation it is today.

From a strategic perspective, the various acquisitions were undertaken to strengthen Magna in terms of technology. Over the years, new and specific competencies have continuously been integrated into the corporate network. As a result, the knowledge about automobiles within the company increased steadily. Magna has thus developed more and more into an outsourcing partner of the most important OEMs.

Following the successful establishment of the company in North America, which was mainly achieved through organic growth, in the late 1980s Magna turned increasingly to the European market. Over the following years and supported by acquisitions, Magna achieved a similarly market-leading position in Europe. A milestone in developing the European market was the acquisition of what was then Steyr-Daimler-Puch AG in 1998, which was the cornerstone for Magna Steyr when it was formed in 2001.

Other groups also expanded their presence in Europe, step by step, partly through greenfield plants, partly by acquisitions intended to enhance and top off their product portfolio. It is noteworthy in this context that Magna's rapid growth was occurring in a market that was considered rather saturated when Magna entered it.

So much for history. But – and this is the decisive question – what have Frank Stronach and Magna done differently from the competition? Or to put it differently, what are the decisive criteria on which OEM customers have increasingly opted for Magna as their supplier partner?

A central aspect in answering this question, besides the strategic acquisitions policy already discussed, is flexibility. Over the years, Frank Stronach has built up an organizational structure that to this day allows for a maximum of flexibility. For Magna the ideas of lean management have never been a management tool which was implemented, but rather part of the organization's basic convictions.

The degrees of freedom resulting from this enabled Magna from the start to focus fully on the needs and desires of its customers, instead of dealing with a high level of internal complexity. At the same time, its flexible structure allowed Magna to pick up new challenges and trends more quickly than its competition, and implement them according to customer requirements, before they became common knowledge in the industry. Paired with growing technological competence, this enabled Magna to capitalize on a special momentum in many business decisions.

Frank Stronach has always relied on the power and the will of his employees to perform. This employee orientation still is a basic value of Magna, and is documented clearly in the corporate constitution.

SUCCESS FACTORS FOR CONTINUED GROWTH

One of the key reasons for the dynamic growth of Magna over the past year is the company's ability to identify changes in the automotive industry early on, and to align itself to the new market conditions. Magna implemented the guidelines of the lean management principle long before they became common knowledge. In parallel, the flexibility of all business processes was supported by a decentralized organizational structure. In addition, the actively driven enhancement of the portfolio through targeted acquisitions that was described above has strengthened the technological positioning of the company.

Over the course of the dynamic growth process, Magna succeeded in maintaining the core principles and values of the company – something many companies have failed to accomplish. Moreover, the distinctive entrepreneurial culture was transferred to the new added business units. In the process, Magna's strong ability to integrate the newly acquired units ensured its success and allowed for fast synergies between the various units.

Success factor: active portfolio management

The targeted acquisition policy and the sustainable, profitable growth of the past years have made Magna one of the leading global suppliers of systems, components and complete modules for the automotive industry. With regard to the range of products and services, Magna in its current group structure – Magna Steyr, Magna Powertrain, Cosma, Magna Donnelly, Decoma, Intier Automotive Interiors, Intier Automotive Seating and Magna Closures – has become the most diversified auto supplier in the world. The product portfolio that Magna can offer its customers ranges from small components to larger modules to complex systems, all the way to a complete vehicle built on a contract assembly base by Magna Steyr at the Graz facility.

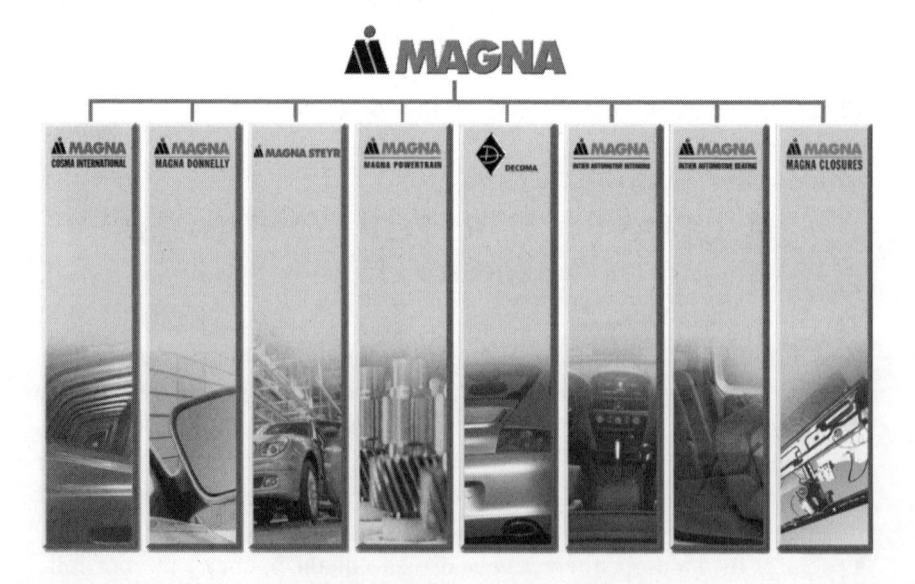

Figure 12.3 *Magna International Group Structure 2005*

Its complete vehicle competence has raised Magna to a new level and created an exceptional competitive advantage. Major projects like the Saab 9–3 Convertible, the BMW X3 and the Jeep Grand Cherokee are proof of the high acceptance **Magna Steyr** has received for its complete vehicle know-how. In 2004 Magna Steyr built more than 227,000 vehicles, a sixfold volume increase over 1998. A former low-volume manufacturer has thus become the world's largest auto maker without a brand of its own. In the process, the number of employees increased from 5,000 to about 10,000.

Magna's all-wheel drive and powertrain competence is organized within **Magna Powertrain**. Here, Magna is a worldwide leader in technology. There is hardly an all-wheel drive vehicle in the premium segment that does not utilize all-wheel drive know-how from Magna Powertrain. With the acquisition of New Venture Gear and the integration of what was previously Magna's Tesma group, one of the worldwide leading powertrain specialists has emerged.

Cosma is the worldwide largest supplier of metal body systems in the auto supplier industry. Its product portfolio ranges from small stampings to structural parts and assemblies and large Class A stampings, all the way to complete bodies-in-white.

The **Magna Donnelly** group, which specializes in mirror systems and electronics, is also the market leader in its business field. Products by Magna Donnelly find their way into more than half of all vehicles produced worldwide. In the booming Chinese market, Magna Donnelly has a market share of about 80 per cent, and about every third mirror actuator is made by Magna Donnelly.

Magna's exteriors group is **Decoma**. As a supplier of complete vehicle exteriors, Decoma has a leading position in the market. Its product portfolio ranges from exterior trim components to bumpers, lighting systems, body side panels, and from tailgates to complete front and rear end modules.

Intier Automotive Interiors covers the entire vehicle interior, its portfolio spanning from complete dashboard systems to side and overhead trim, floor carpets and acoustic systems, to complete vehicle interior integration.

The focus of **Intier Automotive Seating** is on the development and manufacturing of vehicle seats, complete seating systems and seating mechanisms.

The business fields of **Magna Closures** are latching systems, electrical and mechanical window regulators, actuators and mechanisms for doors and tailgates.

Success factor: decentralized organizational structure

The far-reaching changes in the auto industry have made flexibility a more and more important factor over the past few years. The changes in global markets, the dynamics of which will only increase in future, call for organizational structures that allow enterprises to react quickly to new market challenges. The ability to satisfy the needs and expectations of customers within a very short timeframe has become an important criterion for a company in setting itself apart from the competition. This can mean being extraordinarily fast in certain development processes, or achieving the necessary capacity shifts smoothly.

To ensure a maximum level of flexibility in engineering and manufacturing, Magna has been set up in a decentralized structure. This structure also is the most visible element of Magna's special corporate culture: Magna is not structured like a typical large corporation, with its often very static and strict hierarchic architecture. Instead, the company consists of many smaller units. The groups are typically made up of individual divisions whose size is normally limited to 300 to 800 employees. If a unit has grown dynamically and exceeds a certain size, it is usually divided into smaller units again to allow specialization and a focus on its core competences. In their daily business, individual divisions operate with a high level of autonomy and self-organization. On the market, they appear as profit centres. This set-up guarantees each division and its management a maximum of personal freedom. This degree of freedom is what makes Magna an attractive employer for capable and performance-minded heads. The decentralized structure thus has a substantial role in the 'war for talent' as well.

One up from the divisions are the product groups, which organize overall back-office functions in group offices, which are always kept very lean. The groups also coordinate the individual divisions with regard to marketing and eventually operational synergies.

Magna itself, steered by the Magna Executive Management, provides the long-term strategic direction and takes care of financial, but also technological and systemic synergies – like a large umbrella spanning a lot of medium-sized companies. The corporate roof dictates and ensures a high level of customer focus, so Magna always shows 'one face to the customer'.

Despite its size, Magna is thus nothing like a cumbersome supertanker. Instead, the company shows more characteristics of an alliance of small and agile speedboats, manoeuvring highly flexibly and still using the force of the alliance.

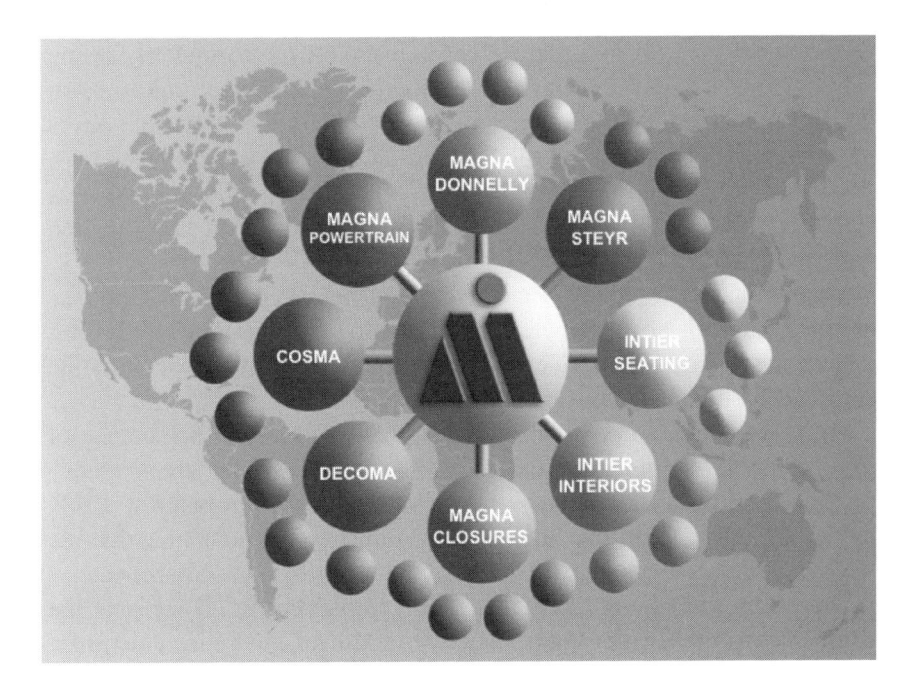

Figure 12.4 *Magna's decentralized structure*

Success factor: entrepreneurship

Because of the changed market situation, high margin and cost pressure and increasing competition, many companies in the automotive industry – suppliers as well as OEMs – have started efficiency improvement programmes again and again over the past years and decades. Often, these programmes were limited to cost savings only, and in retrospect they failed to fully achieve the desired effects. While short-time recoveries were visible, the second and third rounds of many efficiency improvement programmes indicate that the progress made was not sustainable.

One reason for the limited effectiveness is certainly the fact that within the company, such efficiency improvement programmes are experienced negatively, as they are normally linked to severe cuts. In addition, many approaches are falling short of their goals, as they focus on the consequences of problems, but do not go to their source. In a way, these kind of measures are always late and seem to be implemented with very lukewarm motivation.

Magna, in contrast, has a system-active programme to consistently raise profitability. This programme is barely visible to the outside, but of significant importance for the positive performance of the past years, as is the company's decentralized structure: at Magna, there is a particularly strong entrepreneurial culture established over many years. Magna employees on all levels take care that the company advances and that useless jetsam is not generated. This way of entrepreneurial thinking is supported by a system of profit sharing which has proven itself over decades. With its clear commitment to its employees, Magna has an avant-garde function within the industry.

Magna has intentionally been set up and managed as a stakeholder-oriented enterprise over the years. At its centre are investors, employees, management and society. To ensure that the stakeholders, particularly the employees, share in the positive development of the company, Magna has a corporate constitution which exactly predetermines the percentage of profits shared by employees or given to social causes. The transparency and the binding character of the corporate constitution make it a role model not only within the auto supplier industry, and guarantee that the key stakeholders are all partners in Magna's growth and profitability.

Driven by the conviction that it is the employees in all areas of the company who determine the success or failure of the entire enterprise, through their qualifications, motivation and passion, Magna's constitution contains a particularly high social component. In comparison with many competitors, this is certainly an important differentiator. The system, which at Magna also is referred to as 'fair enterprise', ensures the constructive cooperation of management and employees. In a very transparent manner, it also ensures that all employees are interested in a good performance, as they directly participate in the company's profitability.

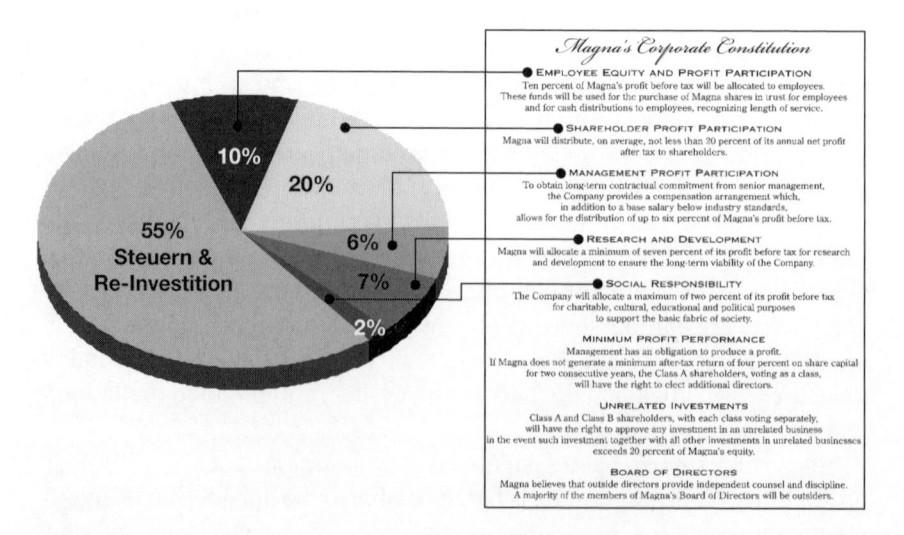

Figure 12.5 *Magna's corporate constitution*

MAGNA'S CORPORATE CONSTITUTION

The Magna corporate constitution defines and describes the central rights of employees and shareholders. At the same time, it regulates the distribution of profits.

In terms of **shareholder profit participation**, the constitution determines that investors receive on average not less than 20 per cent of Magna's annual net profit after tax.

A core element of the specific Magna culture is **employee equity and profit participation**. This participation, which is laid down in the corporate constitution, fosters entrepreneurial thinking and thereby helps reduce inefficiencies. Employees become partial owners and entrepreneurs within the company. That way, they have a very individual interest in offering customers innovative and high-quality solutions, while at the same time holding down costs. With regard to employee equity and profit participation, the constitution provides that 10 per cent of Magna's qualifying profit before tax will be allocated to employees. These funds are used in part for the purchase of Magna shares in trust for employees, and in part for cash distributions to employees, recognizing their length of service.

To obtain long-term contractual commitment from senior management, the constitution also determines **management profit participation**. Thereby, Magna provides a compensation arrangement which, in addition to a base salary below industry standards, allows for the distribution of up to 6 per cent of its profit before tax.

To ensure its long-term and sustainable success and to warrant a continuous innovation process, the constitution spells out that Magna will allocate a minimum of 7 per cent of its profit before tax for **research and development**. This can be interpreted as an indicator how strongly Magna has committed to adding value to its customers through continuous product and process innovations.

As mentioned above, **social responsibility** is a fundamental principle of Magna. To comply with this, Magna allocates a maximum of 2 per cent of its profit before tax for charitable, cultural, educational and political purposes to support the basic fabric of society.

In addition, the constitution requires management to produce a profit. The **minimum profit performance** can be interpreted as an essential contribution to secure the company's long-term viability. If Magna does not generate a minimum after-tax return of 4 per cent on share capital for two consecutive years, Magna's Class A shareholders, voting as a class, have the right to elect additional directors.

To ensure investment is geared to supporting the company's targets, Magna Class A and Class B shareholders, with each class voting separately, have the right to approve any investment in an unrelated business in the event that such an investment, together with all other **investments in unrelated businesses**, exceeds 20 per cent of Magna's equity.

Finally, the constitution also governs the composition of the **board of directors**. As Magna believes that outside directors provide independent counsel and discipline, a majority of the members of Magna's board of directors are required to be outsiders.

THE MAGNA EMPLOYEES' CHARTER

Figure 12.6 *Magna's employees' charter*

Inseparable from Magna's corporate constitution is the Magna employees' charter. The charter clearly defines Magna's commitment to an operating philosophy that is based on fairness and concern for people.

Some of the key elements of the employees' charter illustrate how Magna succeeds in ensuring its distinct entrepreneurial culture over the long term. Magna realizes that the best way to enhance job security is to produce a quality product at a competitive price. The prerequisite for this is the appropriate training and retraining of employees. To encourage individual qualifications and to expand the knowledge network within the company, Magna therefore offers special programmes for human resource development. These include counselling on future professional development; specific training programmes tailored to individual interests and capabilities; and assistance in establishing contact with external institutions.

A further aspect in this context is the company's open communication and information policy. Through a consistent and company-wide open door policy, Magna encourages communication within the company and creates a positive climate for cross-group cooperation.

An instrument like the Magna employees' charter will only show an effect if it is more than lip service. An employee opinion survey guarantees that these principles are adhered to within the divisions and that management is upholding them. All employees are surveyed regularly every 12 to 16 months using a standardized system. The results of the employee opinion survey directly become part of management evaluation by Magna's top executives. They quickly lead to specific action plans to solve the problems pointed out in the survey.

SUCCESS FACTORS TAKEN TOGETHER: OPERATING PRINCIPLES

The corporate constitution and Magna's employees' charter ensure that the 'fair enterprise' principle is not just a theoretical approach, but is realized by management and employees alike on a day-to-day basis. The notion of an 'entrepreneur within the enterprise' is therefore particularly appropriate for Magna employees. The decentralized organization of the company in largely independent profit centres creates the necessary degrees of freedom, reduces administrative expenses and allows for an exceptional closeness to customers. Individual employees within the relatively small and flexible units can be integrated more easily into entrepreneurial responsibilities. This substantially increases employees' own initiative, in particular in terms of internal efficiency.

Allocating 10 per cent of Magna's qualifying profit before tax to employees further strengthens this way of thinking, as performance, quality and efficiency are directly rewarded. Thus the better the quality Magna can offer its customers and the more cost-efficiently this quality can be achieved, the bigger the allocation.

Magna has positioned itself in a way that brings performance and compensation into a fair balance and establishes lean management throughout the company. The dynamic growth over the past decades – often enough in contrast to the general trend of the industry – proves the validity of Magna's basic principles, and shows that entrepreneurial success and fair cooperation between management and employees do not exclude one another.

LOOKING AHEAD: THE FUTURE OF THE INDUSTRY

When looking into the future of the automotive supplier industry, we can identify four important trends. First, many indicators suggest that in future those companies that continuously achieve top performances will be ahead of the competition. This is not only about cost leadership, but more generally about the interplay of cost and quality, which must be considered together. Moreover, a consolidation in the supplier industry will result in performance levels being taken to a new height. The automotive industry will thus remain an industry characterized by top performance, not merely in terms of technology.

Second, there are many signs that outsourcing on the part of OEMs will continue. Industry experts estimate that, by 2015, some 77 per cent of the value will come from suppliers. This is closely related to the efficiency improvement programmes of the OEMs, as well as the steadily growing model diversity.

The third important trend in the automotive industry suggests that the quantity and complexity of engineering projects handled by suppliers will increase further. This results, among other things, in a greater need for financing. To remain competitive in future, many suppliers will continues along their path of relocating manufacturing to countries with lower production costs. Whether these relocations are associated with a different level of quality, or whether they will turn out to be the expected success at all, remains to be seen case by case.

The fourth trend is imminent when the focus of analysis shifts to the development of the global markets. The weight of Asia and particularly China, as well as that of Eastern European markets, will grow in future. China will further develop its position as a low-cost production base as well as a sales market in worldwide competition over the next few years.

In summary, the following four trends can be confirmed:

- The automotive industry will remain an industry of (technological) top performance.
- Outsourcing processes at OEMs will continue.
- The complexity of development processes at suppliers will grow.
- The markets in Eastern Europe and Asia will gain further weight in the global competition.

THE CORNERSTONES OF MAGNA'S GROWTH STRATEGY

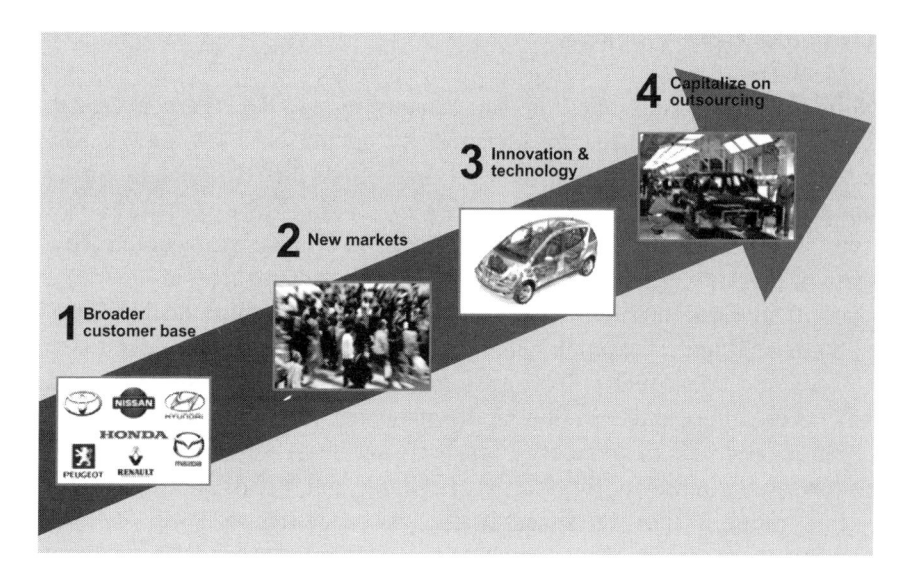

Figure 12.7 *Strategy for further growth*

To continue the successful course of the past years in the light of these new developments, Magna holds on steadily to a step-by-step strategy of disciplined, profitable and self-financed growth. On an operational level, Magna is following four strategic directions:

Continuously broaden the customer base

As a tier 1 supplier, Magna naturally offers its broad product portfolio to all OEMs. In so doing, Magna responds to the noticeable willingness of OEMs to share certain competencies and to capitalize on development partnerships in their non-core business. In future, Magna will use the synergies between its groups even more strongly to establish itself as a qualified value-adding partner and win new customers. In this regard, the French and Asian OEMs have a high priority.

Develop new markets

More than 100 Magna facilities (manufacturing and R&D) are located in Europe, and more than 150 facilities are in the NAFTA region. The company is currently present in Asia, with more than 10 manufacturing and R&D facilities.

In future, Magna will focus on following its OEM customers into new growth markets. Of particular interest in this regard are the emerging markets in Eastern Europe and China. To make the most of these new potentials, Magna is extending its activities into these growth markets step by step and consistently. New customer portals in Seoul and Shanghai have been set up, and capacities at the plants in China and Eastern Europe are gradually being expanded. Every step into these new markets always follows the principle of disciplined, profitable and self-financed growth.

In parallel, Magna continues to align its capacities in North America and Europe to customer needs, and to expand them if needed. As always at Magna, growth means 'in addition to', and not 'instead of'.

Innovations and technological progress

With over 5,000 employees in research, development and engineering, Magna counts among the biggest and most capable engineering service providers in the auto supplier industry. In future, Magna will further expand its role as a driver of innovation within the automotive industry, and support OEMs in managing increasing complexity and technological challenges. To this end, Magna will employ its competencies across the complete vehicle, to proactively offer its OEM customers responses to future technological requirements, new legislative regulations and societal trends. The scope of services ranges from the concept idea, to all phases of product, programme and process engineering, to testing and homologation.

Its complete vehicle competence enables Magna to support auto makers not only on parts or system engineering, but also – if needed – in the engineering and manufacturing of the complete vehicle.

Of key importance to Magna in this process is its highly skilled workforce. The best engineers and innovations are of little use if there is no highly skilled workforce to translate new developments into high-quality products quickly and in a cost-efficient manner. Thus, Magna has established comprehensive training programmes to ensure a 'world-class manufacturing' quality level over the long term.

Some examples of innovation illustrate how Magna is playing a part in the value chain of OEMs, always keeping in mind the needs of the final customer, the vehicle driver. Decoma is developing a 'composite intensive vehicle' which will lower vehicle weight substantially, thereby enabling better vehicle handling and better mileage. Magna's Intier Interiors group, based on its competencies in flat cable systems and integrated airbags, is working to provide solutions for additional hidden load space, thereby further increasing comfort inside the vehicle. Magna Donnelly is pushing the development of a camera-based park assist system, and Cosma is building on its leading-edge know-how in the development and use of light and high-strength steel to decrease vehicle weight and make vehicles safer at the same time. Higher security at a lower weight translates into better mileage and lower insurance rates. At the 2005 Frankfurt Motor Show, Magna Steyr presented the MILA (Magna Innovative Lightweight Auto) concept car, which showcases the group's combined competences in the shape of an impressive prototype. A range of technologies comes together in the MILA concept (Figure 13.8): an eco-friendly CNG (compressed natural gas) powered engine combined with extremely sporty performance (150 HP, over 200 km/h top speed); a consistent lightweight construction; a modular design principle with components and modules developed in advance and optimized in terms of cost and weight; and advanced vehicle safety thanks to the monocoque body's high stiffness. Besides these 'hard facts' it is interesting to note the 'soft fact' that it only took six months to completely develop and build the vehicle on show, as all the development steps up to the complete concept vehicle were modelled virtually.

Figure 12.8 *Concept MILA*

Capitalizing on the ongoing trend of OEM outsourcing

According to several third-party studies, the need for technology partnerships between suppliers and OEMs will increase further. Representatives of suppliers do not need to refer to these studies, though: their day-to-day talks with customers show that they expect ever more sophisticated and comprehensive solutions from their suppliers, and that they presuppose the necessary capabilities to be present at the supplier. With its competences in development and manufacturing, Magna is positioned very well in both operational and strategic terms. The strongly growing model diversity and the rising share of niche vehicles in Europe as well as America and Asia open up excellent opportunities for Magna to capitalize on this outsourcing trend and expand its market position.

Of course, suppliers must not make the mistake of taking these opportunities for future business for granted. In the light of current tendencies to insource, which – particularly in Germany – are partly motivated politically, suppliers are called on to consistently prove to OEMs that they offer economically and technologically superior alternatives.

This latter challenge is not limited to current programmes or specified supply content, but can also relate to new business models and new forms of cooperation.

The concept of a 'peak-shaving' plant, as proposed by Magna Steyr, can be interpreted as a sustainable business model for the future which establishes this kind of technology partnership between OEM and supplier.

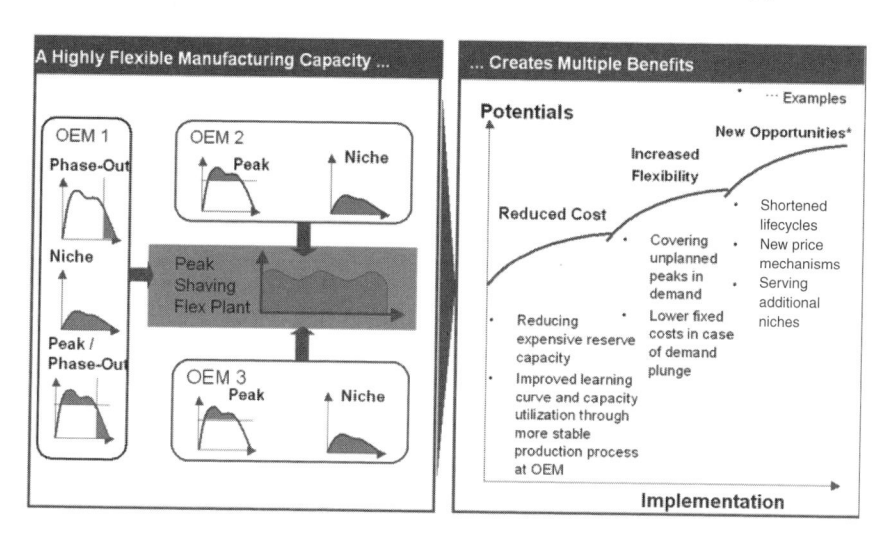

Figure 12.9 *Peak shaving flex plant*
Source: McKinsey, 2004

When we look at the production and sales volumes of various models and different OEMs, it is clear that in order to cover production peaks – or for the production of niche vehicles – capacities are required which are not needed over the full product lifecycle.

Given that strongly varying volumes and inefficient capacity utilization cause disproportionately high costs, Magna Steyr is currently in discussion with several OEMs with regard to a so-called 'peak-shaving' plant. Such a plant would be operated by an external partner – Magna Steyr in this case – and become an integral part of OEM strategies for handling peak levels of production.

The model presupposes that several OEMs would be willing to cooperate with direct competitors, in order to generate a benefit for everyone involved. The current change processes within the automotive industry and the growing readiness for strategic alliances are indications that there is a strong potential for this business model.

The operator of this peak-shaving plant must be capable of building very different vehicles in the same facility. Magna Steyr's Graz plant is the tried and tested role model of such a highly flexible factory ('flex plant'). Graz currently builds seven different vehicles, each on a separate platform, for five different brands, and within three very different OEM

312 Case studies

worlds. It goes without saying that the specific brand characteristics for each brand are maintained. Using the Magna Steyr Production System (MSPS) to bring the capabilities together and put them to work, Magna Steyr presents itself to the OEMs as a qualified operator for that kind of peak-shaving plant.

CONCLUSION

The future of the automotive industry will be characterized by technology partnerships at eye level, with suppliers increasingly moving from parts suppliers to module suppliers to systems integrators. This is another evolutionary step for the automotive industry. The rules of this game are not 'big beats small' or 'strong beats weak', but rather 'flexible beats inflexible', 'fast beats slow', and 'open and willing to learn beats rigid and bureaucratic'.

Magna will expand its leading-edge competences in automotive technology to continue setting the pace for technological progress within the industry. In the interest of a positive evolution of the company and a lasting improvement of its competitive position, this is a necessary step.

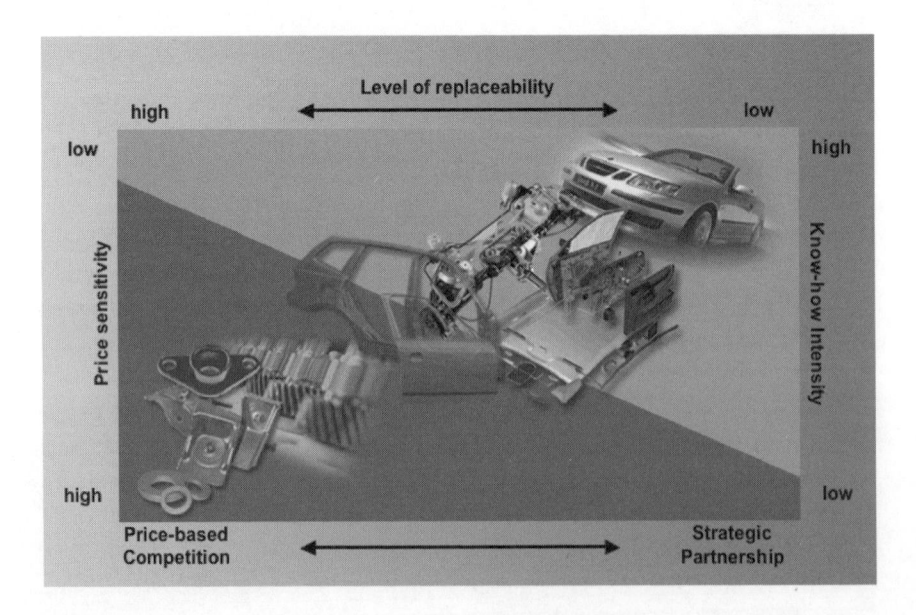

Figure 12.10 *Price-based competition versus strategic partnership*

Price-based competition and strategic partnerships can be considered the end points of a scale within which there are several different stages (commodities – components – modules – systems – complete vehicles). The decision where a supplier positions itself on this scale is paramount for the long-term perspective of the enterprise. For globally active suppliers with a strong presence in the highly industrialized Western countries, the movement can only be towards becoming a strategic partner for OEMs. This means moving away from supplying commodities in a price-based competition and with a high level of replaceability among suppliers, and moving towards innovative comprehensive solutions characterized by a lot of know-how and technological sophistication, where suppliers cannot arbitrarily be replaced. This position must be worked hard for, though, and it takes a clear decision on the strategic direction. It also means the necessary resources in terms of personnel and structures must be put together, along with the innovative solutions with which customers are approached proactively.

Magna has decided to follow that path. In so doing, the maxim for its employees will not change in future: 'Producing a better product for a better price!'

13

BlueTec: the path to the world's cleanest diesel

Dr Thomas Weber, Member of the Board of Management, DaimlerChrysler AG

THE DIESEL DRIVE: A PAST AND FUTURE SUCCESS STORY

The diesel engine is enjoying immense popularity. In Europe it has achieved to date a market share of more than 50 per cent among new vehicles, and this trend – spurred by high fuel prices among other factors – is further on the rise. To give an example, a total of 7.2 million new diesel vehicles were registered in Western Europe in 2005. The share of diesel-powered Mercedes-Benz passenger cars amounted to 54 per cent. But it is not only in Europe that the diesel drive expected to be heading towards a promising future: various studies also detect great potential in 'new' diesel markets, such as the United States. For the year 2012, JD Power forecasts that the diesel share will have at least doubled compared with 2005, so diesel should then account for 10 per cent of newly registered vehicles in the United States.

TRADITION AND MODERN TIMES: THE ORIGINS OF THE DIESEL DRIVE

The history of the diesel engine is closely connected to the Mercedes-Benz brand and the Daimler-Benz company, both the passenger car and truck divisions. Among the pioneers of the diesel engine is Prosper L'Orange, who as a member of the board of Benz & Cie AG developed the prechamber diesel engine and had the technology patented. A milestone in the history of diesel engines was the first test drive with the first serial-production four-cylinder prechamber diesel engine in a road vehicle near Gaggenau on 10 September 1923. The engine delivered a performance of 45 to 50 hp with 8.8 litres displacement, and was used for 5-tonne trucks. The great savings potential of diesel was already apparent during these test drives, and was noted down by the delighted development engineers as follows: 'The fuel consumption is about 25 per cent lower than that of our conventional, gasoline-powered trucks.'

At the Geneva Auto Show in 1932, Daimler-Benz presented the Lo 2000 light truck, called 'Schnell-Lastwagen' (high-speed truck), which was equipped with the newly designed 3.8 litre prechamber diesel OM 59, and which triggered the large-scale breakthrough of the self-ignition engine. The vehicle achieved sales figures of more than 13,000 units – stunning for that time.

It was easy to identify diesel-powered trucks from the outside as well: the word 'diesel' was displayed in large letters on the lower part of the mighty Mercedes star. This pride was justified: Daimler-Benz had long since taken on a leading role in the development of diesel engines.

Boosted by the success of the diesel engine in trucks and convinced by the manifold advantages of the diesel engine over the gasoline engine, Mercedes-Benz was the first vehicle manufacturer to implement the diesel-combustion principle in a passenger car engine more than 70 years ago. In the autumn of 1935, the first 170 diesel-powered passenger cars took to the streets. Almost all of them were taxicabs. One year later, 50 years after the invention of the automobile and 44 years after Rudolf Diesel had obtained the patent for his diesel engine, the first diesel-powered serial-production passenger car was presented to an amazed public in Berlin, in the form of the Mercedes-Benz 260 D. The four-cylinder diesel engine with 2.6 litres displacement yielded 45 hp and, with its five-bearing crankshaft, could effectively dampen vibrations. This allowed an engine speed of 3,200 revolutions per minute, so that experts soon spoke in awe of the 'high-speed engine'. The new and robust engine permitted a maximum speed of 97 kilometres per hour (kph) (60.3 miles per hour) and only consumed between 9 and 11 litres of diesel oil per 100 kilometres (26.1 to 21.4 miles per gallon). Hence a successful start was made to using diesel technology for passenger cars, and the way was paved to further ground-breaking innovations.

In subsequent decades, further milestones followed. The Mercedes-Benz 180 D – better known as the 'Diesel Ponton' – became the cab of the

Figure 13.1 *The first serial-production passenger car with diesel drive, the Mercededs-Benz 260 D*

1950s *par excellence*, and the 'Type 180' could already win the competition with gasoline engines in terms of sales figures. In 1971, the millionth diesel passenger car rolled off the assembly line in Sindelfingen. Over the years, numerous records were set with Mercedes-Benz diesel passenger cars, and the diesel drive made huge progress especially in terms of technology. In 1996, the first passenger car with diesel direct injection was introduced, and 1997 saw a technological quantum leap with the introduction of common-rail direct injection (CDI) in combination with four-valve technology. Since then, the abbreviation CDI – today available in its third generation with piezo-electric injectors – is a symbol for both unrivalled fuel economy and enormous torque boost – a synonym for high propulsion power, which guarantees lots of driving pleasure and often gives diesel engines a competitive edge over gasoline engines.

Until today, the essential advantage of the diesel engine over the gasoline engine was its clearly higher efficiency and the concomitant lower fuel consumption. Thus the diesel requires between 20 and 40 per cent less fuel than a comparable gasoline engine. Over the years, the specific disadvantages, such as the engine-power characteristics and the creation of vibrations and noise, have been significantly improved with a whole range of technical innovations, such as first five-cylinder diesel engines and production-quality turbo-diesel engines.

THE DIESEL ENGINE'S PATH TO LOW EMISSIONS

Emission regulations for diesel engines in passenger cars

Apart from the clear boost in performance and the noticeably reduced fuel consumption, the technological innovations also lead to a significant reduction in emissions. With today's Mercedes-Benz C 220 CDI, for instance, carbon-monoxide (CO) emissions are approximately 92 per cent lower than those of the Mercedes-Benz 190 D 2.5 of 1993. Improvements, especially in the internal combustion process and the oxidation-type catalytic converter, led to a substantial reduction in CO and hydrocarbon emissions. Through these improvements of the internal combustion process, it has been possible to reduce nitrogen oxides (NOx) emissions by about 75 per cent within the last 15 years.

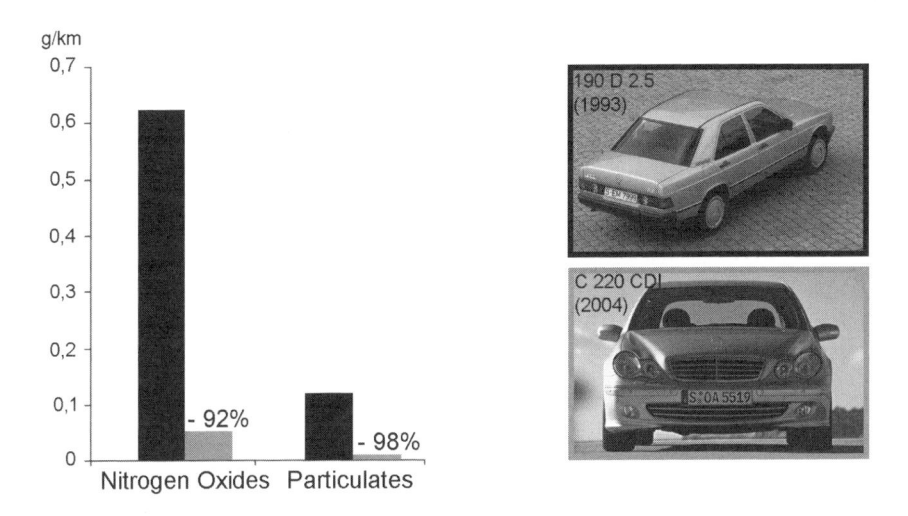

Figure 13.2 *Emission reductions for the diesel engine, 1993–2004*

If the diesel engine still had any disadvantages over the gasoline engine, they were specific diesel-engine emissions, especially particulate matter (PM) and NOx. These two exhaust-gas components are an especial focus of various countries' emission standards, which prescribe a continuous reduction in them over the years, to be implemented via successive stages.

The exact exhaust-gas limit values for the Euro-5 standard are currently being discussed in the European Union, and a further reduction of the limit values for NO and PM prescribed in the Euro-4 standard can be expected.

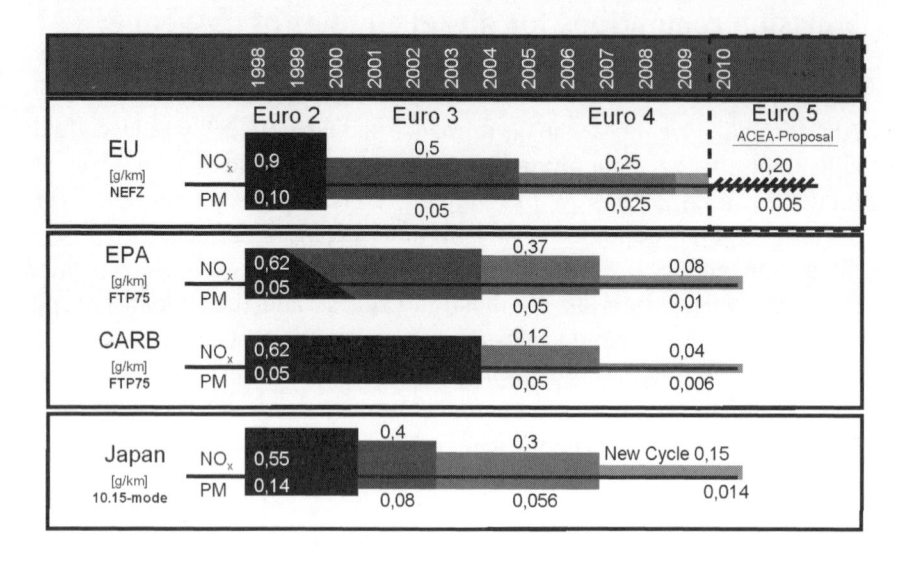

Figure 13.3 *Emission limit values for diesel passenger cars in the European Union, United States and Japan*

For about a year now, the limit values for PM_{10} particulate matter have become an issue of increasing public awareness. This was triggered by the EU's Clean Air Directive, which was transposed into German national law in 2002. As a consequence of this regulation, some cities, such as Stuttgart, will ban truck traffic from passing through, should the daily average values exceed or approach the limit values. This especially concerns high-traffic inner-city routes. Whether these measures will lead to sustainable success must be doubted, especially since various studies have shown that, in Germany, road traffic only accounts for 25 per cent of PM emissions.

A significant reduction in diesel particulate emissions and compliance with future particle limit values could be achieved with the introduction of the service-free diesel particulate filter for diesel passenger cars in autumn 2003. Since summer 2005, Mercedes-Benz has been offering service-free diesel particulate filters as standard equipment for all diesel vehicles in many countries. NOx are the only remaining exhaust-gas component for which the diesel engine shows poorer values than the gasoline engine. For NOx, which can lead to irritation of the respiratory system above a certain concentration and which contribute to the creation of acid rain and the

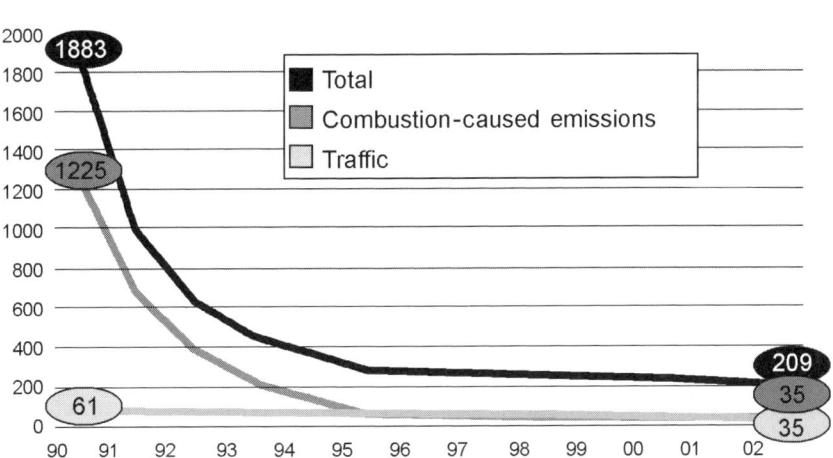

Particulate matter in Germany in kt (1 kt = 1000 tons)

[Chart showing particulate matter emissions in Germany from 1990-2002. Total: 1883 (1990) declining to 209 (2002). Combustion-caused emissions: 1225 (1990) declining to 35 (2002). Traffic: 61 (1990) declining to 35 (2002).]

Figure 13.4 *Development and creators of particulate matter emissions*
Source: Umweltbundesamt 2004

formation of ozone, the strictest exhaust-gas limit values will be valid in the United States and in particular in California starting in 2007.

Emission regulations for diesel engines in trucks

The same challenges in terms of NOx and diesel particle emissions exist for diesel-powered trucks. For these as well, legislators have prescribed the continuous reduction of emissions over various steps. Starting in October 2006, the new exhaust-gas regulation Euro-4 will come into force in the European Union. It will serve to reduce the emission of NOx by about 75 per cent compared with the legal regulations of 1990. In a further step, the Euro-5 standard will then lower the limit values for NOx again from October 2009, an 85 per cent reduction of the limit value compared with the legal regulation of 1990. With both standards, the emission of soot particles will be reduced by approximately 98 per cent compared with 1990. In addition to the European exhaust-gas regulations, there are comparable emission regulations for trucks in the United States and Japan.

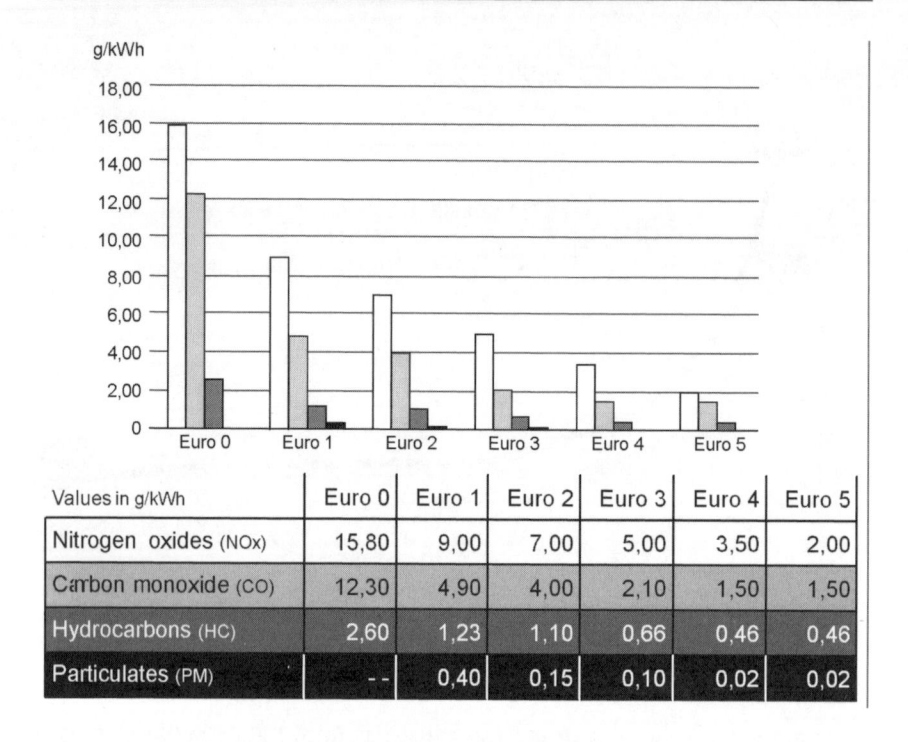

Values in g/kWh	Euro 0	Euro 1	Euro 2	Euro 3	Euro 4	Euro 5
Nitrogen oxides (NOx)	15,80	9,00	7,00	5,00	3,50	2,00
Carbon monoxide (CO)	12,30	4,90	4,00	2,10	1,50	1,50
Hydrocarbons (HC)	2,60	1,23	1,10	0,66	0,46	0,46
Particulates (PM)	--	0,40	0,15	0,10	0,02	0,02

Figure 13.5 *EU emission limit values for trucks*

OUR STRATEGY: THE WORLD'S CLEANEST DIESEL

BLUETEC: modular technology for passenger cars

New solutions for the combustion process and new technologies for the after-treatment of exhaust gases are required if diesel engines are to be competitive in the future and to fulfil the requirements of the exhaust-gas standards. It was already foreseeable that the strict future limit values for NOx could not be fulfilled through improvements in the internal combustion process alone. We therefore decided early on to implement SCR (selective catalytic reduction) technology in order to neutralize the harmful NOx in the exhaust gas, and we can now present a solution package for exhaust-gas after-treatment that enables us to comply with the strictest emission limits worldwide.

Three steps to the world's cleanest passenger car diesel engine

We are pursuing the target of developing the world's cleanest passenger car diesel engine without compromising on the driving pleasure and performance provided by high-torque engines. To achieve an optimal balance of the characteristics of the diesel engine, we are proceeding in three steps:

- Step 1: We further optimize the internal combustion process and apply clean fuels to achieve the cleanest possible and most efficient combustion, thus reducing the raw emissions to a minimum – upstream of any exhaust treatment system. This is achieved by a fine-tuned engine control, four-valve technology, third-generation CDI using piezo injectors, a variable-geometry turbocharger and a high-precision exhaust-gas recirculation system.
- Step 2: An oxidation catalytic converter is used to minimize the emissions of CO and unburned hydrocarbons (HC). Nitrogen monoxide (NO) contained in the raw emissions is converted into nitrogen dioxide (NO_2) by the oxidation catalytic converter, which however does not reduce the total amount of NOx. Subsequently, the particulate filter reduces the particle emissions by up to 98 per cent – a level well below the Euro-4 limit values, which also meets all applicable US emission standards.
- Step 3: The emission of NOx – the concentrations of which are higher in diesel engines than in gasoline engines as a consequence of the diesel design principle – will then be reduced to a level that ensures compliance with the world's strictest emission standards. At this point, the so-called BLUETEC technology is applied, using either a further-developed 'DeNOx' absorption-type catalytic converter or the AdBlue® injection principle. These technologies, in conjunction with the SCR principle, are currently forged into the most effective method of exhaust treatment, resulting in a reduction of NOx emissions of up to 80 per cent.

BLUETEC with AdBlue® injection

Using its design principle, the diesel engine operates on a lean mixture: in other words, on a fuel/air ratio with an excess amount of oxygen. This oxidizing atmosphere however makes it very difficult to chemically reduce unwanted NOx and to convert them into harmless nitrogen by deoxidation. The SCR process is based on the addition of the AdBlue® reductant into the exhaust system. This method is very effective, though technically demanding. AdBlue® is a hydrous urea solution stored in an

322 *Case studies*

Optimization of the engines and combustion processes, clean fuels		Minimize untreated emissions
3-way catalytic converter, particulate filters in all models	Oxi-cat. DPF	Reduction of particles (- 98 %) and emissions
BlueTec technology	SCR-cat.	Reduction of NOx emissions by up to 80 per cent

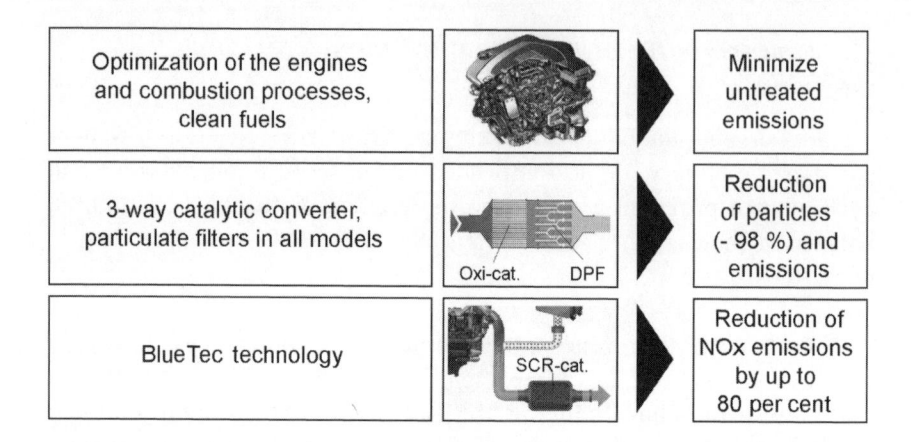

Figure 13.6 *Three steps to the world's cleanest diesel*

on-board container which is injected into the pre-cleaned exhaust flow via a metering valve. The exhaust's thermal energy downgrades the injected AdBlue® into ammonia (NH_3), which then induces the reduction of the NOx into harmless nitrogen and water in the downstream SCR catalytic converter. A high efficiency rate can only be achieved through an accurate adjustment of the injected reductant quantity to the operating conditions of the engine, which is performed with the aid of a sensor at the end of the exhaust system. This process only requires approximately 0.1 litres per 100 kilometres, and hence the storage tank of a passenger car will be designed to hold a sufficiently large quantity that it only needs to be replenished during routine servicing. An electric heating system for the tank and the lines prevents the freeze-up of the AdBlue® solution and ensures reliable system operation even at low ambient temperatures.

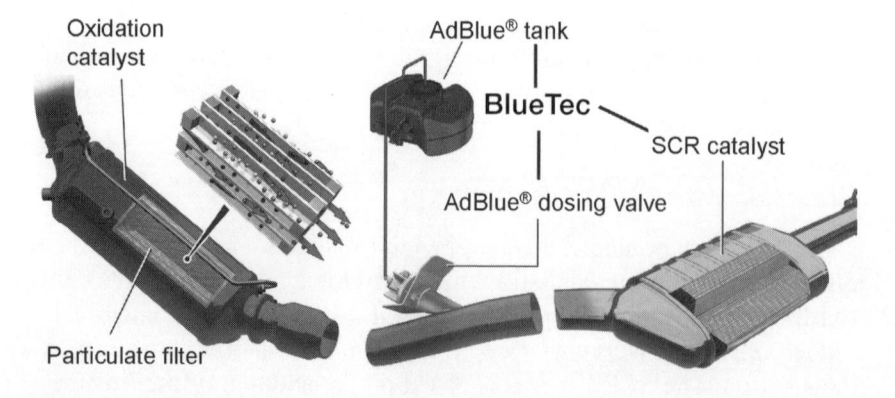

Figure 13.7 *Technology package: BLUETEC with AdBlue® injection*

BLUETEC with an advanced DeNOx catalytic converter

As an alternative principle to the BlueTec variant using AdBlue® to reduce NOx emissions, they can also be trapped in a so-called NOx adsorption-type catalyst, which retains the NOx during the normal lean-mixture operation of the diesel engine. A periodic short-term change to a rich mixture and the corresponding excess of fuel in the fuel/air mixture then creates reduction conditions in which the accumulated NOx are removed. The catalytic converter is however subject to ageing, and its efficiency in reducing NOx decreases in the process. A NOx adsorption catalyst by itself will hence not be able to comply with the increasingly strict emission standards in the long term. One elegant solution is the combination of an improved NOx adsorption catalytic converter (advanced DeNOx catalytic converter) with an SCR catalyst (without AdBlue® injection), which results in a new self-sufficient catalytic-converter system permitting an optimized operating strategy. The design and adjustment of the complete system requires careful consideration of the difficult interaction between the oxidation catalyst, advanced DeNOx catalyst and SCR catalyst, and discontinuous engine operation with a lean and a rich mixture. An optimal adjustment of the system ensures that the regular change between lean and rich mixture operation does not affect engine performance and hence is not noticed by the driver. The result is a significant improvement of the overall system efficiency and a partial compensation for the effects of ageing.

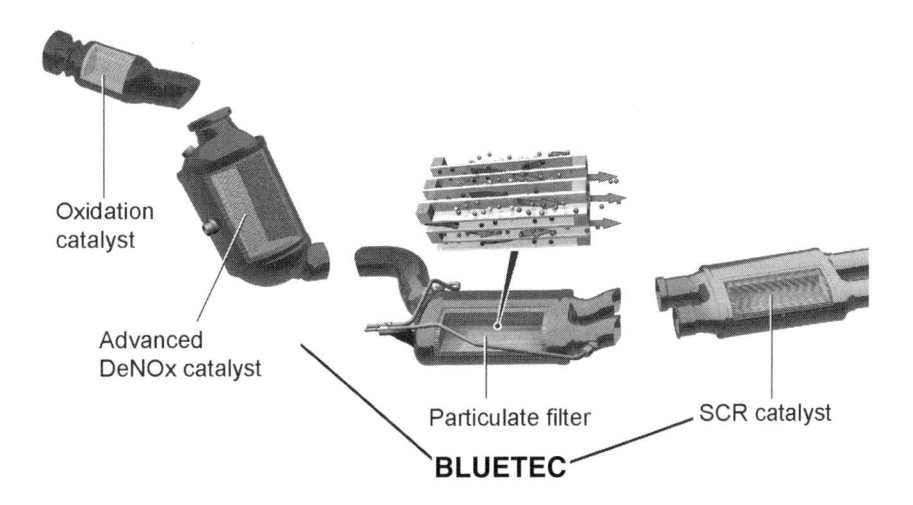

Figure 13.8 *Technology package: BLUETEC with advanced DeNOx catalytic converter*

THE FIRST SERIAL-PRODUCTION PASSENGER CAR: THE E 320 BLUETEC

We started our BLUETEC initiative for passenger cars in June 2005. At the Innovation Symposium in New York, the Mercedes-Benz bionic car was the first vehicle worldwide to show how BLUETEC on the basis of the AdBlue® injection system can drastically reduce NOx emissions even in a passenger car. Thanks to the oxidation-type catalytic converter and the diesel particulate filter, the modern CDI engine with 103 kW/140 hp falls significantly below the strict Euro-4 exhaust-gas limit values and at the same time contributes immensely to improved fuel economy. In the New European Driving Cycle (NEDC), the concept vehicle consumes 4.3 litres of fuel per 100 kilometres (this corresponds to 54.7 mpg) – 20 per cent less than a comparable serial-production model. US measuring procedures (FTP 75) testify a fuel economy of about 70 miles per gallon, which lies about 30 per cent above the value of a serial-production vehicle. At a constant speed of 90 kph, the direct-injection engine consumes 2.8 litres of diesel fuel per 100 kilometres (this equals 84 mpg).

Figure 13.9 *Mercedes-Benz bionic car study*

At the IAA (International Frankfurt Auto Show) 2005, the second passenger car to use this new technology followed, the concept vehicle S 320 BLUETEC hybrid. It proved that this new technology is also feasible in a large sedan. The concept vehicle showed how, in the near future, fuel consumption and emissions can again be drastically reduced while high dynamic driving comfort is offered. The focus was on combining an optimized diesel engine with the BLUETEC technology and a mild-hybrid system. The electric motor which is integrated into the powertrain makes it possible to significantly reduce fuel consumption even more, especially in inner-city stop-and-go traffic. When coasting or braking, the electric motor, working as an alternator, regenerates energy and can make use of it for driving, when the combustion engine has switched off. The measures implemented on the combustion engine and the electric motor hence permit a 20 per cent reduction in the fuel consumption of the S 320 BLUETEC hybrid compared with the corresponding predecessor model.

Figure 13.10 *Vision S 320 BLUETEC hybrid*

At the North American International Auto Show in Detroit in January 2006, DaimlerChrysler presented further BLUETEC vehicles. In the Vision GL 320 BLUETEC and the Jeep® Grand Cherokee BLUETEC concept vehicle, BLUETEC was implemented with the AdBlue® injection system. The two vehicles show that low fuel consumption and the lowest emissions are also possible with large sport utility vehicles (SUVs). With a consumption of 9.9 litres per 100 kilometres (NEDC) (equalling 23.76 mpg), the Vision GL 320 BLUETEC has the potential of being the most economical vehicle and, with BLUETEC, at the same time the cleanest diesel vehicle in this class.

Figure 13.11 *Vision GL 320 BLUETEC and Jeep® Grand Cherokee BLUETEC concept vehicle*

326 Case studies

The E 320 BLUETEC – also presented in Detroit – will be the first serial production passenger car with BLUETEC and will be offered, at first only in the United States and Canada, from autumn 2006 onwards. The BLUETEC serial production vehicle is the cleanest diesel vehicle the customer can buy worldwide and therefore has the potential of fulfilling the world's strictest exhaust-gas limit values and hence also those of all 50 US states. A basic requirement for the successful use of BLUETEC is the use of low-sulphur fuel with a sulphur content of less than 15 parts per million (ppm). This will be available across the United States from autumn 2006.

Figure 13.12 *The E 320 BLUETEC with advanced DeNOx catalytic converter*

The most recent concept vehicle, the Vision CLS 320 BLUETEC, was presented in Geneva in the spring of 2006. With a fuel consumption of 7.9 litres per 100 kilometres (NEDC) (29.77 mpg), the Vision CLS 320 BLUETEC is also one of the most fuel-efficient and cleanest vehicles of its class. In contrast to the Vision GL 320 BLUETEC and the Concept Vehicle Jeep® Grand Cherokee BLUETEC, the E-Class and CLS-Class are equipped with the advanced DeNOx catalytic converter and the SCR catalytic converter.

Figure 13.13 *The Vision CLS 320 BLUETEC*

We are currently preparing this technology for worldwide use in the various models of our vehicle brands. Which BLUETEC variant will be implemented depends on the specific market requirements, the driving cycles and the vehicle design concept. To this end, the technology package must be adapted carefully to the specific external requirements. European requirements, for instance, differ entirely from those of the United States. The development activities for the European market focus on a maximum reduction in NOx emissions and adaptation to European driving profiles, as well as an implementation of the BLUETEC technology with as little effect on fuel consumption (and CO_2 emissions) as possible. In 2008 at the latest, we will offer BLUETEC in passenger cars in Europe.

On the road: BlueTec® in commercial vehicle applications

We were the first commercial vehicle manufacturer to successfully offer the BlueTec® exhaust treatment system with SCR technology and AdBlue® injection for commercial vehicles with a gross vehicle weight rating above 6 tonnes, which we did as early as the beginning of 2005. Since then, this technology has fully proven its worth in more than 14,000 trucks of the Actros, Axor and Atego series. Already today, 96 per cent of these vehicles comply with the Euro-5 emission standards which will become effective in 2009.

Unlike passenger car owners, truck operators must refill the hydrous urea solution supply themselves at regular intervals. Despite frequent assertions to the contrary, the supply of AdBlue® is already ensured on a broad scale by 2,500 service stations across Europe, from the Arctic Circle to the south of Spain, and from Dublin to Moscow. As the AdBlue® consumption amounts to only 2 to 3 per cent of the total diesel fuel consumption, a very long distance can be travelled with only one tank full, and there is hence little risk of running out of AdBlue® en route and not being able to refill in due course.

The BlueTec® diesel technology is essentially based on further-developed engines and the BlueTec® exhaust treatment method outlined above. Here the optimal combustion and the accordingly high rate of efficiency result in extremely low fuel consumption and minimal emissions that – as far as soot particles and PM are concerned – are equivalent to those of exhaust gases treated by diesel particulate filters. These benefits are however compromised by relatively high NOx emissions, which are then treated with the BlueTec® technology. A decision in favour of BlueTec® is hence a decision not only to comply with the upcoming

Euro-4 and Euro-5 emission standards, but also to effectively reduce PM emissions. Independent studies by the TÜV-Nord have proven the effectiveness of this method. Compared to an Actros 1846 with Euro-3 specifications, a BlueTec® 5-equipped Actros showed a reduction of PM emissions of 84 per cent and a reduction in nanoparticles, a constituent of PM, of 80 to 90 per cent. In addition, other legally unregulated emissions were found to be below the verification limit or virtually nonexistent.

BlueTec® not only has environmental benefits, it also cuts operating costs because of lower fuel consumption and subsidies in several European countries. In Germany, for example, the toll per kilometre on the Autobahn is 2 cents lower for a Euro-5 specification vehicle than the toll for a Euro-3 compliant vehicle. In Austria, BlueTec®-equipped trucks are exempt from the prohibition from using the Inntalautobahn at night.

Figure 13.14 *BlueTec®-equipped Actros with Euro-4 or Euro-5 emission level and AdBlue® tank*

A BlueTec®-equipped truck in typical long-haul operation can save approximately 1,500 to 2,000 litres of fuel per year, which has been impressively proven by independent tests: The *Trucker* magazine for example took an Actros 1848 equipped with BlueTec® 5 technology on a 350 kilometre round-trip test drive including gradients of up to 10 per cent. At an average speed of 76 kilometres per hour, the Actros consumed only 31 litres of diesel per 100 kilometres, equalling 7.59 mpg – a dream result, as the magazine states in its July 2005 issue.

The road ahead: BlueTec® to be introduced in buses in late 2006

From October 2006 on, the BlueTec® diesel technology will also be available in Mercedes-Benz and Setra buses for urban transport, chartered and overland operation. Further vehicles equipped with BlueTec® 5 technology are to follow in 2007, already complying with the Euro-5 emission standard that will enter into force in 2009.

With the introduction of the BlueTec® diesel technology in DaimlerChrysler buses we will further boost the success of this young technology in Europe. In Germany alone, more than 5 billion trips are made by bus every year, which according to a VDA study makes the bus the second most important means of transport after the passenger car. The increasingly strict limits of the European emission standards of the recent years have led to a drastic reduction in the emissions of diesel-powered buses – and of all other diesel-powered vehicles as well. By utilizing the BlueTec® technology, we will be able to fulfil the Euro-4 and Euro-5 standards and offer all the economic benefits outlined above for our buses too.

If a further reduction of the particle emissions beyond the very strict Euro-4 and Euro-5 standards as achieved with the BlueTec® technology is required, the BlueTec® emission control system can be combined with a diesel particulate filter, which will be available as an option for buses designed for local public transportation from the beginning of 2007 on. Our system will then comply with the EEV (Enhanced Environmentally friendly Vehicle) requirements, the currently strictest European emission standard for buses and trucks, which even exceeds the requirements of the Euro-5 standard.

Nowadays more than ever, economy and ecology must be reconciled, and this of course also applies to buses. BlueTec® provides the solution to resolve this dilemma: the additional cost over current buses equipped with Euro-3 engines pays off very quickly, as the 6 per cent lower fuel consumption compared with today's Euro-3 vehicles means not only a significant reduction of emissions for the environment, but also a cost reduction to the bus owner.

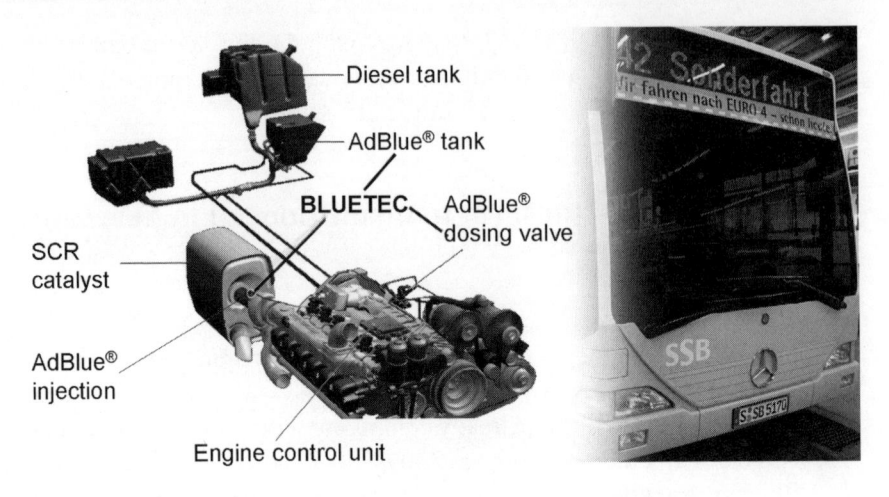

Figure 13.15 *Mercedes-Benz Citaro bus with the BlueTec® system*

CLEAR OUTLOOK: THE FUTURE OF THE DIESEL IS BLUE

Offering the best to our customers is our motto when designing and building our vehicles. This also applies to the diesel drive. This principle was our guideline for the first diesel passenger cars 70 years ago and nothing has changed since then. On the contrary: the diesel's success story provides an obligation and a motivation for us to think ahead and make new technologies available to our customers. With BLUETEC, a further ground-breaking innovation continues the longest diesel tradition among all automotive manufacturers worldwide, and once again highlights our great competence in working out revolutionary solutions in powertrain technology, which at the same time enhance our technological leadership. BLUETEC sends a clear message: the diesel drive has the potential of complying even with the strictest exhaust-gas standards worldwide without compromising vehicle dynamics or driving pleasure.

In the commercial vehicles division, this innovation has proven its suitability for rough everyday conditions and has turned out to be a true win–win situation for the customer and the environment. We consider BLUETEC to be a technology of global importance. We will consistently promote the introduction of this technology in a multitude of vehicle models and markets with dedicated commitment – to the advantage of our customers and to the benefit of our environment.

BLUETEC: PART OF THE ROADMAP FOR INNOVATIVE POWERTRAIN TECHNOLOGIES

Apart from the ecological advantages that vehicles with optimized diesel engines in combination with the innovative BLUETEC technology offer in terms of significantly lower NOx emissions and reduced CO_2 emissions, further potentials for reducing fuel consumption can be opened up on the basis of optimized combustion engines through hybrid vehicles. In this context it needs to be pointed out that every hybrid vehicle is only as good as the combustion engine propelling it. Hence every optimization on the combustion side will also be to the benefit of the hybrid vehicles. One such optimization is for instance the second-generation gasoline engine with direct injection, with which we succeeded in performing an innovation leap with regard to fuel consumption and engine performance. The new, jet-controlled combustion system permits an optimal mixture formation, significantly improving thermodynamic efficiency. With this technology, low fuel consumption and excellent engine-power characteristics are no contradiction. This further development of the combustion engines is supplemented by high-quality alternative and synthetic fuels. Only in combination with optimized fuels can fuel consumption and emissions –for both the gasoline and the diesel engine – be further reduced.

The fact that the hybrid drive is no panacea for a general reduction of fuel consumption and CO_2 emissions has been proved by a German automobile magazine, with a comparison drive between a diesel and a hybrid vehicle on a course across the United States. Over about 5,200 kilometres, a Mercedes-Benz ML 320 CDI with a new V6 diesel engine consumed on average approximately one litre less per 100 kilometres than its hybrid rival. A large part of the course led over freeways and highways, on which the diesel drive clearly outranked the hybrid drive in terms of fuel consumption. Even during city drives, the modern and highly efficient diesel engine showed all its power and only required about 2 per cent more fuel than the comparable hybrid vehicle. The comparison test showed in a quite illustrative manner that the advantages of the hybrid drive mainly come to the fore in inner-city traffic.

In the years to come, the hybrid – either as mild or as full hybrid – can supplement the combustion engine, depending on the region and traffic situation, wherever it is useful and economic for a more efficient use of fuel and for increased vehicle dynamics and comfort. It is therefore our objective to be able to answer the various customer requests with a suitable drive system. With the Two-Mode hybrid system we are developing a full-hybrid technology in cooperation with the General Motors

Corporation and the BMW Group, which will improve the performance characteristics, the fuel consumption and the range of a conventional hybrid vehicle. The advantages of the new system enable us to offer our customers convincing hybrid vehicles with attractive performance, comfort, fuel-consumption and emission characteristics at competitive prices. With the Dodge Durango, we will introduce the first Two-Mode hybrid drive to the market in the beginning of 2008, and shortly after that, we will extend our offer with further models.

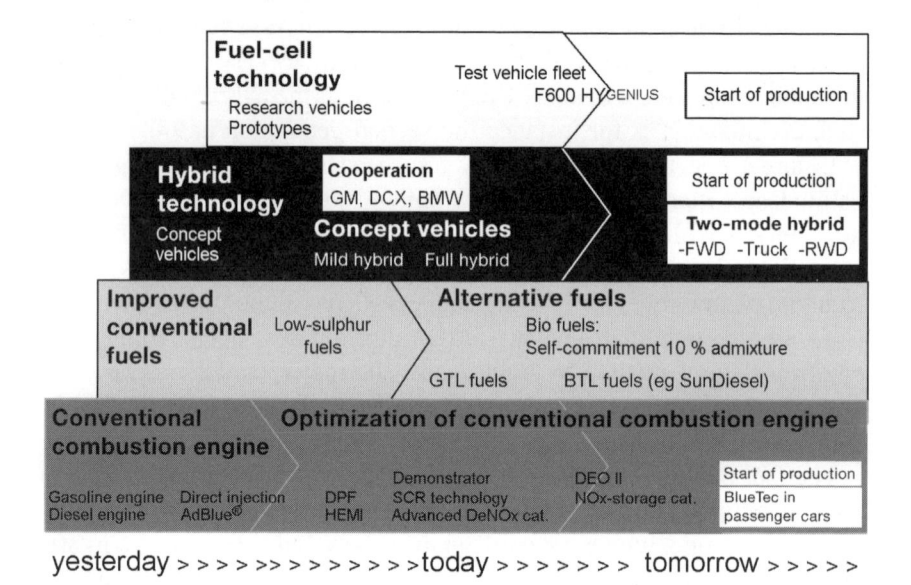

Figure 13.16 *Road map for innovative powertrain technologies*

In the long term, the fuel cell continues to be the future drive system for sustainable mobility. With more than 100 vehicles – passenger cars, buses and vans – DaimlerChrysler has the largest fuel-cell fleet among all automotive manufacturers that is in daily use by customers worldwide. By the end of March 2006, the entire fleet had reached a mileage of almost 2 million kilometres (1,243,000 miles) in more than 100,000 hours of operation. With more than 2,000 hours of operation without loss in performance, the current fuel-cell generation clearly exceeds expectations. The ground-breaking further developments of recent years show the great potential that lies in this comparatively young technology. We believe in this potential and the added value for the customer and the environment. The fuel-cell drive is an integral part of our strategy for innovative drive technologies. We intend to introduce the first fuel-cell vehicles to the market between 2012 and 2015.

Our integrated approach in drive technology thus contains a number of measures and technical innovations that contribute to saving resources and reducing fuel consumption, and that already offer our customers a broad and attractive technology portfolio. We are consistently following the path to more sustainability, step by step. But it is certain that vehicle technology alone will not be able to ensure sustainable mobility. Rather, all parties involved must be included, starting from the automotive manufacturer and heading via the mineral-oil industry and the politicians to the customers.

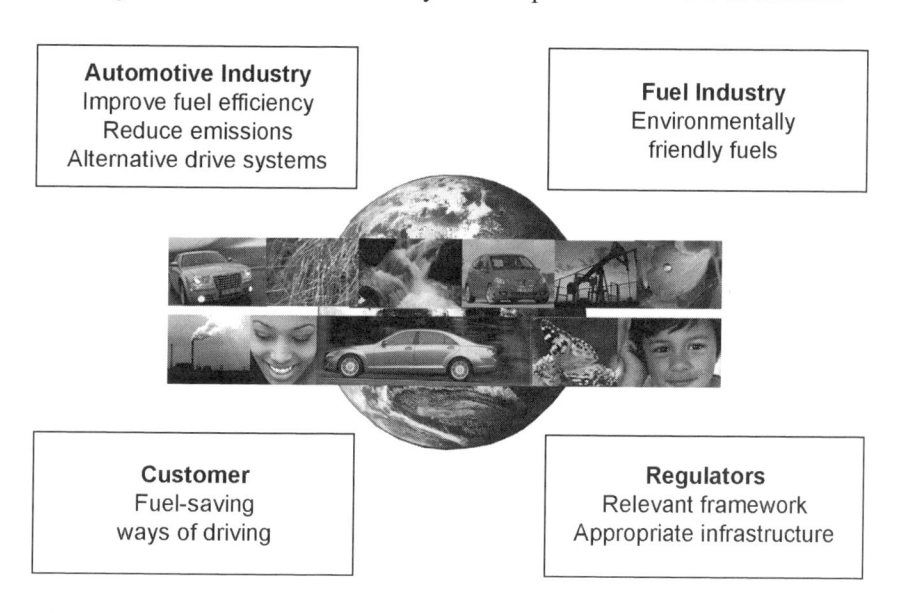

Automotive Industry
Improve fuel efficiency
Reduce emissions
Alternative drive systems

Fuel Industry
Environmentally
friendly fuels

Customer
Fuel-saving
ways of driving

Regulators
Relevant framework
Appropriate infrastructure

Figure 14.17 *An integrated approach: the contribution from all parties*

We as automotive manufacturers are facing this challenge and responsibility every day with the utmost commitment.

14

Bharat Forge: emerging players from emerging regions

Babasaheb N Kalyani, Chairman, Bharat Forge Group

This chapter is about a rapidly growing auto parts company from India that has become a thriving multinational. I review our progress and argue that cost arbitrage is a misplaced notion, and it is the intellectual capital advantage at the macro level, and its management at the micro level, that explains the emergence of players like us in the global arena. I then attempt to explain our management philosophy in terms of vision, focus and action. Through that perspective I dwell on three key business drivers:

- technology;
- scale and growth;
- competitiveness.

Finally I present our perspective about, and plans for, the future, which essentially hinge on harnessing intellectual capital for providing full service, innovation and deriving the synergies of a global organization. With this, the essential proposition to the reader interested in mastering automotive challenges is that there is a lot that is possible at the company level through a fundamental business-driven approach coupled with a risk-taking ability.

The tumultuous macro-level challenges facing the automotive industry are amplified when they confront parts suppliers to that industry. The demand derived from nature, whose prospects are in general cyclic, and are specifically based on the programmes and customers the industry caters for, as well as the structure that sandwiches an already fragmented base between powerful buyers on one side and powerful raw material suppliers on the other, almost seem to make the auto parts industry intrinsically unattractive. Yet we at Bharat Forge can pride ourselves on being a successful global auto parts company. From our largest single-location factory based in India to global footprints through acquisitions in Europe and the United States and a recent joint venture in China, we have achieved visibility beyond the purchasing departments of the automotive industry.

For the information of those who are yet to know us well, we have risen to a leading position in the merchant forging industry in just over 40 years of existence. Today we are the leading supplier to almost all the global OEMs and tier 1 suppliers for forged and machined engine and chassis components which are critical for the safety and performance of automobiles, like crankshafts and axle beams. We have capabilities in steel and aluminum forgings that add value to a significant proportion of these parts through highly complex machining. We support our customers in front-end design and development, and in post-production testing and validation. We supply commercial vehicle and passenger car segments as well as non-automotive sectors such as the oil and gas industry. In certain product categories we already have global market leadership.

Over the last few years we have experienced a scorching organic growth rate of 40–45 per cent per year, then topped this up with a spate of acquisitions. Our consolidated revenue in the financial year ended March 2006 was about US $700 million, of which close to two-thirds was from outside India. The compound annual growth rate (CAGR) of total group sales over the last four years works out to 66 per cent, while the corresponding figure for revenue outside India is 110 per cent. The Indian operation also sells almost half its output abroad (the figure was just about 20 per cent five years ago), and is the largest Indian exporter of auto parts.

The first and commonest reaction to the success of players such as us is that 'they are from LCCs (low cost countries)' and therefore the result of the outsourcing drives of OEMs. Yet which automotive buyer would use cost as the sole consideration? For example, the costs of line downtimes caused by logistics or quality-related problems would be far higher than can be compensated for by any costs saved at the parts level. Lower costs can be necessary as 'qualifiers' but they can never be sufficient by themselves as 'winners'.

One explanation is that the buyers themselves equip suppliers from emerging regions (LCCs) with the other 'hygiene' factors required, such as quality systems and supply chain management, in return for getting lower-cost supplies. While this is true to some extent, it is neither valid for all companies, nor does it fully explain how some suppliers can be better-than-average profitable in a sustainable manner, for this requires that they become world class, and becoming world class has to be result of an urge and effort from within.

So finally what explains the fact that there are some emerging players from emerging regions, like us, who if they have not yet been noticed by customers, competitors and the world in general, will be over the next few years?

Before I get into this, let me digress a bit and unequivocally state that there is an Indian advantage, which indeed provides us with a macro-level edge, but that advantage is different from what it is normally perceived to be. Auto part outsourcing is gathering pace as end-vehicle prices are expected to remain stable in the future while customers expect vehicles to have more and better features. OEMs and tier 1 suppliers in Western Europe and the United States are therefore looking to cut costs by sourcing from or creating bases in the lower-cost economies of Eastern Europe, South America, South-East Asia, China, India and so on.

The Indian auto parts industry has been growing in double digits for the last few years, with the exports driving the growth. However, its annual turnover is still only about US $9 billion, of which about US $1.5 billion is from exports; it has not even scratched the surface of the global outsourcing potential. While self-sufficient in many respects, its large base of more than 6,000 manufacturing units is highly fragmented. Only around 5 per cent of the companies might be organized enough, for various historic reasons, to tap this global opportunity.

At the same time, all the reports, predictions and indicators regarding this industry are highly positive. With every year, a higher proportion of exports is going to OEMs and Tier 1 suppliers rather than to replacement markets. According to a report by McKinsey, India-based automotive component manufacturing has the potential to grow to US $33–40 billion by 2015, of which US $20–25 billion would be in exports. Growth in domestic consumption to US $13–15 billion is also not out of reach if we consider that in numerical terms India has the second largest tractor and two-wheel vehicle, and the fifth largest commercial vehicle, manufacturing base in the world, and also has the fourth largest passenger car market in Asia.

But is this all merely because India has low labour costs? It cannot be denied that Indian labour costs per hour are low, but the net impact on the bottom line after discounting for lower productivity is contestable. Even if productivity levels improve, this labour cost advantage is not structurally sustainable in the long run, especially when compared with countries such as China. Where India scores is in its strong base of intellectual capital, which allows us to deal cost-effectively where the technology intensity is relatively high, even if volumes are relatively low. The quality of engineers and managers available in India in large numbers and with the right age profile is what determines India's competitiveness, and what should continue to determine it in future. A T Kearney's 2004 Offshore Location Attractiveness Index gave India the top position by a comfortable margin because of its strong mix of low costs and rich human resources. A recent KPMG report also suggested that, despite infrastructure issues, India is in an advantageous position for precisely the same reasons.

Let me give you our own example to illustrate the confidence we can have in our intellectual capital. In the late 1980s when we went for a highly automated press line to replace hammer technology, we also decided to replace the blue-collar workforce with college graduates, most of whom were fresh from college. Our rationale for this was that absorption of the technology involved a certain level of intellectual maturity and even a different cultural set-up. Over the years, while the workforce size has gone up, its mix has moved substantially in favour of white-collar workers. Today we employ more than 1,200 engineers, and yet our employee cost as a percentage of the top line has actually gone down.

It is of course one thing to know a fact for oneself and quite another thing for someone else to buy the argument. The Indian engineering industry here must give credit to the domestic IT industry for showing the world that India has an edge in terms of intellectual capital, and for establishing its credibility in terms of quality of products, service and delivery. The Indian engineering industry might not yet have found its rightful place in the global business world, but it is finding its feet and doing so with a confidence reflected in the investments it is making to enhance capacities, productivity and technology. To talk about our own forging industry, it might already be deemed a sunset industry in the Western world, but for us this market, which could be as much as US $15 billion depending upon outsourcing levels, presents a growth opportunity.

Let me come back now to the micro or firm level. In my view if we have been able to achieve something, the explanation for that is quite simple. I believe that it ensues from three basic, sacrosanct management principles: vision, focus and action, though our interpretation of these terms might be a little different from the conventional one. Let me first therefore expand on each of the three, to make it simpler to relate them to key facets of our business, both historical and future.

Vision

To us vision means a dream, a concept that might at the first be met with scepticism. But I feel very strongly that if we have achieved something, it was because we first dreamt really big. At the same time, vision cannot be a pipe dream. Ambitious and yet practical visionary insights can arise only out of the knowledge and rational analysis of the way industry is likely to evolve. Vision therefore is not just a one-time target-setting exercise, but is about the place we must carve for ourselves as the industry evolves. In other words, vision must also be about reinventing ourselves, our own future. (As Alan Kay said, 'The best way to predict the future is to invent it.') This reinvention is required no matter how small or large we are, because external changes are too dynamic, too powerful and overwhelming to control. Rather than turn the tide, we must learn to swim with it. To summarize, vision means dreaming big and constantly inventing newer business models for ourselves.

Focus

Business is all about the judicious allocation of limited resources, such as managerial and financial. Focus is therefore important so that we do not spread these resources too thinly, but it does not necessarily imply that we should be narrow in everything we do. All our resources must be concentrated on the core business and its fundamental drivers. The business drivers might be outside our organization, in terms of what value we must deliver, or they might be inside our organization, in terms of how we must deliver that value. This is also the essence of business strategy.

Action

If there is a difference between developed economies and LCCs, it is here, since LCCs have much ground to catch up, and hence need to be near-fanatical in implementing their business plans. Ambitious dreams have no meaning unless we act upon them with equal aggression. Let me illustrate this with an example. Because of the tooling and set-up costs involved, there is a certain minimum economic quantity at which we can manufacture anything. But when a prospective US buyer visited to evaluate our manufacturing capability, we produced his product physically in front of him and presented him with a sample for testing purposes. Needless to say, we went on to bag a major order. We believe that the risk of (more comfortable) inaction is higher in most cases than the risk of erroneous action. 'Proactive management' is all about astute vision and strategy, which is followed up by agile action.

Let me now deal with the key facets and developments of our business to illustrate the above point. There are three fundamental value drivers: technology, scale and growth, and competitiveness. As I expand upon these, it will be clearer that these have also been cornerstones of our historical development. You might wonder why customer orientation does not find a place here, but the fact is that business is all about delivering value to the customer, and so value drivers have a meaning only in the context of customers.

TECHNOLOGY

I would like to elaborate on this issue at some length since I feel strongly about it, and also because it has a bearing on other aspects that I shall discuss.

Our company was established in the 1960s. Those were the days of the 'licence and permits' era, in which Indian industry was shackled. Though policies favoured self-sufficient indigenous industry and there was an urgent need for it, it took us four years to get an industrial licence to set up forging facilities, so production could only start in the mid-1960s. There was also no technology base available in India. We had to collaborate to obtain it, and rely almost entirely on the inputs of our collaborator.

Slowly and steadily we established ourselves in a leadership position in India by the mid-1980s, yet we were not able to make much mark in the global market, and especially the developed world, despite our almost decade-long concerted efforts. We slowly realized that what we needed was a completely different production technology platform for this purpose, one that ensured a far more reliable process and consistent output.

In the late 1980s we therefore invested in state-of-the-art automated press lines. The technology was so advanced that there were then very few people in the world, and no one internally, who understood it fully. We had to struggle extremely hard to make sure that what was being labelled by our detractors as a 'white elephant' danced to our tune, but dance it did. Our prospective customers soon started realizing what we could achieve, and our capability to supply to them technologically complex products in a highly cost-effective way. Such proactive investments in state-of-the-art technologies and facilities have indeed been our driving force. Today another forging facility, equally technologically modern, has come up for passenger car parts.

Machining is another example. Even today, most forging suppliers do not have machining capabilities of their own. We recognized that forging by itself would be commoditized in the long run, and decided to set up our own machining facilities way back in the early 1970s, for down-the-line value addition. Presently our machining generates almost as much value as forging. Looking at the demand from more and more customers to outsource the production of fully finished products that can go directly on their assembly lines, we have just set up another state-of-the-art facility for machining, which is ahead of the times in terms of ensuring highly enhanced product quality and delivering it in very low cycle times.

Another key technology focus is engineering function. The forging industry has come a long way from the days of toolmakers, who were essentially specialist craftspeople, to computer-aided design, engineering and manufacturing (CAD/CAE/CAM), where a part drawing can be translated into a tooling design, which can be directly used to manufacture a die, and which in turn can produce a physical part as per the original drawing. In this area we have focused on ensuring that our speed to market is the fastest by optimizing this entire cycle.

In the ultimate analysis, then, the technological shift is all about redefining forging from an ancient art to a modern science. The knowledge earlier resided in those who were also required to execute it: that is, those who did the work had the knowledge. Today that execution has been deskilled, as the entire accumulated knowledge has been proceduralized and built into the machines and processes. This is central to ensuring a reliable and consistent output. However, not anyone can simply buy equipment and start producing as efficiently as anyone else. There are many touchpoints involved, and that makes the task of technology management as intricate as the underlying technology.

Scale and growth

Size has its own advantages. It is not, however, merely because there are production economies of scale, but because there are economies of scope: greater and better choices the business has regarding research and development, marketing, human resources (HR) and long-term investments. Scale gives you some stature, it enables you simply to sit across the table with global auto giants. Even today of the more than 300 forging units in India, only a handful have the size and capability to supply to OEMs worldwide. We could have been one of the many that do not, but we pursued scale and growth aggressively. When we decided to go in for automated presses in the late 1980s, we also decided to go in for capacity sufficient to put us directly in league with top manufacturers in the world. The move was fraught with danger: the cutting edge technology and an investment comparable with our top line back then could have bled us dry!

But thanks to such moves, today we have successively reached a global scale of operations that can provide a wide range of products very cost-effectively. Over the last 10 years our forging capacity has been ramped up five times, and it presently stands at 500,000 metric tonnes per annum. Our machining capacity is also impressive (in numbers per annum): 650,000 crankshafts, 500,000 front axle beams and 600,000 steering knuckles. We can manufacture parts ranging from 2 to 250 kg in our closed die forging shop.

Our investments have always been proactive. Further, they have been on a scale and of a technology that the customers would find ever more attractive. Our current investment programme, which has already made us the largest single-location plant, will see this level exceeded by the year-end.

However, even as this investment programme was being conceived, we had started thinking in terms of inorganic growth. We had already made a beginning in 2002 by acquiring the order book of Kirkstall Forge, UK. This move also strengthened our position in the oil and gas sector.

The reason for inorganic growth through capacity acquisition was that we felt that OEMs, especially European companies, preferred to use vendors in their proximity for certain sets of products where they could afford to trade off some cost disadvantages. We actively scouted for acquisition targets, and by the end of 2003 had acquired Carl Dan Peddinghaus (CDP), and by the end of 2004 CDP Aluminiumtechnik, both based in Germany and having about 1,000 employees. CDP is one of the oldest and the largest forging companies in Germany. Founded in 1839, it has plants at Ennepetal and Daun (near Düsseldorf). CDP Aluminiumtechnik was set up in 1997 at Brand Erbisdorf (near Dresden), and specializes in the niche aluminum chassis component segment.

These moves quickly consolidated our position across vehicle and market segments. As soon as the acquisitions were completed, we also started enjoying immense intangible benefits, significantly more than the tangible ones they brought. It was not difficult then to decide to have a global footprint and to shift our attention to the largest market, the United States. Rising steel prices and downward pressure on prices from OEMs have driven a number of suppliers in the United States to Chapter 11 of the US Bankruptcy Code. Federal Forge Inc based in Lansing, Michigan was one such company, which had filed for protection in February 2004. It was on this that we focused our attention. Federal Forge was a 43-year-old established name for designing and manufacturing complex forged steel passenger car parts such as control arms, links, steering knuckles and connecting rods, with a well-regarded client list. From our point of view it presented a significant opportunity to expand our global network and establish a presence in proximity to the Big Three.

In September 2005, we acquired Imatra Kilsta AB, Sweden, along with its wholly owned subsidiary, Scottish Stampings, Scotland (Imatra Forging Group). Imatra Forging Group is the largest manufacturer of front axle beams and the second largest crankshaft producer in Europe. This acquisition completes our global dual-shore capability. We can now produce all our core products – crankshafts, beams, knuckles and pistons – in a minimum of two locations worldwide, and provide design and engineering, and technology front-end support, close to customers for these products.

More recently in March 2006, we have established a Joint Venture (JV) in China with FAW Corporation, the largest automotive group in China. With this JV, Bharat Forge is the largest auto forging company in China. FAW Bharat Forge will progressively position itself as the competitive cost producer of highly engineered forgings for the international market.

All these acquisitions are aligned to the core of our strategy: to enhance our competitive advantage by giving complete service and better value to our global customers, and to continuously strengthen our share of business with them. In all our acquisitions we have focused on leveraging the intrinsic strengths of those businesses to significantly improve their performance. We are happy to note that the same organization and local management have now been able to grow those businesses, and the group as a whole has also benefited.

COMPETITIVENESS

There are number of strategic and operational issues involved in maintaining competitiveness, where to 'maintain' it means to continuously improve upon it. The strategic issue is partly related to the cyclical demand patterns of the industry. Because of the high capital costs involved, a recession is enough to drive a company to bankruptcy. Strategically we have reduced the risk to our business by broadening our customer base. We have also constantly pruned and focused our portfolio on technologically more complex products. On the operational front inculcating excellence is critical, but then the auto industry is a key propagator of its theory and practice. So rather than spending much time here, I would just like to touch on what we have been able to achieve. Over the last four years, our employee productivity has gone up 2.5 times, our cash-to-cash cycle has been cut by one-third through prudent inventory management, while the sales to net fixed assets ratio has almost doubled.

The future poses more challenges, and therefore it also presents greater opportunities. In the next two years, we want to double our top line to reach the US $1 billion mark. That is our ambitious dream. But it is not a mere question of adding capacities, it is more about capabilities. In other words, it is about brain-power rather than brawn-power. This brings us back to intellectual capital-led advantages. With this perspective, my agenda for the future has three main, all 'soft', components: service provider capability, innovation and synergy.

Full service provider capability

I think we are long past being a production-driven organization and have become a technology-driven organization. Rather than physical volume, it is the distinctive product that has become important in this shift. We have already geared ourselves for the next shift, whereby what we will be delivering is not just the product but also all the services around it, such as design and development and validation and testing. We presently have more than 150 engineers working on such services, and as we partner more and more with our key customers, this number is expected to increase manifold.

INNOVATION

So far parts suppliers have focused on innovation in terms of production costs and operational excellence, but gone are the days when auto parts suppliers would merely produce components to the customer's drawings. The domain knowledge related to the parts rests with the parts supplier, and therefore the supplier is in the best position to innovate and add value. This might be from design, which actually controls a significant proportion of final product costs, to quality aspects. The need for proactive co-development is acknowledged today by most OEMs, and is the key to compressing speed to market. Our group has undertaken a number of projects where the knowledge gained by us over the years in the areas of metallurgy, forging and machining can be applied in a systematic fashion, thus making us a true development partner of our key global customers.

SYNERGY

With our global manufacturing network we not only have global capacity, we have added intellectual capital and a valuable set of best global practices.

Just benchmarking within the group and ensuring that the best practices are shared and assimilated by all the units would help further improve value of each of the entities. There are other synergistic benefits that follow, and there are ways to optimize at the system level rather than locally. For example we can provide dual shoring capability to customers' global operations. We are already pooling our R&D and engineering capabilities.

Management of intellectual capital in a cross-cultural setting is a different challenge, and not an easy task, but we are working at it through structured and unstructured integration measures.

I hope I have been able to offer to the reader some insights for mastering automotive challenges. As a final note, in today's competitive world we cannot ever be complacent. Success is not a destination to be arrived at. It is at best a milestone on the trajectory that we chart for ourselves, where we are not allowed to sit and rest!

Conclusion

Ralf Kalmbach, Roland Berger Strategy Consultants

The automotive industry counts as one of the key sectors in most developed economies. It has clearly proven to be among the strongest global drivers of technology, growth and employment. More than 8 million people around the world work directly in the production of vehicles and automotive components. Every year, the industry invests around €70 billion in research and development. These two facts alone provide an impressive insight into the importance of the automotive industry. Nonetheless, the sector is no longer just a driver. Its companies are increasingly being pushed by new and ongoing processes of change. A number of different factors are stepping up the pressure auto makers face today:

- idle capacities;
- new competitors hailing from 'new' automotive markets, such as China or India;
- cost competition between production sites and countries;
- new technologies;
- changing legal requirements.

Combined with a change in the overall economic landscape, these factors translate into an enormous challenge for an industry which requires great stability and solid planning, given its capital intensity and long development and investment cycles.

The automotive industry has always been forced to adjust to significant changes in overall market conditions, technologies and customer preferences. In the past, such crises concerned organizational aspects (such as the R&D and production process crisis of 1992/93). Today, the focus is on globalization-driven adaptation processes. We are facing a new kind of challenge. The emphasis is no longer on isolated elements of the business system. Rather, the technical, political, economic and global structures on which auto makers founded their business systems are changing simultaneously. Hence, the traditional rules no longer apply.

New markets are emerging – markets in which local automotive industries develop rapidly, producing new players (such as Bharat Forge) that instantly take on a prominent global role. These companies appear to know the new success factors and rules very well, frequently even better than traditional manufacturers. They are encroaching upon the very existence of the former market leaders.

Phases of massive change shake industry sectors to their very core, and the automotive industry will share this fate. Not all companies will be able to address the opportunities – but also the risks – of such developments successfully, or even anticipate them. Only a few are in a position to align themselves with novel conditions that they can take advantage of for their own success.

THE SUCCESS FACTORS OF TOP PERFORMERS

In numerous projects, Roland Berger Strategy Consultants has been able to determine which factors are particularly developed in the most successful companies. These top performers:

- have in-depth customer understanding;
- have clear entrepreneurial visions and goals;
- develop long-term prospects;
- place a lot of emphasis on customer loyalty;
- consistently meet the 'value for money' promise in both low and premium price segments;
- consistently deliver first-rate quality;
- boast a global presence, but are regionally oriented;
- are driven by a strong entrepreneurial spirit.

THE PROBLEMS OF LOW PERFORMERS

Low performers have a tough time implementing these success factors. They frequently fail for very similar reasons:

- They miss key trends.
- They either fail to adapt their business system, or do not do so at the right time or consistently enough.

- They lack a sustainable corporate strategy.
- They have no vision, or their vision is not clear enough.
- They are driven by short-term profits.
- They do not possess an autonomous profile.
- They do not provide adequate value for money.
- Their branding is not consistent.
- They lack entrepreneurial courage.
- They do not have an early warning system.

However, the automotive industry has accepted the challenge. Forecasts issued by prophets of doom such as the Club of Rome, and the winner–loser scenarios introduced in James P Womack, Daniel T Jones and Daniel Ross's book *The Machine That Changed The World* (Rawson, New York, 1990), have been made obsolete by reality. Nevertheless, it should be noted that the next round of the 'automotive power play' has already begun. In the next couple of years, automotive executives will have to lay the foundations for the survival and future success of their companies. They will have to overcome crucial challenges and implement conclusive strategies and business systems. In this context, five action areas are key:

- market;
- globalization;
- sales;
- value creation;
- technology.

THE MARKET CHALLENGE

Automotive markets have changed significantly. Not only have new markets in emerging economies been added, but substantial changes in customer behaviour patterns are forcing the industry to pay much closer attention to its clients and to develop a new understanding of their demands. The dictum 'supply generates demand' no longer applies to the automotive industry. Customer preferences have shifted enormously or have even dissolved completely. It was the automotive industry itself, with its excessive product offerings, that laid the groundwork for this scenario. Now it must live with the consequences.

Conventional forecasting models that are based primarily on the interpretation of sociodemographic information simply do not work any more. Income and social status do not lead customers to certain brands, segments or products in a world full of niche vehicles and lifestyle concepts. As a result, the risks for auto makers have increased substantially. After all, huge investments are required to develop and launch new vehicles. This trend is further accelerated by the decline in the number of vehicles produced per type – a tribute to strong product programme differentiation combined with ever shorter product lifecycles.

In Europe and the United States, growth is no longer restricted to the midsize and premium segments – a scenario that has never applied to emerging markets anyway. Instead, a significant 'entry-level segment' is developing. It encompasses vehicles that cost less than €10,000 in Europe and even less in markets such as China or India. In these countries, the entry-level price for 'individual mobility' is around €3,000 for a new car. These market segments are growing disproportionately on the world market, and are forcing the automotive industry to develop suitable market, technology and value creation strategies. New competitors that focus on the entry-level portfolio are emerging, and their low-wage origins afford them crucial advantages in terms of competitive pricing. Car makers must rethink and realign their businesses.

In this environment, accessing customers via sales is increasingly becoming a key success factor. The frequently stiff and multi-level sales systems inherent in a largely unchanged manufacturer–dealer relationship do not accommodate this development, but do offer huge optimization potential. Substantial areas for improvement exist along the entire sales-related value chain, which can increase profits and improve customer loyalty.

The pressure to innovate in the automotive industry continues to increase dramatically, and compels companies to completely realign their development processes and structures to make the complexity and dynamics of product creation manageable. Modular and platform strategies as well as standardization, frequently encompassing several auto makers, are adequate solutions. However, they require deep strategic, process-related and cultural changes. Auto makers are not only challenged by changing customer behaviour patterns, but also by a substantial shift in the importance of market segments.

The key approaches for realignment in this context are explained in more detail in the following.

Identifying and understanding customer needs systematically

If you want to understand your customers' needs you have to know who your customers are. Determining the target group precisely and clearly defining the market position and value proposition are absolutely essential to align product and service portfolios consistently with potential customers. A comprehensive and consistent brand experience can be ensured only if high-quality service portfolios are coherently implemented across all sales phases – from the initial customer contact to the point of sale.

To win customers, create enthusiasm and brand loyalty, companies must create emotional and rational value beyond the mere product itself. The automotive industry has made tremendous efforts and has invested substantial amounts in sales and customer relationship management systems and initiatives. Nonetheless, it has not yet made a major breakthrough in this critical field.

Overcoming the limitations of conventional sales systems

At their core, automotive sales strategies are not sufficiently focused on the needs of customers. Instead of meeting customer needs to the fullest extent possible, excess capacities are pumped into the markets with the assistance of discounts and complex promotions. These activities yield only short-term results, as evidenced by the long list of auto makers that attain only minor success. Not only does this adversely affect profits, it also causes the brand image to decline, which damages the basis of long-term success.

Conventional multi-level sales systems involving importers/national sales companies (NSC) are too time-consuming, too complex and too expensive. Too much money is invested in sales levels without creating value at the customer interface. This is an approach auto makers will no longer be able to afford in markets that are ever more competitive.

To overcome this structural complexity and over-assertiveness, dealers can be integrated as partners nationally or regionally. Cadillac, for example, transferred the responsibility for its European sales to Kroymanns, one of its dealers. Others will emulate this model.

By treading new ground in this way, manufacturers have the opportunity to defy the fundamental 'one nation = one NSC' rule and can use their resources far more efficiently. And if they also rigorously streamline their networks, they will be in a position to optimize sales through professional improvement and standardization.

Gaining control of the sales channel

The consolidation of automotive sales cannot be halted. The actual key issue is how to approach this consolidation. Two main directions are apparent: internationalization and multi-brand sales.

Large, often multinational, dealer groups frequently act as a counterbalance to auto makers. Thanks to multi-brand policies, they are less dependent on manufacturers than traditional single-brand dealers, and are virtually forcing auto makers to cooperate with them and come up with win–win scenarios. They can no longer resort to confrontation to enforce unilateral interests. This type of constellation goes hand in hand with the opportunity to implement the necessary optimization mentioned earlier by entrepreneurial means. Partnership-based collaboration results in the optimum utilization of market potential, and brings business success. The partners have the opportunity to focus on the areas they are best equipped to cover.

Customer relationships and the translation of brand values into unique products and services are elementary core competencies of an original equipment manufacturer (OEM). Implementing these product and service competencies across the entire sales chain requires an uncompromising customer, sales and service orientation. These, in turn, are among dealers' classic core competencies. Bringing these complementary dealer and manufacturer competencies together smoothly enables real value to be created.

When OEMs focus on their key competencies and when larger, more professional dealership partners are created, this development is clearly fostered. Consequently, the recipe for future success is to turn away from competitive thinking and embrace collaborative partnership between manufacturers and dealers. Toyota, for example, uses this partnership approach not only in its supplier relations, but also in its sales organization; a concept that makes it much more successful than many of its competitors.

THE GLOBALIZATION CHALLENGE

The automotive industry is steeped in a tradition of globalization. Driven by General Motors and Ford Motor Company, the development of international markets began in the early 20th century, when distribution companies were established in numerous countries. In subsequent years, production sites were built in Europe and Asia to service the frequently remote sales markets. The globalization of the automotive industry had thus begun. The drivers were the same then as they are now:

- developing sales potential in growing markets;
- taking advantage of lower wages and fixed costs;
- leveraging high fixed costs in R&D and production.

While the drivers of globalization have not changed since the early days, the balance of power and the roles of individual companies in the automotive industry certainly have. GM and Ford may have been the initiators of globalization, steering this development from a position of 'invincible' market power, but markets nowadays are much more fragmented, and the market power of individual companies has declined. No company can bypass the basic trends of the industry: the world has become the market for each and every one of them.

Global expansion happens in waves

Just as demand for vehicles has increased in recent years, particularly in Asia, the balance of power in the automotive industry has also shifted in recent decades. The winners were and still are first and foremost the Japanese, and ultimately also the Korean OEMs. They not only established themselves in the North American market in the early 1980s, they also succeeded in making things very tough for local manufacturers. Their success was based on the attractively priced, high-quality and low-consumption vehicles that US auto makers proved unable to deliver.

In recent years, Asian manufacturers have not only been successful because of their pricing, which was their strongest sales argument until the early 1990s. They successively took advantage of the flexibility attained through the quality image they had created, which is extremely important in North America, and increased their prices. Japanese OEMs can now afford to stay away from cut-throat price wars while still gaining market share.

Following the successful strategy patterns of the Japanese, Korean auto makers have entered the US market. They managed to take advantage of the gap left when their Japanese counterparts 'upgraded', and got a foothold in the American market with less expensive vehicles. From 1994 to 2004, Kia and Hyundai's CAGR grew by more than 30 per cent and 10 per cent respectively, which makes them the fastest-growing car brands in the United States. Like their Japanese role models, they have consistently upgraded and have already arrived in the lower mid-section of the market in terms of brand awareness and price.

Once again, a gap is beginning to open up at the lower end of the market, 'inviting' burgeoning Chinese auto makers to move forward. They will also implement these successful strategies. The outcome is clear, and it will further worsen the crisis for local US manufacturers.

'Déjà vu!'

Japanese and Korean brands have also launched an aggressive attack on Europe. No segment is spared: even in the premium segment, these manufacturers have defined products and strategies that promise success. While the development follows the proven pattern, it is happening more consistently and more quickly than it did in the United States. A gap is already beginning to emerge at the entry level of the market, which once again can be seen as an open invitation.

The first batch of Chinese vehicles has already been launched into Europe. It is only a question of a few years until Chinese auto makers – thanks to the technology procured from their joint venture partners and global suppliers – will be in a position to offer high-quality products and to develop the market from the bottom up. Following the same pattern as in the United States, established European OEMs will find themselves under pressure.

Strategic responses comprising more and more complex technology will no longer do the job, as happened in the early 1990s when Japanese market penetration began to increasingly encroach upon Europe. Customer preferences in volume segments have changed because of environmental conditions. The competition must now be dealt with in all segments of cost and quality, otherwise substantial danger looms.

Even today, Asian auto makers have become permanent players in the European market. Unlike their US counterparts, European manufacturers were, however, able to slow down their success. The reasons can be attributed to the strengths of the Europeans in this competition:

- Europe is the home base of the key premium OEMs.
- Europe has a strong local auto industry with traditionally high brand loyalty and (still) high customer loyalty.
- Southern European manufacturers maintain a stronghold in the entry-level segment.

■ Technology, innovation and prestige play a major role in getting people to buy a car.

However, these strengths are relative. They apply only as long as customers can and must factor them in because of their overall situation. All over Europe, the sluggish economic development and the all-encompassing reform of social systems in key economies will lead to changes in the consumption climate and in consumer behaviour patterns. This will very likely result in people's priorities shifting towards lower-priced offers when it comes to deciding what to buy. The focus of purchase decisions is no longer on 'reasonably priced' but increasingly on 'cheap'. An adequate response to this trend is nothing less than a structural shift in the European auto industry.

Vehicle product portfolios as well as value creation and production site structures will have to be aligned with the new challenges in the home market and the opportunities inherent in emerging markets. All of this will have to occur in a networked business system, which aims to combine the complementary abilities and strengths of partners and sites in such a way that the result is competitive advantages which can be implemented on a global level. Not all auto makers will succeed in this. Some are simply too small, others too inflexible. The current constellation of successful and less successful companies will change forever, partly because some of the players have not been factored in to date. They are only now in the process of entering the global scene, and have quite a few advantages on their side.

SAIC is representative of this group. China's largest OEM recently secured key technology and brand licences from Rover. Nanjing Automobile bought Rover's production lines. Both deals pursue the goal of autonomy from Western joint venture partners, which still dominate the Chinese automotive industry today.

By taking the right strategic steps, China will succeed in developing an independent automotive industry. This industry will have learnt a lot from its Western partners, and will use this know-how as a key strength in competing with its former business partners. At first glance, very little seems to contradict the fast emergence of the Chinese newcomers, especially in view of the enormous progress made in recent years coupled with the will and the economic possibilities that China has to propel itself into a better future.

On the other hand, the game is not lost yet. Many ambitious companies' expansion strategies have failed in the past. The objective now must be to find answers to the following key questions:

■ How can established auto makers take advantage of the opportunities in the emerging markets without fostering unwanted competition?

- What options do European and US manufacturers have to defend their home markets against increased attack from Asian OEMs?
- How can established manufacturers utilize new markets to improve their cost base and thus their competitive positioning on a global level?

Embracing the competition

It is a fact that the impact of globalization is heightening the competition in the automotive industry, and frequently threatens the very existence of its players. Those who do not feel the need to take consistent action given this situation, and who are not willing to question conventional business systems, have already lost the battle. Established manufacturers must react to these new challenges proactively and with a clear strategy.

For OEMs clearly positioned in the premium segment, defending their own market share is less important in the medium term. Their main objective is to take advantage of new opportunities in these markets consistently. Manufacturers who have not attained a premium positioning or are not strongly entrenched in the segment, or those who are suffering from significant cost disadvantages, will first need to eliminate these deficits. At the same time, the growing competitive pressure makes it even more crucial that they steadily take the action necessary on this front, some aspects of which are already known to them. Consequently, it is more important than ever to consistently optimize in-house value creation, which includes – first and foremost – making use of the new markets offering more attractive production costs. As the examples of successful auto makers demonstrate, this can work if firms select the 'right' partners and integrate them into their R&D and production network. A thorough understanding of current and future market needs is indispensable for those wishing to take advantage of the opportunities the new markets yield.

A Roland Berger Strategy Consultants analysis identifies the key success factors in relation to global competition. These are:

- more efficient production systems;
- modular vehicle concepts;
- global market presence manufacturing large volumes on global platforms;
- high quality thanks to proven technology and stable production;
- close and intensive integration of suppliers into a network-oriented business system;
- continuous improvement instead of technology leaps with every new generation;

- understanding of local market requirements;
- focused development of low-cost competencies;
- consistent strategies and strategy implementation with a long-term orientation.

The list of actions is long. However, success on the global market can be achieved only with a business system that factors in these aspects and is consistently implemented by top management.

THE SALES CHALLENGE

Value in the automotive industry comes only partly from developing, manufacturing and selling new vehicles. The after-market is taking on an increasingly important role. This is concerned with generating value from business with the vehicles already on the road, in areas like vehicle financing, maintenance, repair, buying back and reselling used cars, spare parts wholesale and services. These activities are more profitable than vehicle manufacturing: 50 per cent of auto makers' profits stem from the after-market.

In the automotive industry, there is a clear correlation between profit margins achieved in individual value-creation activities and their proximity to the final customers. Often, the closer you are to the customer, the more profitable the business. Consequently, companies selling vehicles, components and related services strive for this closeness. They try to optimize their share in people's 'mobility budgets' and also to increase customer loyalty. As a result, traditional rules, such as 'original components are sold through the original equipment supplier (OES) channel, generic parts through the independent after-market (IAM) channel' or 'spare parts prices are determined by the OEMs and represent binding reference values' are increasingly being ignored and replaced by new provisions, which are strongly affected by a number of crucial factors:

- Product technology and variety: the increasing amounts of technology used in areas such as electronics, electro-mechanical systems and systems integration, as well as the large diversity of brands and models, make after-sales activities more complicated.
- Changes in the vehicle population: the development of the vehicle population impacts the automotive business. Longer model lifecycles,

third cars and high adoption rates cause the vehicle population to grow and to age. As a result, the number of cars that are more than 10 years old is growing at a rate of 3 per cent per year in Germany. The number of seven to nine-year-old cars is growing at 4 per cent in France and a hefty 10 per cent in Spain.

- Development of customer needs: customers' demands in terms of service quality, reliability and customer relations are high and rising. Experiences customers have in other industries will intensify this development.
- Changes in consumer behaviour patterns: the growing number of cars used for business, such as company cars and long-term rentals, in conjunction with a growing and professional portfolio of pre-owned vehicles available for purchase, are changing customer behaviour patterns.
- New regulations: while block exemption impacts primarily the spare parts market, Eurodesign affects components with design patents.
- Specialized prescriber groups: insurance companies and associations such as Thatcham as well as rating agencies such as Euro-NCAP and JD Power are gaining influence.
- Europeanization: in the aftermath of EU expansion, one of the challenges companies face is how to move into other countries while keeping distribution costs as low as possible and avoiding grey markets.
- Sales channel consolidation: in Great Britain and France in particular, large dealer chains control huge swathes of the market. Consolidated IAM wholesalers, repair shops organized in corporate groups or networks, and large fleet operators are also positioned advantageously.
- New market players: for a while, retail chains were expected to enter the automotive industry. However, they failed because of the considerable market entry barriers. Banks and financial institutions are real newcomers, as are leasing companies and fleet operators, which are now trying to gain a foothold in this attractive market.

Consequently, the changed overall framework is challenging the business models of all the companies. In order to secure an attractive share of the value creation in sales and customer service, they will have to redefine their strategies and organizations.

Changing demand structures in the new car market

Fleet managers (professional car buyers, rental car firms, government agencies, private companies) are increasingly becoming intermediaries between OEMs and final customers. Their importance as customers for auto makers is rising dramatically. Consequently, the business is mutating from selling cars to selling mobility.

Having attained this role, they are in a position not just to secure favourable terms and discounts, but they themselves frequently provide profitable services such as financing and leasing. Thus, pressure on auto makers rises on a dual front – they lose out on profits because of lower prices and less value creation.

Setting the used car market lever

Sales of nearly new used cars, or cars less than one year old, are growing at a rate in excess of 6 per cent per year, which is more than one and a half times as fast as the used car market overall. This, in turn, is growing by approximately 4 per cent per year, which is much faster than the new car market. This can partly be attributed to the increasing importance of fleet management companies, which resell nearly new used cars. It is also a result of the common practice of having vehicles registered for one day – a system used by dealers to 'doctor' their official market share by registering vehicles themselves to subsequently sell them as used cars. In Europe a massive 15 per cent of all vehicle registrations fell into this category in 2003.

There are also one-day registrations that are used as an aggressive tool to increase sales. In Germany, they sometimes make up 25 to 30 per cent of all registrations. This volume of intentionally produced used cars makes the professional marketing of used cars indispensable. Although they require professionalism, these transactions are also very attractive for dealers. After all, a used car usually yields a much higher profit than a highly discounted new car.

However, this logic does not apply without restrictions. The flood of one-day car registrations puts intense pressure on genuine used cars, with the result that the value decreases and system profitability across the entire vehicle lifecycle deteriorates substantially. Many auto makers have brought themselves to the brink of collapse with this practice. Apart from manufacturing desirable products, which can be sold with less radical discounts than new cars, auto makers can resolve this issue only by controlling and managing used car sales activities and flows more stringently. To achieve economies of scale and exploit synergies, they have to give their pan-European networks some degree of influence over local and regional dealers, make what they offer transparent, and even out price and demand differences in the used car markets of the individual countries.

Improved service

Through their experiences in other areas of life, such as tourism, the retail trade, telecommunications and financial services, consumers have become accustomed to higher standards of service. In a world full of very similar products, service has become an important, frequently crucial means of differentiation.

The key objective is to increase customer satisfaction levels and consequently create loyal customers. Despite running a range of programmes, the automotive industry lags noticeably behind other sectors, even though there is no lack of insight into what to do and how to do it. What is missing is professional management of service processes through the OEM–dealer–customer interface. At this time, too many individually optimized activities inhibit a thoroughly positive and consistently reproducible customer experience. Mushrooming fast-fit chains are using this deficit to their advantage. Their success is down to excellent service quality, standardized processes, clear rules, flexibility in what they do and when they do it, and good value for money.

Customer satisfaction can frequently be achieved at little cost, but it does require consistent management.

Original spare parts under competitive pressure

In post-accident car repairs, about three-quarters of the spare parts used are purchased from OEMs. The remaining quarter is sourced from the IAM. Given that more than 60 per cent of all repair jobs involve replacing only four to five parts damaged beyond repair, and even wear-and-tear-related repairs centre on a relatively small number of parts (brake pads/discs, exhaust, cooling system, oil filter and the like). IAM dealers and parts manufacturers are eager to expand their share in the supply of components to repair shops. The introduction of the Eurodesign regulation, which allows suppliers to develop original parts without OEM approval, favours this development. This regulation is already in force in Spain and Great Britain; other countries will follow suit.

Suppliers of cheap generic components will therefore enter the market as competitors. Established companies are compelled to offer additional value-added services, such as logistical systems, in addition to attractive prices to help them secure the sustained loyalty of their professional clients.

Tougher competition in repair shops

About 60 per cent of all repair costs are labour costs. Impacting costs in this area requires better organization, more professional structures, and consequently size. Cost savings for customers and profit for workshop operators can be achieved most effectively if the time it takes to carry out repairs is reduced. As a result, more is expected from parts suppliers (be they OEM, OES or wholesaler). Logistics, computerized materials management systems and constant parts availability are key. However, this does not mean that parts prices take a back seat. Only completely optimized business systems will protect the future of the spare parts business.

Financial services as an important source of income

Financial services are not a part of OEMs' core business, yet they make a substantial and consistent contribution to their profits and revenues. One key success factor is customer access at the point of sale. This gives the automotive banks a competitive advantage. With effective customer relationship management and attractive financing offers, automotive banks play an important role in ensuring customer loyalty and winning new customers.

The established system is now feeling the pressure of increasing numbers of fleet and rental car management companies, as well as the growing number of loan-financed used car sales handled by independent financial institutions and commercial banks. Conventional strategies are moving in two directions. First, automotive banks are expanding their service spectrum and acting as commercial banks. Second, commercial banks are forcing their way into the automotive market, primarily through cooperative agreements with large fleet management companies which have tremendous market power. How successful these strategies will be remains to be seen. Both paths are certainly plausible and the results, as so often, hinge on the professional and consistent implementation of business concepts.

Dealer groups play an increasingly important role

The dealer group segment is taking on an ever more prominent role. In some regions dealer groups already dominate the market. Dealer groups will change the structure of the market significantly in the years to come. Many of them are big enough to establish themselves as regional multi-brand dealers offering new and used cars of different brands while also operating efficient repair shops and handling professional financial services.

Their regional presence puts them in a position to develop and maintain close customer relationships. To the OEMs, dealer groups have a significance that elevates them to the role of 'genuine' partners. They are in a position to achieve a win–win situation with manufacturers by personalizing all elements of the sales process. At the same time, these relationships are multilateral. In particular, multi-brands involving several OEMs that are in fierce competition with each other must be properly managed. Nonetheless, it is increasingly only the large retail chains that are in a position to meet the multitude of challenges that automotive sales present. The OEMs' recent consolidation of their distribution networks gives this development an extra push. Auto makers are acquiring and developing mature partners. A paradigm shift is on the horizon.

Taking all relevant aspects into account, OEMs are obviously the only players that can cover the entire value chain with an integrated approach. They encompass everything from new car sales and buying back and reselling used cars to repair and maintenance, spare parts wholesale and financial services. They also have the closest contact with the final customers. Hence, they really do hold all of the trump cards. Nevertheless, the success of companies focusing on individual value chain elements clearly shows that existing structures do not have to stay that way forever. Whether these firms will be able to safeguard their success in the long run depends largely on the development of business models that are even more effectively integrated.

A sales organization that is suitably adapted across all levels will have to be a central element. Many sales and marketing processes may be on a European level, such as pricing for new and used cars as well as marketing. Better control of sales activities can only be achieved with increased integration, which involves reducing the number of autonomous national sales companies or reinforcing alliances and group companies. Overall, sales structures must be more streamlined and traditional national organizations within the new EU of 25 nations must be integrated into these structures to optimize distribution costs. In this context, leaner structures may also involve the regional consolidation of business divisions. Many departments, from call centres to payroll, are ideally suited for outsourcing.

THE VALUE CREATION CHALLENGE

The pressure on costs and output in the automotive value chain has consistently increased in recent years. Auto makers and suppliers were regularly forced to adapt their value creation processes. Whereas initiatives to increase the efficiency of individual elements of the value chain sufficed in the past, this approach will not do today.

To be able to grow in spite of stagnating markets and to accommodate customers' wishes for ever more personalization, car makers have expanded their model spectrums dramatically. In just 10 years, the number of models offered by European OEMs has more than doubled. At the same time as the technical complexity of cars has skyrocketed, development times have been cut by 10 per cent to 20 per cent.

However, recent experience teaches us that higher development costs can no longer be offset by higher product prices, as was possible just a few years ago. Adjusted for the price of technology and equipment, the products are becoming less expensive. Pressure on costs is rising and manufacturers consequently have to raise efficiency levels by any means possible. The automotive value chain offers substantial potential in three areas if it is completely revamped. These areas are outlined below.

Roles in value creation

The roles of all stakeholders in the value creation process – OEMs, suppliers, R&D and production service providers – must be restructured. Although value creation is increasingly being transferred from auto makers to their suppliers, the current form of cooperation is not the optimum approach. Far too often, identical competencies and resources are maintained at both ends, or the outsourcing simply goes too far. As a result, a proper mastery of the ever more complex systems is lacking.

OEMs will have to address a central issue: which competencies need to be covered to what depth in-house, and in what areas will the company want or have to rely to a greater extent on external partners or suppliers? Suppliers and R&D and production service providers, for their part, will have to gain a clear understanding of where their future business opportunities are, which competencies they require and what strategies they intend to follow.

One of the factors driving this development is the compelling need to employ capital more efficiently in all brand-shaping areas. This is essential to free up scarce financial resources to fund growth in new products, technologies and markets.

For the most part, make-or-buy decisions are still made in isolation. All too often there is no overall concept concerning the future value creation structure. Manufacturers will systematically have to review all of their in-house value creation processes and clearly define which services they want to focus on. For suppliers, this entails understanding the value creation strategies of their OEM customers in detail and setting up their own business systems accordingly.

As a consequence, attractive growth opportunities emerge for module and system suppliers, and huge challenges present themselves for R&D and production service providers. The OEMs' greater focus on brand-relevant competencies increases the proportion of suppliers in the overall value chain by about 10 per cent, whereas R&D and production service providers face more difficult times. Given that they primarily serve business segments that are closer to car makers' core competencies, they are more severely affected by insourcing tendencies.

Physical service delivery

OEMs urgently need to optimize their physical R&D, sourcing and production networks in conjunction with their suppliers. In recent years, the focus of automotive industry investments has shifted dramatically in favour of new growth regions (Asia and Eastern Europe). Triad markets are under enormous pressure. Many companies are compelled to establish production sites in low-wage countries simply to ensure their survival. The fact is that as much as 75 per cent of personnel costs can permanently be saved by moving to low-wage locations, in spite of lower productivity levels. Where personnel costs account for 25 per cent to 30 per cent of total production costs, this equates to a total cost reduction of 10 to 15 per cent, even taking all counter-effects into account. In the intense competition of the supplier business, a figure of this magnitude can make or break a company. The trend that sees value creation being offshored to low-wage countries will therefore not only continue in the years to come, it will actually accelerate.

With that said that, what solutions are available for sites in high-wage countries? The main approach is to rigorously adjust controllable costs to suit the given circumstances. The more personnel costs can be reduced – for example by bringing in longer working hours or waiving bonuses – the more insignificant the cost savings of offshoring become. As a result, the savings frequently drop to a level that renders offshoring no longer worthwhile. This may well be the only way for sites in high-wage countries to stay in business.

Business model

Increased cooperation and the conscious shaping of cooperation models between all of the stakeholders in the value chain present significant areas of untapped potential. Closer networking and improved collaboration between all stakeholders represent key levers for optimizing the automotive value chain. Contrary to the demands of the business situation, relations between OEMs and suppliers have deteriorated markedly in recent years. Considering how interdependent the value chain partners are, the amount of mistrust and pressure they feed into their relationships is anything but helpful. The optimized division of value creation and the realignment of physical service delivery hinge on close cooperation with the aim of taking full advantage of the potential available. The industry's approach to collaboration will have to change radically. Intensive cooperation is a must; however, a few important rules must be observed as well. These are:

- Shared projects require clear goals.
- Corporate cultures must be homogeneous and all persons involved must 'fit in' with the goals and teams.
- The assignment of responsibilities must be defined clearly and on the basis of competencies.
- Opportunities and risks must be shared equally.
- Rules for conflict resolution must be clearly defined and contractually stipulated.

In conclusion, only companies that succeed in defining their future core competencies to suit the future markets, and design their site networks to optimize costs, will be able to survive. Greater conscious cooperation is the key.

THE TECHNOLOGY CHALLENGE

Technological progress has been one of the strongest drivers in the development of the automotive industry since its emergence more than 100 years ago. Increasing the performance, comfort, safety, economic life and driving enjoyment as far as practicable while simultaneously managing undesired side-effects such as fuel consumption and emissions is what keeps developers developing and customers buying new vehicles. Hence, technology competency is at the core of any automotive company – for OEMs and suppliers alike. The automotive industry has seen enormous progress in this area in recent years. There is no indication that this development will slow down any time soon. Nowadays, mid-size vehicles perform like only racing cars used to do, and what is considered standard safety equipment today could previously be had for neither love nor money, even in luxury vehicles.

The shifting of value creation structures in the direction of suppliers, which goes hand in hand with technological progress, and the growing importance of specialized R&D service providers, have made key technology accessible to all car makers, regardless of their initial competency. This has resulted in virtually all car brands now having an essentially equal, very high level of technology. However, technology alone no longer serves as a primary differentiation factor as it did in past decades. There are but a few areas of technology that allow auto makers and their suppliers to achieve sustainable differentiation. Aspects such as safety, fuel efficiency, environmental friendliness and driving enjoyment represent such areas of differentiation.

Despite the technology euphoria, it is also apparent that customers have set clear limits to their ambitions for automotive advancement. Customers are no longer accepting of everything that is technically possible, nor are they willing to pay more for it. A painful lesson for auto makers was the realization that less is frequently more. Much of their pain stemmed from the complexity of the technical systems they themselves had created – and especially from the difficulty of integrating them into the overall vehicle system. Here too, necessity drove them to rethink and refocus their approach.

At this time, the automotive industry is undergoing a process of polarization. In the top segment, vehicles boasting 1,000 BHP and more are being developed, and the lower end of the scale is seeing strong growth in the entry-level segment. Entry-level cars are primarily reduced to the basic functions of mobility, and meet these needs robustly and at a reasonable price. The massive increase in demand for such vehicles is driven by the opening up of enormous markets (China, India and Russia) and the breakneck speed of their economic growth. However, these vehicles have a role to play in more than just the emerging markets. Many customers in more mature car markets frequently see the benefits of these concepts and, often under financial pressure, make a conscious decision to buy such a car.

It is important to note that such vehicles do not contain outdated technology despite their moderate price tags. Frequently the safety, performance, consumption and variability standards they have to meet can only be satisfied with enormous technological effort, even though a much more level-headed approach is taken to the subject of new technologies today. That is why the R&D machinery is still running at full speed. The goal is to adapt vehicles to the constantly and quickly changing economic, environmental and legal framework while never losing sight of the issue of customer acceptance.

Auto makers are therefore compelled to participate in the race to find the best solutions for fuel consumption, weight, safety, comfort, performance, emissions, costs and alternative drive concepts. This involves a constantly high level of investment and effort, and those who back down or give up will lose out. However, 'being a part of it' does not mean doing everything yourself. Only intelligently designed partnerships and networks can make this complex world manageable and affordable.

Technology strategy is key

One crucial success factor is the ability to understand which are the areas where customers expect to see technological innovation that differentiates one car from another, as far as their perception of the brand is concerned. These are the areas where the OEM must strive to excel, whereas in other areas the industry standard may well suffice. Furthermore, auto makers must be able to determine which competencies they themselves must possess in order to implement their defined technology strategy, and which can be outsourced to value chain partners. Without this knowledge and a technology/resource strategy developed on this basis, the balancing act between functionality and costs can no longer be mastered.

As a result, the development of suitable technology strategies becomes the key to success. Customers give auto makers plenty of leeway in this respect. They do not require 100 per cent of the technical content of a vehicle to stem from a single brand. They have a focused perception of the elements and functions that are important to them. This provides the necessary breathing space for cooperative ventures and for concentrating on brand-shaping technologies.

The aspect of global markets and requirements must also be taken into account in this context. Auto makers are forced to harmonize the frequently diverse requirements of multiple markets with their business systems, including the emerging markets with their entry-level concepts. What this means is that they must attain global scale by exploiting the possibilities and the needs of the local markets. Decentralized R&D centres and partners as well as local production and supplier partnerships are absolutely indispensable here. Localized products (function, cost, design) with a strong global brand form the basis of success in a global industry.

A compelling need to simplify

Diversity in vehicle portfolios has substantially increased among all OEMs in the past decade, and it continues to rise. Every imaginable niche is being filled, and soon companies will be fighting over even the most minute market potential. As a result, car makers are forced to simplify and accelerate their development processes. They must also reduce development costs substantially, given that the money invested is now spread and amortized over far fewer vehicles per type. Driven by these forces, some auto makers are working systematically and intensively to adapt and/or redesign their R&D structures, processes and strategies. Platform and modular strategies are often the result.

Besides a mastery of the technology itself, the actual organization of technology and vehicle development is becoming a core competency, often representing a crucial success factor. Convincing concepts are strong levers of business success in this context.

Managing technological progress

The automobile in its current format, with a conventional combustion engine, is reaching its limits. Fossil fuel resources will be exhausted in the near future. This puts the very foundations of the industry as a whole in severe jeopardy, and lawmakers as well as the automotive industry find themselves under significant pressure.

The industry is being challenged to develop technologies that provide a prospective solution to the fuel dilemma. The big OEMs fully accept that they are compelled to innovate, this being the only way to safeguard the survival of the automotive industry. Moreover, some auto makers quickly realized that such substantial technological breakthroughs hold a certain amount of differentiation potential. They have thus pulled ahead with concepts such as the hybrid engine, giving them high levels of positive public recognition, which is reflected in high sales figures. This, however, brought things to a head. The entire automotive industry realized that these developments are already being monitored by a public which has been sensitized to high energy prices, and saw that they represent the key to improved market positioning and increased success.

The race to come up with better solutions is on. Hybrid engines, BlueTec, fuel cells, hydrogen – there are many ways to attain substantial improvements in consumption and emissions levels. The task now is to develop them technologically. The automotive industry has pulled out all the stops, and is working toward making the consequences of the automobile more socially acceptable and more environmentally friendly. This is a milestone it will certainly reach.

Technology as an opportunity

An awareness and understanding of technology must extend far beyond research and development. Technology is an essential factor in the positioning of a brand, as it increasingly determines product and brand strategies, in addition to the focused technology strategies described above.

The repositioning of the Lexus in Europe, where it assumed the role of innovator in hybrid technology combined with localized design and customized sales and marketing initiatives, is an example that clearly shows the opportunities this approach can yield. Mercedes-Benz is yet another example. From its very beginnings, the brand has been a pioneer in the segment of 'fast-running diesel engines'. Consequently, Mercedes-Benz is strongly committed to pushing the diesel drive concept in the United States. Mercedes' 'BlueTec' technology, with its superior consumption and emissions performance, is at the heart of this initiative. It provides the technological basis to even undercut the extreme limits in place in some US states, which will help diesel cars gain acceptance. As a brand, Mercedes will reap the benefits.

As both of these examples demonstrate, the concerted effort of all departments across the entire company is required to achieve such goals. How these processes are set up frequently determines whether the technology and the company will be successful. Technology management is synonymous with brand management and value management. It is based on a thorough understanding of customers and their expectations. Only when technology is a priority issue for top management and an integral component to be embedded in departmental strategies can all of this come together.

Index

NB: page numbers in *italic* indicate figures
For directives and regulations *see* European Union (EU) *and* legislation

42V vehicle power system   115–17, 126

acronyms
   ABS: antilock braking system
   EBIT: earnings before interest and tax
   ESP: electronic stability program
   NAFTA: North American Free Trade Area
   NOx: nitrogen oxides
   OEM: original equipment manufacturer
   R&D: research and development
   SCR: selective catalytic reduction
   SUV: sport utility vehicle
ADAC AutoMarxX ratings   42
AdBlue®   15, 125, 328 *see also* BLUETEC and clean diesel
Aisin AW   96
Aisin Seiki   96
ALD   195
Alfa Romeo   163
Allianz Danner test   202–03
AMDEC   200
antilock braking system (ABS)   15, 106, 185, 220, 226, 235, 270
Asia(n)   43, 48, 50, 83, 93, 219, 234, 238, 306–07, 336, 351, 352–53, 362
   crisis (1998)   61
   cultures and long-term relationships   65
   OEMs   49, 51, 66
Audi   58, 109–10, 112, 125, 237
   100 TDI   237
   A8   112
   Electronics Venture   276
   and hybrid engine technology   125
   Q7 SUV   125
   Quattro   110
Auto Distribution   201–02
automotive credit   195
automotive industry
   as role model   291–92

   pioneers of   47–48, *48*
automotive industry, shifting balance of power in   31–37
   and car makers/component suppliers   34–36, *35, 36*
   and customer segments   33–34
   and new suppliers   32, *32*, 33
   and social/environmental issues   36–37, *37*
automotive industry and global economy   3–24 *see also* Germany
global automotive industry   3–4
automotive industry and globalization challenge   46–48, *48, 49*, 49–68
   Japan and Korea: conquest of North America and Europe   48–54
   European markets   50–52, *52*
   and new OEMS from China, India and Eastern Europe   52–54
   North America   49–50, *50*
   new emerging markets, survival and success in *see* emerging markets
automotive industry: winners and losers   38, *38*, 39–45
   Chinese car industry   38–40, *40*
   component suppliers and success factors   44–45, *45*
   top performers and low performers   40, *41*, 42–44
   low performers, problems of   43–44
   top performers and success factors   42
automotive markets, global shifts in   26–31, *27, 28, 29, 30, 31*
Automotive Open Systems Architecture (AUTOSAR)   226–30, 239, 280, 281, *281*
innovative products for new market segments   228
quality, common goal of   227–28

shared market interests   228–30
Automotive Research, Institute for (IFA)
Automotive Research Center (FAW)   65, 254
automotive semiconductor applications   288

Benz & CieAG   315
Berger, R   42, 44
Bharat Forge   64, 68, 334–44
   and acquisitions   341–42
   and action   338–39
   background to   334–37
   and competitiveness   342–43
   and focus   338
   and full service provider capability   343
   and innovation   343
   scale and growth of   340–42
   and synergy   343–44
   and technology   339–42
   vision of   337–38
biofuel   19, 22–23
   and agricultural sectors   22
   biodiesel   23
   bioethanol   22
   and energy crops   22–23
   and raw materials market   23
BLUETEC and clean diesel   15, 125, 314–33
   and commercial vehicle applications   327–30, *328, 330*
   and E320 BLUETEC: first serial-production passenger car   324–27, *324, 325, 326*
   and emission regulations: passenger cars   317–19, *317, 318*
   and emission regulations: trucks   319, *320*
   history of   314–16, *316*
   and modular technology for passenger cars   320–23, *322, 323*
   and outlook and future for diesel   330
   and roadmap for innovative powertrain technologies   331–33, *332, 333*
   and strategy for world's cleanest diesel   320–23
BMW   8, 58, 74, 81, 100, 109, 111–12, 125, 140, 147, 159, 165, 208, 261, 274, 279
   Bank   207–08
   and Brilliance   53
   Car IT   276
   customer satisfaction with   42
   and hybrid engine technology   125
   Mini   33
   sales revenues and EBIT   42
   X3   81
   World (delivery centre)   159
Bosch   66, 116, 205, 219–40, 261, 274
   Competence Centre for Hybrid Systems   230

dominance in diesel injection systems   95
   Engineering   142
   history of   233–34
   and Mercedes A class   222
   Production System   232
   and subsidiary Blaupunkt   236
Bosch, R   233
brand differentiation on basis of platform and module strategies   241–51
   market fragmentation   241–51, *242, 243, 244, 245, 246, 247, 248, 250, 251*
brand(s)   107
   core   243
   identity/image   34, 35, 82
   loyalty   57
   positioning   107, 109, 154
   premium   108
   values   132, 160, 243
Brazil   17, 22, 47, 54, 61, 63, 64, 234, 261–62
breakdowns, automobile   72
Brose Fahrzeugteile GmbH & Co. KG   78–79, *79*
business models   286–89, *287, 288*
business relationships of OEMs and component suppliers, deterioration in   91
by-wire technologies   115–16

capacity and competition   6–7
capacity bottlenecks, unplugging   81
car insurance premiums   151
car lifecycle *see* sales and after-sales challenge
car magazines   105
car makers: core competences that shape the brand   73–75, *74, 75*
   'candidate blocks' and influence on brand promise   74
   defining future core competencies   75
   outsourcing and cost benefits   74–75
CARS 21 group   18–20 *see also* legislation
   and environmental and safety regulations   18, 20
   recommendations of   18–19
   and vehicle safety   19–20
car-related services   17
car-sharing organizations   17
case studies   217–344
   Bharat Forge: emerging players from emerging regions *see* Bharat Forge
   BLUETEC and clean diesel   314–33 *see also main entry*
   brand differentiation   241–51 *see also main entry*
   electronics and change in automotive industry   270–89 *see also main entry*

General Motors in Europe   252–69 *see also* main entry
  partnership as model for success   219–40 *see also* partnerships
  sustainable success: OEMs and suppliers   290–313 *see also* main entry
catalytic converters: DeNOx and SCR   326
challenges
  globalization   46–68, 350–55 *see also* main entry
  market   146–70, 347–50 *see also* market challenge
  sales   355–60 *see also* sales challenge
  sales and after-sales   171–215
  technology   103–45, 363–67 *see also* technology challenge
  value chain   69–102
  value creation   361–63 *see also* value creation challenge
Chevrolet   100, 259, 260, 266
  Taho   100
China   6, 7–8, 16, 26, 29, *29*, 30, 32, 46, 47, 48, 50, 54, 58–60, *60*, 61, 63–64, 66, 73, 81, 82, 84, 87, 213, 219, 228, 236, 238, 264, 269, 289, 291, 306, 308, 336, 342, 348, 352, 353, 364 *see also* Chinese car industry
  as growth market   7–8
  and Buick   57
  and cheap cars   67
  and Chery QQ   30, 65, 67
  and domestic market   8
  and five-year plan   8
  and Geely   46, 65, 67
  and Hyundai   33
  and OEMs   29
  and Rover   353
  and value chain   29
China National Automotive Industry Corporation   39
Chinese car industry   38–40, 151
  and growth of auto market   52–53
  Landwind SIV   66
  Nanjing Automobile   53, 66, 353
  progress of   29
  SAIC   53, 65, 66, 353
Chrysler   14, 46, 47, 101, 109, 157
Citroën C1   99
clean exhaust emissions technologies   14, 21–23
Club of Rome   13, 347
CO_2 emissions   18, 19, 21–23, 327
communication technology segments   119
competition   6–7, 12–13, 151–52, 189–90, 191, 238
competence centres   276

competence inhouse   283
component suppliers   70, 77–78
  focused on components or integration   75–79, *76, 77, 78, 79*
  HBPO   93–94, *94*
  Siemens VDO and Magneti Marelli   94–95, *95*
Concept Vehicle Jeep®   326
conclusion   345–67 *see also* challenges *and* globalization
  low performers, problems of   346–47
  market challenge   347–50 *see also* main entry
  sales challenge   355–60 *see also* main entry
  technology challenge   363–67 *see also* main entry
  top performers, success factors of   346
  value creation challenge   361–63 *see also* main entry
core competence(s)   71–83, 145
core strategy unit   140
Covisint electronic procurement platform   100
cross-border synergies   158
customer loyalty   33, 209, *209*
customer needs   155, 294, 349
customer-focused technology and product strategies   129, *130*, 130–36
  aligning value chain with technology strategy   135–36, *136*
  and changes in customer requirements   129–31
  generating customer-focused innovations   133–34, *135*
  transforming demand to brand-shaping vehicle attributes   131–33, *132, 133*
customer-oriented technology management   127, *127*, 128, *129*, 129–44
  customer-focused technology and product strategies   129–36 *see also* main entry
  networking with external partners   140–44 *see also* main entry
  operational design, forms of   136–40 *see also* main entry
customer relationship management (CRM)   156–57, 164
customer segmentation   33–34
customer satisfaction   114–15, *115*, 131, 166–67
  index (CSI)   253–54
customer, understanding the   154–57
  CRM systems   156–67
  value-based strategies for   154–55, *155, 156*
customers, accessing via sales   348

customers, expectations and behaviour of 146–47, *148*
Czech Republic/Kolin 64, 96, 99–100

Daewoo and Chevrolet brand 66
Daewoo and Kia 53
DaimlerChrysler 8, 34, 43, 52, 64, 70, 107, 115, 120, 125, 159, 261, 325–26, *325, 326*, 332
  Bank 207–08
  buses 329
  and development of hybrid engine with GM 100–01
  E320 125
  and offshoring R&D 64
DaimlerChrysler AG 220–21, 237
dealer groups 161–62, 196–99, *197, 198*, 210, 359–60
Delphi 66, 68, 293–94
  and Chapter 11 protection 293
demo car segment 177, *177*
demographic trends 244
Denso 96
diesel 14–15, 228–29 *see also* BLUETEC and clean diesel
  clean 15, 314–33
  globalization of 229
  and hybrid vehicles 21
  high pressure technology 119
  injection systems 95
  particulate filters 14, 119
diesel cars and market share 125–26
Direct Line 204
digital tachographs 11
Dodge Durango 101
Dresdner Bank 208

earnings before interest and tax (EBIT) 42, 295
Eastern Europe 9–10, 26, 32, 48, 55, 83–85, 162, 170, 189, 219, 234, 306–07, 308, 336, 362
economic cycles 16
economy cars, demand for 219–20
electronic and software development cycles 141
electronic control units (ECUs) 274
electronic continuous damping control (CDC) 267
electronic stability program (ESP) 15, 106, 108, 220–22, 226, 236
  development of 220–21
  learning from example of 222
  and technological challenges 221–22
electronics 15, 72, 80–81, 113, 136, 237
electronics and change in automotive industry 270–89

complex mechanical to complex electronic systems 270, *271*, 272–75
  competence and competition 275
  complexity, growth of 274, *275*
  productivity and challenge 272, *273*, 274
convergence of electronics and car making industry 275–77, *277*, 278–79
  electronics suppliers, importance of 277–78, *278*, 279
knowledge and business model-related dependencies 283–86
  collaboration, new quality of 284–85, *285*, 286
  new business models, need for 286–89, *287, 288*
systems integration 279–83
  responsibility for 282–83
  standardization and competition 280–81, *281*, 282
emerging markets 54–68
  and challenges for OEMs and newcomers 56–61
  diversity in regional markets 58–59
  first time buyers 57–58, *57, 58*
  high fixed costs and operations lacking critical mass 59–61, *60*
  minimal brand loyalty 57–58
  price sensitivity 58–59, *59*
  demand volatility, exchange rate fluctuations and trade barriers 61
  growing demand restricted to 54–56, *55, 56*
  success strategies for established automakers 61–65 *see also main entry*
  success strategies for newcomers 65–67 *see also main entry*
  sustained cost advantages in 55–56
emissions 11, 37, *37*, 228, 262, 317–19 *see also* European Union
engineering service providers 66, 71, 80, *80*, 81
  AVL 66
  EDAG 66, 71
  finding their focus 80, *80*, 81
  Karmann 66, 71, 81
  Magna Steyr 71, 81
  Pininfarina 51, 66, 71
entry-level models 62–63
environmental issues 36–37
ESP: a successful partnership 220–22 *see also* partnerships
Eurodesign 174, 188, *188*, 189, 203, 210, 356, 358
Euro-NCAP 131, 356
  crash test 121–22, *122*, 126, 145

European Commission (EC)   18, 22, 212
European Parliament   18
European Union (EU)   4, 8, 22, 318, 319, 360
    Clean Air Directive   318
    directives   18–19, 37, 229
    E25   175, 210
    e-Safety program   222
    Euro 3 emissions standard for diesel   228
    Euro 4 standard   318, 319
    Euro 5 standard on particulate emissions   229, 318, 319, 327

fast-fitters   202
Fiat   43, 68, 70, 96
financial institutions, captive and non-captive   206–09
    captive banks: the German exception   207, *207*, 208
    non-captives: market share in new growth areas   209
financial services   17, 151, 165, 192–96, 359 *see also* insurance
    automotive trends and change in credit purchasing   194–95, *194, 195, 196*
    banking services   207
    banks and leasing firms   17, 292
    coveted by non-automotive players   192–93, *192, 193*
fleets/fleet management services   176–77, 194, 212, 214, 356–57
Ford Motor Company   32, 43, 46, 47, 52, 68, 70, 100, 157, 163, 293, 350–51
    and hybrid engines   125
France   6, 84, 161, 164, 181, 191, 196, 201–02, 204–05, 208, 211, 213, 356
fuel consumption   37, 228
full-service providers/dedicated production service providers   81–82
    and capacity bottlenecks, unplugging   81
    and new growth markets   82

General Motors (GM)   32, 39–40, *40*, 40, 43, 46, 47, *48*, 52, 57–58, 68, 70, 157, 163, 167, 235, 293, 350–51 *see also* Opel *and* Saab
    Astra   253, 254, 260, 265, 268
    Cadillac   163, 252–53, 259, 260, 264, 349
    Corsa   266
    Corvette   163, 264
    Daewoo   260
    and design and engineering   264
    and development of hybrid engine with DaimlerChrysler   100–01, 293
    and diesel   125
    and European Design Center, Rüsselheim   257–58, 263, 264
    and Fiat powertrain joint venture   125, 261
    and hybrid engine technology   125, 261–62
    and HydroGen3   268
    Hummer   163, 264
    in Sweden   259, 260, 264
    Meriva   253, 265
    and Red X Team   256
    and Rüsselheim Opel factory   255
    share in US market   43
    SUV Graphyte   261
    Tigra Twin Top   265, 268
    Vauxhall   259, 264
    Vectra   253
    Zafira   253, 260, 262, 265
General Motors in Europe   252–69
    customer and dealer satisfaction   254–55
    design expertise   257–59
    design trend-setter Europe   268
    electronics, smart use of   262–63
    employee motivation and success   256
    future-oriented approach   269
    growth above industry trends   263–64
    new market challenges   265–66
    overcoming weak economy   264–65
    portfolio positioning   259–60
    propulsion and hybrid technology   261–62
    quality   257
    single-company strategy   266–68
    specialists and international knowledge-sharing   255–56
    world-class cars: quality and product initiative   253–54
German Association of the Automotive Industry (VDA)   227
    'Quality, the Foundation for Joint Success' agreement   227, 231
German automotive industry   4–7, 9–10, 13–17, 20–24, 150, 159–60, 161, 170, 219, 223, 222, 225, 228, 233–34, 239, 252–53, 289
    and automobile breakdowns   72
    and biofuels   20–23
    and car buyers   147
    and competition and capacity   6–7
    export strategy of   9–10
    and flex fuel vehicles   22
    and future challenges   23–24
    global business location strategy of   9–10
    and road safety   20
    and sales   152
    success strategies of   13–17
    wholesalers   201
German market, the   10–11, 151
    commercial vehicle segment, growth of   10–11
    for diesel vehicles   14
German supply industry   11–13

challenges for   12–13
and clean diesel   15
and financial/car-related services   17
and outsourcing/partnerships   16
and technology leadership   12, 15
Germany   4–17, 20–24, 79, 84, 118, 180, 181, 191, 204, 211, 213, 229, 235, 310, 318, 356 *see also* German automotive industry; German market *and* German supply industry
   ADAC (automobile association)   113, 254
   as business location   4–6
   and banks   151, 208
   business model   6
   GDV insurance association   151
   and German Civil Code (HGB)   160
   KBS Federal Motor Vehicle Office   72
   and new market opportunities   6
   and Pforzheim 2004 wage agreement   5
   and production sites   9
   Weller Group   161–62
global business location strategy   9–10
global market(s)   15, 47 *see also* automotive markets, global shifts in
   and biofuels   22
   for premium products   15
global sourcing   64
globalization   6–7, 47–48, 64, 350–55, 290, 292, 293 *see also see* automotive industry and globalization challenge
   and Asian automotive industry   352–54
   and changing times   47
   and competition and key success factors   354–55
   driven adaptation processes   345
   and global expansion   351–52
Goldman Sachs   114
green engine technologies   123

Hella Behr Plastic Omnium (HBPO)   93–94, *94*, 205
Honda   97, 100, 114, 124
hybrid engine technology   119, 123, 124–25, 230, 261–62, 366
Hyundai   33, 50, 52, 63, 64, 66, 67, 83, 351
hub models   158
hubs   169–70

IAM repairers/wholesalers: technology challenge   199–202
   repair level: consolidation towards affiliated networks   199–200, *200*
   wholesale level: consolidation towards large buying groups   201–02, *201*
iDrive system   42, 111–12
India(n)   6, 7–8, 16, 17, 26, 32, 33, 39, 54, 58, 63–64, 66, 73, 81, 82, 84, 213, 219, 228, 236, 238, 269, 335–36, 348, 364
   as growth market   7–8
   car makers   151
   engineering industry   337
   and global IT supremacy   8
   growth of auto market   52–53
   low labour costs   336–37
   and Mahindra   53
Infineon   285
information technology (IT)   111
   and software for car makers   276–77
insurance   17, 151, 202–05
integrated chassis control (ICC)   267
intellectual property, safeguarding   64–65
International Technical Development Center (ITDC) Rüsselsheim   257, 265
internet and private trading   152
in-vehicle technology   80–81
Italy   51, 84, 189, 211

Jaguar   34, 43, 109
Japan   6, 8, 11, 26, 46, 47, 49, 53, 54, 66, 96, 105, 170, 213, 225, 230, 235, 238, 291, 351
   and hybrid engine technology   123
   and *keiretsu(s)*   96–97, *97*, 98
Japanese   46, 49, 66
   automotive industry   32, 39, 44, 234–35, 351–53
   brands   50
   supplier (Zexel)   234
JD Power & Associates   131, 166–67, 253, 268, 356
Jeep Grand Cherokee   81, 325
joint ventures   142

Kia   50, 52, 53, 83, 351
Korea(n)   6, 8, 46, 47, 51, 53, 66, 225, 235, 260, 289, 291, 351–53
   cars/brands   39, 49, 50
   car manufacturers   32, 151, 234–35
Kroymans Group   163, 167, 349

labour cost savings   55
lean management principle   297
lean retailing   292
legislation   18–19 *see also* European Union (EU)
   Block Exemption Regulation   151–52, 160, 165, 173–74, 186, 198, 210
   Design Protection Regulation   152
   ECE regulations   18–19
Lexus   50–51
liability   282
location decisions   89
logistical costs   89

low-labour-cost locations and
  survival 87–90, 336–37
  and detailed location plan 90
  production location, choosing 88–89, *88, 89*
  products, choosing 87, *87*, 88
low-pollutant vehicles 11

Machine that Changed the World, The 13, 347
macroeconomic trends 131
Magna Innovative Lightweight Auto (MILA) concept car 309, *310*
Magna International 294–313, *295, 296, 312*
  as example of sustainable growth 294
  and active portfolio management 298–99
  and corporate development 296–97
  corporate constitution of *302*, 303–04
  decentralized organizational structure of 300, *301*
  and entrepreneurship 301–02
  employees' charter of *304*, 304–05
  group structure of 298, *298*, 299
  growth strategy of 297–98, *307*, 307–12
    broadening customer base 308
    capitalizing on OEM outsourcing trend 310–11, *311*, 312
    development of new markets 308
    innovations and technical progress 308–09, *310*
  operating principles of 305–06
Magna Steyr 296, 298, 299
  Production System (MSPS) 312
Magna Powertrain 298, 299
Magneti Marelli 94–95, *95*, 96 *see also* Fiat *and* Siemens VDO
market challenge 347–50
  controlling sales channel 350
  conventional sales systems, overcoming limitations of 349–50
  customer needs, identifying and understanding 349
market challenge and strategic control 146–70
  competition outside new car market 151–52
  competitive pressure 150–51, *150*
  customer, understanding the 154–57 *see also main entry*
  customers: expectations and behaviour 146–47, *148*
  offers and costs, manufacturers' approach to 147–49, *149*, 150
  sales activities as key to success 152–53, *153*

sales: power play and control 161–67 *see also main entry*
sales systems, overcoming limitations of 157–60 *see also main entry*
separate tiers to single network 167–70
  collaboration with suppliers/ dealers 168–69
  from static multi-tiered model to dynamic network 169–70
  outlook 170
market research institutes 131
markets 21, 93, 219, 230, 306–07
  global 15
  growth of 7–8, 17, 82
  liberalization of 12
  niche 33, 77
  triad 26, 33, 53, 61, 82, 84, 103, 105
Mercedes-Benz 51, 58, 62, 74, 101, 109, 114, 124, 147, 148, 234, 314–16, *316*, 317–19, 331
  bionic car 324, *324*
  BlueTec 367
  buses 329, *330*
  CLK 81
  S class 112, 120–21, 237
Mini 33, 109, 154–55
Mitsubishi 43, 44
module and system suppliers, growth opportunities for 82, *83*, 83
module strategy 249, *250*
multi-brand sales 162–64
multi-brand strategy 243, 250

network management 128
network restructuring 158
networking with external partners 140–44
  and brand-shaping value chain elements 141–42
  and competences and competitive capabilities 142, *143*
  from hierarchies to genuine partnerships 143–44, *144*
  and outsourcing of value chain elements 141
new cars
  fleets 176–77, *176, 177*
  full mobility service solutions 178, *178*
  market and changing demand 356–57
  product to mobility 176–78
niche markets/products 33, 77
Nissan 51, 97, 114, 125
  Infinity 51
nitrogen oxides (NOx) 15, 317, 318–19, 320, 327
non-governmental organizations (NGOs) 18

North America 54, 93, 101, 225, 238, 293, 342, 351
North American Free Trade Area (NAFTA) 9

Offshore Local Attractiveness Index (A K Kearney, 2004) 337
offshoring 55, 84
Opel 67, 252, 253–55, 256, 258, 259, 260, 263–66, 267, 268
operational design, forms of 128, 136–37, *137*, 138–40
   component-oriented development organizations drive complexity 137
   functional teams reduce complexity 137–38
   function-oriented development organizations guarantee customer focus 138, *139*, 140
outsourcing 12, 16, 75, 210, 310

particulate matter (PM) 14, 37, 119, 229, 317, 318–19
partnership(s) 219–40
   and AUTOSAR *see* Automotive Open Systems Architecture (AUTOSAR)
   and cost-effective structures and processes 230–33
      and balancing innovation and cost leadership 231–32
      and importance of geographical proximity 231
      and mix of high-cost and low-cost countries 232–33
      and process optimization 232
   and ESP 220–22 *see also* electronic stability program (ESP)
   and global change 238–40
      and joint responses to future challenges 239–40
      and trust 240
   independence and responsibility in 223–37
      competence and broad footing support independence 224–25
      inequality of power 224
   and international presence 233–36
      and Bosch 233–34, 236
      and global responses to local requirements 235
      and shifting growth regions 234–35
   and long-term perspective 236–37
   and need for stamina/perseverance 237
   and technological leadership, common goal of 225–26
      suppliers and responsibilities 226

Patterns of Success for Automotive Component Suppliers 44
peak-shaving plant 311, *311*, 312
Peugeot 37, 99
   107 99
   and diesel particle filters 37
political framework: CARS 21
   group 18–19 *see also* CARS 21 group *and* legislation
Porsche 81, 109, 125, 162, 276, 292, 293
   Boxster 81
   Cayenne SUV and hybrid engines 125, 293
   Engineering Group 276
platform strategy 246–48, *247, 248*, 249
premium vehicle brands 109
production sites 9–10, 55, 83–91, 258–59, 351
Production Technology, Fraunhofer Institute for 255

quality promotion and assurance 256

R&D 5, 7, 8, 15, 21, 24, 44, 61, 107, 144, 226, 308, 344, 345, 351, 354, 261, 362, 364, 366
   global networks 64
Renault 19, 121–22, 145, 181, 191, 203
   Clio 181
   design to cost approach 63
   Laguna 121
Renault/Nissan: Dacia Logan 53, 63, 151
repair and service 182–87, 359
   car pool: six- to nine-year-old segment 185, *185*, 186
   car technology: threat or opportunity? 186, *186*, 187
   customer demand for reliability/satisfaction 182–85, *183, 184*
return on capital employed (ROCE) 44, 75, 172, *172*, 193
return on equity (ROE) 152
Roland Berger Strategy Consultants 67, 77, 85, 113, 152–53, 154, 162, 271, 354
   RB Profiler 154, *155*
Rover 53, 66, 353
Russia 54, 64, 66, 73, 82, 87, 364

Saab 109, 253, 258, 259, 260, 261, 264–65, 268
   BioPower 261
   Brand Center, Trollhätten 258–59
   Technical Development Center, Trollhätten 265
safety features 15, 106, 119
   ABS 15, 106, 185, 220, 226, 235, 270

airbags 15, 51, 106, 108, 270
belt warning indicators 20
ISOFIX child restraint systems 20
passenger protection systems 108
sales and after-sales challenge 171–215
  acceleration of change, factors in 173–74
  automotive value chain during car lifecycle 172, *172*, 173
  capture of value along car lifecycle 211–15
    fully captive scenario 211–12
    fully non-captive scenario 212–13
    retail scenario 213
    striking the balance 213–15
  demand shifts and redefining market rules 176–96
    new cars: product to mobility 176–78 *see also* new cars
    repair and service 182–87 *see also main entry*
    spare parts 187–91 *see also main entry*
    used cars 179–82 *see also main entry*
    'user chooser' business model 179
    financial services challenge 192–96 *see also* financial services
  threats and opportunities for market players 175–76
  threats/opportunities and new challenges 196–210
    dealer groups: relationship challenge 196–99, *197, 198 see also* dealer groups
    financial institutions, captive and non-captive 206–09 *see also main entry*
    IAM repairers/wholesalers: technology challenge *see main entry*
    insurers: the influential challenge 202–05, *205*
    OEMs: captive business model challenge 209, *209*, 210
    parts suppliers: market access challenge 205–06, *206*
sales challenge 355–60
  dealer groups, importance of 359–60
  financial services as source of income 359
  improved service 358
  new car market and changing demand structures 356–57
  original spare parts and competitive pressure 358
  repair shops and tougher competition 359
  used car market: setting the lever 357

sales: power play and control 161–67
  auto makers 164, *164*, 165
  dealers 161–64
  new players 165
  partnerships 166–67
sales systems, overcoming limitations of 157–60
  and optimization programmes, limited success of 159–60
  and potential for improvement 157–58, *158*, 159
segmentation 33–34, 93, 219
selective catalytic reduction (SCR) 14–15, 320
Schuh, Prof Dr G 255
Seger, K 109
Siemens VDO 66, 94–95, *95 see also* Magneti Marelli
Skoda 8
Slovakia 64
small and medium-sized enterprises 12, 285
Smart car 34
software 136
  architecture 280
  development process 113
South Africa 61, 63
South America 26
Spain 84, 161, 189, 208, 211, 356, 358
spare parts 187–91, 358
  captive parts/accident-driven market 187–88, *188*, 189
  wholesaling and competition 189–90, *190*, 191
Steyr-Daimler-Puch 295, 296
strategic alliances 94–95, 293
strategies
  expansion 353
  export 9–10
  module 249, *250*
  multi-brand 163–64, 243, 250
  platform 246–48, *247, 248*, 249
  success 13–15, 61–65
  technology/product 127–28, 135
  value-based 154
  value chain 140
studies/surveys
  Cap Gemini Car Online Study (2005) 42
  on BlueTec® exhaust treatment (TÜV-Nord) 328
  on car manufacturers and automotive suppliers (RWTH) 254
  on customer satisfaction 166–67
  on electronics 113
  on electronics value and suppliers/car makers (McKinsey) 277
  on export strategies 67

Index 377

on India-based automotive component manufacture (McKinsey) 336
on low-labour-cost locations 85
on multi-brand sales 162
on patterns of success in component supply industry 77
on process management in retail industry (McKinsey) 292
success strategies for established automakers 61–65
  developing low-cost competencies 62–63
  global R&D, production and sourcing system 63–64
  globalizing mangement structures and personnel development 65
  local market requirements, understanding and meeting 61–62
  safeguarding know-how 64–65
success strategies for newcomers 65–67
  developing autonomous technology competences 66–67
  developing independent brands 66
  developing products fit for global market 66–67
  implementing export strategies 67
sustainable success: OEMs and suppliers 290–313 *see also* Magna International
  and automotive industry as role model 291–92
  and future of the industry 306–07
system suppliers 142
systems integration 279–80, 282–83

Tata 46, 53, 65, 66
technology challenge 363–67
  managing technological progress 366–67
  progress or pitfall 103–45 *see also* customer-oriented technology management *and* technology development
  simplification 366
  strategy as key 365–66
  technology as opportunity 367
technology development 105–26 *see also* technology development and customer
  and ecology, safety and convenience 119
  and focus on customer 119–26, *122, 124*
  from demand to value 117–18, *118*
  in transition 105–10
    and competitive pressure 105–06, *106*, 107
    emotion and innovation 109–10
    innovation as standard 107–08, *108*
    without customer focus 110–17

failure, reasons for 110–13, *111, 112*
mature technologies 113–15, *114, 115*
non-establishment of technologies 115, *116*, 116–17
Thatcham 174, 205, 356
tiger economies (Asian) 26, 27
Toyota 32, 42, 46, 49, 52, 96, 97, 98–99, 100, 114–15, 123–25, 131, 166–67, 228, 230, 350
  and business relationships with component suppliers 96
  Aygo 99
  compared with GM 39–40, *40*
  and hybrid engine technology 123, 126
  and joint ventures 96
  and key customer opinion leaders 124
  Lexus/Lexus RX400h 123, 124, 145
  plant with PSA in Kolin (CR) 96, 99–100
  Prius 33, 37, 123
  and PSA Peugeot-Citröen 293
triad markets 26, 33, 53, 61, 82, 84, 103, 105

unique selling points (USPs) 35, 169, 282
United States of America (USA) 11, 21, 26, 32, 51–52, 67, 105, 158, 213, 222, 229, 234, 234–35, 283, 348
used cars 179–82
  and creation of vicious circle 180–82
  and 'nearly new car' system 179–80
  and professionalism in management 180, *181*
  and setting the lever 357

value chain 35, 128, 135–36, 167, 215, 276, 287, *287*, 288, 309
  strategies 140
value chain automotive, paradigm shift in 272, 274
value chain breakdown: focus on core competence 71–83 *see also individual subject entries*
  car makers: focused on core competences that shape the brand 73–75
  component suppliers: focused on components or integration 75–79
  engineering service providers: finding their focus 80–81
  full-service providers/dedicated production service providers 81–82
  module and system suppliers, growth opportunities for 82–83, *83*
value chain: business model and networking 91–92, *92*–101
  closer collaboration, need for 101

collaboration and cross-shareholdings:
    OEMs and component suppliers
    (Japan's *keiretsus*) 96–97, *96, 97*
collaboration between OEMs and
    component suppliers without cross-
    shareholdings: Toyota 98, *98*, 99
collaboration between OEMs:
    DaimlerChyrsler, GM and
    BMW 100–01
joint ventures between component
    suppliers: HBPO 93–94, *94*
joint ventures between OEMs: Toyota
    Peugeot Citroën Automobile
    (TPCA) 99–100
strategic alliances between component
    suppliers: Siemens VDO and Magneti
    Marelli 94–95, *95*
value chain challenge: networks 69, *69*,
    70–71, *71*, 72–102
    and key challenges 102
value chain: footprint, growing pressure on
    existing locations 83–91
    low-labour-cost locations and
        survival 85–90 *see also main entry*
    solutions for locations in countries with
        high labour costs 90, *91*
value chain, key levers of 70, *71*
value creation 12
    business model 363
    challenge 361–63
    physical service delivery 362–63
    roles in 361–62
VDA and Ad Blue® 15
vehicle model cycles 113, *114*, 141
vehicle safety 19–20, 37
vehicle types
    4x4s 16
    compact 15, 16
    convertibles 16

cost of 17
cross-over models 148
flex fuel 22
hybrid 21
low-pollutant 11
minivans 27, 105
MPVs 44, 105
niche 16, 81–82, 265
pick-ups 27, 49
premium 17
roadsters 265
sport utility (SUV) 15, 16, 27, 34, 44,
    49, 105, 148, 252, 260, 265
supermini 16
vans 49, 105
Verheugen, G 18
Volkswagen 14, 43, 44, 51, 52, 64, 81, 83,
    110, 125, 147–48, 151, 165, 234, 235,
    292, 293
    Beetle 61
    Fox 30, 62
    Golf/IV/V/City 61, 62, 110–111, 148
    Jetta 62
    Phaeton 34, 110, 147
    Polo 62
Volkswagen Financial Services 195, 207,
    207, 208
Volvo 109

wages, hourly 55–56, *56*
Weber, T 120
Western Europe 26, 84, 159
Womach, J P; Jones, D T, and Ross, D 13,
    347
World Trade Organization (WTO) 63

ZVEI: German electrical engineering
    and electronics industry
    association 279